APPLIED DISCRETE-CHOICE MODELLING

David A. Hensher
Lester W. Johnson

SCHOOL OF ECONOMIC AND FINANCIAL STUDIES
MACQUARIE UNIVERSITY, SYDNEY, AUSTRALIA.

With contributions by J.J. Louviere and J. Horowitz

A HALSTED PRESS BOOK

CROOM HELM LONDON

JOHN WILEY & SONS
NEW YORK

© 1981 David A. Hensher and Lester W. Johnson
Croom Helm Ltd, 2-10 St John's Road, London SW11

British Library Cataloguing in Publication Data

Hensher, David A
    Applied discrete choice modelling.
    1. Consumption (Economics) -
    Mathematical models
    I. Title   II. Johnson, Lester W
    339.4'7   HB801   80-41192
    ISBN 0-7099-0330-8
          0-7099-1203-7 Pbk

Published in the U.S.A.
by Halsted Press, a Division of
John Wiley & Sons, Inc., New York

Hensher, David A   1947-
    Applied discrete-choice modelling.

    1. Decision-making—Mathematical models. 1. Johnson,
Lester W., joint author. II. Title.
HD30.23.H46   658.4'033   80-23517
ISBN 0-470-27078-0

Printed and bound in Great Britain

CONTENTS

List of Figures

List of Tables

PREFACE

This book is offered primarily as a text for a one-semester course in the theory and application of individual choice models when the objects of choice are discrete. The book is also of use to the general reader and practitioner who wishes to obtain a working knowledge of the essential elements underlying operational discrete choice models, especially the conditional logit model, and who desires a series of case studies as a source of guidance in using such procedures. A test case study complete with data and the manual of a computer program and results is given in Chapter 10 so that students, lecturers and practitioners can apply the models during the learning phase.

The text has been used in the teaching of senior undergraduates and junior postgraduates in the economics discipline. The level has been set on the assumption that the reader has a knowledge of elementary consumer demand theory (usually taught in first year economic principles courses) and elementary statistics (up to an awareness of linear regression and statistical tests of goodness of fit).

We assume an elementary knowledge of calculus, but do not, like so many books, develop difficult mathematical proofs; rather for the sake of appreciation of the procedures being applied, the mathematical detail has been kept to a minimum. The reader interested in more clarification and extension of a particular topic is guided in further reading to the major references.

A book of this type, by its own design, is only original in concept not content. A great deal of debt must be paid to the pioneers of individual choice modelling, especially the researchers who have taken the statistical contributions of the past decades and developed their contribution in an economics framework. The recognition of contributors is acknowledged in the references, although particular debt is owed to Daniel McFadden, Charles Manski and Moshe Ben-Akiva, who have been notably responsible for clarifying and extending the large amount of technical literature on individual choice modelling which is spread widely across a number of disciplines, especially psychology, economics, statistics and engineering.

At various stages in the authors' pursuance of the topic of the text a number of people have provided advice and encouragement, in particular Peter Stopher, Jordan Louviere, Marc Gaudry, Quasim Dalvi, Dick Bullock and Andrew Daly. James Crittle was instrumental in development and testing of the computer program and Truong P. Truong provided much assistance in identifying any looseness in the explanations during the course of preparing the book. Richard Galbraith conducted extensive empirical tests using the computer program discussed in Chapter 10 in order to eliminate errors. Peter Barnard read the final manuscript and made some useful comments to improve the presentation.

We thank the authors of the papers which are used in Sections 9.2 to 9.7. Their comments on our presentation of their contribution to the literature and support in the exposure of their work is gratefully acknowledged. Our particular thanks go to the Australian Road Research Board for their financial assistance in the development of the computer program and the support service for its distribution. We accept responsibility for errors that still remain.

We are grateful to the Literary Executor of the late Sir Ronald A. Fisher, F.R.S., to Dr. Frank Yates, F.R.S. and to Longman Group Ltd., London, for permission to reprint Table III from their book <u>Statistical Tables for Biological, Agricultural and Medical Research</u> (6th edition, 1974). Permission from the author (C.M. Thompson) and Biometrika Trustees to reprint the Table of percentage points of the Chi-Square distribution from Biometrika (Volume 32, 1941) is gratefully acknowledged.

Finally, we are indebted to Sue Beskin for typing and Irene Young for artwork, especially their patience in deciphering the drafts and transforming them into a readable product.

DECEMBER 1979

David A. Hensher
Lester W. Johnson

Interest in discrete data has been stimulated by a growing interest in microeconomic problems and a growing availability of good microeconomic data. As economists attempt to make greater use of their theory to solve such practical problems as estimating the demand for new modes of travel and ascertaining the determinants of the labor supply of women, the analytical fiction of the representative consumer and its econometric analogue - the classical regression model - have become less useful. Increasingly, economists have begun to recognize that the analysis of choices at the extensive margin (i.e., discrete choices) are just as interesting and often of greater empirical importance than the analysis of choices at the intensive margin that is treated in traditional analysis. Because the source of sample variation critically affects the formulation and estimation of many models of discrete choice, the traditional schizophrenia of "Marshallian econometrics" that separates the formulation of an economic model for a "typical individual" from its stochastic specification is absent from many of the best papers in this literature.

(Heckman, 1976: i)

CHAPTER 1

Introduction

1·1 The Aims of the Book

Applied discrete-choice modelling can be viewed as the use of a variety of statistical techniques to quantify in a meaningful way a relationship between a discrete choice and a set of explanatory variables. The term 'meaningful' is fundamental to this statement and is the link with the requirement that a model have a behaviourally reasonably derivation from some theory. A behaviourally reasonable derivation entails the specification of a set of assumptions underlying a theory, which are used in the solution of an estimatable model and a test of a theory's predictive capability. Since a model implies a simplification or abstraction from reality, modelling should be interpreted as an objective, an approach to explaining and predicting the particular features of the analysis unit's behaviour most relevant to the issue under study. Hence the aims in this book of such a modelling exercise are to estimate the effects of changes in (one or more of) the explanatory variables on the probability of choice and to be able to use the estimated models as predictive tools.

The literature on discrete-choice modelling is spread widely across several disciplines, notably statistics, economics, psychology, engineering and sociology. The predominant emphasis of this literature is on the statistical requirements, with a limited concern for the underlying behavioural derivatives. Exceptions are found in economics and psychology. We believe that a knowledge and understanding of the relevance of alternative statistical specifications of discrete-choice models is dependent on exposure to a theoretical framework within which the behavioural assumptions associated with alternative statistical specifications are made explicit. Thus the emphasis in this book is on getting the theory clear and knowing the behavioural strengths and weaknesses of a particular statistical specification. For this reason, a great deal of effort is devoted to the economic and behavioural theory underlying discrete-choice models.

If a particular model formulation is to survive, it should be derived from a theory whose predictions correspond most nearly with actuality (implying it is also operational in a real-world environment (in contrast to a research environment)). One of the difficulties in the survival stakes is the ability of the analyst, as the observer of individual behaviour, to postulate a modelling framework that provides an appropriate reflection of such behaviour. This is a major limitation in modelling; and as will be outlined in the book, we have to consider ways of accommodating this weakness so as to minimise the error in prediction. The translation of the homo economicus assumption (namely, if an object is chosen then it must maximise utility as the chooser perceives it) into a suitable empirical model is the essence of the modelling task.

The satisfying feature of the discrete-choice modelling approaches presented in the following chapters is that they have a definite operational capability, even if there is concern about some of the translational assumptions, and hence, a practitioner will find the style and scope suited for applications in the real-world. We have to, however, guard against the inappropriate use of the models, limiting their application to contexts where the assumptions underlying a theory are likely to be a reasonable approximation to reality. The emphasis is on knowing and applying; hence there is a sense about this book that makes it an introductory manual for practitioners. The range of applications provided and the test case study adequately illustrate the diversity of relevant applications of discrete-choice modelling procedures. It is thus intended that the book exposes, in the simplest manner possible, given the nature of the topic, the range of significant assumptions underlying the structure of the set of discrete-choice models that are of operational relevance, and in so doing anticipate a more selective use of this modelling capability in the spirit in which it has been developed.

1·2 Outline and Scope

The theme of this book is presented in four stages. Stage One introduces the necessary contextual prerequisites (Chapter 2) that provide a link with the established economic theory of consumer demand and a point of departure for the main thrust of the choice theory central to discrete-choice modelling. A paradigm of choice is proposed in Chapter 2.3 which outlines the relationship between the elements of the models in subsequent chapters and the 'characteristics' approach to consumer demand, the latter approach being an appropriate source of linkage with established economic theory. We are interested in predicting population behaviour, but argue that the hetero-geneous mix of individuals and likely responses in a choice environment supports a microeconomic disaggregate approach to modelling choice behaviour and a procedure for aggregation (post-estimation) to obtain population predictions. The emphasis on the individual in a choice environment is outlined in Chapter 2.

The second stage, embodied in Chapter 3 entails a detailed development of a basic choice model, which will become the point of reference for discussion in Chapters 4 onwards on the adequacy of a range of important behavioural assumptions. The best way to teach a subject is to develop a simple structure initially and then critically appraise it as part of a process of developing alternative and often more realistic structures. The basic choice model in Chapter 3 is a single equation, single decision model. Initially the established demand model with continuous commodities is outlined and shown to be unsuitable when commodities are discrete. An alternative approach is developed to handle discrete commodities, drawing on a specialised set of theory now referred to as random utility theory, and a procedure for maintaining many of the mathematical niceties of established demand theory is discussed, in particular the notion of a margin. A choice-theoretic modelling approach is developed with a minimum of assumptions in order to provide the most general framework. However, in order to solve for an operationally tractable model structure, some strong behavioural assumptions are introduced, notably the independence from irrelevant alterna-tives property. The structural solution for the basic choice model in its most basic form can be derived from first principles, making a particularly

3

useful reference model. This model is referred to
as the basic multinomial logit model.

In Chapter 3 we select one statistical procedure
for estimating the parameters of the basic choice
model, so that an empirical link between selection
probabilities associated with each discrete alternative and the utility associated with each alternative can be established. The maximum-likelihood
estimation technique is outlined for any number of
alternatives, it being the most appropriate
procedure, provided computer subroutines are
available. Chapter 3 is concluded with a discussion
of the measures used to test for statistical
significance, and a simple illustration of the
application of the basic choice model. It is
essential that the contents of Chapter 3 are understood before going to Chapter 4 and the next stage.

Chapters 4 to 8 introduce the additional
conceptual issues necessary in an introduction to
applied discrete-choice modelling. In Chapter 3 we
have assumed a choice set of a predefined number of
alternatives without asking about the actual number
and the basis for generating the choice set. How
do we generate a choice set? Theoretically a
procedure can be postulated for selecting a set of
choice sets in a probabilistic choice environment
(as outlined in Chapter 4.2), and for selecting
elements in each choice set; but from an empirical
perspective we are a long way from systematic
identification of choice sets. This issue is very
important since once a choice set is defined, the
analyst's empirical work becomes conditional on the
relevance of the choice set, and in the formulation
of the basic choice model on the acceptance of each
and every alternative being mutually exclusive and
collectively exhaustive.

In theory and practice the number of alternatives may be either excessive and/or subsets so
similar that there are good reasons for grouping
alternatives. This might also be a mechanism for
satisfying strong behavioural assumptions related
to the similarity of alternatives (the independence
from irrelevant alternatives property - introduced
in Chapter 3.3 and developed in detail in Chapter 5).
In Chapter 4.2 we discuss, within the framework of
the basic choice model, ways of handling grouped
alternatives. The entire chapter is devoted to
extending the basic choice model within a logit
context. In Chapter 3 we assumed a single equation
choice model based on a single decision. For a
number of reasons given in Chapter 4 it is more
realistic to consider a decision process as the
interaction of a number of choices, which should be

4

modelled either simultaneously or recursively.
Alternative decision structures are outlined in
Sections 4.3 and 4.4 Ways are suggested to
decompose a simultaneous decision structure into a
set of sequential-recursive models by invoking
separability of choice. The notion of a choice
hierarchy is used to tie all the discussion on
decision structure together. Section 4.4 is
included with an overview of more complex (yet
potentially more behaviourally plausible) logit
model forms; which is designed in part to highlight
the strong assumptions underlying the basic logit
choice model. The brief discussion of the similarity of alternatives in a choice set provides a
basis for justifying an extensive assessment in
Chapter 5 of the validity of the independence
assumption in the basic choice model.
    Having decided on a suitable decision structure,
the analyst has to decide on the form of the utility
expression which contains the set of attributes and
weights reflecting the relative importance of each
attribute. In Chapter 4.5 we take the simple
linear-in-parameters additive utility function and
discuss alternative specifications of the attributes. An extended discussion of this important
element of model specification is given in Appendix
B. The chapter concludes with a simple example of
two choices which utilises the main tools introduced
in this chapter.
    A central behavioural assumption of many share
models, of which the basic choice model is a member,
is that the ratio of the odds of selecting an alternative to that of another alternative remains
unchanged as other alternatives are added or deleted
from the choice set. This assumption is both a
strength and a weakness of such models; it is a
strength in that it enables the development of a
simply estimated and applied model (see Chapter 3),
and it is a weakness in that it is a somewhat
restrictive assumption in many applications. Chapter
5 is devoted to a detailed discussion of the
independence from irrelevant alternatives (IIA)
property, in particular procedures to determine if
it is violated in a particular application and if
so, proposals to remedy violation. The advantages
of a simple model are such that all efforts should
be made to assist in maintaining a simple, yet
suitable, structure prior to having to move to more
complex structures such as multinomial probit (as
discussed in Chapter 6), or nested logit (summarised
in Chapter 4).

Chapter 6 introduces a range of variants on the basic choice model, giving attention to the alternative statistical estimation techniques such as weighted least-squares regression and maximum likelihood. Modifications to the basic choice model are introduced which are designed to handle situations where pairs of alternatives violate the IIA property. The particular model is known as dogit,* ('d' referring to "dodging IIA"). A nonlogit procedure that does not require the IIA property is briefly discussed, referred to as multinomial probit, although we cannot develop it in this book. It is an advanced procedure which has recently been extensively outlined by Daganzo (1979) and evaluated by Horowitz (1980). Chapter 6 is concluded with an outline of ways of testing for alternative functional forms of the linear-in-parameters utility function.

The next two chapters present a range of issues that require some appreciation in a book on choice modelling, even though they are of more general relevance. Since the prime aim of discrete-choice modelling is to develop a forecasting capability, it is necessary to understand the issue of aggregating individual predictions to yield population predictions. The aggregation issue focusses on sources of bias due to defining nonhomogeneous decision units prior to estimation, and the use of aggregate measures of attributes. Two particular levels of aggregation are: (1) the use of group and intergroup averages in the definition of the magnitudes of explanatory variables for each individual and (2) the use of the average level of a variable for all individuals in a sample in obtaining the average probability of choice, both before and after a policy change, and in the calculation of elasticities of choice. A second important general issue is the transferability potential of a model estimated say in one location or time period and applied in another location or time period. Procedures are outlined that argue for transferability of model parameters subject to some modifications. Note that it is the functional form of the model and the estimated coefficients that are transferred, not the levels of the explanatory variables. Section 7.4 discusses alternative sample designs and their implications in choice modelling, and clarifies the sources of error that the modeller must minimize. Sampling is one of the

---

*This model is also known as the 'capture' model because of its relation to a special case of choice set generation. See Ben-Akiva (1977a).

most important elements of modelling, providing a
link between the analytical model and the data
environment. The last two sections of Chapter 7
illustrate a mechanism for obtaining from a choice
model behavioural shadow prices for variables that
are not expressed in monetary units; and raises
the possibility that behavioural phenomena such as
habit and threshold in choice may be important and
should be included in the formulation of more
relevant choice models.

Up to this point, all explanatory variables
have been assumed to be exogenous; however it is
reasonable to consider some variables as endogenous.
Simultaneous equation models are introduced in
Chapter 8 which incorporate endogenous variables,
and also the possibility of incomplete information.
The latter issue is closely related to endogenous
variables, since in practice many situations arise
where a variable is only identifiable on a subsample of the data, namely the subsample associated
with a particular alternative. An example is a
choice model of women working and nonworking where
the market wage is only identifiable with working
women. Sample separation is assumed and suitable
procedures are adopted to handle bias due to
selectivity of information. This chapter completes
Stage 3.

The final stage includes discussion of a number
of applications from a wide range of areas such as
employment, child care, transport and education;
and a detailed test case study complete with a
computer program, a data set listing, directions
to use the program and interpretation of the
output.

Two appendices have been prepared by Louviere
and Horowitz, with the aim of expanding on two
important areas of applied modelling, namely the
measurement and specification of attributes in a
utility function.

The book is designed primarily to provide an
introduction to the key issues in discrete-choice
modelling. Completion of this book by the reader
should enable him/her to go to the more detailed
literature at large (e.g. Manski and McFadden, 1980)
and place it in an appropriate context.

The reader will quickly realise that the book
is oriented towards the theory and application of
the logit form of discrete-choice models with cross-
sectional data. This is justified on a number of
grounds:

7

(a)   In a book on applied discrete-choice modelling the technique which appears to have the most suitable and definite application (so far) in a binary and multiple-alternative situation for either a single equation or multiple equation model is logit in its basic and complex forms.

(b)   Other techniques such as independent probit (see Section 6.5) are easy to apply in a binary context, although the empirical results are so similar to binary logit, but more difficult to interpret; thus it seems unnecessary to pursue this in any detail (it is briefly discussed in Chapter 6)

(c)   In a multiple-alternative context multinomial-covariance probit has been proposed as an alternative to the basic multinomial logit model (of Chapter 3). It is, however, still a research procedure, and does not appear at this stage to have any major advantages over the modified (or nested) logit model.   Furthermore computer costs become excessive, given current software, when the number of alternatives in a choice set goes beyond four. The nested logit model (discussed in Chapter 4) is an alternative logit specification which relaxes the independence-from-irrelevant alternatives property. McFadden (1980) has synthesised the research on nested logit. Daganzo (1979) has given a complete introduction to multinomial probit for those interested in this particular procedure or curious about how it differs from multinomial logit (see also Ortuzar and Williams, 1978).

(d)   The development of theory associated with discrete-choice models, when the data is time-series or panel has only recently been given any serious consideration (Heckman, 1980). While the 1980's should provide a full set of theory and empirical experience in the area of dynamic discrete-choice modelling it would be premature in an introductory book to even attempt a discussion on the few extant contributions. The major problem faced in this area is suitable data (Leplastrier, 1980).

CHAPTER 2

Contextual Prerequisites

2·1 Emphasis on the Individual

Societies typified by the U.S.A., Australia and Western Europe operate in an environment conditioned on the value judgement that individual preferences count; social choice being to a great extent the outcome of the accommodation of individual preferences and the welfare significance of such preferences. This value judgement is derived from the moral notion of democracy.

In its most general form the notion of an individual would be an atomistic unit - the individual person; although in reality we have a number of alternative bases such as the household, the family, the firm and the organisation. These societal-derived 'units' are best thought of as physical entities comprising a heterogeneous set of members each of whom maximises personal utility subject to unit-environment constraints. Unit-environment constraints reflect the fact that several factors (e.g. legal, social, etc.), as well as the individual budgets (time and money) must be considered when an individual attempts to maximise utility. Therefore, admitting of joint decision-making, the perspective adopted here is that allowance for jointness is reflected in the constraints. For example, member A of a two-person household knows that the other member's utility is maximised if, *ceteris paribus*, commodity X is consumed, and that member A will have to forego the consumption of commodity Y. The utility of member A, in a joint decision-making situation, is maximised in part with the knowledge of the other member's attainment of a maximum utility level, the index of the other member's maximum level of utility being an element in member A's set of constraints.

9

Selection of the 'strict' individual as the unit of analysis provides a more general basis on which to develop a theoretical framework. Furthermore the choice method presented in this book assumes selection of an alternative out of a predetermined choice set (see Section 4.2) hence all the constraints have been accommodated in the determination of the choice set, not in the selection of the utility maximising alternative from a given choice set.

An important aspect of all planning is to predict the demand for a particular service. While recognising that an ultimate aim is the determination of population choice (i.e. aggregate demand); since observed aggregate behaviour is the result of individual decision-making by many individuals the assumed heterogeneity of tastes and individual behaviour rules in the population makes the individual-based approach an appealing starting point for the study of consumer and producer choice behaviour. Grouping of individuals (referred to as aggregation) which display heterogeneity should be delayed as long as is possible and desirably only used, given the state of the art, after model analysis.[1] Furthermore, it is likely that the factors influencing a particular choice outcome will differ in value and range across the population such that any basis for market segmentation (see Section 7.2.3) must emanate from a detailed knowledge at the level of the decision-making unit. These premises are part of the rationale that argues for the relevance of studying the individual's behaviour in the prediction of market demand. That is, the 'true' measurement of the variation in the explanatory variables is a necessary condition for determining the influence of those variables on the behaviour of concern. At this level of data analysis, we have maximum flexibility in the way we combine model outputs in aggregate forecasting.[2]

In addition to the predictive output of a study of individual choice, we may very often be able to obtain an estimate of the utility derived by an individual (rather than some 'average' individual) which provides a source of information on the benefits associated with a specific project. The estimated change in utility as a result of some alteration in environment is an approximation of the change in benefit which in theoretical terms is the change in what is termed consumer surplus (see Note 3, Chapter 4). Approximate weighting to allow for any undesirable distributional implications can be easily handled at this level, and then aggregation obtains the total change in user benefit.

Therefore, the need to link utility with the services provided by commodities is best done at the individual level.

So far, the notion of utility has been freely used on the assumption that it is understood by the majority of readers. The notion of utility is a convenient theoretical construct that provides an index of the relative levels of satisfaction associated with the consumption of particular commodities per unit of time. Since commodities *per se* do not yield utility (unless there is some intrinsic value of a particular commodity which cannot be obtained in any other way), the utility being derived from the services associated with the commodity, then we are interested in identifying the services provided. Services are conveniently described in terms of a set of attributes (e.g. in-vehicle time, comfort, convenience, associated with travel by a mode; number of bedrooms, money price, garage facilities, frontage width, associated with housing). The level of utility obtained is some appropriately defined combination of the attributes (by level) each weighted by the relative importance of that attribute in contributing to total utility of the particular commodity. The important point is that individuals maximise utility by consuming bundles of attributes which define levels of service. Society attaches labels to commodities for convenience. In theory, every bundle of attributes is in the eyes of the individual a unique commodity. Thus a realistic study of demand must emphasise the relationship between utility and service, and this is only satisfactorily accommodated in a theoretical and empirical framework which adopts the individual as the unit of analysis. This is a central theme of the book.

2·2 Individual Choice and Individual Demand

Caution see errata sheet

We are interested in individual choice, but before continuing, a distinction between the terms 'choice' and 'demand' must be made. The word choice will be consistently used to refer to the selection decision by an individual between commodities which are perceived to be discrete and which are contained in a relevant choice set (i.e. 'what' or 'whether' as opposed to 'how much'). Examples of this type of decision are choice of occupation, what mode of travel to use, and whether to strike or not. However, this is not the only way in which the term choice is used in economics.

For example, choice axioms are used in the building
of a general theory of the consumer (e.g. the axiom
of rational choice), the net results of which are
normally a set of consumer demand functions. This
is a much more general use of the term choice in
that it refers to the choice between different
bundles of commodities, none of which are necessarily
perceived to be discrete.

Individual demand, for our purposes, will be
defined as the selection decision between
commodities which are perceived to be available in
a measurable continuum. On a more aggregate level,
the sum of individual choice situations may in
fact be considered a demand modelling problem.
For example, we may consider an individual contemplating whether to use public transport or car as
the mode to work as being faced with a choice
problem and model it as such, but on an aggregate
(e.g. zonal or city) level consider the demand for
public transport since the variable in question
(total public transport patronage) can be considered
continuous. It is quite easy to fall into the trap
of using the terms choice and demand interchangeably
and many authors seem to do so. In specifically
defining each of these, we hope to provide a
consistent thread throughout this book which will
be as free as possible of ambiguity.

The traditional economic assumption is that
commodities are finely divisible and the arguments
entering the utility expression of the individual
are quantities of various commodities consumed.
This assumption assures that a change in price will
have an observable effect on the quantity of the
good demanded by any individual. There are many
commodities for which this assumption does not hold.
For those commodities a change in price may either
leave the consumption of that commodity unaffected
or involve zero consumption of that commodity in
preference for another discrete option.

The essential difference between the two
'types' of commodities is that optimising behaviour
by the consumer when commodities are finely
divisible is defined by an individual demand
function that reflects marginal adjustments by the
consumer in response to changes in the levels of
attributes; when commodities are not finely
divisible marginal adjustments are not feasible
consequences. The unqualified term "marginal" is
defined precisely in economics to reflect small
changes. Thus the individual in consuming discrete
commodities is better represented by an individual
choice function. The individual demand function is
characterised by selection at an intensive margin;

12

we might usefully say that the individual choice function is characterised by selection at an _extensive_ margin. The notion of an extensive margin will be explained in detail in Chapter 3.

When is a commodity a member of an individual choice function or an individual demand function? Alternatively, when does a commodity become discrete? This is in part a function of the individual's perception of a commodity (as a bundle of attributes), and the uniqueness of such a commodity. Remember that a commodity is defined in terms of the mix of attributes, thus 5 kilograms of beef may be a different commodity to 20 kilograms of beef in that the difference is more than simply the weight. A useful categorisation is one which is based on individual decision rules:

(a)   individual demand functions are defined on commodities perceived to have an intensive margin;

(b)   individual choice functions are defined on commodities with an extensive margin; and can include categorical (i.e. those for which there is no doubt that they have an extensive margin) or other commodities perceived by an individual to have an extensive margin.

Some points of clarification are required to improve the understanding of when a commodity is a member of (a) or (b). Conceptually noncategorical commodities are continuously measurable, but an individual may perceive the amount of a particular commodity chosen as based on a selection out of a limited set of levels. For example, the quantity of beef demanded per unit of time can be perceived by the consumer as continuous (1 kg, 1.1 kg, 1.2 kg ...), hence there is an intensive margin with respect to the relevant attributes such as money, price; alternatively the consumer can perceive the quantity of beef demanded per unit of time as a selection out of 5 kg vs. 10 kg vs. 15 kg up to an amount defining the threshold of consumption of the particular commodity. The latter is a situation with an extensive margin in terms of the level of an attribute such as purchase price and thus individual choice. In a sense individual choice is defined in terms of the _thresholds_ of an individual demand function. The essential assumption is that the commodity must be assigned to a function to depict the utility space in which the maximising individual perceives the commodity.

2·3 Choice and Utility

the traditional economic model of consumer behaviour has disappointingly few implications for empirical research

(Muth, 1966: 699)

Although the theoretical underpinnings of discrete choice models contain elements of the traditional microeconomic theory of consumer behaviour, such as the formal definition of rational choice and other assumptions of traditional preference theory, the essential point of departure from traditional economic theory of consumer demand for the topic of this book is the postulate that utility is derived from the properties of things, or in the now classical work of Lancaster (1966, 1971) from the characteristics (in an objective dimension) which goods possess rather than goods *per se*. Goods are employed either singly or in combination to <u>produce</u> the characteristics which are the source of a consumer's utility.

The emphasis of this section is to take Lancaster's contribution as a point of departure from conventional consumer behaviour theory in economics, and to modify it so that the connection between the spirit of Lancaster's precise approach and the approach pursued in this book is clear. The connection with the characteristics approach is strong although Lancaster and others (e.g. Rosen, 1974) are only concerned in developing in detail a subset of the elements of what we will refer to as the paradigm of choice.

To appreciate the connection between the 'standard Lancaster approach' (or SLA) and modifications, let us briefly outline the SLA for the situations where goods are divisible (Lancaster, 1966, 1971) and indivisible (Rosen, 1974). Furthermore, so that the reader is able to interpret (and assess) the arguments in terms of the relationship to discrete-choice models, it is appropriate to formally state the paradigm of choice now and discuss its elements later. Formally the paradigm of choice underlying discrete-choice models is a set of three interconnected equations:

$$s_k = f_{kr}(t_r) \qquad (2.1(a))$$

$$u_j = g(s_{kj}) \qquad (2.1(b))$$

$$P_j = h(u_j) \qquad (2.1(c))$$

$$\text{and} \quad P_j = h(g(f_{kr}(t_r)\,)\,) \qquad (2.1(d))$$

where s_k is the perceived (marginal) utility of
         consumption service k
        t_r is the observable value of objective
         characteristic r
        u_j is the overall utility (preference)
         associated with the jth alternative
        s_{kj} is the level of attribute k
         (representing consumption service k)
         associated with alternative j
        P_j is the likelihood of choices allocated
         to alternative j

        f,g,h are functions yet to be determined
        (see Chapters 3 and 4).

The standard Lancaster approach postulates that
goods (X) are transformed into objective characteristics, t, through the relation

$$t = BX \qquad (2.2)$$

where B is an R by J matrix which transforms the J
goods into R objective characteristics. Hence B
defines what may be termed the consumption tech-
nology, assumed to be objective in that it is
invariant for all consumers. A range of mappings
exists such that several goods are capable of
producing one characteristic, and several characteristics are produced by one good. Lancaster asserts
that the relevant characteristics should be
defined not in terms of an individual's reaction to
the good (which we will refer to as consumption
service or attribute) but rather in terms of
objective measurement; that is, in terms of the
properties of the good itself. Lancaster is not
saying, however, that there can be no differences
between consumers in their perceptions of an
objective characteristic, but only that these
differences (if they exist) relate to the formation
of a preference function for t which is outside the
domain of his theory.

The rationale given for the emphasis on t is
that the interest of economists is on how people
will react to changes in prices or objective characteristics embodied in the goods that produce t, and

not in how the function U(t) is formed. The implication must be that the functions h, g and f_{kr} in
equations 2.1(a) to (c) can be reduced to a function
B( ) without any loss of information; that is
there is a one-to-one correspondence in content and
form between s_k and t_r, u_j and s_{kj}, which implies
that utility is a function of commodity characteristics:

$$u = U(t_1, t_2, \ldots, t_R) \qquad (2.3)$$

where t_r is the amount of the rth characteristic
that a consumer obtains from consumption
of commodities r = 1,...,R.

The particular formulation outlined above
assumes that goods are infinitely divisible,
frequently purchased and of low unit value. Many
goods are lumpy, i.e. not perfectly divisible,
particularly goods of relevance in discrete-choice
models, many of which are also infrequently
purchased. Rosen (1974) has developed a goods-
characteristics model when goods are indivisible
(or discrete), assuming that alternatives are
available for a continuous range of objective
characteristics. This latter assumption enables
elimination of Lancaster's transformation from goods
to characteristics and the ability to state a model
directly in terms of prices and quantities of
characteristics, still defined objectively in
Rosen's model. Invoking Hicks's composite good
theorem (Hicks, 1946) (allowing us to hold the
prices of all other goods constant except those
under study), we can assume one intrinsic group of
goods (e.g. modes of transport, residential accommodation) yielding objective characteristics
$(t_1, t_2, \ldots, t_R)$ and define the other goods consumed
as d. Then Rosen's model may be stated as

Maximise $\qquad U(t_1, t_2 \ldots, t_R) \qquad (2.4)$

subject to $\qquad p(t_1, t_2, \ldots, t_R) + d = M \qquad (2.5)$

where the price of d is arbitrarily set equal to
one dollar, M is the consumer's income, and
$p(t_1, t_2, \ldots, t_R)$ represents the price of one good
yielding objective characteristics $t_1, t_2, \ldots, t_R$
which are actually acquired. The budget constraint,
defined in terms of the objective characteristics
is non-linear. When goods are not divisible then

16

$p(t_1, t_2, \ldots, t_R)$ need not be linear, and hence it is not appropriate to define objective characteristics in terms of characteristics per dollar (or any other unit price), but instead in terms of their absolute levels. Price must be represented as a separate dimension, as it will be in the discrete-choice models.

Rosen's model is more appropriate in a discrete-choice theoretical framework, although it still links utility directly to the objective characteristics of goods. The paradigm of choice links utility to goods and utility to objective characteristics via a complex function of function(s). Herein is the point of departure from the Lancaster-Rosen contribution, although we take with us the spirit of the approach and use it as the starting point for developing the full set of relationships outlined in the paradigm of choice. In particular, discrete-choice modelling focusses principally on equations 2.1(b) and 2.1(c), and accepts the need to map attributes (or consumption services) into objective characteristics (often referred to as features or facilities) and vice versa in the development of predictive capability. In practice, it is common for analysts to assume a one-to-one correspondence between s_k and t_r such that s_k is a perfect estimate of t_r.

The relationship between utility and the sources of utility is clearly central to the decision on selection of commodities. Let us now outline in theoretical terms the alternative ways in which we can represent the sources of utility, given that we accept the limitations of using the Lancaster-Rosen Standard approach. We will present three modifications, the subsequent one building directly on the preceding, and use the final modified formalisation as the link with the basic choice model developed in Chapter 3. You are reminded at this stage that the discrete-choice model is essentially an analytical representation of equations 2.1(b) and 2.1(c), with alternative assumptions on g and h.

Since the objective properties of commodities may not be an appropriate measure of services, especially given that individuals maximise utility based on the perception of the characteristics, then an alternative 'modified Lancaster-Rosen approach' (MLRA) would assume that an individual consumes commodities by consuming the services provided by the commodities; that is, utility is a function of services rendered by commodities:

17

$$u = U(s_1, s_2, \ldots, s_K) \tag{2.6}$$

where s_k is the amount of kth consumption
service that a consumer obtains
from consumption of commodities.
$k = 1, \ldots, K$

Furthermore, given the uncertainty of the level
of service offered by commodities a 'further
modified Lancaster-Rosen approach' (FMLRA) would
assume that an individual consumes commodities by
consuming the expected services provided by the
characteristics associated with commodities; that
is, utility (assuming deterministic utility
maximisation) is a function of the expectation of
consuming a required level of service provided by
characteristics which group to define a commodity:

$$u = U((se + su)_1, (se + su)_2, \ldots, (se + su)_K) \tag{2.7}$$

where se_k = the expected amount of kth consumption
service that a consumer obtains from
consumption of commodity characteristics.
$k = 1, \ldots, K$

su_k = the unexpected amount of kth consumption
service that an individual obtains from
consumption of commodity characteristics.
$k = 1, \ldots, K.$

Equation (2.7) represents the individual's
decision calculus. However analysts are seldom
able to 'peep-into-the-head' of the individual and
accurately report this calculus, and so to make
explicit this restriction we can define the utility
function as given in equation (2.8):

$$u = U((se_o + se_{uo} + su_o + su_{uo})_1, \ldots,$$
$$(se_o + se_{uo} + su_o + su_{uo})_K) \tag{2.8}$$

where the subscripts 'o' and 'uo' indicate the
division of expected and unexpected consumption
services that a consumer obtains from the
consumption of commodity characteristics that is
observed and unobserved by the analyst. In
practice, we are not able to separate out the four
elements as is depicted in equation (2.8); rather
at best we can define an element that is observed
(denoted as V - see Chapter 3) and an element
that is unobserved (denoted as ε or epsilon), the
latter assumed to be distributed across the population in some defined way (see Section 3.3). It
is not likely to be possible to separate se_o and su_o,

18

hence V is simply the representation of the
composite of these two types of sources of utility;
likewise for ε with respect to se_{uo} and su_{uo}.

The four formulations (2.3, 2.6, 2.7 and 2.8)
are not independent, and can be combined to define
part of a paradigm of choice. Let us refer to the
objective characteristics as features, and attributes as the quantitative dimension in which consumption services are defined. There are many attributes
which map exactly into a feature; however an
attribute may be functionally related to more than
one feature and vice versa. For example, a feature
on private automatic branch exchanges (PABXs) might
be 'call holding while attending another call':
two attributes related to this feature would be
'the making of an enquiry call to another extension
while holding an outside call' and 'the holding of
an existing call while dealing with an incoming
outside call'. Throughout the book the separation
of supply 'price' into a vector of features and the
demand 'price' into a vector of attributes is used
to account for the important distinction between
the value of a commodity to an individual and the
objective nature of the commodity. This provides
one useful mechanism for identifying the possible
source of bias in using supply 'prices' as
determinants of choice; such prices have an
indirect influence via their role in the definition
of demand price. An important element in choice
modelling is the translation of features into
attributes so as to assess the impact of a change in
the objective properties of commodities; and the
translation of an attribute-level change into a
feature-level change to provide a basis for
determining the appropriate supply change. In some
circumstances the attribute and the feature only
differ in terms of magnitude. In other situations
the difference could be one of dimension - two
different characteristics. Thus the term
'characteristics' is usefully defined on both the
feature and the attribute dimensions, the mapping
of feature into attribute and/or attribute into
feature may involve one or more characteristics.

The subset of the paradigm of choice is
summarised overleaf (excluding equation 2.8 for
simplicity, without removing the essential
argument):

$$u = U((se + su)_1, (se + su)_2, \ldots,$$
$$(se + su)_K), \tag{2.9}$$

$$(se + su)_k = f_k(t_1, t_2, \ldots, t_R), \quad k = 1, \ldots, K \tag{2.10}$$

$$\text{or} \quad s_k = f(t_{11}, t_{21}, \ldots, t_{R1}, t_{12}, t_{22}, \ldots, t_{RJ}) \tag{2.11}$$

or

$$(se + su)_k = f_k(t_{11}, t_{21}, \ldots, t_{R1}, t_{12}, t_{22}, \ldots, t_{RJ})$$
$$r = 1, \ldots, R$$
$$j = 1, \ldots, J \tag{2.12}$$

t_r, in equation (2.10) is defined as the rth feature, assumed independent of the jth commodity, and is an appropriate formulation when explicit commodities cannot be formally defined in a choice framework; that is, where each mix of features is a (potentially) unique commodity. Alternatively, since a particular consumption service (defined in terms of atrributes) can be obtained from various bundles of features and varying levels of features, service can be defined across a range of R features, as shown in equation (2.10) in a framework of J commodities. Equation (2.9) is a commodity-independent relationship between attributes and features. Equation (2.11) is a commodity-specific relationship. To complete the paradigm two additional expressions are required. The first, equation (2.13), indicates the dependence of t_{rj} on the unit offering by the jth commodity of the total quantity of feature r:

$$t_{rj} = g_{rj}(y_{rj}), \ldots \quad r = 1, \ldots, R; \quad j = 1, \ldots, J \tag{2.13}$$

where y_{rj} is the quantity of feature r available in one unit of commodity j. The final equation (2.14) relates the total amount of the rth feature obtained from the jth commodity to the quantity of the commodity consumed (i.e. G_j):

$$t_{rj} = g_{rj}(G_1, G_2, \ldots, G_J) \quad j = 1, \ldots, J \tag{2.14}$$

The approach assumes that a particular consumption service (defined on one or a set of attributes) can be met by one or more objective characteristics (defined on one or a set of features and translated into a perceived set of attributes), and that a particular objective characteristic can exist in one or more commodities.

The paradigm of choice, together with alternative specifications of the relationship between u_j, s_{kj} and t_r, is consistent with the general approach to consumer behaviour in economics, although the analysis of the relationship between consumption of commodities and sources of utility begins further back in the individual's decision process. We accept that a consumer does not directly acquire objective characteristics or consumption services; rather he purchases commodities. Commodities are acquired in those amounts that provide the quantities of t_{rj}'s that provide the amount of desired s_k's (or $(se + su)_k$ or $(se_o + se_{uo} + su_o + su_{uo})_k$) that maximises utility. This gives

$$('price'_j)(\partial u / \partial \text{ expenditure on } j)$$

$$= \sum_j \sum_k (\partial u / \partial (se + su)_k)(\partial (se + su)_k / \partial t_r)(\partial (se + su)_k / \partial t_{rj}).$$

$$.(\partial t_{rj} / \partial G_j) \, , \, G_j > 0$$

In words, given a positive level of consumption of the jth commodity, the value of a commodity j, equal to the product of the price of j and the marginal utility derived from the expenditure on j is equal to the product of the marginal utility of the kth attribute, the marginal rate of substitution between the kth attribute and the rth objective characteristic, the marginal rate of substitution between the kth attribute and the rth objective characteristic contained in commodity j; and the marginal rate of substitution between the rth objective characteristic contained in the jth commodity and the quantity of the jth commodity consumed, all other things being equal.

We are now in a position to develop the basic choice model, by taking the paradigm of choice as central to the formulation, and adding assumptions as required to qualify the particular analytical form of the model's specification of the relationship between P_j, u_j and s_{kj}.

NOTES — CHAPTER 2

1. Because the aggregation problem (see Chapter
    7.2) is not currently resolved in terms of the
    explicit inclusion of a distributional
    assumption on the within-unit variance when
    grouped data is used, such that the macro and
    micro approaches will result in the same
    predictions of market demand, the best way of
    allowing for the aggregation problem is to
    approach the modelling task with individual-
    level data; this assumed to be a desirable
    prerequisite to the satisfactory exploration
    of market or macro-behaviour.

2. Hence, the approach in this book to modelling
    involves one particular interpretation of the
    way a model interfaces with the data, namely
    at the disaggregate or individual level; in
    contrast to the aggregate or market level.
    Both approaches are interested in aggregate
    demand; the individual approach opting for a
    direct mechanism for representing the
    relationship between the individual's choice
    alternatives and the attributes which have an
    influence on the choice outcome, and then
    drawing on some aggregation rules to combine
    individual outcomes to arrive at a market
    demand.

CHAPTER 3

A Basic Discrete Choice Model

3·1 Introduction

Two elements of the paradigm of choice proposed in Chapter 2 are central to the development of a basic choice model. These elements are the function which relates the probability of an outcome to the utility associated with each alternative; and the function which relates the utility of each alternative to a set of attributes that, together with suitable weights, determine the level of utility of each alternative. In this chapter, we develop in detail a basic choice model, known as the multinomial logit model, in the belief that the most effective way of understanding discrete choice modelling is to build up a basic model in detail, then to appraise this model and build on it by way of introducing a wide range of relevant issues.

In Section 3.2 the conventional microeconomic demand model with continuous commodities is outlined and used as a basis for demonstrating its inadequacy when commodities are discrete. A general theory of discrete choice is developed around the notion of the existence of population choice behaviour defined in terms of a set of individual behaviour rules, and a structure of the utility function that contains a random utility component. The random utility model is then developed to arrive at a formulation for obtaining selection probabilities. Section 3.3 takes the analytically intractable general model and introduces a number of assumptions on the distribution and form of the relationship between utility and probability of selection, resulting in a computationally feasible basic choice model, the multinomial-logit model.

Having derived the basic choice model in adequate detail, a procedure for estimating the parameters in the utility expression of the logit model known as maximum-likelihood estimation is introduced in Section 3.4. Various statistical measures of goodness-of-fit are outlined in Section 3.5, along with the main policy outputs such as elasticities and probabilities. The chapter concludes with a simple example of the application of the basic choice model.

Chapter 3 represents a comprehensive introduction to the basic elements of a choice model, and is in sufficient detail that the reader should be able to obtain a clear appreciation of how the final model is derived.

3·2 The Theoretical Framework

In conventional consumer analysis with a continuum of alternatives, one can often plausibly assume that all individuals in a population have a common behaviour rule, except for purely random 'optimisation' errors, and that systematic variations in aggregate choice reflect common variations in individual choice at the intensive margin. By contrast, systematic variations in aggregate choice among lumpy alternatives must reflect shifts in individual choice at the extensive margin, resulting from a distribution of decision rules in the population.

(McFadden, 1974: 106)

Many economic decisions are complex and involve choices that are non-marginal. Typical examples include the choice of occupation, choice of ownership of particular consumer durables, choice of house type and residential location, and choice of transport mode for the journey to and from work. Although economists are primarily interested in market demand, which is the result of the sum of individual demands over the population according to a rule of aggregation;[1] given that each individual is making individual consumption decisions based on individual needs and environment, the complexity of these individual decisions makes the relationship between market and individual demand even more complex.

Within a framework of economic rationality and a postulated structure of utility maximisation the possibility exists of the presence of unobserved attributes of individuals such as tastes and unmeasured attributes of alternatives which vary over the population in such a way that they obscure the implications of the individual behaviour model.

Given this state, is it feasible to deduce from an individual choice model properties of population choice behaviour which have empirical content? The answer is yes, the justification for which is given in this chapter. Data can be obtained on the behaviour of a cross-section of consumers selected from a population with common observed socioeconomic characteristics (but differing levels), money budgets M_q and demands G_q associated with each individual ($q = 1,...,Q$). A reasonable behavioural model, derived from the individual's utility function $u = U(G,\omega)$ which is maximised subject to the budget constraint (M) is $G = h(M;\omega)$ where ω is a representation of the tastes of an individual. The model may be used to test behavioural hypotheses such as those relating to the structural features of parametric demand functions, particularly price and income elasticities, and the revealed preference hypothesis that the observed data are generated by utility-maximising consumers (Leibenstein, 1976). Because of measurement errors in G_q, consumer optimisation errors, and unobserved variations in the population, the observed data can be expected not to fit the behavioural equation exactly (Hensher & Dalvi, 1978). The procedure of most empirical demand studies is to ignore the possibility of taste variations in the sample and assume that the sample has randomly distributed observed demands about the exact values G for some representative tastes $\bar{\omega}$, i.e. $G_q = h(M_q ; \bar{\omega}) + \varepsilon_q$ where ε_q is an unobserved random term distributed independently of M_q. Hence $\bar{\omega}$ has no distribution itself.

In a population of consumers who are homogeneous with respect to monetary budgets, aggregate demand in this specification will equal individual demand in the aggregate and all systematic variations in market demand can be interpreted as generated by a common variation at the intensive margin of the identical individual demands. In the absence of unobserved variations in tastes or budgets there is no extensive margin affecting aggregate demand (McFadden, 1974a; Hensher, 1974). Conventional statistical techniques can be applied to

$G_q = h(M_q ; \bar{\omega}) + \varepsilon_q$ under the specification above to test hypotheses on the structure of h. In a conventional economic demand study where quantities demanded vary continuously such that marginal optimisation errors and measurement errors are likely to be particularly important, and possibly dominate the effect of taste variations, the specification above is realistic.

When the set of alternative choices is finite, how do we have to interpret the traditional model, and what role can it play? With discrete alternatives the standard utility maximisation model with the corresponding demand equation $G_q = h(M_q ; \omega)$

predicts a single chosen G (referred to as an alternative) when tastes and unobserved attributes of alternatives are assumed uniform across the population. The conventional statistical specification in $G_q = h(M_q ; \bar{\omega}) + \varepsilon$ would then imply that all observed variation G_q in demand over the finite set of alternatives is the result of behaviour described by some global disturbance term. That is, heavy demands are imposed on the random disturbance term. Continuing this line of argument, McFadden states:

> *Aggregate demand can usually be treated as a continuous variable, as the effect of the discreteness of individuals' alternatives is negligible. As a result, aggregate demand may superficially resemble the demand for a population of identical individuals for a divisible commodity. However, systematic variations in the aggregate demand for the lumpy commodity are all due to shifts at the extensive margin where individuals are switching from one alternative to another, and not at the intensive margin as in the divisible commodity, identical individual case. Thus it is incorrect to apply the latter model to obtain specifications of aggregate demand for discrete alternatives.*

(McFadden, 1974a: 309)

When commodities are not continuous there is no intensive margin at which changes in the magnitudes of attributes produce responses measured by a change in the criterion variable. That is, small marginal adjustments are not feasible consequences at the level of the individual. Although it is not possible (when the unit of analysis is the individual or household) with cross-sectional revealed preference data to accommodate discrete choice in an atomistic individual choice framework (current practice being limited to such data), the invoking of population choice behaviour as a model defined on a set of individual behaviour rules permits maintenance of the marginal calculus through a redefinition of the margin. The margin is now seen as the extensive margin for the population, and it is relevant to each individual member of the population because the individual behaviour rule is contained within the set of individual behaviour rules. This is guaranteed because of the assumption that an element of utility is random, is individual-specific, and is connected to the criterion variable (i.e. probability of selection) via a defined distribution. This defined distribution is that which will accommodate the way in which the individual behaviour rule is mapped into the set of individual behaviour rules. It is the individual-specificity due to idiosyncrasies in tastes, conditioned on the representative utility, which produces a distribution of decision rules in the population.[2] This permits the population margin to be used to assess the effect on each individual of a change in an observable attribute.

What is required is a formulation of the model in which the effects of individual difference in tastes and optimization behaviour on the error structure in the conventional specification are made explicit. Alternatively, we need a general procedure for formulating models of population choice behaviour from distributions of decision rules in the population where commodities are discrete. This is developed in the next section.

3·2·1   A General Approach in Terms of Random Utility

A study of individual choice behaviour requires three primary ingredients:

(1)   objects of choice and sets of alternatives available to decision makers (DM) known as choice set definition;
(2)   the observed attributes of DMs and a rule for combining them;
(3)   a model of individual choice and behaviour, and the distribution of behaviour patterns in the population.

Introducing some notation, let G indicate the set of alternatives in the (global) choice set, and S the set of vectors of measured attributes of the

decision makers. Then an individual, drawr randomly
(in a simple random sample) from the population,
will have some attribute vector s ∈ S, and will face
some set of available alternatives A ⊆ G. (From now
on G and S are not required.)[3] Hence the actual
choice for one individual, described by particular
levels of a common set of attributes s and alternatives A across the sampled population[4] can be
defined as drawing from a multinomial distribution
with selection probabilities (multinomial refers
to the existence of two or more possible outcomes).

$$P(x|s,A) \ \forall \ x \in A \quad \text{(The probabilities} \qquad (3.1)$$
$$\text{of each alternative)}$$

In words, equation (3.1) states the probability of
selecting alternative x, given the individual's
socioeconomic background and set of alternatives A,
for each and every alternative contained in the set
A. x, the notation for consumption services or
attributes, is used to emphasise that the alternative is defined in terms of a set of attributes.

   To operationalise this condition, we need to
establish an individual behaviour rule, defined as
a function 'IBR', which maps each vector of observed
attributes s and a possible alternative set A into
a selected alternative of A. We are interested in
a model of individual behaviour, which is an
analytical device for representing the set of
behaviour rules 'SIBR' relevant to all the individuals defining the sampled population. For example,
IBR may be a particular choice function resulting
from the maximisation of a specific utility function,
whereas SIBR may be the set of choice functions
which result from the maximisation of some utility
function. When unmeasured attributes (often
referred to as tastes) vary across the sampled
population, there exist many possible behaviour
rules in a model SIBR.
   With multiple behavioural rules in the population a model SIBR which describes a population,
must have a probability defined on the measurable
subsets of SIBR specifying the distribution of the
SIBRs in the population.
   The selection probability that an individual
drawn at random from the population will choose
alternative x, given the observed attributes s and
the alternative set A, is given by equation (3.2).

$$P(x|s,A) \ = \ P\{\text{IBR} \in \text{SIBR}|\text{IBR}(s,A) = x\} \qquad (3.2)$$

The right-hand side is, in words, the probability of choosing a particular individual behaviour rule contained in the model given that the particular individual behaviour rule, defined on s and A, is to choose x. Hence the right-hand side defines the probability of occurrence of a behavioural rule producing this choice. It is not the probability that the IBR is contained in the set, but the probability of choosing that IBR within the SIBR, given that the IBR maps the attributes into the choice x. This relationship is an initial condition for a model of choice behaviour. If P is assumed to be a member of a parametric family of probability distributions (e.g. normal, Weibull, Gumbell, gamma - see Section 3.3), and the actual choices are multinomially distributed with probabilities as given in equation (3.2), then estimates of the parameters may potentially be obtained.

Having postulated the SIBR model, we need to relate the selection probabilities to the utility maximisation assumption which is central to the classical rational economic consumer (refer to Chapter 2.3). How do we represent the sources of utility in the choice model? Initially, we can assume that each individual defines utility in terms of attributes according to a common functional form.

Let U_{iq} be the utility of the ith alternative for the qth individual. Further assume each utility value can be partitioned into two components: a systematic component or 'representative utility', V_{iq} and a random component, ε_{iq} which is a reflection of the individual idiosyncrasies of tastes. Then,

$$U_{iq} = V_{iq} + \varepsilon_{iq} \tag{3.3}$$

V_{iq} is subscripted q, even though we define V as representative, because the level of an attribute contained in the expansion of

$$V_{iq} \ (= \sum_{k=1}^{K} \beta_{ik} s_{ikq})$$ varies across individuals.

Only βs are assumed constant across individuals (although they can vary across alternatives), i.e. only the coefficients, not the levels of attributes are independent of q.[5]

This dichotomisation is undertaken for operational reasons when populations of individuals are being modelled. It is assumed that one part of utility is common to all individuals while the other part is individual-specific. This is a very crucial assumption, implying the existence of a significant element of the full attribute set which is associated with homogeneous utility across the population under study. That is, one element, V_{iq} is assumed to take on a homogeneity interpretation across the population in terms of the relative importance of those attributes that are contained in V_{iq}, hence β_i, not β_{iq}. Clearly, the particular definition of the dimensions of V_{iq} will depend largely on the population being studied, the ability to segment the sampled population if it is consistent with achieving homogeneity of utility (see Section 7.2), and the extent to which known or assumed attributes yielding representative utility can be measured. This is discussed further in Chapter Four.

It is assumed that the systematic component is that part of utility contributed by attributes that can be observed by the analyst and the random component is the utility contributed by the attributes unobserved by the analyst. This should not be interpreted to mean that individuals maximise utility in a random manner, rather they are deterministic utility maximisers (however see page 136, Section 5.2). Yet the analyst does not have the capability of 'peeping into the head' of each individual and fully observing the set of influencing factors and hence the complete decision calculus, making it necessary to assign a probability to any event selection. The deterministic utility maximisation function is better thought of as a 'perceived maximisation' function, since the existence of an imperfect market results in the individual seeking to maximise utility to a level that he perceives as maximum. We now have most of the basic concepts necessary in the formulation of a model.

Individuals are assumed to choose the alternative that yields the highest utility. For this reason, the empirical structure of the utility function is of central concern in individual choice modelling, and represents the mechanism by which the attributes of the alternatives and the individual socioeconomic environment influence the choice probabilities and hence the predictive capability of the model. Details on alternative specifications of the relationship between V_{iq} and the attributes are developed in Section 4.5. Individual q will choose alternative i if and only if (iff)

$$U_{iq} > U_{jq} \qquad j \neq i \in A \tag{3.4}$$

The interesting conditions of $U_{iq} = U_{jq}$ or $U_{iq} \approx U_{jq}$ are discussed in a later Chapter (Section 7.6). From equations (3.3) and (3.4) alternative i is chosen iff

$$(V_{iq} + \varepsilon_{iq}) > (V_{jq} + \varepsilon_{jq}) \tag{3.5}$$

or rearranging to place the observables together and the unobservables together,

$$(V_{iq} - V_{jq}) > (\varepsilon_{jq} - \varepsilon_{iq}) \tag{3.6}$$

Since the analyst does not know $(\varepsilon_{jq} - \varepsilon_{iq})$ and hence cannot determine with certainty if $(V_{iq} - V_{jq}) > (\varepsilon_{jq} - \varepsilon_{iq})$, he has to assign a probability with which $(\varepsilon_{jq} - \varepsilon_{iq})$ is likely to be less than $(V_{iq} - V_{jq})$. Thus we have the following equations:

$$P_{iq} \equiv P(x_i | s, A) = P[IBR_\varepsilon \in SIBR | IBR_\varepsilon \ (s, A) = x_i] \tag{3.7}$$

$$P(x_{iq} | s_q, A) = P_{iq} = P[\{\varepsilon(s, x_j) - \varepsilon(s, x_i)\} < \{V(s, x_i) - V(s, x_j)\}]$$

$$\text{for all } j \neq i \tag{3.8}$$

with (3.8) being one interpretation or definition of the translation of equation (3.7) into an expression in terms of V and ε. Moving from (3.7) to (3.8) is not a straight substitution as such. We have taken the conceptual notion of an IBR as given in (3.2) and given it an operational flavour. Equation (3.8) is not equal to (3.7), but one translation in terms of V and ε. That is, given utility written in two components, and given that an individual is going to choose i over j if $U_i > U_j$ then IBR implies equation (3.8).

In other words, the probability that an individual drawn randomly from the sampled population, with attributes s and choice set A will choose x_i equals the probability that the difference between the random utility of alternative j and alternative

31

i is less than the difference between the representative utility levels of alternative i and
alternative j for all alternatives in the choice
set. We do not know the actual distribution of
$\varepsilon(s,x_j) - \varepsilon(s,x_i)$ across the population, but assume
that it is random and is related to the probability
according to a distribution yet to be defined.
Possible statistical distributions are the cumulative normal or the Weibull. We will discuss this
later. The model given in equation (3.8) is known
as a random utility model (RUM). Unlike the
traditional economic model of consumer demand, we
are introducing a more complex yet more realistic
assumption on individual behaviour to account for
the inability of the analyst to fully represent
the dimensions determining preference in the utility
function.

So far we have developed a theoretical
specification of the relationship between the
selection of an alternative and the sources of
utility which influence the final choice. No
assumptions have been made as to the distribution of
the elements of utility across the population. In
order to begin relating equation (3.8), the random
utility model, to a useful statistical specification
for purposes of empirical measurement, two fundamental notions have to be understood: the
distribution function, particularly in a cumulative
form and the density function in its joint form.
These concepts are discussed now, and then we will
be in a position to specify the structure of the
random utility model which requires solution for
empirical application. Intuitively, we have
utility space and IBRs, and want to formulate the
model in an n-dimensional space.

Consider a continuous random variable Z and
define the function F(Z) to be such that F(a) is
the probability that Z takes on a value less than
or equal to a (i.e. $F(a) = P(Z \leq a)$). We call
F(Z) a cumulative distribution function (CDF),
since it accumulates the probability of Z up to the
value a. It is monotonically increasing over all
values of Z. Limiting ourselves to cases where
the CDF is continuous, we define the derivative of
F(Z) to be given by F'(Z) (or $\partial F/\partial Z$) = f(Z) and
call this the probability density function (PDF) of
the random variable Z. An example of a PDF is
given in Figure 3.1. For a continuous function at
a given point, f is not interpreted as a probability, but the height of the curve.

FIGURE 3·1 :
An Example of a Probability Density Function

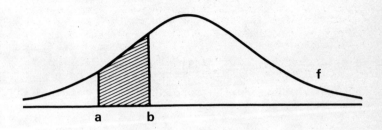

The probability of Z being between any two points, a and b, is simply given by the area under f between the points a and b. This may be calculated by the formula

$$P\ (a \leq Z \leq b) = \int_a^b f(z)\,dz$$

where z is a dummy variable of integration. From this, the probability of Z being less than or equal to a (our definition of the CDF F(a)) is given by

$$F(a) = \int_{-\infty}^a f(z)\,dz.$$

Extending these notions to the case of n random variables $Z_1, Z_2, \ldots, Z_n$, the probability that $Z_1 \leq a_1$, $Z_2 \leq a_2, \ldots Z_n \leq a_n$ <u>simultaneously</u> (jointly) is equal to

$$F(a_1, a_2, \ldots, a_n) = \int_{-\infty}^{a_1} \int_{-\infty}^{a_2} \ldots \int_{-\infty}^{a_n} f(z_1, z_2, \ldots, z_n)$$

$$dz_1 dz_2 \ldots \ldots dz_n.$$

We call $F(a_1, a_2 \ldots a_n)$ the <u>joint CDF</u> and $f(z_1, z_2, \ldots, z_n)$ the <u>joint PDF</u> for the random variables $Z_1, Z_2, \ldots, Z_n$.

Finally, given the joint PDF of n random variables, we can find the joint marginal PDF of any subset of k of these random variables by integrating out (from $-\infty$ to ∞), the other $n - k$ variables. For example, if we are interested in the joint marginal PDF of Z_1 and Z_2, this is given by

$$\int_{-\infty}^{\infty} \cdots \int_{-\infty}^{\infty} f(z_1, z_2, \ldots, z_n) \, dz_3 dz_4 \cdots dz_n$$

This leaves the joint marginal density (PDF) of Z_1 and Z_2 since all other variables have been integrated out. Furthermore, the joint marginal CDF of Z_1 and Z_2 is given by

$$\int_{-\infty}^{a_1} \int_{-\infty}^{a_2} \int_{-\infty}^{\infty} \cdots \int_{-\infty}^{\infty} f(z_1, z_2, \ldots, z_n) \, dz_1 dz_2 \cdots dz_n$$

This is the case since we have taken the joint marginal PDF of Z_1, and Z_2 and integrated this over Z_1 and Z_2 from $-\infty$ to a_1 and a_2 respectively. In other words, the joint marginal CDF of Z_1 and Z_2 can be interpreted as $F(a_1, a_2, \infty, \infty, \ldots, \infty)$. For a further discussion of this, see Freund (1962, Chapter 5).

We are now in a position to specify the structure of the choice model in more detail. The meaningfulness of distributional and density assumptions will become apparent if the aims of choice model development are briefly recapped. The aim of a choice model is to estimate the significance of the determinants of $V(s,x)$ in equation (3.8). For each individual q the analyst observes some ordering (see next paragraph) of the alternatives and from these data has to infer the influence of various attributes in the utility expression on $V(s,x)$, shortened to V_{jq}. The specification of the functional form of V_{jq} in terms of attributes (i.e. the relationship between decision attributes and observed choice behaviour) has to be determined since this has an influence on the significance of attributes. However we will assume a form that is linear additive. By linear additive, we mean a composition rule for mapping the multidimensional attribute vector into a unidimensional overall

34

utility of the form $V_{jq} = \beta_{1j} f_1 (s_{1jq})$
$$+ \ldots + \beta_{kj} f_k (s_{kjq}).$$ Note

that the characteristics may enter in straight
linear form, as logarithms or as various powers. By
linear we mean linear in parameters. For clarity
of exposition, however, we will continue to use V_{jq}
rather than the expression in terms of attributes.

The procedure being developed for the basic
choice model requires that the analyst only observe
the individual's choice and the defined choice set,
not the rank order of all alternatives. Alternative
approaches could have been adopted such as the rank
order of all alternatives (see Section 9.6),
although it is argued that such information is
relatively unreliable where alternatives are not
frequently used. This alternative procedure
increases the total information from a given individual (you are 'exploding' the data), permitting
more than one observation per individual, but at the
expense of increased unreliability of output. At
this juncture in the state of the art, such an
alternative approach should be relegated to the
area of future research.

The next step is to specify a probabilistic
model of the observed data (as a function of the
parameters associated with each attribute), and to
use probabilistic assumptions which will enable
adequate statistical testing. A statistical
estimation technique is required in the process of
obtaining estimates of the parameters associated
with attributes. In the basic choice model we have
selected a technique referred to as 'maximum-
likelihood estimation' (MLE), which will be outlined
in detail in Section 3.4. The maximum-likelihood
estimates are obtained by maximisation of a
probabilistic function with respect to the parameters.

The choice model development proceeds in a
series of logical steps: (a) initially we assume
that an individual q will select alternative i if
and only if U_{iq} is greater than the level of
utility associated with any other alternative in
the choice set (equation (3.4)); (b) then the
probability that the individual would observe
alternative i being ranked higher than any other
alternative j in the choice set is determined,
conditional on knowing the V_{jq}'s for all j in the
individual's choice set.

35

Assuming that the known value of V_{jq} is v_j, then equation (3.8) can be expressed as

$$P_{iq} = P(U_{iq} > U_{jq} | V_{jq} = v_j, j \in A_q) \; \forall \; j \neq i \qquad (3.9)$$

This is a statement about the probability that the random elements (ε_{iq}'s) take on a specific relationship with respect to the quantities of interest, the V_{jq}'s. Once an assumption is made about the joint distribution of the ε_{jq}'s and the V_{jq}'s are specified in terms of parameters, we can then apply the maximum-likelihood estimation procedure.

Given equation (3.8), let us rearrange it to express the right-hand side in terms of the relationship between ε_{jq} and the other elements.

$$P_{iq} = P[\varepsilon_{jq} < V_{iq} - V_{jq} + \varepsilon_{iq}, \forall j \in A_q, j \neq i]$$

For a particular alternative, i, we need to identify the level of ε_i. Since ε_i has a distribution of values in the sampled population, denote all possible values of ε_{iq} by b_ℓ ($\ell = 1, \ldots, r$) and assume initially some discrete distribution (i.e. a limited number of levels of ε_{iq}). Then

$$P_{iq} = P[\varepsilon_{iq} = b_\ell, \; \varepsilon_{jq} < V_{iq} - V_{jq} + b_\ell,$$

$$\forall j \in A_q, j \neq i] \qquad (b_\ell = b_1, b_2, \ldots, b_r) \qquad (3.10)$$

This equation can be expanded:

$$P_{iq} = P[\varepsilon_{iq} = b_1, \text{ and } \varepsilon_{jq} < V_{iq} - V_{jq} + b_1,$$

$$\forall j \in A_q, j \neq i]$$

$$+ P[\varepsilon_{iq} = b_2 \text{ and } \varepsilon_{jq} < V_{iq} - V_{jq} + b_2,$$

$$\forall j \in A_q, j \neq i]$$

$$+ \ldots$$

$$+ P[\varepsilon_{iq} = b_r \text{ and } \varepsilon_{jq} < V_{iq} - V_{jq} + b_r,$$

$$\forall j \in A_q, j \neq i]$$

Alternatively,

$$P_{iq} = P[\varepsilon_{iq} = b_1][P(\varepsilon_{jq} < V_{iq} - V_{jq} + b_1,$$

$$\forall j \in A_q, \ j \neq i)]$$

$$+ \ldots$$

$$+ P[\varepsilon_{iq} = b_r][P(\varepsilon_{jq} < V_{iq} - V_{jq} + b_r,$$

$$\forall j \in A_q, \ j \neq i)]$$

or

$$P_{iq} = \sum_{\ell=1}^{r} P[\varepsilon_{iq} = b_\ell][P(\varepsilon_{jq} < V_{iq} - V_{jq} + b_\ell),$$

$$\forall j \in A_q, \ j \neq i] \tag{3.11}$$

Equation (3.11) can be modified further by assuming a continuous distribution of b_ℓ's ($-\infty$ to $+\infty$), giving equation (3.12)

$$P_{iq} = \sum_{g=1}^{\infty} P[\varepsilon_{iq} = b_g] \ \Delta b_g \ [P(\varepsilon_{jq} < V_{iq} - V_{jq} + b_g),$$

$$\forall j \in A_q, \ j \neq i] \tag{3.12}$$

Thus, in the limit, as $\Delta b_g \to 0$

$$\lim_{\Delta b \to 0} P_{iq} = \int_{-\infty}^{\infty} P[\varepsilon_{iq} = b_g][P(\varepsilon_{jq} < V_{iq} - V_{jq} + b_g),$$

$$\forall j \in A_q, \ j \neq i] \tag{3.13}$$

Equation (3.13) is a general expression for the relationship between a selection probability and the attributes of the alternatives in the choice set for a utility maximising consumer under the assumed condition of random utility, the randomness due to the information gap between the utility maximiser and the analyst. This equation is a most general formulation of a choice model. A number of assumptions have to be introduced to convert equation (3.13) to an operational model. In the rest of this chapter, we introduce assumptions that permit a very simple (or basic) operational model; in later chapters other assumptions are made that

37

result in more complex although behaviourally more appealing model forms.

3·3 The Basic Choice Model—A Particular Model Formulation

To make the individual choice model operationally tractable, a number of axioms have been developed to condition the interpretation placed on the empirically identifiable selection probabilities. Another way of expressing this is to say that in practice formulae are specified for the selection probabilities, and then the question of whether these formulae could be obtained via equation (3.13) from some distribution of utility-maximising consumers is examined. The defined parametric specifications associated with the particular operational models used to obtain selection probabilities do not have a strict choice-theoretic foundation.

The main axiom of selection probability developed to assist in the formulation of a simple operational model, is known as The Independence-from-Irrelevant Alternatives (IIA). This axiom states that the ratio of the probabilities of choosing one alternative over another (where both alternatives have a non-zero probability of choice) is unaffected by the presence or absence of any additional alternatives in the choice set.

This condition is both a strength and weakness of a model: it is a strength in that it provides a computationally convenient choice model, and permits the introduction and/or elimination of alternatives in the choice set without re-estimation; it is a weakness if the observed and unobserved attributes of utility are not independent of one another and/or if there is correlation of the unobserved components of utility among alternatives (Hensher & Stopher, 1979). The presence of the IIA condition, however, should not be of general concern:

> The independence assumption is a priori
> neither desirable not undesirable, but
> should be accepted or rejected on
> empirical grounds depending on the
> circumstances.

(Charles River Associates 1976: D-104)

Further discussion of this axiom, together with tests to determine when the IIA property is violated and remedies in the case of violation are presented in Chapter Five.

McFadden (1974) introduces two additional assumptions for completeness:

(a) <u>positivity</u>. The probability that a particular alternative is chosen, given the socio-economic characteristics and the alternatives in the choice set, has to be greater than zero for all possible alternative sets A, vectors of measured atrributes s, and x∈A.

(b) <u>irrelevance of alternative set effect</u>. In the absence of replications on each individual, it is not possible to identify an 'alternative choice set effect' (z), so we then have to introduce a further restriction to isolate the 'choice alternative effect'. We assume that $V(s,x,z) = V(s,x) - V(s,z)$, that is, the function $V(s,x,z)$ used in determining selection probabilities has the additive separable form. Provided the model is limited to situations where the alternatives can plausibly be assumed to be distinct and weighted independently in the eyes of each decision maker, and that there is, across replications, one alternative set (the present choice alternatives), then the selection probabilities can be obtained with some degree of confidence, although this is not a guarantee that the selection probabilities structure conforms precisely with the choice theory.

The IIA property implies that the random elements in utility (i.e. ε_j's) are <u>independent</u> across alternatives. If we can also assume that they are identically distributed, then a suitable distribution is the double exponential or Weibull distribution. The starting point for our derivation of the structural solution for the basic choice model is a definition of the Weibull distribution in terms of ε_j's, given in equation (3.14)

$$P(\varepsilon_j \leqslant \varepsilon) = \exp(-\exp -\varepsilon) = e^{-e^{-\varepsilon}} \qquad (3.14)$$

In equation (3.8) we indicated that

$$P_{iq} = P((\varepsilon_{jq} - \varepsilon_{iq}) < (V_{iq} - V_{jq})) \text{ for all } j \neq i$$

$$j = 1,\ldots,J$$

$$q = 1,\ldots,Q \qquad (3.15)$$

Re-arranging equation (3.15) to reflect the condition in equation (3.14), and dropping the

39

subscript q (for clarity of exposition without loss of information), we obtain equation (3.16), which is a respecification of the left-hand side of equation (3.14)

$$P_i = P(\varepsilon_j < (\varepsilon_i + V_i - V_j)), \text{ assuming that}$$

$$U_j \neq U_i \text{ (hence < not } \leqslant) \tag{3.16}$$

Since each ε_j is assumed to be independently distributed, the probability of choosing alternative i, P_i, may be written as the product of J-1 terms

specified using (3.14) as follows for some given value of ε_i (say b):

$$P_i = P(\varepsilon_j < (b + V_i - V_j) \text{ for all } j \neq i)$$

$$= \prod_{\substack{j=1 \\ j \neq i}}^{J} \exp(-\exp -[b + V_i - V_j]) \tag{3.17}$$

But (3.17) is true for an arbitrary value of ε_i and so in order to write the joint density function for ε_i we must multiply (3.17) by the density of ε_i which may be written as $\exp(-\exp(-\varepsilon_i) - \varepsilon_i)$ (obtained by taking the derivative of the CDF (3.14) with respect to ε_i) or in terms of b as $\exp(-\exp(-b) - b)$.

This yields the joint density, denoted as $\partial F / \partial b$ and given by

$$\exp(-\exp(-b) - b) \prod_{\substack{j=1 \\ j \neq i}}^{J} \exp(-\exp - [b + V_i - V_j])$$

which may be simplified to

$$\exp(-b) \exp [-\sum_{j=1}^{J} \exp(-b + V_i - V_j)] \tag{3.18}$$

Thus, analogous to equation (3.13), the probability of choosing a particular alternative i, obtained by integrating the probability density function (3.18) over all possible values of ε is

$$P_i = \int_{b=-\infty}^{b=\infty} \exp(-b) \exp\left[-\sum_{j=1}^{J} \exp - (b + V_i - V_j)\right] db$$

(3.19)

In the search for a final solution, we need to rearrange equation (3.19), as follows, so as to separate out elements containing b:

$$P_i = \int_{b=-\infty}^{b=\infty} \exp(-b) \exp\{-\exp(-b) \cdot$$

$$\left[\sum_{j=1}^{J} \exp(V_j - V_i)\right]\} db$$

(3.20)

We need to integrate equation (3.20) which has a definite integral from $-\infty$ to $+\infty$. This expression is not easy to integrate as it is given above, so the first step is to apply a transformation of variables.

Let $\exp(-b)$ be replaced by z, noting that z does not replace b but the exponential of the negative of b. Thus $b = -\ln z$. The expression to be integrated becomes

$$z \exp[-za] \quad \text{where } a = \sum_{j=1}^{J} \exp(V_j - V_i), \text{ a}$$

constant because it only contains Vs.

However, since we are integrating in equation (3.20) over the random utility space with respect to db, not $d(\exp(-b))$, then a transformation has to occur so that db can be replaced by dz.

Since $\exp(-b) = z$ implies that $b = -\ln z$, we may replace db by $-(1/z)dz$ in (3.20). We also have to change the limits of integration since db is now $-(1/z)dz$.

Noting that $z = \infty$ when $b = -\infty$ (from $z = \exp(-(-\infty))$) and $z = 0$ when $b = \infty$, equation (3.20) may now be rewritten in terms of z as

$$P_i = \int_{\infty}^{0} z \exp[-za] \quad (-1/z) dz$$

(3.21)

Upon simplifying and reversing the order of integration (the latter simply changes the sign), we obtain equation (3.22)

41

$$P_i = \int_0^\infty [\exp(-za)] \, dz \qquad (3.22)$$

This is a more conventional form of a definite integral, so now we can integrate

$$P_i = -\exp(-za)/a \Big|_0^\infty \quad \text{(noting that}$$

$$\int \exp(-az) = \frac{-\exp(-az)}{a} \quad \text{and that when}$$

$z = \infty$, $\exp(-\infty) = 0$, when $z = 0$, $\exp(0) = 1$ and that we integrate from 0 to ∞, evaluating the area up to ∞ and subtracting the area up to 0).

$$P_i = -\left[\frac{1}{a}(0-1)\right] = \frac{1}{a}, \text{ where } a = \sum_{j=1}^J (V_j - V_i)$$

$$(3.23)$$

Rearranging equation (3.23), we obtain

$$P_i = \frac{1}{\displaystyle\sum_{j=1}^J \exp-(V_i - V_j)} \quad . \quad \text{By rules of}$$

exponentiation, the final model form is

$$P_i = \frac{\exp V_i}{\displaystyle\sum_{j=1}^J \exp V_j} \qquad (3.24)$$

Equation (3.24) is the basic choice model, given the assumptions outlined above, and is referred to as the conditional logit-choice model or multinomial logit (MNL) model. Some authors refer to this formulation as a nonlinear-logit model to distinguish it from other logit specifications (see Chapter 6.3). In the remaining sections of Chapter 3 the procedure for estimating the MNL model is outlined, the important outputs are identified and a simple empirical illustration is developed to provide a complete framework for a basic choice model. The remaining chapters in the book take the basic model as a point of departure for a more detailed discussion of a wide range of issues.

3·4 Statistical Estimation Procedure

Given the basic multinomial logit (MNL) choice model developed in the preceding section, we will now consider the estimation of the parameters of the utility expressions in equation (3.24). There are several alternative statistical approaches to choice model estimation, a survey of which will be presented in Chapter 6. Our purpose here is to develop one particular procedure known as <u>maximum-likelihood estimation</u> which in many cases is preferable to any of the other available methods. To do this, we will first develop the general concept of maximum likelihood and then apply it to the specific case of the multinomial logit model. In the following Section (3.5) we will describe the different model outputs and provide interpretation for them and then in Section 3.6 present a simple illustration of the estimation methodology so that the reader may, at this relatively early stage, see the results of an actual empirical application of choice modelling.

The method of maximum likelihood is based on the idea that a given sample could be generated by different populations and that a particular sample is more likely to come from one population than another. Therefore, maximum likelihood estimates are the set of population parameters which would generate the observed sample most often. To illustrate this principle, suppose that we have a random sample of n observations on some random variable Z denoted by $(z_1, \ldots, z_n)$ from a population characterised by an unknown parameter θ (which may be a mean, a variance, etc.).

Since Z is a random variable, it has a probability density function (PDF) associated with it which may be written $f(Z|\theta)$. This means that the probability distribution of Z depends upon the value of θ. ($f(Z|\theta)$ is read "a function of Z <u>given</u> some value for θ"). Assuming all of the n values of Z in the sample are independent, we can then write the joint (conditional) probability density function (PDF) of the sample as

$$f(z_1, z_2, \ldots, z_n | \theta) = f(z_1|\theta) f(z_2|\theta), \ldots, f(z_n|\theta) \qquad (3.25)$$

In the usual interpretation of this joint PDF, the Zs are considered variable for a fixed value of θ. However, if we consider the Zs to be fixed and θ to be variable, we may interpret equation (3.25) as a likelihood function instead of a joint PDF. In the situation at hand, we have a single sample of Zs so that treating Zs as fixed seems reasonable. If we then maximise equation (3.25) with respect to θ (allow θ to vary), the resulting estimate of θ which maximises equation (3.25) is called the maximum likelihood estimate (MLE) of θ. In other words, it is the value of θ (i.e. characteristic of the population) which is most likely to have generated the sample of Zs that we observed.

This idea of maximum likelihood is easily extended to the situation where the population is characterised by more than a single parameter θ. For example, if the Zs above followed a normal probability distribution, then, in the absence of any further knowledge, the population is characterised by a mean (μ) and a variance (σ^2). If we define θ to be a 2-dimensional <u>vector</u> of elements (μ, σ^2) instead of a single parameter, the likelihood function of the sample may still be written in the form given by equation (3.25) and we then maximise the function with respect to the vector θ. The parameter values which maximise equation (3.25) are the MLEs of the elements of the vector θ.

To maximise a likelihood function, one proceeds in exactly the same way as in the maximisation of any function. The estimates of θ which will be MLEs are those values at which $\partial L/\partial\theta_i = 0$, where i indexes the elements of θ and L is the notation used to designate the likelihood function. Often, it is mathematically simpler to work with the (natural) logarithm of the likelihood function since the MLEs of θ are invariant to monotonically increasing transformations of L. Hence, we look for values of θ which maximise $\ln L = L^*$ (i.e. those values of θ_i where $\partial L^*/\partial\theta_i = 0$). For completeness one should check the second-order conditions for a maximum at this point. However, so as not to unduly complicate matters here, we will assume that L (or L*) is such that a maximum will exist and be unique. Furthermore, McFadden (1968) has shown that a unique maximum does exist for the basic MNL model except in very special conditions not usually encountered in practice.

The next step in a discussion of maximum likelihood is the estimation of the parameters of the basic MNL choice model developed in the last section. Recall that the probability of individual q choosing alternative i can be written in the MNL model as

$P_{iq} = \exp(V_{iq})/\sum_{j=1}^{J} \exp(V_{jq})$. Assume that the

V_{jq} are linear additive functions in the attributes (Xs) which determine the utility of the jth alternative. In other words, let V_{jq} be written as

$$V_{jq} = \sum_{k=1}^{K} \beta_{jk} X_{jkq} \qquad (3.26)$$

It is possible, for a given j, that one of the Xs (say X_{j1q}) is set equal to 1 for all q. In this case, the coefficient β_{j1} is interpreted as an alternative-specific constant (specific to alternative j). However, we cannot specify a constant to appear in each V_j since the result is essentially that of perfect multicollinearity in a linear regression context and no estimator may be found for any βs. Therefore, we may specify at most (J-1) alternative-specific constants in the model. As for the other Xs in equation (3.26), if X_{jk} appears in the utility expression (V_{jq}) for all J alternatives, the variable is termed generic and β_{jk} may be replaced by β_k (i.e. the coefficient of X_{jk} is the same for all j). On the other hand, if X_{jk} appears only in V_{jq} it is called alternative specific. We will continue, for the moment using the notation of equation (3.26) which implies alternative-specific variables since generic variables are essentially more restrictive in the sense that we impose equality of coefficients. We will say more about this later (Section 4.5).

Suppose we have a random sample of Q individuals and for each we observe the choice actually made as well as the values of X_{jkq} for all alternatives. Given that individual q is observed to have chosen alternative i, the PDF for that observed data point is $f(Data_q|\beta)$ where $Data_q$ is the observed data for individual q and β is the vector of parameters contained in the functions V_{jq}. But this PDF is simply represented by P_{iq} given in equation (3.24). Therefore, to write the likelihood function for the sample, if all observations are independent we may replace $f(Data_q|\beta)$ by the expression for the probability of the alternative actually chosen by individual q. Hence, if we order our observations so that the first n_1 individuals are observed to have chosen alternative 1, the next n_2 to have chosen alternative 2, etc., the likelihood function of our sample may be written as

$$L = \prod_{q=1}^{n_1} P_{1q} \cdot \prod_{q=n_1+1}^{n_1+n_2} P_{2q} \cdots \prod_{q=Q-n_J+1}^{Q} P_{Jq}$$

(3.27)

where $\prod$ is an operator implying multiplication in the same way as $\sum$ refers to addition.

It is possible to simplify this expression for L slightly by defining a dummy variable f_{jq} such that $f_{jq} = 1$ if alternative j is chosen and $f_{jq} = 0$ otherwise. Doing this, we may write equation (3.27) as

$$L = \prod_{q=1}^{Q} \prod_{j=1}^{J} P_{jq}^{f_{jq}}$$

(3.28)

To see that equation (3.28) is the same as (3.27), let us examine a few observations. First, consider one of the n_1 observations where we assume the individual has chosen alternative 1, so we want P_1 to appear in L for that value of q. For that q in equation (3.28) we multiply over j the terms $P_{jq}^{f_{jq}}$. The first term will be P_{1q}^{1} since alternative one was chosen and hence $f_{1q} = 1$. The next (and all terms subsequent) will be $P_{2q}^{0} = 1$ ($P_{jq}^{0} = 1$) since $f_{2q}, \ldots, f_{Jq}$ will be zero because alternative 1 was chosen. For one of the n_2 individuals who chose alternative 2, $f_{2q} = 1$ and all other $f_{jq} = 0$ so only P_{2q} will enter equation (3.28) for that observation. In this way, we can see that equation (3.28) is exactly the same as equation (3.27).

Now, given L in equation (3.28), the log-likelihood function L* may be written

46

$$L^* = \sum_{q=1}^{Q} \sum_{j=1}^{J} f_{jq} \ln P_{jq} \qquad (3.29)$$

If we now replace P_{jq} in equation (3.29) by the expression (3.24) the result is an equation which is a function of the unknown βs contained in the expression V_{jq} since all other quantities in equation (3.28) are known (the Xs and f_{jq}'s).

L^* is then maximised with respect to the βs in the usual manner, the resulting estimates being the MLEs for the model's parameters. It is possible to derive the set of first-order conditions necessary for the maximisation of L^*. However, these conditions are not particularly instructive at this point since the important thing is to understand the basic methodology. Hence, we will end the discussion of maximum-likelihood estimation of the MNL model by noting that equation (3.29) should be maximised with respect to the parameters (βs) using some nonlinear maximisation algorithm. These algorithms are usually iterative in nature, the analyst being required to provide an initial guess as to the values of β. These values are used in equation (3.26) to calculate V_{jq}'s which are inserted in equation (3.24) to calculate P_{iq}'s. These are then used in equation (3.29) to calculate a starting value of L^*. The usual procedure is then to search in some fashion for "better" values of βs to use in equation (3.26) to then get new P_{iq}'s in equation (3.24) which will cause the value of L^* in equation (3.29) to increase. The iterative procedure will continue until some predetermined level of tolerance is reached (i.e. either L^* increases by an amount less than a given tolerance or the βs change by less than some predetermined amount (see Chapter 10)). There are several methods which may be used to search for the optimal value of β. The interested reader is referred to Goldfeld & Quandt (1972) for a survey of many of the algorithms which may be used.

3·5 Model Outputs

Having derived the maximum likelihood estimation method for the basic MNL choice model in the previous section, attention is now turned to the various results which emerge as a consequence of the application of such a procedure. These include not only the estimated βs and hence predicted probabilities but also estimated standard errors associated with these estimated βs, measures of goodness of fit for the model as a whole, and estimated elasticities of choice, both individual and aggregate, with respect to the various attributes (Xs).

3·5·1 Coefficient Estimates

First of all, an estimated β_{jk} (say $\hat{\beta}_{jk}$) can be interpreted as an estimate of the weighting applied to attribute k in the utility expression V_j of alternative j. Once we have estimates of βs, an estimate of V_{iq} (say $\hat{V}_{iq}$) can be calculated by taking the βs and the Xs for individual q and alternative i and using equation (3.26). The resulting $\hat{V}_{iq}$ can be interpreted as an estimate of the utility U_{iq} of alternative i to individual q.

3·5·2 Significance of Coefficients

It would be advantageous if we could statistically test whether a particular $\hat{\beta}_{jk}$ was significantly different from zero in much the same way as a regression coefficient is tested using a t-test. As it happens, the choice of the MLE method allows this to be done asymptotically (i.e. strictly valid only in very large samples). To do this, we need to calculate the matrix of second partial derivatives of L (or L*) with respect to the βs. The negative of the inverse of this matrix evaluated at the estimated values is the asymptotic variance-covariance matrix for the MLEs. The square roots of the diagonal elements can be treated as asymptotic standard errors (see, for example, Theil, 1971). For those not familiar with matrices, the above discussion is probably confusing. It is sufficient to note, then, that using the maximum-likelihood procedure, we can calculate asymptotic standard errors for the βs in the MNL model and use

48

these to test the significance of the βs using an
asymptotic t-test. These standard errors and
t-statistics are normally produced as part of the
output in any MNL computer program (e.g. the program
described in Chapter 10).

3·5·3 Goodness – of – Fit Tests

At this point, it might be useful to consider
a statement made by Frisch almost 30 years ago
concerning statistical tests.

> *Mathematical tests of significance,*
> *confidence intervals etc. are highly*
> *useful concepts ... All these concepts*
> *are, however, of relative merit only.*
> *They have a clearly defined meaning only*
> *within the narrow confines of the model*
> *in question ... As we dig into the foun-*
> *dation of any economic ... model we will*
> *always find a line of demarcation which*
> *we cannot transgress unless we introduce*
> *another type of test of Significance*
> *(this time written with a capital S), a*
> *test of the applicability of the model*
> *itself ... Something of relevance for*
> *this question can, of course, be deduced*
> *from mathematical tests properly*
> *interpreted, but no such test can ever*
> *do anything more than just push the*
> *final question one step further back.*
> *The final, the highest level of test can*
> *never be formulated in mathematical terms.*

(Frisch, 1951: 9-10)

This quote serves to remind us of the relative
role of statistical tests of model significance,
since far too often statistical measures are used
as the dominant criteria for acceptance or
rejection of a particular model. Nevertheless there
are a number of statistical measures of model
validity which can assist in the assessment of
empirically estimatable individual-choice models.
The object here is to describe these measures.

In order to determine the goodness-of-fit for
the basic MNL model, we would like to compare, in
some sense, the predicted dependent variable with
the observed dependent variable. In discrete
choice models, however, this is virtually
meaningless since we observe the actual choices
made (denoted by f_{jq} in the previous section) while
the estimated model produces probabilities P_{jq}.

Hence, to use "residuals" (i.e. the difference between P_{iq} and f_{iq}) in the calculation of a measure of fit analogous to R^2 in regression does not make sense.

The log-likelihood function evaluated at the mean of the estimated parameters is a suitable overall criterion for goodness-of-fit when the maximum-likelihood estimation method is being used in model estimation. This function is used in tests of the importance of particular sets of variables, the procedure being referred to as the likelihood-ratio test.

To test the significance of the logit function with large samples, the generalised likelihood-ratio test is used. This test proposes a null hypothesis that the probability, P_i of an individual choosing alternative i is independent of the value of the parameters in the MNL function (equation 3.24). If this hypothesis cannot be rejected, we take the coefficients to be zero. That is, it tests the hypothesis that all βs in equation (3.26) are zero (except for alternative-specific constants). As is the case with testing the significance of R^2 in regression analysis, for a reasonably specified model we almost always reject the hypothesis of independence. Therefore, the usefulness of the likelihood-ratio test is its ability to test whether subsets of the βs are significant. The generalised likelihood-ratio criterion is of the form

$$\lambda = \max L(\omega) \, / \, \max L(\Omega) \qquad (3.30)$$

where λ is called the likelihood ratio, $\max L(\omega)$ is the maximum of the likelihood function where M elements of the parameter space have been constrained by the null hypothesis (e.g. if testing for significance of a set of βs in the MNL model, the maximum of L with these βs set equal to zero), and $\max L(\Omega)$ is the unconstrained maximum of the likelihood function. Wilks (1962) shows that $-2 \ln \lambda$ is approximately distributed like chi-square with M degrees of freedom for large samples when the null hypothesis is true. Therefore, one maximises L for the full MNL model and then for the MNL model with some βs set to zero (i.e. eliminate some Xs). Next, calculate λ and then see whether $-2 \ln \lambda$ is greater than the critical value of χ_M^2 from some preselected significance level. If so, one may reject the null hypothesis that the particular set of βs being tested are equal to zero.

For the basic MNL choice model, the likelihood function L will take on some value between zero and one since L is the product of Q probabilities. Therefore, the log-likelihood function L* will be negative. Let us define $L^*(\hat{\beta})$ as the maximised value of the log-likehood and $L^*(0)$ as the value of the log-likelihood evaluated such that the probability of choosing the ith alternative is exactly equal to the observed aggregate share in the sample of the ith alternative (call this S_i). In other words, let

$$L^*(0) = \sum_{q=1}^{Q} \sum_{j=1}^{J} f_{jq} \ln S_i \qquad (3.31)$$

Clearly, L* will be larger when evaluated at $\hat{\beta}$ than when the explanatory variables (Xs) are ignored as in equation (3.31). Intuitively, the greater the explanatory power of the Xs, the larger $L^*(\hat{\beta})$ will be in comparison to $L^*(0)$. We can use this idea to form what has been termed a likelihood-ratio index which can be used, much as R^2 is in ordinary regression, to measure the goodness-of-fit of the MNL model. To do this we calculate the statistic

$$\rho^2 = 1 - (L^*(\hat{\beta})/L^*(0)) \qquad (3.32)$$

We noted that $L^*(\hat{\beta})$ will be larger than $L^*(0)$ but for the MNL this means a smaller negative number so that $L^*(\hat{\beta})/L^*(0)$ will be between zero and one. The smaller this ratio, the better the fit of the model (i.e. the greater the explanatory power of the Xs over the aggregate constant-share prediction model) and hence, the larger 1 minus this ratio. Therefore, we may use ρ^2 (rho squared) as a type of pseudo-R^2 to measure the goodness-of-fit for the model. It should be noted, however, that values of ρ^2 of between 0.2 and 0.4 are considered extremely good fits so that the analyst should not be looking for values in excess of 0.9 as is often the case when using R^2 in ordinary regression.

McFadden (1979) points out that some MNL computer programs compute ρ^2 not on the basis of $L^*(0)$ assuming that P_i is equal to S_i, the sample aggregate share, but assuming equal aggregate shares for each alternative (e.g. if J = 3, using $S_i = 1/3$ in equation (3.31)). ρ^2 defined as we have here is preferable since we at least know from the

Q observations the share of each alternative in the sample and would use these as predictions of P_i's if we did not attempt to use a choice model to improve the predictions.

We may improve on ρ^2 given in equation (3.32) by adjusting it for degrees of freedom, a process which is especially useful if we want to compare different models. The corrected ρ^2, given by $\bar{\rho}^2$ (rho-bar squared) is

$$\bar{\rho}^2 = 1 - \frac{L^*(\hat{\beta}) / \sum\limits_{q=1}^{Q} (J_q - 1) - K}{L^*(0) / \sum\limits_{q=1}^{Q} (J_q - 1)} \qquad (3.33)$$

where J_q refers to the number of alternatives faced by individual q (n.b. so far J has been assumed as the same for all Q individuals but this need not be the case; we will discuss this later) and K is the total number of variables (Xs) in the model.

A number of studies have proposed tests of prediction success which involve a comparison of the summed probabilities from the models (i.e. expected number choosing a particular alternative) with the actuality for the sample. It is possible however that a model might be good in prediction with respect to the estimation sample, while not necessarily predicting well the outcome of any policy change which can be defined in terms of movement in one or more of the independent variables. The best test of predictive strength is a before-and-after assessment procedure (e.g. Hensher & Bullock, 1979).

McFadden (1979) has synthesised the prediction tests into a prediction success table (Table 3.1). Each entry (N_{ij}) in the central matrix of the table gives the expected number of individuals who are observed to choose i and who are predicted to choose j. Alternatively, it is the probability of individual q selecting alternative j summed over all individuals who actually select alternative i. Thus

$$N_{ij} = \sum_{q=1}^{Q} f_{iq} P_{jq} = \sum_{q \in Q_i} P_q(j \mid A_q) \text{ where } f_{iq}$$

equals one if i is chosen, zero otherwise. A_q is the set of alternatives out of which individual q chooses, and Q_i is the set of individuals in the sample who actually choose alternative i. Column sums (predicted count)

$$= \sum_{i \in A_q} [\sum_{q \in Q_i} P_q(j|A_q)] = \sum_{q=1}^{Q} P_q(j|A_q) = N_{.j}$$

are used to calculate predicted shares; row sums (observed count)

$$= \sum_{q \in Q_i} [\sum_{j \in A_q} P_q(j|A_q)] = \sum_{q \in Q_i} 1 = N_{i.}$$

are used to calculate observed shares. $N_{ii}/N_{.i}$ indicates the proportion of the predicted count (i.e. individuals expected to choose an alternative) who actually choose that alternative. $(N_{11} +...+ N_{JJ})/N_{..}$ gives the overall proportion successfully predicted.

To interpret the per cent correct, it is useful to compare it to the per cent correct that would be obtained by chance. Any model which assigns the same probability of choosing an alternative to all individuals in the sample would obtain a percentage correct for each alternative equal to the actual share for that alternative.

The prediction success index is an appropriate goodness-of-fit measure to account for the fact that the proportion successfully predicted for an alternative varies with the aggregate share of that alternative. This index may be written as

$$\sigma_i = \frac{N_{ii}}{N_{.i}} - \frac{N_{.i}}{N_{..}} \tag{3.34}$$

where $N_{ii}/N_{.i}$ is the proportion of individuals expected to choose an alternative who actually choose that alternative, and $N_{.i}/N_{..}$ is the proportion which would be successfully predicted if the choice probabilities for each sampled individual were assumed to equal the predicted aggregate share. Hence, if σ_i is equal to zero, the model does no better in prediction for alternative i than the market-share hypothesis.

An overall prediction success index may be formed by summing σ_i's over the J alternatives,

TABLE 3·1: Prediction Success Table

	Predicted Choice			Observed Count	Observed Share
	1	2 ...	J		
1	N_{11}	N_{12}	N_{1J}	$N_{1.}$	$N_{1.}/N_{..}$
2	N_{21}	N_{22}	N_{2J}	$N_{2.}$	$N_{2.}/N_{..}$
... J	N_{J1}	N_{J2}	N_{JJ}	$N_{J.}$	$N_{J.}/N_{..}$
Predicted Count	$N_{.1}$	$N_{.2}$	$N_{.J}$	$N_{..}$	1
Predicted Share	$\dfrac{N_{.1}}{N_{..}}$	$\dfrac{N_{.2}}{N_{..}}$	$\dfrac{N_{.J}}{N_{..}}$	1	
Proportion Successfully Predicted	$\dfrac{N_{11}}{N_{.1}}$	$\dfrac{N_{22}}{N_{.2}}$	$\dfrac{N_{JJ}}{N_{.J}}$	$\dfrac{N_{11}+...+N_{JJ}}{N_{..}}$	
Success Index	$\dfrac{N_{11}}{N_{.1}} - \dfrac{N_{.1}}{N_{..}}$	$\dfrac{N_{22}}{N_{.2}} - \dfrac{N_{.2}}{N_{..}}$	$\dfrac{N_{JJ}}{N_{.J}} - \dfrac{N_{.J}}{N_{..}}$	$\sum\limits_{i=1}^{J}\left[\dfrac{N_{ii}}{N_{..}} - \left(\dfrac{N_{.i}}{N_{..}}\right)^2 \right]$	
Proportional Error in Predicted Share	$\dfrac{N_{.1}-N_{1.}}{N_{..}}$	$\dfrac{N_{.2}-N_{2.}}{N_{..}}$	$\dfrac{N_{.J}-N_{J.}}{N_{..}}$		

54

weighting each σ_i by $N_{.i}/N_{..}$. This may be written

$$\sigma = \sum_{i=1}^{J} (N_{.i}/N_{..}) \, \sigma_i \qquad (3.35)$$

We may expand equation (3.35) as follows:

$$\sigma = \sum_{i=1}^{J} (N_{.i}/N_{..}) (\frac{N_{ii}}{N_{.i}} - \frac{N_{.i}}{N_{..}})$$

$$\sigma = \sum_{i=1}^{J} (\frac{N_{ii}}{N_{..}} - (\frac{N_{.i}}{N_{..}})^2)$$

This index will generally be non-negative with a maximum value (when $\sum_{i=1}^{J} N_{ii} = N_{..}$ so that the model perfectly predicts) of

$$1 - \sum_{i=1}^{J} (N_{.i}/N_{..})^2 \qquad (3.36)$$

Hence, we can normalise σ so as to have a maximum value of one. The higher the value, the greater the predictive capability of the model. An example of the typical output of a prediction success test is given in Table 3.2 for the choice of establishment type.

The random utility model as represented in the multinomial logit function provides a very powerful mechanism for assessing the effects of a wide range of policies. Since policies impact on individuals with varying degrees of force, it is desirable that we are able to determine the individual-specific impact prior to the determination of the market-share effects. If the estimated model has been carefully developed such that the representative-utility condition is empirically sound, which implies that the choice set definition and the structural representation of the decision process is reasonable (see Chapter 4), then we have a very flexible policy-sensitive analytical tool.

We now outline the main policy-related outputs of individual-choice models, and comment on the types of policy issues which are ideally investigated in this choice framework. It is important to state that errors associated with any modelling

TABLE 3·2 : Prediction Success Table — An Example

Actual Alternatives	Predicted Alternatives (1)	(2)	(3)	Row Total	Observed Share %
(1) fully detached house	100	20	30	150	50.0
(2) town house	30	50	20	100	33.3
(3) flat	20	10	20	50	16.7
Column Total	150	80	70	300	100.0
Predicted Share (%)	$50 = \frac{150}{300}$	26.6	23.3	100	
Per cent Correct	66.6	62.5	28.6	56.6 ((100+50+20) /300)	
Success Index (Not normalised)	.166	.359	.053	.19	
Predicted Share less Observed Share	0	-6.7	6.7		

Overall normalised-success index is 0.2533

approach are not necessarily a result of the modelling approach, but can frequently be accounted for by the errors in exogenously supplied data. The best examples of this are exogenous forecasts of future levels of population (by occupation and income levels), and future levels of transport and housing services. Given that smaller samples are required for individual modelling in contrast to aggregate modelling (the latter using grouped data based initially on information from many individual interviews/questionnaires), the additional cost in obtaining such detail is more than compensated by cost savings and increased accuracy of predictive performance and policy indicators.

The types of policy outputs are similar to those of most econometric models, although the validity of the output is usually much stronger. The models can be used to obtain measures of the responsiveness of a population group to changes in levels of particular attributes (i.e. elasticities of particular choices with respect to particular attributes), and to obtain individual and grouped estimates of the likelihood of undertaking a particular activity, given the levels of the attri- butes offered as the significant choice discrimin- ators.

Guidance on the appropriateness of various policies can be obtained from the measures of

responsiveness of demand to changes in each of the
attributes which influence the demand. Direct and
cross elasticities can be obtained from the models.
Direct elasticity is the percentage change in the
probability of choosing a particular alternative in
the choice set with respect to a given per cent
change in an attribute which describes the utility
of that alternative. A cross elasticity is the
percentage change in the probability of choosing a
particular alternative in the choice set with
respect to a given percentage change in an attribute
which describes the utility of a competing alternative. The size of the change in the level of an
attribute has an important bearing on whether the
elasticity measure should be point or arc (see
below).

To derive a general formula for the calculation
of elasticities in the basic MNL model, consider
the equation for P_{iq} given by equation (3.24) and
recall the definition of V_{jq} given by equation
(3.26). The elasticity of any variable Y with
respect to another variable Z is $(\Delta Y/Y)/(\Delta Z/Z)$,
which reduces to $(\partial Y/\partial Z)(Z/Y)$ as ΔZ approaches zero.
Therefore, direct point elasticities in the MNL
model can be written

$$E^{P_{iq}}_{X_{ikq}} = \frac{\partial P_{iq}}{\partial X_{ikq}} \cdot \frac{X_{ikq}}{P_{iq}} \tag{3.37}$$

This is interpreted as the elasticity of probability of choosing alternative i for individual q
with respect to a marginal (or 'small') change in
the kth variable which describes the utility of
the ith alternative for individual q.

An operational formulation for this elasticity
requires that we evaluate the partial derivative in
equation (3.37). This may be done as follows:

$$\frac{\partial P_{iq}}{\partial X_{ikq}} = \frac{(\sum_j e^{V_{jq}}) \frac{\partial (e^{V_{iq}})}{\partial X_{ikq}} - (e^{V_{iq}}) \frac{\partial (\sum_j e^{V_{jq}})}{\partial X_{ikq}}}{(\sum_j e^{V_{jq}})^2}$$

(using the quotient rule for derivatives)

$$= \frac{(\Sigma_j e^{V_{jq}})(e^{V_{iq}})\beta_{ik} - (e^{V_{iq}})(e^{V_{iq}})\beta_{ik}}{(\Sigma_j e^{V_{jq}})^2} \quad (3.38)$$

(using the rule: $\partial e^{az}/\partial Z = ae^{az}$).

Simplifying equation (3.38), we get

$$\frac{\partial P_{iq}}{\partial X_{ikq}} = P_{iq}\beta_{ik} - P_{iq}{}^2\beta_{ik} \quad (3.39)$$

and so the direct point elasticity in equation (3.37) becomes for the MNL model

$$E_{X_{ikq}}^{P_{iq}} = P_{iq}\beta_{ik} (1-P_{iq}) X_{ikq}/P_{iq} = \beta_{ik}X_{ikq} (1-P_{iq}) \quad (3.40)$$

For cross point elasticities, we follow a similar path by evaluating $\partial P_{iq}/\partial X_{jkq}$ as follows:

$$\frac{\partial P_{iq}}{\partial X_{jkq}} = \frac{(\Sigma_j e^{V_{jq}})(0) - (e^{V_{iq}})(e^{V_{jq}})\beta_{jk}}{(\Sigma_j e^{V_{jq}})^2} = -P_{iq}P_{jq}\beta_{jk} \quad (3.41)$$

We then evaluate the cross elasticity as

$$E_{X_{jkq}}^{P_{iq}} = \frac{\partial P_{iq}}{\partial X_{jkq}} \cdot \frac{X_{jkq}}{P_{iq}} = -P_{iq}P_{jq}\beta_{jk}X_{jkq}/P_{iq} = -\beta_{jk}X_{jkq}P_{jq}$$

$$(3.42)$$

Notice that this cross elasticity only depends on variables associated with alternative j and is independent of i. Therefore, cross elasticities with respect to a variable associated with alternative j are the same for all $i \neq j$. This constrained result arises because of the assumption that the actual utilities are distributed about their means with distributions that are independent and identical.

A simple way in which equation (3.40) and equation (3.42) may be combined to yield a single point elasticity formula for the basic MNL model is given by

$$E_{X_{jkq}}^{P_{iq}} = \beta_{jk}X_{jkq}(\delta_{ij} - P_{jq}) \qquad (3.43)$$

where $\delta_{ij} = \begin{cases} 1 & \text{if } i = j \text{ (a direct point} \\ & \qquad\qquad\text{elasticity)} \\ 0 & \text{if } i \neq j \text{ (a cross point} \\ & \qquad\qquad\text{elasticity)} \end{cases}$

The direct elasticity approaches zero as P_{jq} approaches unity, and approaches $\beta_{jk}X_{jkq}$ as P_{jq} approaches zero. The converse applies for the cross elasticity.

Equation (3.43) gives elasticities for each individual. To find aggregate elasticities, one is tempted to evaluate equation (3.43) at the sample average X_{jk} and $\hat{P}_j$ (average estimated P_j). However, since the MNL model is nonlinear, the estimated logit function need not pass through the point defined by these sample averages. It is not uncommon to find errors of up to 20% (usually over-estimates) in estimating the responsiveness of probability of choice with respect to some variable X_{jk}. Therefore, a more preferable approach is to evaluate equation (3.43) for each individual q and then aggregate, weighting each individual elasticity by the individual's estimated probability of choice. This technique is known as the sample enumeration method, the formula for which is

$$E_{X_{jkq}}^{\bar{P}_i} = \left(\sum_{q=1}^{Q} \hat{P}_{iq}E_{jkq}^{P_{iq}} \right) / \sum_{q=1}^{Q} \hat{P}_{iq} \qquad (3.44)$$

where $\hat{P}_{iq}$ in an estimated choice probability and $\bar{P}_i$ refers to aggregate probability of choice of alternative i.

The elasticity formulation above is derived from partial differentiation of the choice function, on the assumption that any changes in X are marginal. When nonmarginal changes occur, as is frequently the situation in practice, then provided that the change in the level of the independent variable does not result in a level of X outside of the distribution of values used in estimation, an arc elasticity formula is appropriate. This is calculated using differences (X^1, X ; P^1, P) rather than differentials:

$$E_{X_{ikq}}^{P_{iq}} = [(P_{iq}^1 - P_{iq})/(X_{ikq}^1 - X_{ikq})]/[P_{iq}/X_{ikq}] \quad (3.45)$$

$$E_{X_{jkq}}^{P_{iq}} = [(P_{iq}^1 - P_{iq})/(X_{jkq}^1 - X_{jkq})]/[P_{iq}/X_{jkq}] \quad (3.46)$$

The elasticities can be combined in many ways, which is particularly convenient and useful when we want the average level of responsiveness across a number of market segments, for example.

McFadden (1979) has summarised some aggregation rules which are listed here for reference:

(1)   Aggregate elasticity over market segments equals the sum of segment elasticities weighted by segment shares of the market. This rule assumes that the per cent change in the policy variable is the same in each segment.

(2)   Aggregate elasticities over alternatives equals the sum of component alternative elasticities weighted by the component share of the compared alternative (e.g. all public transport). This rule assumes an equal per cent change in each component alternative as the result of a policy.

(3)   Elasticity with respect to a component of a variable equals the elasticity with respect to the variable times the component's share in the variable. An example would be the elasticity with respect to bus fare when we only have estimated elasticity with respect to total trip cost.

(4)   Elasticity with respect to a policy that causes an equal per cent change in several variables equals the sum of elasticities with respect to each variable.

McFadden continues to discuss how these rules may be combined to arrive at the elasticity needed for policy analysis.

3·6 A Simple Illustration of the Basic Model

The previous two sections have presented an estimation procedure and the model outputs for the basic MNL choice model. To conclude this chapter, it is appropriate to provide a single empirical example of the use of the basic model.

The example concerns the choice of means of transport to school for students in Hobart, Australia in June 1977 (see Hensher, 1979a for a more complete discussion of the Hobart problem and data). The data consists of Q = 502 observations where the choice set available to each individual includes the alternatives of the student travelling by car to school as a driver via a temporary bailey bridge (the main Tasman Bridge linking the east and west banks of the Derwent River in Hobart had collapsed in 1975 and was being rebuilt) or to travel as a ferry passenger (i.e. J = 2). Five variables (Xs) were considered to determine the utility of each mode and were defined as generic so that the coefficient of X_k was the same in each utility expression (i.e. $\beta_{jk} = \beta_k$ for all j = 1,2). These variables were:

WLK   =   total walk time   (minutes)
WT   =   total wait time   (minutes)
INVT =   total in-vehicle time   (minutes)
INVC =   total in-vehicle cost   (cents)
PKC   =   parking cost   (cents)

In addition, a constant specific to the car-driver mode was specified in the model.

The results of maximum likelihood estimation of the model (which took 3 iterations before the desired level of tolerance - L* changing by less than 0.01 - was reached) are given in Table 3.3. Coefficients reported refer to choice of the car driver mode.

TABLE 3·3 : Parameter Estimates for the Illustrative Example

Variable	$\hat{\beta}$	Standard Error	T-Ratio
WLK	-0.064	0.0186	-3.44
WT	-0.174	0.0346	-5.02
INVT	0.002	0.0097	0.19
INVC	-0.012	0.0032	-3.61
PKC	-0.001	0.0064	-1.37
CONSTANT	-2.563	0.3638	-7.04

All of the variables were expected to have a negative sign but the coefficient of INVT has a positive sign in our results. However, its coefficient is very insignificant (t-ratio of only 0.19) so little should be made of the incorrect sign of the variable. Normally the analyst would search out the causes of nonsignificance; and re-estimate the model without this variable if such a variable is truly nonsignificant. However, other considerations may lead the analyst to conclude that the model itself is inappropriate and/or bias due to measurement, specification or sampling is the main cause (see Section 7.4). All of the other coefficients have the *a priori* correct sign and all are significant except for PKC although its t-statistic is still greater than one in absolute value. The pseudo-R^2 for the model is 0.226 which implies a reasonably good fit, especially when the presence of several significant t-statistics is considered along with the ρ^2.

Aggregate point elasticities calculated using the full sample-enumeration method discussed in the last section were calculated for all variables and choices. The results are presented in Table 3.4.

TABLE 3·4 : **Direct and Cross Point Elasticities Associated with Choice of Mode to School Trip in Hobart, Tasmania**

Explanatory Variables	Direct Elasticities		Cross Elasticities	
	E_{11}	E_{00}	E_{10}	E_{01}
WLK	-.053	-.119	.749	.008
WT	$-.803 \times 10^{-5}$	-.064	.399	$.128 \times 10^{-5}$
INVT	.068	.007	-.044	-.011
INVC	-.898	-.085	.530	.143
PKC	-.041	$-.113 \times 10^{-3}$	$.711 \times 10^{-3}$	.007

The more dispersed the distribution of the values of explanatory variables the lower will be the weighted aggregate elasticity relative to the aggregate elasticity, the latter calculated at the sample average (X_{jk} and $\hat{P}_j$); since the greater the differential in the relative levels of an attribute the lower would be the response of aggregate demand to any changes in the variable (Westin, 1974). Gillen (1977) calculates weighted and unweighted aggregate elasticities for four variables as respectively (-.29, -.34), (-0.59, -0.68), (-.31, -.38) and (-.19 and .25) to illustrate this.

In Table 3.4, E_{11} refers to the elasticity of P_1 (probability of car driver) with respect to the variable listed, while E_{00} refers to direct elasticities of P_0 (ferry passenger). E_{10} and E_{01} refer to cross elasticities of P_1 and P_0 (car driver and ferry) respectively with respect to variables affecting the utility of the other choice. Since INVT had an estimated wrong sign in Table 3.3, the elasticities with respect to in invehicle time also have the wrong sign.

Interpreting the estimated elasticities is a straightforward task. For example, E_{11} for INVC = -.898 means that a one per cent increase in the cost of travelling by car as a driver will, all else remaining constant, cause a 0.898% decrease in the overall probability of car-driver choice of mode to school. Other elasticities may be interpreted in a similar manner.

NOTES — CHAPTER 3

1. Aggregation is itself a complex issue, and is discussed in Chapter 7.

2. By implication, there is another element that is not individual specific, known as the representative element that belongs to the whole sampled population. There is a distribution around the representative element that will accommodate all the idiosyncrasies of taste across the individuals in the sampled population, known as the random element. In other words, we are going to make the assumption that there must be some relationship between members of the sampled population, we assume that there are some elements that can be combined and defined as representative utility, and the rest are distributed around the representative element. The assignment of a distribution to the random element provides the link between an individual behaviour rule and a set of individual behaviour rules, or population choice behaviour.

3. In Chapter 2, lower case s defines an attribute. In Chapter 3, this notation is reserved for a particular type of 'attribute', those which define the individual decision maker and his

63

environment. These 'attributes' are commonly
referred to as socioeconomic variables, and
are included in the formal model to represent
the heterogeneous nature of decision makers
and unobservable atrributes of the alternatives
(see Section 4.5).

4. At least two elements or alternatives must exist
in an individual's choice set, otherwise you
are not modelling individual <u>choice</u>.

5. Covariance probit (see Section 6.5) replaces
β_{ik} with β_{ikq}; however the utility expression
is defined in such a way that a representative
component of the same form as above results,
together with a more complex random component,
the latter including a deviation term to allow
each individual's response to the attribute X_{ki}
to vary around a mean response β_{ki} (see equation
6.35).

CHAPTER 4

Choice Set Definition and Decision Structures

4·1 Introduction

So far we have assumed a decision environment in which a single equation specifies the relationship between the probability of selecting an alternative out of a collectively exhaustive set of alternatives, and the levels of utility associated with each and every alternative. All the attributes that are measurable are assumed to enter the utility expression in a linear additive manner (see Section 3.2.1). Furthermore the basic choice model requires that the alternatives in a choice set should be distinct and independent, avoiding inclusion of any two alternatives which are almost identical or very similar (a term yet to be defined precisely) in their unmeasured attributes, or two alternatives where one always dominates the other.

In this chapter and the next the plan is to take a number of the strong assumptions associated with the basic model, to discuss them in more detail (if appropriate to the argument) and then to extend the basic model to accommodate more realistic, and possibly more complex, structures. Chapter 5 is devoted to the important assumption of the independence from irrelevant alternatives. In the present chapter we will accept the independence assumption for most of the discussion, and introduce a number of issues relevant to the accommodation of alternative structural relations between more than one decision, given the assertion that many choice situations cannot be adequately represented by a single choice equation either because the set of interrelated decisions are too complex to handle at this level, there is a hierarchical relationship between a set of interdependent choices, or a decision entails the simultaneous choice of a complex alternative.

65

The chapter is arranged in the following order. Central to a discussion on decision structures is the generation of choice sets, hence in Section 4.2 we outline, in a theoretical manner, the notion of a choice set and its selection. Empirical research on systematic identification of choice sets at the individual level is somewhat unsatisfactory, hence we are left with criteria, but no adequate measurement basis for empirically defining a choice set for a particular individual and a particular issue. The similarity of alternatives (including non-overlapping subsets of alternatives) is discussed. This issue pertains in part to Chapter 5, although it is appropriate to introduce it here because of the possibility of having choice sets defined on an unmanageable number of alternatives. Equipped with a knowledge of the choice set generating process, the next task is to define a decision structure within which various choices operate. In Section 4.3 we outline alternative decision structures (such as fully independent, sequential, sequential recursive and simultaneous), and introduce a number of concepts which underlie the alternative structures and are necessary for specifying the relationship between alternatives in a given choice set. These notions are separability (in its various forms), marginal, joint and conditional probability.

Once the alternative decision structures are understood, the next step is to decide on the appropriate choice hierarchy and a mechanism for linking decisions if interdependency exists. In Section 4.3 the notion of an inclusive value, variously referred to as inclusive price or expected maximum utility is introduced and used as the basis for connecting a hierarchy of choice models. This concept in the context of the basic (multinomial logit) choice model is a central feature of applied discrete choice modelling. In Section 4.4 we introduce the notion of a choice hierarchy and the modelling implications of this assumption; and then provide a brief overview of the range of model specifications in the logit family together with a test for structural sensitivity. The final section discusses ways in which the attributes in the utility expression (assumed to be linearly additive in its parameters) can be specified, in particular the distinction between generic attributes, alternative specific attributes and alternative specific constants.

4·2 Choice Set Generation

The definition and identification of choice sets relevant to a particular issue is one of the least understood areas in discrete choice modelling. Although a formal definition of a choice-set generation process can be offered (see below), and used in the specification of choice models incorporating a range of types of constraints (such as the unavailability of one alternative or captivity to one alternative), we still face the problem of identifying suitable empirical criteria that can be used in the evaluation of alternative assumptions on the relationship between the individual and the set of alternatives of potential relevance. Often simple rules have been used in choice-set generating models such as 'public transport is unavailable if access to it requires a walk in excess of two kilometres', or 'house locations in a quadrant of the urban area that the individual does not reside in are not relevant in the residential location decision' or 'an organisation with more than 200 office employees in the one location is captive to the large telecommunication facilities, and Key Telephone Systems are not relevant'. There is no guarantee, however, that these are behaviourally valid rules.

Despite the lack of knowledge of the elements defining a choice set in an empirical context, we can offer a realistic theoretical structure that describes choice-set generation, and a discussion on the grouping of alternatives in a predefined choice set if the number of elemental alternatives is either too many for practical application, or there is concern over the level of similarity between subsets of alternatives (a concern relevant to the basic choice model when the independence-from-irrelevant alternatives property applies), or data on the variables in the utility expressions are only available at an aggregate level (e.g. average travel time by public transport, rather than for rail and bus separately). The discussion in this section is an outline of the theoretical structure and the grouping of alternatives. This is adequate background for the remaining sections of the chapter which assume generated choice sets and then develop alternative decision structures and ways of linking sets of related choices.

Manski (1977) has formulated a general outcome of the entire choice process. For every element (j) in a finite set of alternatives (A):

$$P_j = \sum_{C \in T} \sum_{q \in Q} C_{TQ}(C,q) \; P_q(j \in C) \qquad (4.1)$$

where (C,q) is a choice problem, C being a non-null choice set, q a rational individual contained in Q, a population of individually rational decision makers. If the set of all non-null choice sets is T, then a choice problem is a pair (C,q) drawn from the space TxQ according to the probability measure C_{TQ} defined over T x Q. C_{TQ} is referred to as the

choice-problem generating process. In words, equation (4.1) states that with a probabilistic choice-set generating process, the marginal probability of choice of selecting alternative j contained in the finite set of alternatives (A) is equal to the product of the probability of the choice set being C and the conditional probability of selecting alternative j given a choice set C. Hence, given particular choice conditions (such as captivity or the unavailability of one alternative or the similarity of two alternatives) the choice-set generating process can be used in the reformulation of a choice model, but still within a multinomial logit framework. The basic choice model in Chapter 3 can be thought of as a special case of the MNL model. To illustrate this assertion let us take one example where captivity to a particular alternative is an outcome, develop the model formulation and then relate it to the basic choice model.

Equation (4.1) can be simplified as equation (4.2), deleting summation over individuals,

$$P_j = \sum_{C \in T} P(C) \; P(j|C) \qquad j = 1,\ldots,J \qquad (4.2)$$

Capital C is a general term referring to a choice set, and we have a set of choice sets, T, where A defines a choice set with all alternatives, and $1,\ldots,J$ are J choice sets each with one element.

Assuming that an individual can be captive to a specific alternative, then the number of feasible choice sets is given as

$$T = (1,2,\ldots,J,A) \qquad 1,2,\ldots,J \in A,$$

$$T \text{ has } J + 1 \text{ elements} \qquad (4.3)$$

Equation (4.3) is a reduced set of choices in the sense that there are other combinations, for example 1 and 2, or 1 and 3 etc. To understand the process it is only necessary to include the choice sets with one element and all elements. Equation (4.3) now replaces $T = (A)$ in Chapter 3 where we had a single choice set containing all J elements.

To obtain the probabilities of the choice sets assume that they are functions of the elements of the utility function, and are denoted by μ_j (non-negative parameters). Thus, in the basic choice model, we can relate by assumption, μ_j to the set of attributes in a utility expression:

$$\mu_j = \exp W_j \quad , \quad W_j \neq V_j \tag{4.4}$$

V_j being the representative utility associated with the jth alternative in the basic choice model (equation 3.26), and

$$W_j = \gamma_j V_j + \delta_j, \ \gamma_j \text{ are parameters, and } \delta_j$$

is a constant parameter (not the same as δ_j in the derivation of elasticities in Chapter 3). Ben-Akiva (1977a) has defined (but not proven) the probability of being captive to a specific alternative as[1]

$$\mu_i / (1 + \mu), \ \mu = \mu_1 + \mu_2 + \ldots + \mu_J \quad i = 1,\ldots,J \tag{4.5}$$

which is equivalent to

$$\exp W_i /(1 + \sum_{j=1}^{J} \exp W_j) \tag{4.6}$$

Each μ reflects the utility of the jth alternative, thus μ_1 reflects the utility from the first alternative, and μ_J the utility from alternative J. Given

$$\mu_1, \mu_2, \ldots, \mu_J$$

let us define μ, some parameter which reflects the utility of the choice set containing all alterna-tives. Because $u_1,\ldots,\mu_J$ are relative, depending on γ_j and δ_j, then if we change the scale of the parameters we just change the scale of the μ_j's; thus, in order to get a unique set of μ_j's, we need to normalise by defining μ associated with the choice set containing all alternatives as equal to unity. What is the probability of selecting any of

these J + 1 choice sets? The sum of
$\mu_1 + \mu_2 + \ldots + \mu_J + 1$ is the total utility of all
choice sets, T. Thus the probability of selecting
choice set 1 is $\mu_1/(\mu_1 + \mu_2 + \ldots + \mu_J + 1)$.
Simplifying by defining $\mu_1 + \mu_2 + \ldots + \mu_J = \mu$, then
the probability of selecting choice set i is
$\mu_i/(1 + \mu)$. The probability of selecting choice set
A is $1/(1 + \mu)$.

The choice set probabilities are given by
(referring to equation 4.3):

$$P_T = \left[\frac{\exp W_1}{(1 + \sum\limits_{j=1}^{J} \exp W_j)} \quad , \quad \frac{\exp W_2}{1 + \sum\limits_{j=1}^{J} \exp W_j} \quad , \ldots \right.$$

$$\left. \ldots , \quad \frac{\exp W_J}{(1 + \sum\limits_{j=1}^{J} \exp W_j)} \quad , \quad \frac{1}{(1 + \sum\limits_{j=1}^{J} \exp W_j)} \right] \qquad (4.7)$$

Since we want to relate the choice outcome to
the choice-set generating process, then we need to
relate equations (4.3) and (4.7) to equation (4.2)
or (4.1). When we do this the following result
emerges:

$$P_i = \frac{\exp W_i}{(1 + \sum\limits_{j=1}^{J} \exp W_j)} . 1 + \frac{1}{(1 + \sum\limits_{j=1}^{J} \exp W_j)} . P(i|A)$$

$$(4.8)$$

Procedure to arrive at (4.8): an individual is
assumed to be captive to a specific alternative or
to have a choice from A (expression (4.3) where
the first J choice sets have one element and the
last one has all J alternatives). This yields
(4.7). Now to obtain the marginal choice probability, say for alternative i, which is assumed to
be the first element in A or the choice set
1 (i = 1), we note that the probability of selecting
alternative i(=1) out of choice sets 2,...,J is
zero. The probability of selecting alternative i
out of choice set 1 is:

$$\exp W_1 / (1 + \sum_{j=1}^{J} \exp W_j). \qquad (4.9)$$

However, i = 1 is contained in A, hence the probability of selecting alternative i is equal to the sum of the probability of selecting i out of choice set 1 and the probability of selecting i out of choice set A, the latter equal to

$$(1/(1 + \sum_{j=1}^{J} \exp W_j)) \, P(i|A).$$

$\sum_{j=1}^{J} \exp W_j$ can be interpreted as the odds of being captive to having a choice;

$\exp W_i / (1 + \sum_{j=1}^{J} \exp W_j)$ is the probability of being captive to alternative i and

$1/(1 + \sum_{j=1}^{J} \exp W_j)$ is the probability of a full choice set.

To get (4.8), we substitute into (4.2). Assume i=1, for equation (4.2) we need the probability of selecting choice set 1, containing a single element,

$$\frac{\exp W_i}{(1 + \sum_{j=1}^{J} \exp W_j)}$$

times the probability of choosing alternative 1 when the choice set consists of one element (i.e. $P(i=1|1)=1$); the second part of equation (4.8) is the probability of choosing choice set A times the probability of choosing alternative i given it is contained in the choice set A.

Since $(P(i|A) = \exp V_i / (\sum_{j=1}^{J} \exp V_j)$, then

(noting $V_i \neq W_i$)

$$P_i = \frac{\exp W_i}{(1 + \sum\limits_{j=1}^{J} \exp W_j)} + \frac{\exp V_i / (\sum\limits_{j=1}^{J} \exp V_j)}{(1 + \sum\limits_{j=1}^{J} \exp W_j)}$$

$$= \frac{(\exp W_i)(\sum\limits_{j=1}^{J} \exp V_j) + \exp V_i}{(1 + \sum\limits_{j=1}^{J} \exp W_j)(\sum\limits_{j=1}^{J} \exp V_j)} \qquad (4.10)$$

From equation (4.4), $W_i = \gamma_i V_i + \delta_i$, thus

$$P_i = \frac{\exp(\gamma_i V_i + \delta_i)(\sum\limits_{j=1}^{J} \exp V_j) + \exp V_i}{(1 + \sum\limits_{j=1}^{J} \exp (\gamma_j V_j + \delta_j))(\sum\limits_{j=1}^{J} \exp V_j)}$$

$$= \frac{1 + \exp (\gamma_i V_i + \delta_i) \dfrac{\sum\limits_{j=1}^{J} \exp V_j}{\exp V_i}}{1 + \sum\limits_{j=1}^{J} \exp (\gamma_j V_j + \delta_j)} \cdot \frac{\exp V_i}{\sum\limits_{j=1}^{J} \exp V_j} \qquad (4.11)$$

If $\gamma_j = 1$, $j = 1,\ldots,J$ and $\delta_j = \delta$ for $j = 1,\ldots J$, then (4.11) becomes the basic choice model (equation 3.24). Alternative specifications of the logit model are briefly discussed in Sections 4.4 and 6.6. The sole purpose of the discussion above is to illustrate the way in which the choice-set generating process works under an illustrative condition of captivity.

The crucial equations are 4.2, 4.3, 4.4 and 4.5. The remaining equations in this section are manipulations to arrive at 4.11. Equation (4.11) is a general form of the logit model in which our basic choice model in Chapter 3 is a special case. In concluding the discussion on the choice set generating process, it must be pointed out that the presentation is couched in terms of a logit formulation, although other formulations could be used such as multinomial probit (see Section 6.5).

So far we have presented the notion of a choice set generating process and alternative assumptions on the elements in a choice set. In practice, it becomes necessary to limit the number of alternatives in a choice set, regardless of the knowledge of the full set of elemental alternatives. In other words, it is necessary to group alternatives by design or randomly select a subset of relevant alternatives. Furthermore, data availability is such that often it is not possible to empirically specify a choice set containing elemental alternatives but only a lesser number of alternatives with some implicit relationship between a "grouped" alternative and a subset of elemental alternatives. In concluding section 4.2, it is appropriate to outline ways of accomodating large numbers of alternatives and/or biases that occur when the alternatives are limited to non-elemental alternatives. A consideration of subsampling fits more appropriately in a later section (4.4), because it involves a more complex likelihood function than that in the basic choice model.

When an individual makes a decision based on the selection of an alternative out of a set of alternatives, he/she has an interpretation of the alternatives that might differ from the definitions of alternatives that the analyst often adopts. Examples are car-pooling, which has many possible individual interpretations including multiple occupancy in same car with same driver or varying car and driver; and public transport which can be train or bus or even taxi or dial-a-bus. Each of these possible alternatives might vary significantly in terms of service offered, yet are frequently combined as a single representative alternative with representative attributes. The possibility for error in estimates of parameters is highly likely if the conventional modelling approach in Chapter 3 is adopted without questioning the definition of the alternatives in the choice set. Conventionally we assume randomly selected "representative" alternatives for each "class" of elemental alternatives where classes are defined by the analyst.

One way of handling this problem is to seek out the relationship between so-called representative alternatives, and the fuller range of relevant alternatives and to accommodate any bias due to grouping. The notion of an elemental alternative can be used to distinguish the explicit alternatives of relevance to the decision-making

unit in contrast to the grouped or 'set of assumed
identical alternatives' (SIA) which are used in the
definition of the choice set for model estimation
and application.

If we were able to identify for each individual,
the particular elemental alternatives, expressed in
terms of a range of attributes (by level), then the
correct determination of choice probabilities for
SIAs involves calculation of the probability of an
individual selecting each alternative, and then
arranging the calculations in a way in which summing
will produce the relevant probabilities for a
particular SIA. Thus if the jth SIA has N_j
elemental alternatives and subsets are non
overlapping, then the choice probabilities for SIA
alternatives are

$$P_{qi} = \sum_{n=1}^{N_i} \exp V_{qn} \Big/ \sum_{j=1}^{J} \sum_{n=1}^{N_j} \exp V_{qn} \qquad (4.12)$$

$$\text{and} \quad \sum_{j=1}^{J} N_j = N$$

Note that the denominator is summed across all
elemental alternatives in each SIA, $n = 1,\ldots,N_j$
and all the SIAs, $j = 1,\ldots,J$.

When sets of assumed identical alternatives
are defined instead of elemental alternatives,
which is often the only option in practice, then
V_{qn} is not observed. To estimate the choice model
in terms of known levels of the explanatory
variables, we need to express the numerator and
denominator of the right-hand side of equation
(4.12) in terms of variables subscripted by
q_i and q_j respectively.

If we knew V_{qn}, then we could calculate $\tilde{V}_{qi}$
(as an approximation) using equation (4.13).

Define

$$\exp \tilde{V}_{qi} = \left(\sum_{n=1}^{N_i} \exp V_{qn} \right) / N_i \qquad (4.13)$$

noting that

$$\tilde{V}_{qi} \neq \sum_{n=1}^{N_i} V_{qn} / N_i$$

74

Rearranging, taking logarithms and exponentiating yields

$$\exp(\tilde{V}_{qi} + \ln N_i) = \sum_{n=1}^{N_i} \exp V_{qn} \qquad (4.14)$$

For J alternatives, we have

$$\sum_{j=1}^{J} \exp(\tilde{V}_{qj} + \ln N_j) = \sum_{j=1}^{J} \sum_{n=1}^{N_i} \exp V_{qn} \qquad (4.15)$$

Thus substitution of the left-hand side of (4.14) and (4.15) into (4.12), defining $V_{qi} \approx V_{qi}^{*}$ (explained below) gives

$$P_{qi} = \exp(V_{qi}^{*} + \ln N_i) / \sum_{j=1}^{J} \exp(V_{qj}^{*} + \ln N_j) \qquad (4.16)$$

The basic choice model (3.24) is a special case of equation (4.16) when all the Ns = 1. Since the natural logarithm of 1 is zero, this leaves $\exp V_{qi}^{*}$ which equals $\exp V_{qn}$, thus giving (3.24).

The formulation in equation (4.16) relies on the number of elemental alternatives as the basis for approximating the error in grouping alternatives. This error is in fact an error variance and hence if we can estimate it, rather than approximate it, then we have a basis for assessing the suitability of the size-proxy. Taking the relation in equation (4.13), we can specify V_{qi}^{*} in terms of the mean of V_{qi} and dispersion around it for the set of elemental alternatives:

$$V_{qi}^{*} = \tilde{V}_{qi} + \ln \left(\sum_{n=1}^{N_i} \exp(V_{qn} - \tilde{V}_{qi})/N_i \right) \qquad (4.17)$$

It can be shown (McFadden, 1978) that $V_{qi}^{*} - \tilde{V}_{qi}$ approaches $\sigma_{qi}^2/2$ when V_{qn} is assumed to be standard normally distributed, and thus σ_{qi}^2 is the within-group variance of the utility V_{qn}. Thus we can conclude that equation (4.16) is a suitable expression for a multinomial logit model where SIAs are defined as elements in the choice set.[2]

The formulation above has made no allowance for the degree of similarity between elemental alternatives defining an SIA (or the degree of similarity between SIAs). This issue is discussed in Section 4.4. It is not a necessary part of the discussion on choice set generation or the grouping of alternatives in a choice set, but does have an important role in the application of the basic choice model when the IIA property is thought to be violated.

4·3 Alternative Decision Structures and Decision Linking

Section 4.2 introduced the idea of a choice-set generating process and a procedure for grouping alternatives in a given choice set for the multinomial logit model. The discussion continued to assume a single equation, like Chapter 3. The complexity of decision making and the reality of the process are such that single-equation representation of the full set of relevant decisions is either unrealistic or imposes far too heavy a computational burden on the analyst. There are a number of procedures available for 'simplifying' the modelling task without adding significantly to the loss of information, and in some instances adding to the realism of the representation of the decision structure. In very simplistic terms the discussion centres around whether the choice process can be characterised by a simultaneous choice or a sequential choice structure although the criteria for selection of structure are not limited solely to characterisation of the true choice process. In practice it is often difficult to identify the true structure and hence alternative structures should be tested (although invariably this is not performed).

The section continues to adopt the multinomial logit model framework, and to use the strengths of the technique in formulating a range of decision structures. A suitable starting position is to note that the independence-from-irrelevant alternatives property implies that the probability of selecting a particular alternative is proportional to the representative utility of that alternative (V_j) and thus the idea of separability of choice is consistent with the application of the basic choice model. This permits a decomposition of any complex decision process into a series of structually related decisions.

Separability is concerned with the possibility of dividing up the commodity bundle into a number of sub-bundles in such a way that the level of utility afforded by a particular commodity bundle depends only on the levels of utility yielded by various subcollections of the given commodity bundle and on a uniform relationship between goods in different subcollections. Alternatives within a subgroup may bear any relationship with another, but alternatives from different subcollections must bear a similar relationship with one another. The IIA property embodies both functional separability and separability of choices, requiring that proportional representative utilities are preserved within and between choice sets. Functional (Leontief) separability assumes that the marginal rate of substitution among a set of variables is independent of other variables (that is,

$$\partial(u_k 1/u_k 2)/\partial X_k 3 = 0 \quad k^1 \neq k^2, k^3$$

where

$$u_k 1 = \partial u/\partial X_k 1$$

and

$$u_k 2 = \partial u/\partial X_k 2).$$

Separability of choice assumes that the conditional probability associated with a given choice is dependent on only part of the full utility function. Maintenance of representative utilities through all choices implies that the choice models must be estimated in the reverse sequence from that in which the choices are seen to be made (Stopher & Meyburg, 1976).

A number of alternative structures can be proposed, although it should be stated that the structures do not necessarily have strong behavioural implications, analytical convenience often being a major consideration. The main structures are called the independent structure, the sequential structure, the recursive structure and the simultaneous structure. The dependency among choices is a function of the commonality of the attributes, and can be unidirectional or two-way directional. We will discuss these structures in terms of three decisions associated respectively with the selection of a $\in$ A, b $\in$ B and d $\in$ D. It is important that the attribute types are also spelled out since it is necessary that the appropriate attributes enter into each of the equations so that the models are correctly linked.

The simplest structure assumes that choices are independent such that any joint probability of choice is the product of separately estimated models. Separate utility functions for each choice are defined, and assumed to be of an additive separable form. Thus for the three choices

$$u_{abd} = u_a + u_b + u_d \qquad (4.18)$$

$$P_{a \in A} = P(u_a \geq u_{a'}, \quad \forall a' \in A) \qquad (4.19a)$$

$$P_{b \in B} = P(u_b \geq u_{b'}, \quad \forall b' \in B) \qquad (4.19b)$$

$$P_{d \in D} = P(u_d \geq u_{d'}, \quad \forall d' \in D) \qquad (4.19c)$$

and $\quad P_{abd \in ABD} = P_{a \in A} \cdot P_{b \in B} \cdot P_{d \in D} \qquad (4.20)$

(4.19a) has the following interpretation:

> *the probability of selecting alternative a out of the full set of alternatives A equals the probability that the utility associated with a is greater than, or equal to the utility associated with another alternative a', for each and every alternative contained in the choice set A.*

The independence assumption implies that the sets of attributes defining each of u_a, u_b and u_d (i.e. $\sum_k x_{ak}$, $\sum_k x_{bk}$, $\sum_k x_{dk}$ respectively) are independent across the choices. Thus any joint probability is equal to the product of the marginal probabilities (equation 4.20). There are many situations where the attributes that define probabilities of various choices are not independent and mutually exclusive and thus a conditional setting is more realistic. There are two conditional decision structures known as the sequential structure and the recursive (sequential) structure.

In the sequential structure, an individual is assumed to make one decision independent of any other choice and then to make subsequent choices conditional on the previous choices. There are no feedback loops or mutual interactions between decisions and it is implied that there exists some form of hierarchical structuring to the decision process. A sequential structure also assumes that the utility function is additive separable. One example of an additive utility function is

$$u_{abd} = u_a + u_{b|a} + u_{d|ab} \qquad (4.21)$$

where u_a is the utility of alternative a, $a \in A$

$u_{b|a}$ is the utility of alternative b given alternative a, $b \in B$, $A \cap B = \emptyset$

$u_{d|ab}$ is the utility of alternative d given alternatives a and b, $d \in D$, $A \cap B \cap C = \emptyset$

79

$A \cap B = \emptyset$ indicates that the intersection of A and B is empty, i.e. choice sets A and B are disjoint.

An example of a sequential structure with no feedback effects is given in equation (4.22).

$$P_{a \epsilon A} = P(u_a \geq u_{a'}, \; \forall a' \epsilon A) \qquad (4.22a)$$

$$P_{b \epsilon Ba} = P(u_{b|a} \geq u_{b'|a} \; \forall b' \epsilon B) \qquad (4.22b)$$

$$P_{d \epsilon D_{ab}} = P(u_{d|ab} \geq u_{d'|ab} \; \forall d' \epsilon D) \qquad (4.22c)$$

Although a particular sequence is assumed in equations (4.21) and (4.22), since the equations above are not mutually interactive they can be estimated in any order. Since we have one marginal probability, $P_{a \epsilon A}$ and at least one conditional probability, $P_{b \epsilon B_a}$, $P_{d \epsilon D_{ab}}$, then a joint probability can be obtained:

$$P_{abd \; \epsilon \; ABD} = P_{a \epsilon A} \cdot P_{b \epsilon B_a} \cdot P_{d \epsilon D_{ab}} \qquad (4.23)$$

It is important to note that all the attributes in choice set A are independent of the attributes in B and D, the attributes in choice set B are conditioned on the selection of a particular alternative in choice set A, and the attributes in choice set D are conditioned on the selection of a particular alternative in A and in B. There is no feedback loop.

The third decision structure is an extension of the sequential structure to incorporate feedback effects, and is referred to as the recursive (sequential) structure. At each decision level the choice is assumed to be conditioned on the previous choice in totality rather than a single alternative in a previous decision. The feedback is incorporated into the utility function in the form of an additional variable, variously referred to as inclusive price, inclusive value, or expected maximum utility. Since the representative utilities must be estimated and maintained throughout the entire sequential recursive structure, estimation begins with the latest decision and proceeds back to the initial decision, maintaining relative weights of the individual attributes in each previous decision.

*It is clear that the partitioning and
sequencing of choices will, therefore,
affect the estimation of strict utilities
(Luce, 1959). In particular, the decision
on which choice is last will have a
considerable influence on the estimated
models. If the decisions are sequential
in reality, then it is mandatory that the
correct sequence be determined. If
sequential models are an analytical
convenience then sensitively testing of
the sequential assumptions is necessary.
Clearly, the recursive, sequential
structure is analytically convenient since
it permits considerable simplification of
the choice sets for the modeling.*

(Stopher & Meyburg, 1976: 17)

In practice it is necessary to ensure that the
sequential recursive structure selected is correct,
since evidence has shown that the results are
sensitive to the sequence (Ben-Akiva, 1973).

In the structure of the sequential model given
in equation (4.22) the utility function for u_a
would be modified to accommodate the feedback; and
might be given as expression (4.24):

$$u_a = \tilde{u}_a + \sum_{b \in B_a} P_{b|B_a} \cdot u_{b|a} \qquad (4.24)$$

where $\tilde{u}_a$ is the utility function without feedback,
i.e. using attributes specific to a. The second
term on the right hand side of (4.24) can be
expressed in a number of forms, one example being

$$\sum_{b \in B_a} P_{b \in B_a} \cdot u_{b|a} = \ln \sum_{b \in B_a} \exp u_{b|a} \qquad (4.25)$$

Constructing such an index involves maintaining
equal marginal rates of substitution among those
attributes in the different probabilities of a
recursive structure, i.e. functional separability.
The procedure for inclusion of equation (4.25) in
a series of structural equations is developed
later in this section. However to obtain an
intuitive feel for this concept, assume the choice
of transport mode ($a \in A$) is a function of the
destination choice decision ($b \in B$) (not a
particular destination as such). That is, P_a is

81

constrained by the entire decision process which
relates to the destination choice process. This
is a mechanism for accommodating some of the unit
environment constraints (see Chapter 2.1). The
estimation is undertaken in the reverse order to
decision seniority so as to incorporate the
empirical index in the initial decision.

To expand on this discussion of inclusive value
as the feedback linking mechanism, one might ask:
why does the inclusive value variable have to take
such a complicated form; perhaps a simple
translation of the sum of the attributes associated
with choice of model weighted each by externally
provided weights, summed across all modal alternatives would be adequate in accounting for feedback?

For the example above, we might define the
influence of mode choice on destination choice by
a composite value variable equal to

$$\sum_{a=1}^{A} \sum_{k=1}^{K} \gamma_k x_{ka},$$ where the γ_k's are independently

derived weights used in converting all attributes to
a common metric (some γ's possibly being unity if
they are already in the common metric). What is
wrong with this approach? The inclusive value
variable must be constructed within the theoretical
framework used to formulate the model (in this case
it is multinomial logit), which is itself founded on
the notion of 'value' dispersion about representative (mean) values, denoted as $IV_{a=1}$ to $IV_{a=A}$.
The inclusive value IV_a is determined by aggregating
over those utilities associated with selected
choices which are actually perceived by rational
decision makers - namely the individuals - and not
over the utility values attributed by the analyst
to the choice making population as a whole, which
might give the incorrect form assumed above.

To derive the correct form of the feedback
variable for the basic logit model, we assume that
the influence of one decision on another is defined
in a random utility modelling context as the
expected value of the maximum of the components in
U_q, which is

$$E \left[\max_{i \in A_q} U_{iq} \right]$$

(this is proven in Williams, 1977). That is the
feedback variables represent expectations of the
outcomes of lower-level choices that could be
different among alternatives of higher-level
choices.

Given that

$$\frac{\partial F(\varepsilon_q)}{\partial V_{iq}} = 0 \quad \text{and} \quad \frac{\partial U_{iq}}{\partial V_{iq}} = 1$$

(from Chapter 3) then for the basic choice model

$$\frac{\partial E\,[\max\,U_q]}{\partial V_{iq}} = P_{iq} = \frac{\exp V_{iq}}{\sum\limits_{j=1}^{J} \exp V_{jq}}$$

We can re-express this equation as

$$E\,[\max_{i \in A_q}\,U_q] = \int \frac{\exp V_{iq}}{\exp V_{iq} + \sum\limits_{j \neq i} \exp V_{jq}}\ dV_{iq}$$

Let $x = \exp V_{iq}$ and $a = \sum\limits_{j \neq i} \exp V_{jq}$

Then $dx = \exp V_{iq}\ dV_{iq} = x\,dV_{iq}$

That is, $dV_{iq} = dx/x$, and hence

$$
\begin{aligned}
E[\max\,U_q] &= \int \frac{x}{x+a}\ \frac{dx}{x} \\[2mm]
&= \int \frac{dx}{x+a} \\[2mm]
&= \ell n\ (x+a) + \text{constant} \\[2mm]
&= \ell n\ \sum_{j=1}^{J} \exp V_{jq} + \text{constant} = (4.25)
\end{aligned}
$$

Since we are interested in the relative values of this expected value, then the constant can be ignored, leaving us with the natural logarithm of the denominator of the basic logit model, referred to as inclusive value (IV). An inclusive value form other than that in equation (4.25) can be shown (e.g. Williams, 1977) to be inconsistent with the behavioural basis for the logit-share model developed in Chapter 3. (This model assumes that all selected alternatives are independent; in Section 4.4 we introduce a modification to equation (4.25) when degrees of similarity are permitted).[3]

This result has a useful role in the development of the basic choice model with grouped alternatives (equation 4.16). In general, for a logit model as given in equation (3.24),

$$P_i = P(SIA_i) = P(\max_{n \in N_i} U_{iq} > \max_{n \notin N_i} U_{jq}) \qquad (4.26)$$

$$\text{where} \quad \max_{(n \in N_i)_q} U = U_{iq}^\Delta = V_{iq}^\Delta + \varepsilon_{iq}^\Delta \qquad (4.27)$$

where Δ defines some aggregation across alternatives. Since the expected-maximum utility associated with a set of alternatives is the logarithm of the sum of the exponential of representative utility of each and every alternative in a choice set, then the expected maximum utility associated with a set of (assumed) identical alternatives is

$$V_i^\Delta = \ln \sum_{n=1}^{N_i} \exp V_{nq} \qquad (4.28)$$

Thus $P_i = \exp V_i^\Delta / \sum\limits_{j=1}^{J} \exp V_j^\Delta$

$$= \exp (\ln \sum_{n=1}^{N_i} \exp V_{nq}) / \sum_{j=1}^{J} \exp (\ln \sum_{n=1}^{N_j} \exp V_{nq})$$

(or equation 4.12).

Since V_{nq} is not observed, or more precisely, X_{nq} is not observed, only X_{iq}, then we need to develop some "approximation".

Define $\bar{X}_{iq} = \sum\limits_{n=1}^{N_i} X_{nq}/N_i$ and let $\delta_{nq} = X_{nq} - \bar{X}_{iq}$

that is, δ_{nq} is the deviation of the "true" level of an attribute associated with an elemental alternative from the mean level of the attribute that is associated with the grouped alternative. Replacing X_{nq} with $\delta_{nq} + \bar{X}_{iq}$,

$$V_i^\Delta = \ln \sum_{n=1}^{N_i} \exp \beta_i(\bar{X}_{iq} + \delta_{nq}) = \beta\bar{X}_{iq} + \ln \sum_{n=1}^{N_i} \exp \beta_i \delta_{nq} \qquad (4.29)$$

We can expand $\exp \beta_i \delta_{nq}$ (using the expansion of powers of exp and assuming the series remain equal as r (in $(1 + \frac{1}{r})^r$) is indefinitely increased)

$$\exp \beta_i \delta_{nq} = 1 + \beta_i \delta + \frac{\beta_i^2 \delta^2}{2!} + \frac{\beta_i^3 \delta^3}{3!} + \ldots$$

Thus $V_i^\Delta = \beta \bar{X}_{iq} + \ln \sum_{n=1}^{N_i} (1 + \beta_i \delta + \frac{\beta_i^2 \delta^2}{2!} + \ldots + \ldots)$

Since $\ln \sum_{n=1}^{N_i} 1 = \ln N_i$ and δs are deviations from means such that $\ln \sum_{n=1}^{N_i} \beta_i \delta = 0$ and $\ln \sum_{n=1}^{N_i} \frac{\beta_i^2 \delta^2}{2!}$

is assumed negligible (as are higher order terms in δ), then

$$V_i^\Delta \simeq \beta_i X_{iq} + \ln N_i$$

However, since elemental alternatives are the real sources of utility, then an error is still likely to exist in the probabilities. Recall that

$$V_i^\Delta = \ln \sum_{n=1}^{N_i} \exp V_{nq} = \beta_i \bar{X}_{iq} + \ln \sum_{n=1}^{N_i} \exp \beta_i (X_{nq} - \bar{X}_{iq})$$

$$= \beta_i \bar{X}_{iq} + \ln N_i + \ln \frac{1}{N_i} \sum_{n=1}^{N_i} \exp \beta_i (X_{nq} - \bar{X}_{iq}) \quad (4.30)$$

Then the error is the last term. As N_i approaches unity the error is reduced such that at $N_i = 1$, $V_{nq} = \bar{V}_{iq}$ and the error is eliminated. As the number of elemental alternatives approaches infinity, the error approaches the expectation of $\exp \beta_i (X_{nq} - \bar{X}_{iq})$. On the assumption that $X_{nq} - \bar{X}_{iq}$ is standard normally distributed, then this is the expectation of a log-normal variable, equal to $\exp (0.5 \sigma_{iq}^2)$. That is, the error asymptotically approaches $\exp (0.5 \sigma_{iq}^2)$; the error being the within-group variance of the representative utility (as assumed but not proven in Section 4.2). A fully specified representative utility with grouped alternatives would be

$$V_{iq}^{\Delta} = \beta_i \bar{x}_{iq} + \ell n \, N_{iq} + \sigma_{iq}^2/2 \qquad (4.31)$$

In equation (4.16), $\beta_i \bar{x}_{iq} + \sigma_{iq}^2/2 = V_{iq}^*$, but since $\sigma_{iq}^2/2$ is not known in practice, then $V_{iq}^* \simeq \bar{V}_{iq}$. This completes the discussion of grouped alternatives. Let us now introduce the final decision structure.

The final structure is fully simultaneous
This is the most general of the decision structures:

> *The problem with ... decisions is that we cannot find a unique 'natural' sequence of partitions that will be generally applicable. Therefore a simultaneous structure is superior to a recursive structure.*

(Ben Akiva & Koppelman, 1974: 140)

The individual is assumed to make all decisions simultaneously and the joint probability distribution is predicted directly. No assumptions are made about independence or the hierarchical structure of the decision process:

$$P_{abd \in ABD} = P(u_{abd} \geq u_{a'b'd'} \quad \forall a'b'd' \in ABD) \qquad (4.32).$$

While this structure may be appealing because of its generality, there are many empirical situations where the structure is not realistic, and a recursive structure is preferable. However, even if equation (4.32) were deemed to be a realistic representation of the decision structure, the possible combinations of alternatives between choice sets is likely to make estimation very costly and computationally very demanding. For example, if there are 20 residential locations in a choice set, six establishment types, four occupant statuses, and four residential mobility levels, then we have 1920 combinations of alternatives, which is both unmanageable and possibly unrealistic. There is a need to prune the alternatives and to hypothesise simplified and indirect-simultaneous structures if the simultaneous form is preferred. For practical reasons, the simultaneous approach can be simplified by assuming separability of choice, implying that the conditional probability for a given choice depends only on part of the full utility function. An example for two decisions is that the conditional probability of choosing to rent or buy is a function of the variables for both occupant statuses, but for only one level of establishment type (e.g. a flat).

Thus a fully, but indirect, simultaneous model would be:

$$P_{a \in A_{bd}} = P(u_{a|bd} \geq u_{a' \, bd} \quad \forall a' \in A_{bd}) \qquad (4.33a)$$

$$P_{b \in B_{ad}} = P(u_{b|ad} \geq u_{b' \, ad} \quad \forall b' \in B_{ad}) \qquad (4.33b)$$

$$P_{d \in D_{ab}} = P(u_{d|ab} \geq u_{d' \, ab} \quad \forall d' \in D_{ab}) \qquad (4.33c)$$

$$P_{abd \in ABD} \neq P_{a \in A_{bd}} \cdot P_{b \in B_{ad}} \cdot P_{d \in D_{ab}} \qquad (4.34)$$

In the simultaneous-indirect structure the conditional probabilities provide insufficient information to predict the joint probability, P_{abd}; thus we need either to estimate a marginal probability (i.e. the probability of one decision of a joint distribution), such as $P_{a \in A}$, or to estimate directly the joint probability, as in equation (4.32). We do not have a capability of estimating a marginal probability in a model structure which is fully simultaneous in its indirect specification. The only alternative procedures available are the specification of the joint utility directly or some recursive structure that is equivalent to a simultaneous structure

If the directly joint-utility specification (4.32) is adopted, then we can obtain any marginal or conditional probability; e.g.

$$P_{a \in A} = \sum_{bd \in BD_a} P_{abd \in ABD} \qquad \begin{array}{l}\text{marginal probability} \\ \text{of selecting} \\ \text{alternative a, } a \in A\end{array} \qquad (4.35)$$

$$P_{d \in D} = \sum_{ab \in AB_d} P_{abd \in ABD} \qquad \begin{array}{l}\text{marginal probability} \\ \text{of selecting} \\ \text{alternative d, } d \in D\end{array} \qquad (4.36)$$

$$P_{a\in A_{bd}} = P_{abd\in ABD} \Big/ P_{bd\in BD} \qquad \begin{array}{l}\text{conditional probability} \\ \text{of selecting} \\ \text{alternative a, } a\in A \\ \text{(Bayes Theorem)}\end{array} \qquad (4.37)$$

$$P_{d\in D_{ab}} = P_{abd\in ABD} \Big/ P_{ab\in AB} \qquad \begin{array}{l}\text{conditional probability} \\ \text{of selecting} \\ \text{alternative d, } d\in D\end{array} \qquad (4.38)$$

where

$$P_{bd\in BD} = \sum_{a\in A_{bd}} P_{abd\in ABD} \qquad (4.39)$$

$$P_{ab\in AB} = \sum_{d\in D_{ab}} P_{abd\in ABD} \qquad (4.40)$$

How do we convert a simultaneous structure into a recursive structure that is equivalent, given that a simultaneous structure is preferable from theoretical considerations but a recursive structure has computational advantages?

Define the choice model as equation (4.41)

$$(P_{abd\in ABD})_q = \frac{\exp v_{abdq}}{\displaystyle\sum_{a'b'd'\in ABD} \exp v_{a'b'd'q}} \qquad (4.41)$$

and

$$v_{abdq} = \sum_{k=1}^{10} \beta_{abdk} x_{abdkq} + \sum_{k=11}^{20} \beta_{abk} x_{abkq}$$

$$+ \sum_{k=21}^{30} \beta_{adk} x_{adkq} + \sum_{k=31}^{40} \beta_{bdk} x_{bdkq} + \sum_{k=41}^{50} \beta_{ak} x_{akq}$$

$$+ \sum_{k=51}^{60} \beta_{bk} x_{bkq} + \sum_{k=61}^{70} \beta_{dk} x_{dkq} \qquad (4.42)$$

assuming 10 attributes of each of seven types

where x_{abdkq} is a vector of attributes that differ for all alternatives (e.g. if A = mode choice, B = destination choice, D = time of day travel choice, then travel time depends on all three choices).

x_{bdkq}, x_{abkq}, x_{adkq} are vectors of attributes that only differ for two alternatives, respectively bd, ab and ad (e.g. for ab, walking distance from house to railway station).

x_{akq}, x_{bkq}, x_{dkq} are vectors of attributes that only differ for a single alternative (e.g. alternative-specific dummy variables - see Section 4.5).

Let us <u>assume</u> a particular recursive structure

$$P_{abd \in ABD} = P_{d \in D_{ab}} \cdot P_{b \in B_a} \cdot P_{a \in A} \tag{4.43}$$

where equation (4.43) is (4.22) reordered on the right-hand side to reflect the estimation sequence, since equation (4.22) has no feedback loops and order is of no consequence.

Attributes which do not vary for alternatives in D have no effect on $P_{d \in D_{ab}}$, thus the model can be formulated as equation (4.44) which excludes x_{bkq}, x_{akq}, and x_{abk}:

$$(P_{d \in D_{ab}})_q = \frac{\exp \left(\sum_{k=1}^{10} \beta_{abdk} x_{abdkq} + \sum_{k=21}^{30} \beta_{adk} x_{adkq} \right.}{\sum_{d' \in D_{ab}} \exp \left(\sum_{k=1}^{10} \beta_{abd'k} x_{abd'kq} + \sum_{k=21}^{30} \beta_{ad'k} x_{ad'kq} \right.}$$

$$\frac{+ \sum_{k=31}^{40} \beta_{bdk} x_{bdkq} + \sum_{k=61}^{70} \beta_{dk} x_{dkq} \right)}{+ \sum_{k=31}^{40} \beta_{bd'k} x_{bd'kq} + \sum_{k=61}^{70} \beta_{d'k} x_{d'kq} \right)} \tag{4.44}$$

This is the basic choice model in Chapter 3 expanded out to clarify the contents of the utility expression for a single decision conditional on two other decisions.

The logarithm of the denominator of equation (4.44) can be simplified to equal

$$IV_{abd'}, \, d' \in D_{ab} \tag{4.45}$$

where (4.45) denotes the inclusive value (IV) for choice defined on set D given a and b, and is to be included in the next model to provide a suitable feedback loop. The logarithm of the denominator is a measure of expected-maximum utility associated with that decision or utility attached to the set of opportunities available to the individual, given that the choice set is defined to contain all relevant alternatives.

Inclusive value provides a summary measure of the desirability of a set of alternatives related directly to a higher level decision; and can be interpreted as a utility for the opportunity set of alternatives associated with choices lower in the hierarchy, regardless of which alternative is actually selected.

The next model is $P_{b \in B_a}$, and is developed in an analogous way.

$$
(P_{b \in B_a})_q = \frac{\exp \left(\sum_{k=11}^{20} \beta_{abk} x_{abkq} + \sum_{k=51}^{60} \beta_{bk} x_{bkq} + IV_{abd'} \right)}{\sum_{d' \in D_{ab'}} \exp \left[\sum_{k=1}^{10} \hat{\beta}_{ab'd'k} x_{ab'd'kq} + \sum_{k=21}^{30} \hat{\beta}_{ad'k} x_{ad'kq} \right. }
$$

$$
\left. + \sum_{k=31}^{40} \hat{\beta}_{b'd'k} x_{b'd'kq} + \sum_{k=61}^{70} \hat{\beta}_{d'k} x_{d'kq} \right] \cdot
$$

$$
\cdot \sum_{b' \in B_a} \exp \left(\sum_{k=11}^{20} \beta_{ab'k} x_{ab'kq} + \sum_{k=51}^{60} \beta_{b'k} x_{b'kq} \right) \quad (4.46)
$$

noting that the additional attributes in equation (4.46) are those which vary for b. The only attribute type not yet included is x_a. Equation (4.46) can be simplified, along the same lines as equation (4.44).

Let us simplify the denominator, defining

$$
\ln \sum_{d' \in D_{ab'}} \exp \left(\sum_{k=1}^{10} \hat{\beta}_{ab'd'k} x_{ab'd'kq} + \cdots + \sum_{k=61}^{70} \hat{\beta}_{d'k} x_{d'kq} \right)
$$

$$
= IV_{ab'd'}, \quad d' \in D_{ab'} \quad (4.47)
$$

90

Then

$$
(P_{b \in B_a})_q = \frac{\exp \left(\sum_{k=11}^{20} \beta_{abk} x_{abkq} + \sum_{k=51}^{60} \beta_{bk} x_{bkq} + IV_{abd'} \right)}{\sum_{b' \in B_a} \exp \left(\sum_{k=11}^{20} \beta_{ab'k} x_{ab'kq} \right.}
$$

$$
\left. + \sum_{k=51}^{60} \beta_{b'k} x_{b'kq} + IV_{ab'd'} \right) \qquad (4.48)
$$

The logarithm of the denominator in equation (4.48) can be simplified as

$$
IV_{ab'}, \; b' \in B_a \qquad (4.49)
$$

which is the inclusive value associated with choice set B for the particular alternative a in A, and is used as the feedback link for the choice model associated with the set of alternatives $a' \in A$. Thus

$$
(P_{a \in A})_q
$$

$$
= \frac{\exp \left(\sum_{k=41}^{50} \beta_{ak} x_{akq} + \ln (\text{denominator of } 4.48) \right)}{\sum_{a' \in A} \exp \left(\sum_{k=41}^{50} \beta_{a'k} x_{a'kq} \right) \cdot \left(\sum_{b' \in B_{a'}} \exp \left(\sum_{k=11}^{20} \hat{\beta}_{a'b'k} x_{a'b'kq} \right. \right.}
$$

$$
\left. \left. + \sum_{k=51}^{60} \hat{\beta}_{b'k} x_{b'kq} + IV_{a'b'} \right) \right) \qquad (4.50)
$$

$$
= \frac{\exp \left(\sum_{k=41}^{50} \beta_{ak} x_{akq} + IV_{ab'} \right)}{\sum_{a' \in A} \exp \left(\sum_{k=41}^{50} \beta_{a'k} x_{a'kq} + IV_{a'b'} \right)} \qquad (4.51)
$$

We can now demonstrate the equivalence of the recursive structure and the simultaneous structure. From above, given equations (4.35) to (4.38),

$$P_{d \in D_{ab}} \cdot P_{b \in B_a} \cdot P_{a \in A}$$

$$= \frac{P_{abd}}{\sum_{d' \in D_{ab}} P_{abd'}} \cdot \frac{P_{ab}}{\sum_{b' \in B_a} P_{ab'}} \cdot$$

$$\frac{\exp\left(\sum_{k=41}^{50} \beta_{ak} x_{akq} + IV_{ab'}\right)}{\sum_{a' \in A} \exp\left(\sum_{k=41}^{50} \beta_{a'k} x_{a'kq} + IV_{a'b'}\right)} \qquad (4.52)$$

Replacement of the right-hand side with the right-hand sides of equations (4.44), (4.48) and (4.50) and simplification will produce $P_{abd \in ABD}$. The reader is given the task of showing this.

In the example above only one ordering was presented for the recursive equivalent of the simultaneous choice outcome; however other orderings are feasible; and indeed it is necessary to test for alternative orderings because it is not necessarily true that the estimates of parameters obtained by a directly joint-simultaneous model (equation 4.32) would be the same as those obtained by using an indirect estimation procedure (equations 4.44, 4.48 and 4.50) because of errors introduced at each stage. Given that a simultaneously estimated model is not likely to be available for comparison with alternative orderings of choices, then how can we test for equivalence between a particular recursive structure and the simultaneous model? A test is outlined in the next section, based on work by Daly & Zachary (1978).

When we have a sequential-recursive structure, it is no longer valid to automatically apply the simple elasticity formulae given in Chapter 3 (equations 3.43, 3.45 and 3.46). These formulae are suitable for attributes in the initial equation of an estimation sequence within which they appear. Since attributes in an initial equation are carried forward (via inclusive value) to a subsequent equation, then in calculating an elasticity in a subsequent equation for an attribute that appears in a previous equation (or equations) we need to include an allowance for the impact of the previous choice outcome(s). The range of formulae associated with the calculation of point elasticities for the choice outcomes a, b, d are given below. Derivations are lengthy and so are omitted here, but they follow the same principles used in Chapter 3 to calculate simple elasticities. Let us assume that attribute type X appears in all equations, attribute type Y in equations associated with b and a, and attribute type Z only in the a equation. Thus we have, suppressing the q subscript, <u>six</u> direct point elasticity formulae:

for choice $d \in D_{ab}$

$$E_{X_{d'abk}}^{P_{d|ab}} = \beta_{d'k} X_{d'abk} (\delta_{dd'} - P_{d'|ab}) \tag{4.53a}$$

for choice $b \in B_a$

$$E_{Y_{b'ak}}^{P_{b|a}} = \alpha_{b'k} Y_{b'ak} (\delta_{bb'} - P_{b'|a}) \tag{4.53b}$$

$$E_{X_{dab'k}}^{P_{b|a}} = \gamma\beta_{d'k} X_{dab'k} \ P_{d|ab'} (\delta_{bb'} - P_{b'|a}) \tag{4.53c}$$

for choice $a \in A$

$$E_{Z_{a'k}}^{P_a} = \Delta_{a'k} Z_{a'k} (\delta_{aa'} - P_{a'}) \tag{4.53d}$$

$$E_{Y_{ba'k}}^{P_a} = \theta\alpha_{b'k} Y_{ba'k} P_{b|a'} (\delta_{aa'} - P_{a'}) \tag{4.53e}$$

$$E_{X_{da'bk}}^{P_a} = \theta \gamma \beta_{d'k} X_{da'bk} \ P_{d|a'b} P_{b|a'} (\delta_{aa'} - P_{a'}) \tag{4.53f}$$

where $\delta_{ij} = 1$ if $i = j$ (a direct elasticity), and $= 0$ if $i \neq j$ (a cross elasticity).

$E_{X_{d'abk}}^{P_{d|ab}}$ = choice d elasticity with respect to the kth atribute of the vector $X_{d'abk}$

$E_{Y_{b'ak}}^{P_{b|a}}$ = choice b elasticity with respect to the kth attribute of the vector $Y_{b'ak}$

The other elasticities have similar interpretations.

γ and θ are respectively coefficients associated with IV_{abd}, and IV_{ab}, assumed in equations (4.48) and (4.51) to be equal to unity. The aggregate elasticities can then be calculated using the sample enumeration procedure in Chapter 3. The resulting elasticities associated with the use of the formulae (4.53c) and (4.53f) will be lower than those obtained if the simple formulae were applied in the calculation of elasticity associated with attribute type X in choices associated with b and a. This is because the additional probabilities will be less than unity. The same interpretation applies in comparing equation (4.53e) with equation (4.53c). Hence decisions associated with a and b are less sensitive to changes in an attribute that varies across the alternatives in choice set D (i.e. X type attributes) than is the decision associated with d.

This section is lengthy, although it is justified given the importance of a knowledge of alternative decision structures. All the structures outlined above can be readily applied using the estimation procedure of the basic choice model without any changes. The notion of an inclusive value has been used in linking decisions. We now turn to a more detailed discussion of the linking of decisions, and provide a test for a 'correct' recursive structure.

4·4 Choice Hierarchy and Model Classification

In this section we introduce the notion of a choice hierarchy and the implications of grouping sets of decisions (referred to as blocking) from the viewpoint of modelling. A range of joint choice logit-type models are then introduced that adopt alternative assumptions on the relationship between decisions and alternatives within choice sets. These models range from the simplest form termed basic multinomial logit (BMNL) where the parameters of the inclusive values are constrained to equal one, through to the nested logit and generalised extreme value model.

In Section 4.3, the application of an inclusive value index implied that it was constrained to have a parameter of unit value and that no account was taken of the possibility of varying degrees of similarity between the unobserved terms in the preceding level of a hierarchical model structure. By suitable modifications, we can obtain a logit model which is not constrained by the independence-from-irrelevant alternatives property. The section is concluded with an outline of a procedure to test for the 'correct' sequencing of the recursive structure, given that a recursive structure is the most likely specification when joint choice is to be modelled.

In Section 4.3 the discussion of a decision structure was in terms of three decisions related to the choice of a, b and d. However, often empirical situations entail many more interacting decisions such that the modelling task can become overdemanding on the analyst. An example of a set of travel-related household decisions is

(1)   employment location
(2)   residential location
(3)   housing type
(4)   house occupancy status
(5)   car ownership
(6)   car availability (for all workers)
(7)   mode to work (for all workers)
(8)   mode to nonwork (for all nonworkers)
(9)   frequency (for nonwork trips of
         each purpose)
(10)   destination (for nonwork trips of
         each purpose)
(11)   time of day (for all trips)
(12)   route (for all trips)

The estimation of models pertaining to these twelve decisions in a sequential recursive structure, with feedback loops at every stage is an enormous task; furthermore it implies that each decision is dependent on the rest (see discussion on equivalence of simultaneous and recursive structure in Section 4.3). An alternative and possibly more realistic approach, is to seek out which decisions are of a much different character than other decisions and which are relatively more similar in nature. In the example above, stability over a time interval is a logical criterion for identifying degrees of difference between the decisions. Thus residential location choice and housing choice are costly decisions and are stable over relatively long time intervals, whereas in contrast the destination choice for nonwork trips is often made on a trip basis, sometimes daily.

There is a behavioural basis for treating certain decisions (or bundles of decisions) as

95

having a joint structure and another bundle of decisions as being block conditional on this joint decision. This statement implies that there exists some choice hierarchy formulated in terms of specific behavioural hypotheses, which will represent the structure of the total vector of choices as a logical working hypothesis. This hierarchy differs from that referred to in Section 4.3 in that we have groups of decisions such that within each group of choices, decisions are assumed to be made by a joint process in which the full range of possible trade-offs is considered (Ben-Akiva & Lerman, 1979), and where the blocks of choices as single units have a conditional structure. The hierarchical decision structures are a function of explicit behavioural hypotheses about individual behaviour, and thus for the twelve decision types above, there are conceivably many choice hierarchies. Two examples of choice hierarchies for the decisions in the example are:

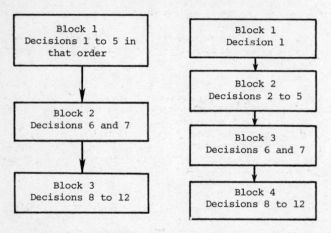

The senior block (i.e. 1 for 1, 2; 2 for 2, 3 etc.) of decisions are made with the junior blocks indeterminate, and the junior block decisions are made conditional on the outcome of the senior block choice process.

A block recursive choice hierarchy is similar to the unblocked recursive structure although the modelling implications do need to be represented in terms of blocks of decisions. Ben-Akiva & Lerman (1979) have provided a useful discussion on the modelling implications of choice hierarchies in the context of a three-block recursive model (Figure 4.1). We draw on their work in the

96

following paragraphs. Assume choice b from set B which is part of a hierarchy, preceded by a choice of a from set A and followed by a choice of d from set D.

FIGURE 4·1:

A Three Block Recursive Model

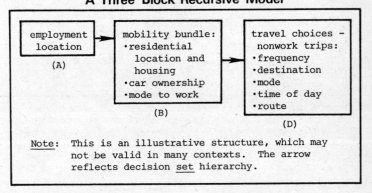

employment location

(A)

mobility bundle:
• residential location and housing
• car ownership
• mode to work

(B)

travel choices - nonwork trips:
• frequency
• destination
• mode
• time of day
• route

(D)

Note: This is an illustrative structure, which may not be valid in many contexts. The arrow reflects decision set hierarchy.

The relevant variables can be represented by four classes of variable which influence the choice from B:

(1) those that directly affect the choice of b, such as direct attributes of alternative B, but do not directly influence the choice of a or d. For example, rent or house price in the mobility bundle which varies according to residential location and house-type combination.

(2) those that directly affect the choice of b as well as higher level choice a and lower level choice d. For example, level of service attributes by public transport for work trip, which is an attribute of an alternative mobility bundle, and of employment location alternatives, which corresponds to a, and of time of day of travel by public transport for nonwork trips.

(3) those that are determined by the outcome of the higher level choice a and affect the choice of b, such as an attribute of the chosen a which is treated as a socioeconomic factor affecting the choice among alternatives in B. For example, variables resulting from the employment location decision such as that indicating whether or not a worker in the household is employed in the city centre. This variable is predetermined in the mobility choice process, and it is an attribute of the household which does not vary among alternative

mobility bundles, i.e. to include it requires a particular specification in the mobility bundle model (see Section 4.5 - discussion on alternative-specific variables).

(4) those that express expectations from the outcome of the lower level choice from set D. Those expectations may vary among alternatives in B and can be treated as attribures of the alternatives in B. An example would be variables describing travel decisions made conditional on the mobility choice such as level of service by public transport for social trips from a given residential location. This variable depends on how the household will choose to travel for social trips, a decision which is made only conditional on household's mobility choices. Thus, social trip level of service is indeterminate in the mobility decision, i.e. the household does not know the specific social trips it will make. This does not imply that it does not enter into the household's evaluation of mobility alternatives.

Like the representation of types of variables in the example of a recursive structure in Section 4.3, a logically consistent block-recursive model system requires that each of the four types of variables be properly represented. That is, appropriate linkages within and between components of a choice hierarchy are required. The procedure is identical to that in Section 4.3. For example, in modelling the choice from B, attributes which are specific to a combination abd (class 2 above) or to bd combination (class 4 above) must be summed across alternative choices in D so as to be included in the model for the choice from B conditional on the choice of a. Inclusive values are used to accomplish this. The general structure, given this choice hierarchy is:

$$u_{abd} = u_{d|ab} + u_{b|a} + u_a \tag{4.54}$$

$$P_{d \in D_{ab}} = P(u_{d|ab} \geq u_{d'|ab} \quad \forall\, d' \in D) \tag{4.54a}$$

$$P_{b \in B_a} = P(u_{b|a} + \ell n \sum_{d \in D_{ab}} \exp u_{d|ab} \geq u_{b'|a}$$

$$+ \ell n \sum_{d \in D_{ab'}} \exp u_{d|ab'} \quad \forall\, b' \in B) \tag{4.54b}$$

$$P_{a \in A} = P(u_a + \ln \sum_{b \in B_a} \exp (u_{b|a} + \ln \sum_{d \in D_{ab}} \exp u_{d|ab})$$

$$\geqslant u_a{}' + \ln \sum_{b \in B_{a'}} \exp (u_{b|a'}$$

$$+ \ln \sum_{d \in D_{db}} \exp u_{d|a'b}) \, \forall \, a' \in A) \qquad (4.54c)$$

The notion of a choice hierarchy with blocks of choices is a useful working tool for formulating the strengths of interdependencies between sets of choices.

There is another issue which has yet to be considered, namely the similarity of alternatives in a choice set and a procedure for reflecting this in a model system. This particular topic is also a link to Chapter 5 where the independence-from-irrelevant alternatives property is discussed as an assumption of the basic logit model; which requires that no alternative is dominant and that no two alternatives are more similar to each other than each is to another alternative. The procedure outlined below provides one way of overcoming the IIA problem by specifying a formulation in which degrees of similarity are permissible.

4·4·1 Classification of Logit Models

It will be useful, at this point, to outline a range of logit models to show the connection between the basic logit model and the more complex yet potentially more realistic specifications. The alternative logit specifications are given for two decisions in ascending order of complexity. They are summarised in Table 4.1 for situations where alternatives are grouped and ungrouped (see Section 4.2). The discussion in this section and Section 4.4.2 is considered to be advanced, yet included because the issues are important in current research and for future applications. Comprehensive discussion of the state of the art is given in McFadden (1979, 1980); Williams & Ortuzar (1979) and Ortuzar & Williams (1978).

The differences between logit forms relate to the assumptions on the random components of the set of utility expressions. In the basic logit model the ε_j's are assumed to be independent and identically distributed with a type 1 extreme value

TABLE 4·1: Alternative Logit Model Recursive Specifications for Two Decisions

TITLE	A. SPECIFICATION WITHOUT GROUPED ALTERNATIVES
BASIC MULTINOMIAL LOGIT (BMNL)*	$$P_{b \in B_a} = \frac{\exp\left[\sum_k \beta_k X_{abk} + \sum_k \beta_k X_{bk}\right]}{\sum_{b' \in B_a} \exp\left[\sum_k \beta_k X_{ab'k} + \sum_k \beta_k X_{b'k}\right]}$$ $$P_{a \in A} = \frac{\exp\left[\sum_k \beta_k X_{ak} + \ell n \sum_{b \in B_a} \exp\left(\sum_k \beta_k X_{ab'k} + \sum_k \beta_k X_{b'k}\right)\right]}{\sum_{a' \in A} \exp\left[\sum_k \beta_k X_{a'k} + \ell n \sum_{b \in B_{a'}} \exp\left(\sum_k \beta_k X_{a'b'k} + \sum_k \beta_k X_{b'k}\right)\right]}$$
SEQUENTIAL NESTED LOGIT (SL)**	$$P_{b \in B_a} = \text{as per BMNL}$$ $$P_{a \in A} = \frac{\exp\left[\sum_k \beta_k X_{ak} + \theta \, \ell n \sum_{b \in B_a} \exp\left(\sum_k \beta_k X_{ab'k} + \sum_k \beta_k X_{b'k}\right)\right]}{\sum_{a' \in A} \exp\left[\sum_k \beta_k X_{a'k} + \theta \, \ell n \sum_{b \in B_{a'}} \exp\left(\sum_k \beta_k X_{a'b'k} + \sum_k \beta_k X_{b'k}\right)\right]}$$

100

A. SPECIFICATION WITHOUT GROUPED ALTERNATIVES

GENERALISED EXTREME VALUE NESTED LOGIT (NL)***

$$P_{b \in B_a} = \frac{\exp\left[\dfrac{\sum_k \beta_k X_{abk} + \sum_k \beta_k X_{bk}}{1 - \sigma}\right]}{\sum_{b' \in B_a} \exp\left[\dfrac{\sum_k \beta_k X_{ab'k} + \sum_k \beta_k X_{b'k}}{1 - \sigma}\right]} \qquad \text{if } b \in B_a$$

$$P_{b \in B_a} = 0 \qquad \text{if } b \notin B_a$$

$$P_{a \in A} = \frac{\exp\left[\sum_k \beta_k X_{ak} + (1-\sigma)\ln \sum_{b' \in B_a} \exp\left(\dfrac{\sum_k \beta_k X_{ab'k} + \sum_k \beta_k X_{b'k}}{1 - \sigma}\right)\right]}{\sum_{a' \in A} \exp\left[\sum_k \beta_k X_{a'k} + (1-\sigma)\ln \sum_{b' \in B_{a'}} \exp\left(\dfrac{\sum_k \beta_k X_{a'b'k} + \sum_k \beta_k X_{b'k}}{1 - \sigma}\right)\right]}$$

101

TABLE 4-1 (cont.)

TITLE	B. SPECIFICATION WITH GROUPED ALTERNATIVES
BASIC MULTINOMIAL LOGIT (BMNL)*	$P_{b \in B_a} = \dfrac{\exp\left[\sum\limits_k \beta_k X^*_{abk} + \sum\limits_k \beta_k X^*_{bk} + \ln N_b\right]}{\sum\limits_{b' \in B_a} \exp\left[\sum\limits_k \beta_k X^*_{ab'k} + \sum\limits_k \beta_k X^*_{b'k} + \ln N_{b'}\right]}$
	$P_{a \in A} = \dfrac{\exp\left[\sum\limits_k \beta_k X^*_{ak} + \ln \sum\limits_{b' \in B_a} \exp(\sum\limits_k \beta_k X_{ab'k} + \sum\limits_k \beta_k X_{b'k} + \ln N_{b'}) + \ln N_a\right]}{\sum\limits_{a' \in A} \exp\left[\sum\limits_k \beta_k X^*_{a'k} + \ln \sum\limits_{b' \in B_{a'}} \exp(\sum\limits_k \beta_k X_{a'b'k} + \sum\limits_k \beta_k X^*_{b'k} + \ln N_{b'}) + \ln N_{a'}\right]}$
SEQUENTIAL NESTED LOGIT (SL)**	$P_{b \in B_a} = $ as per BMNL
	$P_{b \in B_a} = \dfrac{\exp\left[\sum\limits_k \beta_k X^*_{ak} + \theta \ln \sum\limits_{b' \in B_a} \exp(\sum\limits_k \beta_k X^*_{ab'k} + \sum\limits_k \beta_k X^*_{b'k} + \ln N_{b'}) + \ln N_a\right]}{\sum\limits_{a' \in A} \exp\left[\sum\limits_k \beta_k X^*_{a'k} + \theta \ln \sum\limits_{b' \in B_{a'}} \exp(\sum\limits_k \beta_k X^*_{a'b'k} + \sum\limits_k \beta_k X^*_{b'k} + \ln N_{b'}) + \ln N_{a'}\right]}$

TITLE	B. SPECIFICATION WITH GROUPED ALTERNATIVES

GENERALISED EXTREME VALUE NESTED LOGIT (NL) ***

$$P_{b \in B_a} = \frac{\exp\left[\dfrac{\sum_k \beta_k X^*_{abk} + \sum_k \beta_k X^*_{bk}}{1-\sigma} + \ln N_b\right]}{\sum_{b' \in B_a} \exp\left[\dfrac{\sum_k \beta_k X^*_{ab'k} + \sum_k \beta_k X^*_{b'k}}{1-\sigma} + \ln N_{b'}\right]} \quad \text{if } b \in B_a$$

$$P_{b \in B_a} = 0 \quad \text{if } b \in B_a$$

$$P_{a \in A} = \frac{\exp\left[\sum_k \beta_k X^*_{ak} + (1-\sigma)\ln \sum_{b' \in B_a} \exp\left(\dfrac{\sum_k \beta_k X^*_{ab'k} + \sum_k \beta_k X^*_{b'k}}{1-\sigma} + \ln N_{b'}\right) + \ln N_a\right]}{\sum_{a' \in A} \exp\left[\sum_k \beta_k X^*_{a'k} + (1-\sigma)\ln \sum_{b' \in B_{a'}} \exp\left(\dfrac{\sum_k \beta_k X^*_{a'b'k} + \sum_k \beta_k X^*_{b'k}}{1-\sigma} + \ln N_{b'}\right) + \ln N_{a'}\right]}$$

(this last specification assumes that the grouped alternative, a, is homogeneous in terms of observed attributes - see text)

103

TABLE 4·1 — NOTES

*BMNL

The coefficient of inclusive value is constrained to unity. Inclusive value is

$$\ell n \sum_{b' \in B_a} \exp \left(\sum_k \beta_k x_{ab'k} + \sum_k \beta_k x_{b'k} \right).$$

Separability of choice is assumed.
See equation (4.16) for grouped alternatives.

BMNL is a linear restriction on a sequential model; i.e. $\theta = 1$.

**SL

SL is an empirical generalisation of the BMNL.

***NL

Also referred to as structured logit model (Daly & Zachary, 1978; Daly, 1979).

GEV provides conditions under which NL model can be derived from a theory of stochastic utility maximisation (McFadden, 1979).

Major contribution is that a general pattern of dependence among the unobserved attributes of alternatives is obtained, helping to overcome restriction imposed in BMNL by IIA property.

σ is an index of similarity of the unobserved attributes of alternatives, when

$$0 < \theta \leqslant 1$$

$$\theta = 1 - \sigma \quad \text{or} \quad \sigma = 1 - \theta.$$

distribution. 'Independence' indicates that the
correlation between the unobserved attributes
associated with each and every pair of alternatives
in a choice set and across choice sets is zero.
'Identically distributed' says that taste variation
exists over the observed attributes (and is allowed
for in the random component), yet it is neutral
between alternatives, having the same distribution
(i.e. equal variance) around the mean (or
representative) utility level. In practice it is
difficult to distinguish the influence of taste
variation from that of unobserved attributes (e.g.
is the selection of car, with $V_i = V_j$, due to it
being more comfortable - this being an observed
attribute, and/or the individual having a value of
travel time savings different to the mean value -
the latter related to the observed attributes time
and money?). However, to appreciate the two
elements of the assumption it is useful to keep
the two types of components in the random term
distinct.

The basic multinomial-logit (BMNL) model in
Table 4.1 is a representation of the basic choice
model with inclusive value for a two-decision
sequential-recursive structure. The model assumes
that the coefficient of inclusive value is unity,
making it a special case (referred to as joint logit
because it is the equivalent of a simultaneous
choice in the sequential recursive form - see
below). The sequential nested-logit (SL) model in
Table 4.1 generalises the BMNL model by allowing the
coefficient of inclusive value (= θ) to vary within
limits ($0 \leqslant \theta \leqslant 1$). It permits pairwise
(unobserved) attribute correlation while maintaining
the equal-variance assumption within and between all
choice levels in a hierarchy. The final
specification, generalised-extreme-value nested
logit (NL), incorporates a measure, $(1 - \sigma)$, to
allow for the relative degrees of dissimilarity
between the unobserved attributes of alternatives
and nonequal variance. The latter condition is
accommodated by having a multilevel (hence nested)
structure with equal-variance within a level but
differing variances between levels. σ is
proportional to the inverse of the variance of
$\varepsilon_i - \varepsilon_j$ (see Section 4.4.2) and hence is an index
of the degree of independence of the random
components associated with alternatives in the same
level of a nested structure.[4] Ben-Akiva & Lerman
(1979), Williams (1977) and Daly & Zachary (1978)
have independently shown that parameterisation of

inclusive value is a necessary condition for a SL
model to be consistent with utility maximisation.
To assume $\theta = 1$ for all situations, as in the BMNL
model, is theoretically (and possibly empirically)
unsound as a <u>general</u> behavioural assumption of
inclusive value. Under certain conditions, the SL
and the NL models' respective parameters θ and $1-\sigma$
are equivalent. McFadden (1979) investigated the
relationship between θ and $1-\sigma$ and concluded that
the coefficient of inclusive value in the SL model
can be used to obtain an estimate of σ provided the
following sufficient and necessary conditions hold:

> ... a <u>sufficient</u> condition for a nested
> logit model to be consistent with
> individual utility maximisation is that
> the coefficient of each inclusive value
> lie between zero and one ... [and that
> these coefficients not decline as one
> moves up the decision tree to more
> inclusive nodes (McFadden, 1978)] ...
> this condition is also <u>necessary</u> for
> consistency with random utility
> maximisation if the domain of
> $(V_2-V_1,...,V_J-V_1)$ is unrestricted.

(McFadden, 1979: 287)

When the necessary and sufficient condition
$0 \leqslant \theta \leqslant 1$ is satisfied, $1-\theta$ (equal to σ) is an
index of the similarity of alternatives in choice
set B (Table 4.1).

Since θ is an important parameter in the link
between choices, we need to investigate its
behavioural interpretation. Given the two choices
(a from A and b from B), for any attribute (x)
defined in terms of an alternative b in choice set
B, the logit model implies

$$\frac{\partial P_{b \in B_a}}{\partial x_{bk}} = \frac{\partial P_b}{\partial V_b} \cdot \frac{\partial V_b}{\partial x_{bk}} \quad \text{and} \quad (4.55)$$

$$\frac{\partial P_{b \in B_a}}{\partial x_{b'k}} = \frac{\partial P_b}{\partial V_{b'}} \cdot \frac{\partial V_{b'}}{\partial x_{b'k}} \quad (4.56)$$

where $(\partial V_b)/(\partial x_{bk}) = \beta_k$. To obtain simple formulae
for $(\partial P_b)/(\partial V_b)$ and $(\partial P_b)/(\partial V_{b'})$, we use the
quotient rule (noting that $(\partial \exp X)/(\partial X) = \exp X$):

106

$$(\partial P_b)/(\partial V_b) = \frac{(\sum_{b' \in B} \exp V_{b'})(\exp V_b) - (\exp V_b)(\exp V_b)}{(\sum_{b' \in B} \exp V_{b'})^2}$$

$$= \frac{\exp V_b}{\sum_{b' \in B} \exp V_{b'}} - \frac{(\exp V_b)(\exp V_b)}{(\sum_{b' \in B} \exp V_{b'})^2}$$

$$= P_b - P_b^{\,2} = P_b(1 - P_b) \qquad (4.57)$$

and

$$(\partial P_b)/(\partial V_{b'}) = \frac{(\exp V_{b'})(0) - (\exp V_b)(\exp V_{b'})}{(\sum_{b' \in B} \exp V_{b'})^2}$$

$$= \frac{- (\exp V_b)(\exp V_{b'})}{(\sum_{b' \in B} \exp V_{b'})^2}$$

$$= - P_b\, P_{b'} \qquad (4.58)$$

$$(\text{since } P_{b'} = (\exp V_{b'})/(\sum_{b' \in B} \exp V_{b'}))$$

Equations (4.55) and (4.56) can be simplified as equations (4.59) and (4.60).

$$\frac{\partial P_{b \in B_a}}{\partial x_{bk}} = \beta_k P_b(1 - P_b) \qquad (4.59)$$

$$\frac{\partial P_{b \in B_a}}{\partial x_{b'k}} = -\beta_k P_b\, P_{b'} \qquad (4.60)$$

Given $P_{ab \in AB} = P_{b \in B_a} \cdot P_{a \in A}$ and the inclusive value index, Silman (1977) has shown that

$$(\partial P_a)/(\partial V_{b|a}) = \theta P_{b \in B_a} P_a(1 - P_a) \qquad (4.61)$$

To derive this result, we use the equations for the sequential (nested) logit model with ungrouped alternatives (Table 4.1).
Define

$$P_{b \in B_a} = \frac{\exp (V_{ab} + V_b)}{\sum\limits_{b' \in B_a} \exp (V_{ab'} + V_{b'})} = \frac{\text{top B}}{\text{bottom B}} \quad \text{and}$$

$$P_a = \frac{\exp (V_a + \theta \ln \sum\limits_{b' \in B_a} \exp (V_{ab'} + V_{b'}))}{\sum\limits_{a' \in A} \exp (V_{a'} + \theta \ln \sum\limits_{b' \in B_a} \exp (V_{a'b'} + V_{b'}))}$$

$$= \frac{\text{top A}}{\text{bottom A}}$$

$$\frac{\partial P_a}{\partial V_{ab}} = \frac{\text{bottom A} \cdot \dfrac{\partial \text{ top A}}{\partial V_{ab}} - \text{top A} \cdot \dfrac{\partial \text{ bottom A}}{\partial V_{ab}}}{(\text{bottom A})^2}$$

where $V_{ab} = V_{b|a}$ a specific (a,b) pair.

$$\frac{\partial \text{ top A}}{\partial V_{ab}} = (\text{top A}) \theta \; \frac{\partial \; (\ln \sum\limits_{b' \in B_a} \exp (V_{ab'} + V_{b'}))}{\partial V_{ab}}$$

$$= (\text{top A}) \theta \; (\sum\limits_{b' \in B_a} \exp (V_{ab'} + V_{b'}))^{-1}$$

$$\cdot \exp (V_{ab} + V_b)$$

$$(\text{since } \frac{\partial \; \ln(f(x))}{\partial x} = \frac{1}{f(x)} \cdot \frac{\partial \; f(x)}{\partial x}$$

$$\text{where } f(x) = \sum\limits_{b' \in B_a} \exp (V_{ab'} + V_{b'})$$

$$\text{and } x = V_{ab})$$

$$\frac{\partial \text{ bottom A}}{\partial V_{ab}} = (\text{top A})\theta \left(\sum_{b' \in B_a} \exp (V_{ab'} + V_{b'}) \right)^{-1}$$
$$\cdot (\exp (V_{ab} + V_b))$$

Substituting into the right-hand side of $\partial P_a / \partial V_{ab}$ we get

$$\frac{\partial P_a}{\partial V_{ab}} = \frac{(\text{bottom A})(\text{top A})\theta \left(\sum_{b' \in B_a} \exp (V_{ab'} + V_{b'}) \right)^{-1} \cdot \exp (V_{ab} + V_b)}{(\text{bottom A})^2}$$

$$- \frac{(\text{top A})^2 \theta \left(\sum_{b' \in B_a} \exp (V_{ab'} + V_{b'}) \right)^{-1} (\exp(V_{ab} + V_b))}{(\text{bottom A})^2}$$

$$= \frac{\text{top A}}{\text{bottom A}} \cdot \theta \cdot \frac{\text{top B}}{\text{bottom B}}$$

$$- \left(\frac{\text{top A}}{\text{bottom A}} \right)^2 \cdot \theta \cdot \frac{\text{top B}}{\text{bottom B}}$$

$$= P_a \theta P_{b \in B_a} - P_a^2 \theta P_{b \in B_a}$$

$$\frac{\partial P_a}{\partial V_{b|a}} = \theta P_{b \in B_a} P_a (1 - P_a)$$

The following conditions must hold for a meaningful interpretation:

(1) P_a and $V_{b|a}$ are positively related for any b

(2) $P_a \geqslant 0$

(3) $(1 - P_a) \geqslant 0$

Then θ must be greater than or equal to zero. If $\theta = 0$, then $(\partial P_a)/(\partial V_{b|a}) = 0$ and hence the utility associated with an alternative in choice set B, defined conditional of an alternative in A has no influence on the selection of an alternative a in the choice set A.

It can also be stated that

$$\frac{\partial P_{ab}}{\partial V_{b'|a}} = \frac{\partial P_a}{\partial V_{b'|a}} \; P_{b|a} + P_a \; \frac{\partial P_{b|a}}{\partial V_{b'|a}} \quad \text{For } b' \neq b$$

(using 4.58 and 4.61)

$$= \theta P_{b'|a} \; P_a (1 - P_a) \; P_{b|a} + P_a (-P_{b|a} \cdot P_{b'|a})$$

$$= P_{b'|a} \; P_a \; P_{b|a} (\theta (1 - P_a) - 1)$$

$$= -(\theta P_a + (1 - \theta)) \; P_{b'|a} \; P_{ab}$$

$$= -[\theta + \frac{(1-\theta)}{P_a}] \; P_{b'|a} \; P_{ab} \; P_a$$

$$= -[\theta + \frac{(1-\theta)}{P_a}] \; P_{ab'} \; P_{ab} \qquad (4.62)$$

It can be assumed that $(\partial P_{ab})/(\partial V_{b'|a})$ is less than or equal to zero; i.e. a positive change in the level of utility associated with alternative b' associated with alternative a will not lead to an increase in the likelihood of selecting alternative b associated with alternative a. Hence equation (4.62) can be defined as $\leqslant$ zero. Rearranging (4.62) to express it in terms of θ, we obtain

$$-[\theta + \frac{(1-\theta)}{P_a}] \ P_{ab}, \ P_{ab} \leqslant 0$$

$$\theta + \frac{(1-\theta)}{P_a} \geqslant 0$$

$$\theta P_a + 1-\theta \geqslant 0$$

$$\theta(P_a-1) + 1 \geqslant 0$$

$$\theta(P_a-1) \geqslant -1$$

thus
$$\theta \leqslant 1/(1-P_a) \tag{4.63}$$

Thus we have shown that θ has no upper bound. However, as mentioned before, McFadden (1979) has shown that a sufficient condition for consistency with individual utility maximisation is that $0 \leqslant \theta \leqslant 1$.

θ (in the SL model) and $(1-\sigma)$ (in the NL model) are equivalent when the sufficient condition $0 < \theta \leqslant 1$ is satisfied. The behavioural interpretation of bounded θ assists in determining whether the relationship between decisions is joint (θ close to 1), independent (θ close to 0), or a particular sequence (θ does not decline at higher level decisions).

Since θ is a mechanism for accommodating differential rates of substitution among all ab combinations it provides a means of relaxing the IIA property of the BMNL model. We can clarify this statement. From equation (4.62), an increase in the utility associated with V_{ab} (= ΔV_{ab}) results in equation (4.64) (Silman, 1977)

$$\Delta P_{b'a} \quad \begin{matrix} \text{(i.e. other b's} \\ \text{to same a)} \end{matrix} = -[\theta + \frac{1-\theta}{P_a}] \ P_{ab}, \ P_{ab} \ \Delta V_{b|a}$$

$$\text{for } b' \neq b \tag{4.64}$$

Since $\quad \Delta P_{b'a'} = \Delta[P_{b'|a'} \ P_{a'}] = P_{b'|a'} \ \Delta P_{a'}, \ a' \neq a$

then $\quad \dfrac{\partial P_{a'}}{\partial V_{b|a}} = -\theta \ P_{a'} \ P_a \ P_{b|a} = -\theta \ P_a \ P_{ab}$

thus $\quad \Delta P_{a'b'} \quad \begin{matrix} \text{(i.e. other b's} \\ \text{to other a's)} \end{matrix} = -\theta \ P_{a'b'} \ P_{ab} \ \Delta V_{b|a} \tag{4.65}$

111

In equation (4.64) we have a constant of proportion-
ality equal to $(\theta + \frac{1-\theta}{P_a})$ and in equation (4.65) it
is equal to θ. Since $P_a \geqslant 0$, then $(\theta + \frac{1-\theta}{P_a}) > 0$.

Cambridge Systematics Inc. (1977) have
clarified the behavioural meaning associated with
the level of θ. When $\theta = 1$, assuming two decisions
(a, b), an allocation to b of alternative a will
occur in equal proportions from all other,
a' $\neq$ a and b' $\neq$ b pairs and from all other alternatives a' associated with alternative b. Hence the
choice sets A and B can be modelled jointly, with
the relative shares of all ab combinations
remaining unchanged. When $0 < \theta < 1$
improvement in alternative a associated with
alternative b will result in a greater move from
a'b to ab than from other b' alternatives. As θ
approaches zero most of the reallocation of
alternative a will come from a' for the same b; as
θ approaches unity most of the reallocation from
alternative b' will approach reallocation from a'b
to ab. That is, choice sets A and B can be
modelled as sequential recursive. Finally, when
$\theta = 0$, improving alternative a which is associated
with alternative b would reallocate to ab but only
from a'b; there is no reallocation from b'. The
choice sets can be treated independently. Thus, the
coefficient of the inclusive value variable accounts
for the relative effect of a group of attributes
that appear in more than one model and which can
differ among choices.

As indicated earlier, taste variation is
incorporated in the random component. Hence,
defining $V_b = \theta \, \ell n \sum_{a' \in A} \exp V_{a'|b} \quad \theta (= 1-\sigma)$ can also
be thought of as a measure of bias of perception of
V_b and $V_{a'|b}$ since for the qth individual
$V_{bq} = V_b + \varepsilon_{bq}$ and $V_{aq|b} = V_{a|b} + \varepsilon_{aq|b}$, with
$E(\varepsilon_{bq}) = 0$ and $E(\varepsilon_{aq|b}) = 0$. Since the ε variables
represent deviations from the mean then θ is equal
to $(\text{var } \varepsilon_{aq|b} / \text{var } \varepsilon_{bq})^{\frac{1}{2}}$.

Hence when the variance associated with
decision b is greater than that for decision a
given b, the hierarchical sequence structure is
suitable (even though we might be unsure of the
sequence), and as the ratio (i.e. θ) approaches
unity a true simultaneous structure might be
preferable which can be modelled as an equivalent
sequential-recursive structure with $\theta = 1$. The

112

issue of sequence sensitivity when $0 < \theta < 1$ is developed in Section 4.4.2. The advancements in specification of the logit form give us a useful mechanism for testing dependency amongst alternatives and hence a way of identifying possible violation of IIA, and tests for suitable recursive structure.

The specifications in Table 4.1 without grouped alternatives accommodate similarity between alternatives on the assumption that estimation is carried out using randomly selected 'representative' alternatives from each type of elemental alternatives, where the types are defined by the analyst. For grouped alternatives, allowance has to be made for within group variance (see Section 4.1). This is a straightforward application of equation (4.17), when the model is a BMNL. However when we introduce a nested logit (and the simpler sequential logit model), the specification is not quite so obvious. In the nested logit model with grouped alternatives, inclusive value has been defined in terms of the expression (4.16) which accommodates the mean and within-grouped-alternative variance. Thus, given equation (4.17), reproduced here

$$v^*_{qj} = \tilde{v}_{qj} + \ln \left(\sum_{n=1}^{N_j} \exp \left(V_{qn} - \tilde{v}_{qj} \right) \mid N_j \right)$$

the analogous expression for the right-hand side of equation (4.17) in the present context is

$$\frac{\left(\sum_k \beta_k x^*_{ab'k} + \sum_k \beta_k x^*_{b'k} \right)}{1 - \sigma} + \ln N^{-b'} \cdot$$

$$\cdot \sum_{n=1}^{N_{b'}} \exp \left[\frac{\left(\sum_k \beta_k^0 x_{ank}^0 + \sum_k \beta_k^0 x_{nk}^0 \right) - \left(\sum_k \beta_k x^*_{ab'k} + \sum_k \beta_k x^*_{b'k} \right)}{1 - \sigma} \right]$$

$$(4.66)$$

where the 0 denotes the level associated with an elemental alternative, not a representative level defined on the 'set of assumed identical alternatives'. To obtain the inclusive value variable, we have to add to equation (4.66) the equivalent of $\ln N_j$ in equation (4.16). Hence,

113

$$\text{Inclusive Value} = \ln \sum_{b' \in B_a} \exp \left(\frac{(\sum_k \beta_k x^*_{ab'k} + \sum_k \beta_k x^*_{b'k})}{1 - \sigma} \right.$$

$$\left. + \ln N_{b'}) + N^{-b'} \cdot \right.$$

$$\sum_{n=1}^{N_{b'}} \exp \left(\frac{(\sum_k \beta_k^0 x_{ank}^0 + \sum_k \beta_k^0 x_{nk}^0) - (\sum_k \beta_k x^*_{ab'k} + \sum_k \beta_k x^*_{b'k})}{1 - \sigma} \right)$$

$$(4.67)$$

In practice it is usually not possible to identify
the levels of the observed variables for each
elemental alternative, and so the alternatives are
assumed (by default) homogeneous in terms of the
observed attributes. Hence the last term in
equation (4.67) cancels, leaving inclusive value
defined as given in equation (4.68).

$$\text{Inclusive Value} = \ln \sum_{b' \in B_a} \left(\frac{\sum_k \beta_k x^*_{ab'k} + \sum_k \beta_k x^*_{b'k}}{1 - \sigma} + \ln N_{b'} \right)$$

$$(4.68)$$

Thus expression (4.68) replaces the inclusive value
given in the last equation in the second column of
Table 4.1, namely

$$\ln \sum_{b' \in B_a} \exp \left(\frac{\sum_k \beta_k x_{ab'k} + \sum_k \beta_k x_{b'k}}{1 - \sigma} \right)$$

This results in the last equation in column 3 of
Table 4.1. An alternative maximum-likelihood
procedure to that outlined in Chapter 3.4 is
required to obtain estimates of the parameters β_k

and σ. This issue is beyond the scope of this book
(see Cosslett, 1978, 1980; Williams, 1977;
McFadden, 1980).
    Another 'grouping-type' issue concerns the
accommodation of choice issues where the number of
alternatives are regarded as excessive, imposing
data and computational requirements on the analyst.
It would be desirable if the model could be
estimated on a subset of the alternatives without
loss of predictive accuracy. McFadden (1978) has
shown that the likelihood function of the BMNL model

can still be used to estimate a model on subsets of the alternatives and obtain consistent estimates of the parameters provided the following assumptions hold:

(a) if $j \epsilon A \subseteq C$ and $\pi (A|i,x) > 0$, then

$\pi (A|j,x) > 0$ (positivity)

(b) if $j \epsilon A \subseteq C$, then $\pi (A|i,x) = \pi (A|j,x)$,

(uniformity)

where A is a subset of alternatives selected by fixed or random sampling (including or excluding the chosen alternative), and π is a probability distribution function (PDF).

However, this requires that the selection-of-alternatives mechanism effect is accounted for by suitable inclusion of class-specific parameters (i.e. suitable alternative class-specific variables). If suitable class-specific parameters cannot accommodate the selection mechanism effects, a modified likelihood function has to be specified, which explicitly accounts for the non-uniformity of the PDF's. This alternative function is

$$L_Q = \frac{1}{Q} \sum_{q=1}^{Q} \log \left(\frac{\exp (\sum_k \beta_k x_{ikq} + \log \pi (A_q|i_q,x_q))}{\sum_{j \epsilon A} \exp (\sum_k \beta_k x_{jkq} + \log \pi (A_q|j,x_q))} \right) \quad (4.69)$$

$\pi (A_q|i_q,x_q)$ might, for example, be defined as the number of education establishments in class i. It is a relatively simple operation for a programmer to include this modified likelihood function in a BMNL model computer program. It becomes more complicated when a nested logit formulation is also required. This concludes the discussion of extensions to the BMNL model. The next section uses the nested logit specification to demonstrate its power in assessing the sequence sensitivity of the sequential-recursive model.

4·4·2 A Test for Suitable Recursive Structure (when $0 < \theta < 1$)

Assuming a consistency of a structure with utility maximisation, Daly & Zachary (1978) noted that since the variance of the Weibull distribution (see Chapter 3.3) is inversely proportional to $(1-\sigma)$, the recursive model represents a decomposition of the alternatives such that the

utilities of the lowest stage of a hierarchy have
the smallest variance. Given this condition, we
can use it to test for an appropriate recursive
structure, i.e. a test for sequence. We can
incorporate one degree of freedom in the logit model
by assuming that the error in estimating the
utility function has a Weibull distribution given
by $P(u_a \leqslant V_a + \varepsilon_a) = \exp(-\exp -zt)$ where z is a
constant. The model is thus

$$P_{a \in A} = \frac{\exp(zV_a)}{\sum\limits_{a' \in A} \exp(zV_{a'})} \qquad (4.70)$$

Since the utility scale has an arbitrary zero,
implying that the model is measuring utility
differences, then the variance is the variance
associated with differences of utilities (Daly &
Zachary, 1978):

$$\text{var}(u_a - u_{a'}) = \pi^2/6z^2 \qquad (4.71)$$

Varying z will change the variance of the
difference between the two utility functions. Thus
allowing for this would enable the model to include
choices between similar alternatives as well as
between diverse alternatives, and help to overcome
the restrictions imposed by the IIA property. A
model capable of doing this is equivalent to the
nested model in Table 4.1.

Prior to changing the sequence in a recursive
structure, the analyst may wish to consider the
specification of the utility expression in terms of
the particular variables, their form or the overall
functional form of the utility expression. The
reason why this is a real option is that via the
inclusive value variable, measurement error in
variables, for example, can be compounded and
carried through subsequent models; the error
increasing as we move to higher level models.
Changing the sequence to satisfy the conditions
required for z (or θ) without testing for measurement, specification and possibly sampling error
would possibly never reveal the real error. In
practice, however, separation of sources of error
is difficult (see Chapter 7.4 and Appendix C).

Let S* be a subset of the set of alternatives
whose elements are closely comparable. Thus
equation (4.70) can be rewritten as

$$P_{a \in A} = \begin{cases} P_{a \in A} & \text{if } a \notin S* \\ \\ g P_{a \in S*} & \text{if } a \in S* \end{cases} \qquad (4.72)$$

where g = probability that choice lies in

$$S* = \exp zV_{S*} / (\exp zV_{S*} + \sum_{a' \in S*} \exp zV_{a'})$$

$$P_{a \in S*} = \exp zV_a / \sum_{a' \in S*} \exp zV_{a'}$$

and V_{S*} is defined by

$$\sum_{a' \in S*} \exp zV_{a'} = \exp (zV_{S*})$$

The model, referred to by Daly & Zachary as structured logit, allows the sensitivity parameter z to take a new value z* for choices within the subset S*. Thus we can redefine $P_{a \in S*}$ and V_{S*}:

$$\exp (z*V_{S*}) = \sum_{a' \in S*} \exp (z*V_{a'}), \qquad \text{with}$$

$$V_{S*} = \frac{1}{z*} \ln \sum_{a' \in S*} \exp (z*V_{a'}), \qquad \text{and}$$

$P_{a \in S*} = \exp z*V_a / \sum_{a' \in S*} \exp z*V_{a'}$. Respecified equation

(4.72) is equation (4.73):

$$P_{a \in A} = \begin{cases} \dfrac{\exp zV_a}{\exp zV_{S*} + \sum_{a' \notin S*} \exp zV_{a'}}, & a \notin S* \qquad (4.73) \\ \\ \dfrac{\exp zV_{S*}}{\exp zV_{S*} + \sum_{a' \in S*} \exp zV_{a'}} \cdot \dfrac{\exp z*V_a}{\sum_{a' \in S*} \exp z*V_{a'}}, & a \in S* \end{cases}$$

An important result is the equivalence to inclusive value of V_{S*}. The model is consistent with utility maximisation provided $z* \geqslant z$. The variances of the model will be

$$\text{var} (u_a - u_{a'}) = \begin{cases} \dfrac{\pi^2}{6z^2} & \text{if } a,a' \text{ not both in } S^*, \ a \neq a' \\[3mm] \dfrac{\pi^2}{6(z^*)^2} & \text{if } a,a' \text{ both in } S^*, \ a \neq a' \end{cases}$$

If we have two decisions, associated with a and b say, then if it is thought that the choice associated with selection of a out of A is more variable than choice associated with b out of B, then the structure of the model would be

$$P_{ab \in AB} = P_{b \in B_a} \cdot P_{a \in A}$$

In terms of the discussion above, the decision associated with b is modelled first, that is z^* and the coefficients of utility functions for choice b are estimated in the model

$$P_{b \in B_a} = P_{b \in S^*}$$

The calculation of the inclusive value V_{S^*} can be used in the choice model associated with a. If the recursive structure chosen is correct, then $z^* > z$. The model can be extended to allow for any number of subsets, each with its own internal parameter, and thus a hierarchy of choices can be developed. The only restriction is that the sensitivity parameter at one level must be greater than the parameter at the next higher level. This is the sufficiency condition quoted from McFadden earlier in this section.

Hence if S^* is chosen to consist of the subset of almost identical choices, the structured logit model will allow for the small variance by assigning a very large value to z^*. If necessary, the total choice set can be divided into one element subsets so that the IIA property will not invalidate the model. This concludes the detailed outline of decision structures and choice hierarchies.

4·5 Specification of the Attributes in the Utility Expression

There are two main types of explanatory variables, 'generic variables' (GV) and 'alternative -specific variables' (ASV). The distinction relates

to the way a variable enters the data, not the way
it is estimated.

Generic variables vary in level across choice
alternatives whereas ASVs have an identifiable
correspondence between choice alternatives. An ASV
is a result of interaction between an alternative-
specific dummy variable (ASDV) and an attribute
contained in the X and/or S vector set for an
individual. An ASDV takes on the value one for a
particular alternative and zero otherwise. An
example of an ASV is one which gives the appropriate
level of establishment size for the 'flat'
alternative, and which takes a zero value for all
other alternative establishment types. A generic
variable, for example, would be one which gives the
relevant level of establishment size for all the
alternatives in the set.

It is important to note that all variables must
be defined with respect to the dependent variable;
i.e. have some testable causal relationship with
choice. If all the variables in a model are
generic, then the model can be described as an
abstract-alternative model. Desirably, individual
utility, expressed as a function of observed and
unobserved variables should depend only on GVs;
because

> *Individual utility* depends on the
> constellation of physical experiences
> associated with an alternative, and
> cannot depend on labels ... attached
> to alternatives by the planner.
>
> (McFadden, 1976a: 23)
> (our emphasis)

Average utility, however, may depend on ASVs which
represent the influence of unobserved GVs. It is
only because of an inability to observe all GVs
which influence the behaviour being studied that
ASVs are used. It is in this context in particular,
that the need for more research into the determinants of choice and their measurement becomes
vital (Hensher & McLeod, 1977; Hensher & Dalvi,
1978; Horowitz, 1980).

If all variables were generic, such that they
relate to attributes common to all alternatives,
then the model can be applied for prediction
purposes to situations much different from those
used for model estimation, especially to systems
not currently in use.

119

Even if we were able to fully specify a GV model, it is implicit in the specification that the representative utility assumption holds across the population being studied. In practice it is often not possible to ascertain a priori whether choice models are sufficiently well specified (i.e. parameters have the same values in each utility expression for a particular attribute) to justify use of generic attributes. This is where market segmentation is of value (see Chapter 7.2.3; Charles River Associates, 1978; Hensher, 1974a; Dobson, 1979).

Given the state-of-the-art, even though in utility theory one dollar spent on alternative A should be valued the same as one dollar spent on alternative B (given a perfect market), there are likely in practice to be differences, attributed to non-pure cost distortions. Hence some ASVs should be introduced to account for alternatives-biases or other environmental biases on the opportunity cost of money (Hensher & Dalvi, 1978).

Since socioeconomic and environmental attributes do not vary across choice alternatives (e.g. a person is of a given age regardless of his location and establishment type), they must be entered into the specification of the model in one of two ways:

(a)   pure ASVs (or ASDVs) which have the described value or one for the attributes of one (or more) alternative(s), and zero otherwise. The behavioural interpretation is that the particular attribute exerts a pure shift effect on choice; and hence, ceteris paribus, higher income families (for example) have a higher preference for a particular alternative in the choice set.

(b)   interactive (indirect) ASVs, which influence choice via their interactive influence on another explanatory variable. For example, cost of an establishment type weighted by family income, where detached and semi-detached houses take on the relevant cost level and all other alternatives are zero. It is legitimate to also weight the cost of all establishment types by income, producing a GV. The behavioural interpretation is that individuals with different income circumstances value cost savings or outlays differently.

Because of the alternative behavioural implications, a particular variable can be redefined and entered into the model specification both ways.

120

Alternative-specific constants (ASCs) can also be included to capture the effect of unobserved factors influencing choice decisions. These should be included for all but one of the estimation alternatives. Inclusion of ASCs for all alternatives creates a condition analogous to perfect multicollinearity in regression analysis, thereby preventing estimation of the model.

ASVs are relevant only when there is a direct correspondence among the alternatives available to different individuals. Otherwise GVs have to be used. If the set of alternative establishment types at one location is entirely different from the establishment type set at another location, then there is no correspondence among sets of alternatives, and hence those alternatives can be described only through the use of GVs. But if only one of those establishment types is common to every individual's set of alternatives, then ASVs can be used to describe that one establishment type.

The discussion so far on specification of attributes has concentrated on the relationship between one attribute and the alternative ways in which it can enter a utility expression so that a meaningful interpretation can be placed on the expected choice outcome as a result of an attributes presence in one or more utility expressions. While this is very important, there is another more general issue concerning the form of the relationship between utility and attributes, which has a bearing on the final presentation of the attributes regardless of whether they are generic or alternative-specific. The general issue of form can be developed in the context of the neoclassical theory of consumer behaviour; that is we can use theory to assist in the specification of the utility function. This emphasis for discrete choice modelling has recently been outlined by Train & McFadden (1978) and Truong & Hensher (1980).

At the outset a distinction should be made between the types of attributes (the issue under study here) and the range of attributes in each type category; in particular we make the conventional distinction between the attributes that are inherent in the alternatives themselves ('price' effects) and the attributes that define the unit environment ('income' effects). It is common practice in discrete choice modelling to include in the utility function variables which in neoclassical choice theory are constraints on utility maximisation; hence there are grounds for concern and a need to justify the inclusion of constraint-variables in

the utility function. The common inclusions are
the wage of the individual, and other socioeconomic
variables.
    There is thus a need for a theoretical proof of
the legitimacy of including such variables. Let us
define the utility function associated with the ith
activity as

$$U_i = U(G_i, L_i) \qquad (4.74)$$

such that utility is obtained in the consumption of
goods (G) and leisure (L). The quantity of goods
and leisure available are given by the identities

$$G_i = w(T-t_L) + Y \qquad (4.75)$$

$$L_i = T-t_w \qquad (4.76)$$

where w is the hourly wage rate, T is the total
amount of resource time, t_L is the total amount of
leisure time, Y is nonwage income, and t_w is the
total quantity of work time. In developing the
theoretical justification, let us assume three
types of activities - work, leisure and activity i;
and also concentrate on the specification of the
utility function associated with this ith activity
(for example, modal transport to work, or search
for a new residential location). The conduct of an
activity involves the foregoing of work (and hence
goods consumption) and/or leisure (defined in time
units). Let us assume that the individual will not
forego goods consumption, and thus the tradeoff
will be between the activity i and leisure.
Furthermore, to avoid unnecessary confounding of the
complexity of the proof, we will assume that
activity i's utility is defined by the attributes
homogeneous time and homogeneous cost; thus other
potentially important attributes (such as
convenience, effort, heterogeneous time-walk,
sitting etc.) are assumed unimportant. It is a
simple matter (see below) to include additional
attributes once the form of the utility expression is
determined.
    Define the individual's money budget as

$$M = w(T-t_L-t_i) + Y = G = C_i + S \qquad (4.77)$$

where the terms as yet defined are S (= savings),
t_i (= the total time allocated to the activity i)

and C_i is the total monetary cost allocated to activity i. Assuming a leisure-activity i tradoff only (that is, $\partial G/\partial (w.t_w) = 0$ implying additional income is taken up as leisure) and that the disutility of work = disutility of leisure, the utility maximisation condition is

$$\partial U/\partial t_L - w(\partial U/\partial G) = 0 \qquad (4.78)$$

That is, the marginal utility of leisure equals the marginal utility of goods consumption. Alternatively, this says that the leisure-work tradeoff is in equilibrium and substitution will have to occur between activity i and leisure. Hence, the utility associated with a unit of activity i is

$$U_i = (\partial U/\partial G)(G_{i1} - G_{i2}) + (\partial U/\partial t_L)(t_{Li1} - t_{Li2})$$

$$+ (\partial U/\partial t_i)(t_{i1} - 0) \qquad (4.79)$$

where the subscript 1 refers to the situation in the presence of a unit of activity i and 2 the situation in the absence of the unit. Rearranging (4.78) and multiplying both sides by $(G_{i1} - G_{i2})$ yields

$$(\partial U/\partial G)(G_{i1} - G_{i2}) = \frac{\partial U/\partial t_L}{w}(G_{i1} - G_{i2})$$

Given that T, Y and S are exogeneous (and cancel out when taking differences), from (4.77) we get

$$G_{i1} - G_{i2} = (-wt_{Li1} - wt_{i1} - C_{i1}) - (-wt_{Li2})$$

Since only leisure time varies as a result of the change in goods consumption, activity time and money outlays remain unchanged; thus

$$U_i = (\partial U/\partial t_L)(w^{-1}(-wt_{Li1} - wt_{i1} - C_{i1} + wt_{Li2}) + t_{Li1} - t_{Li2})$$

$$+ (\partial U/\partial t_i)t_{i1}$$

$$= -(\partial U/\partial t_L)(t_{i1} + C_{i1}/w) + (\partial U/\partial t_i)t_{i1} \cdots$$

$$= -(\partial U/\partial t_L) C_{i1}/w + t_{i1}(\partial U/\partial t_i - \partial U/\partial t_L) \cdots$$

$$= - \text{(marginal utility } (C_{i1}/w) + t_{i1} [\text{Marginal utility}$$
$$\quad \text{of leisure)} \qquad\qquad\qquad\qquad \text{of activity i}$$

$$\quad - \text{marginal utility }]$$
$$\quad \text{of leisure} \qquad\qquad\qquad\qquad\qquad\qquad (4.80)$$

123

Thus from equation (4.80), the utility associated with a unit of activity i is defined as a function of t_i and C_i/w. Hence the utility expression would be

$$U_i = \beta_1 t_i + \beta_2 (C_i/w) \qquad (4.81)$$

If we had assumed a work-activity i tradeoff, then $\partial L/\partial (w.t_w) = 0$ and the additional income is taken up in goods, and the utility expression would be

$$U_i = \beta_i (t_i w) + \beta_2 C_i \qquad (4.82)$$

Train & McFadden (1978) have developed a more general formulation which permits tradeoffs between goods, leisure and activity i. We now present the general formulation in terms of homogeneous (fully accounted for) time and money, and then generalise it further to include variables that are not attributes of the alternatives associated with the activity itself, but which improve the specification of the model in the presence of unobservable (or nonmeasured) attributes of the alternatives.

Define expenditure (E) as a function of utility and the wage rate:

$$E = E(U,w)$$

and for utility maximisation, the following identity holds:

$$E = Y + w(T-t_i) - C_i \qquad (4.83)$$

The development of a general form of the utility function for activity i requires an initial assumption about the function $U(G,L)$. Train & McFadden assume a Cobb-Douglas function:

$$U = AG^{1-\alpha}L^{\alpha} \qquad 0 < \alpha < 1 \qquad (4.84)$$

with an expenditure function

$$E = Ua^{-1}w^{\alpha} \qquad (4.85)$$

when a is a constant. Given equation (4.83), we can define

$$Y + w(T-t_i) - C_i = Ua^{-1}w^\alpha$$

therefore

$$U = a(Yw^{-\alpha} - C_i w^{-\alpha} + Tw^{1-\alpha} - t_i w^{1-\alpha}) \qquad (4.86)$$

Since the terms not including C_i and t_i cancel out in a model defined on the utility expressions of the competing alternatives associated with activity i, then

$$U = -a(C_i w^{-\alpha} + t_i w^{1-\alpha}) \qquad (4.87)$$

The correspondence between equations (4.87), (4.81) and (4.82) needs to be noted. When $\alpha = 1$, then equation (4.87) becomes equation (4.81) and when $\alpha = 0$, equation (4.87) becomes equation (4.82). When $0 < \alpha < 1$, then $\partial L/\partial(w.t_w)$ and $\partial G/\partial(w.t_w) > 0$.

In the derivation above of the utility expression, we assumed two attributes - homogeneous time and homogeneous cost. These attributes were also implicitly taken to have no measurement error and accounted for the sources of utility. In the specification of an empirically estimatable function, however, it might not be valid to assume only two perfectly measured attributes as the sole source of utility; indeed it is usually the case that both measurement error and specification error exists when a utility expression is defined solely in terms of attributes of the alternatives (approximately weighted by $w^{-\alpha}$ or $w^{1-\alpha}$). Furthermore, even if we were confident in limiting the specification to attributes of the alternatives, we could improve the specification by defining a range of attributes when the homogeneity assumption is invalid; for example the number of rooms in a house might be replaced with three attributes - the number of bedrooms, number of toilets and bathrooms, and number of garages. Similarly, it is common practice in transport mode-choice studies to distinguish types of travel time (wait, walk, in-vehicle). This disaggregation acknowledges the existence of heterogeneity in the contribution of a unit of each type of attribute to utility. Suitable behavioural weights would have to be assigned to each attribute treated separately so as to reflect the differential valuations.

125

A major source of specification error is the exclusion of relevant attributes (Horowitz, 1980). This is a common problem where some attribute has not been measured, and is thus unobserved by the analyst. Rather than assign this attribute's contribution to the random component of the utility expression (that is, an additional dimension in the singular ε term, assumed to be Weibull distributed in the population for the logit model), alternative-specific constants and socioeconomic variables can be included in the representative utility function as proxies for the unobserved attributes associated with the alternatives. Since such variables are attribute proxies then in accordance with the theoretical arguments above, they must be weighted by either $w^{-\alpha}$ or $w^{1-\alpha}$, depending on whether they are cost-related or time-related. As a general rule, we are proposing that any socioeconomic variable or alternative-specific dummy variable which is a proxy for an unobserved component of a goods-related variable should be weighted by $w^{-\alpha}$; any such variable which is a proxy for an unobserved component of a leisure-related (or nongoods) variable should be weighted by $w^{1-\alpha}$. For example, in a study of accommodation choice, number of individuals in a household' (HS) is a proxy for 'size of the accommodation' and would be defined as (HS)$(w^{1-\alpha})$.

The general form of the utility function can now be written out fully (equation 4.88)

$$U = -a \sum_{k=1}^{N} \beta_k g_k w^{-\alpha} - a \sum_{k=1}^{M} \theta_k \ell_k w^{1-\alpha} - a \sum_{k=1}^{R} \gamma_k (pg)_{ik} w^{-\alpha}$$

$$- a \sum_{k=1}^{T} \delta_k (p\ell) w^{1-\alpha} - a(\lambda+\mu) \qquad (4.88)$$

where
a	=	a constant
$\beta, \theta, \gamma, \delta$	=	parameters
g_k	=	the kth goods-related attribute associated with the alternatives
ℓ_k	=	the kth non-goods related attribute associated with the alternatives
$(pg)_k$	=	the kth goods-related proxy variable associated with unobserved goods-related attribute of the ith alternative

$$\text{(i.e. } \sum_{k=1}^{R} \gamma_k (pg)_{ik} + \lambda_i$$

$$= \sum_{k=1}^{Z} \beta_{(k+N)} (ug)_{ik})$$

$(ug)_{ik}$ = the kth unmeasured goods-related attribute

$(p\ell)_{ik}$ = the kth non-goods related proxy variable associated with unobserved non-goods related attribute of the ith alternative

$$\text{(i.e. } \sum_{k=1}^{T} \delta_k (p\ell)_{ik} + \mu_i$$

$$= \sum_{k=1}^{Y} \beta_{(k+M)} (u\ell)_{ik})$$

$(u\ell)_{ik}$ = the kth unmeasured non-goods related attribute

λ_i, μ_i = errors required so that equation (4.88) is exact.

The representative utility component, V is obtained from equation (4.88) by assuming that $-a(\lambda + \mu)$ is an element of the random component of utility, suitably distributed in the population to conform with the assumption of the particular model being estimated.

Since the attributes include an additional parameter (α), we no longer have a linear-in-parameters utility expression (except when $\alpha = 0$ or 1). This creates estimation problems. Given the available computer software[5] an iterative procedure of assigning values for α would have to be used; and the final value selected would be that associated with the largest value of the likelihood function. Added to this iterative requirement is the unambiguous allocation of socio-economic variables to the goods-related and non-goods related proxy, attribute categories. In practice the analyst will have to experiment with alternative specifications.

The terms 'ranked' and 'unranked' alternatives have often been used to describe respectively the existence and nonexistence of correspondence. A ranked alternative can be described by ASVs, GVs or both; an unranked alternative can be described only by GVs. In the logit model (basic choice model), j, the number assigned to each of the alternatives from which each individual in the sample can choose, is fixed, and these alternatives are the same for all the individuals, e.g. in a particular sample j = 1 may always be the car alternative, j = 2 the bus, j = 3 the train alternative. This is shown as a ranked set of alternatives and so permits ASVs.

However, alternatives available to each individual in the sample are not necessarily the same in number or kind, e.g. alternatives may be shops or shopping centres available to an individual. If the sample includes individuals from different areas, the available shopping alternatives will differ from individual to individual, called unranked alternatives. It is not meaningful to allow ASVs, but only GVs.

To conclude the discussion on variable representation, we should clarify the important distinction between ASVs and 'alternative-specific values', which is implicit in the arguments presented. If a variable such as income does not vary in value across the alternatives, then we have the same term multiplying the numerator and each member of the sum in the denominator of the logit (or any share) model. Thus it will cancel out. Hence such variables must have alternative-specific values and can enter the model only when they are transformed [(a), (b) above] to have such values.

In Chapter 10, the way in which variables are coded for estimation is outlined.

4·5·1 Internal Structure of Attributes

In any study of individual behaviour it is important to identify the relevant dimension in which variables are assessed by the individual in arriving at a choice decision. When the unit of analysis is the individual this is especially relevant since with maximum exposure to the estimation technique the parameters are often sensitive to mismeasurement of the level of an attribute. When a group of individuals is the unit of analysis (such as the members of a census collector's district - ccd) this is of lesser concern since any variability between the perceptual dimension and, say, the actual dimension are lost in the aggregation. This is not a justification for aggregation, for as will be demonstrated in a later section (7.2), early aggregation reduces variance and relevance by 'sweeping the problem under the carpet'.

A priori, it has been argued convincingly that individuals base their decisions on their perceived estimates of attributes of alternatives. It is not possible, however, to directly measure how people perceive a situation or the relevance of an attribute, and thus a method of reporting is used to obtain the information indirectly. In the translation from perception to 'reported perception' it is generally argued that a significant measurement error is introduced (due to, for example, question wording, rounding of response, 'post-utilisation bias', forcing of response to a predetermined response scale, interviewer distortion in the case of an interview, etc.). We will never know the full extent of such error. All that we can do is to seek out any possible systematic errors thought due to one of the measurement constraints and seek to remove the constraint. For example, there is evidence that self-administered survey forms contribute relatively less reporting bias than an interview (and as a bonus are less costly to conduct); a genuine stamp on a return-mail envelope yields a better content response than a franking stamp on the grounds that individuality is being demonstrated in the survey. As a result of much theoretical argument and a substantial even if somewhat incompletely convincing empirical search in recent years, it is generally accepted that some form of reported perception data is desirable in modelling individual choice behaviour.

What is not clear, however, is the extent of error (assumedly in terms of elasticities and probabilities of choice) when 'objective', 'manufactured' or 'synthesised' levels are used (Talvitie, 1980; Horowitz, 1980). The reported-perception levels may not be the yardstick for error since we have no guidance on its relationship with the true perceptual level. Synthesis usually involves the objective manufacturing by analysts of average levels of variables for various types of individuals and/or particular groups of individuals with approximately homogeneous levels of spatial and nonspatial attributes of alternatives. Examples are zonal interchange travel times derived from tree (network) matrices as proxies for point-to-point travel time; and the average income level of the group of individuals living in a ccd as proxy for individual income. Quite clearly, if the loss of sensitivity resulting from using synthesised group means is negligible then there are significant cost economies from using them as proxies. The

129

evidence however is generally limited. Two studies
in transport have concluded on the basis of once-off
investigations that the loss of sensitivity is
negligible compared to other forecasting errors
(Johnson, 1975), and that provided a policy will
have a homogeneous impact within a zone, then the
errors are minimal. A study by Horowitz (1980)
suggests that the inclusion of synthesised group
means is the major source of bias out of six
possible types of bias investigated in a basic logit
model. The six types and their associated root-
mean-square error are: sampling errors (.015),
correlated disturbances (.044), disturbances with
unequal variances (.049), random parameter
variation (.135), omission of relevant explanatory
variables (.264) and grouped-averaged explanatory
variables (.381). (See also note 1 in Chapter 7
and Appendix C).

While the evidence, limited as it is, tends to
point towards ambiguity in the internal structure
of variables as a major source of prediction error,
even if this is a relatively minor or major source
of error it is a source that can be allowed for.
To the extent that this might be the case, then
the analyst should explore the implications of the
simplifying assumption.

So far we have only referred to the relationship between levels of perception (true and
reported) and synthesis. Neither of these levels
need be the 'true' reality with respect to each
individual. There is a logical fundamental
distinction between 'perceived' reality and 'true'
reality. True reality is not of any interest in
the estimation of a behavioural model. It is of
critical relevance, however, in the application of
the model since any policy proposal involves a
supply change which is not equated in level to the
particular level that an individual perceives as
the input into his behavioural response (see also
Chapter 7.2). The supply change is likely to be
a general change in level which has to be in some
way converted from a true change to a perceived
change. However, given that the true reality is
not known since it is not general but individual-
specific, analysts usually only have knowledge of
the approximated synthesised-group level. This
level should not be fed into a model that is
estimated on reported-perceived data. Rather it
should be adjusted to make the new level of the
variable dimensionally consistent with the model.
Ideally a relation between the reported-perception
level and the synthesised level should be used to

130

adjust the input. However, this is clearly not possible since it has never been possible to estimate the relationship when the synthesised level is invariant across the individuals in the group. The correct method is an estimated relationship between the reported-perceived level and 'true' reality; and between the synthesised level and 'true' reality, using a distribution of groups in order to have variability in the synthesised level. In summary form:

RP (reported-perceived level)

$$= \alpha_0 + \alpha_1 \quad \text{(true reality - TR)} \qquad (4.89)$$

$$TR \quad = \beta_0 + \beta_1 \quad \text{(synthesised level - S)} \qquad (4.90)$$

The only known possible way of measuring TR is to identify for each individual his detailed activity pattern etc., and then objectively measure.

A further dimension worthy of consideration relates to the evaluation of proposed policies. Evaluation is concerned with the aggregate net social welfare associated with a policy. It draws on the demand models for a measure of change in demand and also as a source of data for assessing the extent of resource savings (see note 3, Chapter 4). Since resource savings involves levels of variable change which are net of nonresource components (e.g. tax), then the levels of variables used in the estimation of the model and in changes in demand are not appropriate for the evaluation model. A resource correction factor has to be introduced. Let us assume that the correction process is straightforward, since it is not a concern here.

What is of concern, however, is that when economic evaluation requires a common metric for expressing the costs and benefits (usually in dollar terms), a procedure is required to convert non-dollar variables into dollar equivalents. This involves the assignment of shadow prices. An extensive literature has developed in the area, especially for valuing the savings (Hensher & Dalvi, 1978; Bruzelius, 1979).

As will be outlined in a later section, the individual choice model can be used to derive shadow prices for various 'benefits', provided there is a cost-variable in the model, since the change in utility identified in the model is the appropriate definition of benefit change. This can be easily related to the consumer surplus literature on benefit assessment (Bruzelius, 1979). However, since the relationship between a cost variable and another explanatory variable yields a behavioural shadow price and not a resource shadow price, we have a problem of deciding if there will be any error (over or underestimation of dollar benefits) by using the behavioural value. Given that we have little idea of the proportion of the 'reported-perceived' level of a variable that is a non-resource component, it is not a simple matter to adjust the behavioural value by a resource correction factor. Nevertheless, individual choice models have been shown to be a theoretically and empirically sound mechanism for obtaining behavioural shadow prices for noncost variables. Theoretically a relationship between behavioural and resource values does exist within the same framework (as illustrated in theories of the allocation of time; Hensher, 1978; DeSerpa, 1971; DeDonnea, 1970; Burzelius, 1979). However, because of the practical difficulties of operationalising such theories to obtain an empirical relationship between behavioural and resource values, analysts have either assumed a one-to-one correspondence between behavioural and resource shadow prices (but not for the level of attributes), presumably on the implicit judgement that the error in reported-perception from true reality cancels out any nonresource component; or developed alternative ways of valuing resource shadow prices without the use of statistical models (e.g. Hensher, 1977a).

NOTES — CHAPTER 4

1. 1 in the denominator is a scaling constant, $\mu_{123} = 1$, enabling $\mu = \mu_1 + \mu_2 + \mu_3 + \mu_{12} + \mu_{13} + \mu_{23}$ if there are 3 alternatives. Thus

    $1 + \mu$ = a probability of unity, thus the probability of a full choice set is $1/(1 + \mu)$.

2. $\ln N_i$ implies that all elemental alternatives in a group are relatively homogeneous, and that this variable is only accounting for the size (quantity) of a group, not its quality per se. Ceteris paribus, a large group alternative would have a higher probability of being selected than a very small one, since the number of elemental alternatives is greater.

3. This example is not trivial. It has an important implication beyond choice or demand modelling. In economic evaluation where measures of user benefit are formulated in terms of consumer surplus, the area under the demand curve above the price of the quantity demanded is theoretically the measure of net benefit. In practice a change in net benefit as a result of some policy change (usually a change expressed in terms of an attribute in a utility expression of an alternative on which demand is defined) is often calculated by a formula not derived directly (i.e. inconsistent with) from the theory underlying the demand function. Formulating an independent measure of benefit results in a misuse of the demand function and thus is an inexact measure of benefit. The example in the text illustrates this point. In the United Kingdom a measure of benefit associated with changes in the transport system is given as

$$\tfrac{1}{2} \sum_{odm} (T^1_{odm} + T^2_{odm}) \ (C^1_{odm} - C^2_{odm})$$

where o is origin, d is destination, m is mode, T^1 is trips before, T^2 is trips after the change, and C^1 and C^2 respectively cost (money and time) associated with the before and after situations respectively. Williams (1977) has shown that this formula is not an exact measure of the benefit and cannot be derived using the behavioural theory underlying the particular demand models from which Ts are obtained. The correct measure of direct user benefits, if the basic logit model is being used is

$$(1/\lambda_q) \ \ell n \sum_{j=1}^{J} \exp V_{jq}$$ where λ is the marginal utility of money; that is the scale parameter $(1/\lambda_q)$ used to convert all attributes to a common monetary metric.

4. The literature on logit models contains many nomenclatures to define particular model forms. The equivalences between our categorisation and the range of titles are: BMNL MNL, joint logit; SL is the same as used in studies by, for example, Cambridge Systematics (1977, 1979).

NL ≈ Hierarchical Logit (HL), Structured Logit (StrL), Multi-Level Logit (MLL). McFadden (1980) and Bullock (1979) have, respectively, applied the NL and MLL model. There is another category which is not discussed in Table 4.1, referred to as Generalised Extreme Value (GEV) Logit by McFadden (1979, 1980), Tree Extreme Value by Cosslett (1978), and Cross-Correlated Logit (CCL) by Williams (1977). These latter forms permit more complex correlation patterns. NL is a specialisation of GEV (hence we also call it GEVNL) which allows nonequal variance only between levels in a model hierarchy. The GEV model has recently been programmed at Macquarie University; and research directed by McFadden in the U.S.A. and Williams in the U.K. is also developing appropriate computer software for the GEV model.

5. Daly (1979a) has developed computer software to handle nonlinear-in-parameters utility expressions for maximum-likelihood logit. The programmes have been applied in a Dutch Study of destination choice (Daly, 1978a, 1980).

CHAPTER 5

The Choice Axiom and Independence from Irrelevant Alternatives Property

Perhaps the greatest strength of the choice axiom, and the one reason it continues to be used, is as a canon of probabilistic rationality. It is a natural probabilistic formulation of K. J. Arrow's famed principle of the independence of irrelevant alternatives, and as such it is a possible underpinning for rational, probabilistic theories of social behaviour. Thus, in the development of economic theory based on the assumption of probabilistic individual choice behaviour, it can play a role analogous to the algebraic rationality postulates of the traditional theory.

(Luce 1977: 229-230)

5·1 Introduction

A central property of the basic choice model and the sequential logit model (see Table 4.1) is the independence from irrelevant alternatives (IIA). In Chapter 3 this property was briefly outlined so that it could be applied in the derivation of the logit model. It was also referred to in Chapter 4 when introducing the dependency among alternatives in a choice set. Since the IIA condition is both a strength and a potential weakness of the basic and sequential logit models, imposing restrictions on the structure of selection probabilities which may or may not be valid in particular applications, it is necessary to discuss the property in more detail.

The most appropriate starting position for a discussion is the theory of individual choice developed in psychology, associated principally with Thurstone (1927) and Luce (1959). Economists have drawn heavily on this contribution, modifying it to suit their needs, and some would argue distorting the true interpretation of an individual choice probability (Bullen & Boekenkroeger, 1979). In the next section the IIA property is introduced against a background of psychological choice theory, the latter being a composite of Thurstone's theory of comparative judgement and Luce's choice axiom, given particular distribution assumptions. This background from a set of antecedents is also useful more generally in that it provides one basis for demonstrating the link between the IIA property and the fundamental behavioural assumption that an individuals will select that alternative, out of the choice set which is consistent with the maximisation of utility, given the analyst's level of information. This should not be interpreted as stating that the IIA property is the only condition consistent with the fundamental assumption; only that in a particular modelling context (set out below and in Chapter 3) it can be shown to be consistent.

Once the background is outlined, then we can show in Section 5.3 how the property operates in a logit model and identify some of the concerns that modellers have when taking advantage of this property's strengths. Section 5.4 sets out procedures to determine violations of and to propose remedies for the IIA property. The concluding section presents an empirical illustration of a basic choice model and the use of the proposed tests for violation and recommended remedies. These tests should be applied in all applications of logit models, although we know that in practice this seldom occurs.

5·2 Existence of the Independence from Irrelevant Alternatives Property – The Antecedents

In Chapter 3 we postulated the existence of a utility maximising individual and then derived an estimatable model, the basic choice model. The major concepts used in this derivation were the idea of random utility, the independence-from-irrelevant alternatives property (which implied the choice axiom) and a Weibull (or double exponential) distribution for the independent and identically distributed random components (ε_j's).

It was not shown, however, that the Weibull distribution is the only distribution in a multiple alternative environment which guarantees a utility maximum solution when the choice axiom is used as the basis for an analytically tractable model.

To understand the IIA property and its central role in the basic choice model, it is necessary to seek out the background antecedents that have provided a particular interpretation of a maximum utility behavioural environment and to show how this can be linked into the basic choice model as a result of assuming the Weibull distribution which guarantees equivalence with the choice axiom (and thus the basic logit model) and hence the existence of the IIA property. Once these relationships are clear then a solid basis for discussing the IIA property is available. Since the IIA property imposes a particular structure on choice probabilities (given in its origins) it requires special consideration to decide whether it is a suitable assumption in an application. The realisation that IIA is an essential ingredient in deriving an analytically tractable and easily estimatable model means that it should not be casually rejected without first applying suitable tests of violation and attempts to remedy the violation if one is found. Failure to remedy the violation would then require use of alternative model forms such as multinomial probit (see Chapter 6) or nested logit (see Chapter 4).

The beginnings of the choice theory relevant to the book emanate from Thurstone's theory of comparative judgement, published in 1927 (Thurstone, 1927, 1927a):

> A term is needed for that process by which
> the organism identifies, distinguishes,
> discriminates, or reacts to stimuli, a
> term which is innocuous and as noncommittal
> as possible, because we are not now
> interested in the nature of that process
> ..... In order to avoid any implications,
> I shall call the psychological values of
> psychophysics _discriminal_ processes.

Although the discriminal process is not directly observable, it plays a central role in Thurstone's judgement model. The idea is that there exists an imaginary psychological process underlying revealed behaviour, wherein choice alternatives are

137

represented as random variables (or discriminal processes) which the individual compares in the process of making a choice. These random variables correspond to a set of A alternatives and take the form (using our notation)

$$V_1 + \varepsilon_1, \; V_2 + \varepsilon_2, \ldots, \; V_J + \varepsilon_J, \text{ where}$$

$$V_j (j = 1, \ldots, J)$$

are real constants defined herein as representative utilities (or scale values) of the alternatives and $\varepsilon_j (j = 1, \ldots, J)$ are independently and identically distributed (iid) <u>normal</u> random variables with mean zero, unit variance and zero covariance. Identical variances and common covariances means that the marginal distributions differ only in their locations along the axis; that is they are independently and identically normally distributed about their mean values V_j, the latter being some numerical scale function of the different attributes of the alternative (Figure 5.1).

FIGURE 5·1:

Marginal Distributions of V_1, V_2 and V_3 for Thurstone's Normal (Case V) Model

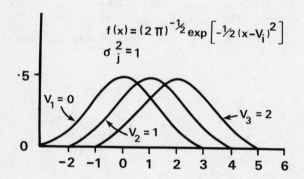

$$f(x) = (2\pi)^{-\frac{1}{2}} \exp\left[-\frac{1}{2}(x-V_i)^2\right]$$

$$\sigma_j^2 = 1$$

An essential feature of Thurstone's theory of comparative judgement in the formulation outlined above (known as Case V) with independent discriminal processes is that a complete set of choice probabilities satisfies the model if and only if there exist scale values V_1, V_2, $\ldots V_J$, $\ldots V_{J+n}$ such that for every alternative i and set of relevant alternatives (A), $i \in A \subseteq B$

$$P_{i \in A} = P[V_i + \varepsilon_i = \text{Max}\{V_j + \varepsilon_j | j \in A\}] \qquad (5.1)$$

(equivalent to $P_{i \in A} = P(V_i + \varepsilon_i > V_j + \varepsilon_j \quad \forall j \in A)$

(equation 3.8) with no ties).

Yellott (1977: 118) has proven that every Case V model $T(\mu, \sigma^2, r)$ is completely equivalent to $T(0,1,0)$. r is the covariance. Thus we now have a basis for admitting that our basic choice model is a utility maximisation model provided the other imposed assumptions are consistent. Alternatively, we need to demonstrate that the choice axiom is equivalent to Thurstone's Case V model with $T(0,1,0)$. Looking ahead, this is true for the general case of A alternatives only when the random components are Weibull distributed, and not normal as in Thurstone's original formulation.

The other major contribution from psychological choice theory is embodied in Luce's theory of choice (Luce 1959) and is referred to as the choice axiom. The basic choice axiom is stated formally as:

Let B be the full set of alternatives $(1, \ldots, J, \ldots, J + n)$ and let A be some offered set of B containing alternative i, for example $A = (i, j)$. The Luce choice axiom states that

$$P(i \in B) = P(A \in B) \ P(i \in A), \ P(A \in B) = \sum_{j \in A} P(j \in B) \qquad (5.2)$$

In words, the probability that i is chosen from the entire set B is given by the product of the likelihood that some element of A is chosen when all B is presented, and the probability of choosing i when the choice is restricted by presenting only alternatives of the set A. $P(i \in B)$ and $P(i \in A)$ come from two different empirical observations. The first involves presentation of the whole set B, and the second, presentation of the reduced set A. Luce's axiom makes a directly testable prediction about the relationship that should be found among the probabilities.

Another way of referring to Luce's axiom is to say that it looks at the relationship among choice probabilities as the number of alternatives involved in the choice are changed. In particular, the assumption is that the ratio of the likelihood of choosing i to likelihood of choosing j is a constant irrespective of the number and composition of other alternatives in the set presented for choice. This is variously referred to as the constant ratio rule (Clark, 1957) or the 'independence-from-irrelevant alternatives' Lemma (Luce, 1959; Arrow, 1951). This relationship needs further comment. Let B be a larger set containing i and j. Then

$$\frac{P(i,j,z \in B)}{P(j,i,z \in B)} = \frac{P(i \in B)}{P(j \in B)} \quad , \quad B = (i,j,z) \tag{5.3}$$

From Luce's choice axiom, by defining A to be a set A = (i,j) with $P(i) \neq 0$, $P(j) \neq 0$ then from equation (5.2)

$$P(i \in B) = P(i \in A) \cdot P(A \in B)$$
$$P(j \in B) = P(j \in A) \cdot P(A \in B) \tag{5.4}$$

By taking ratios, equation (5.3) is obtained. That is, the ratio of the proportion of i choices to the proportion of j choices is independent of what other elements, and how many, are in B. In order to consider the relationship of pairwise choices to choices from larger sets, define B = (i,i), P(i \in B) = 0.5. Then,

$$P(i \in B) = \frac{1}{\sum\limits_{j \in B} \frac{P(j \in B)}{P(i \in B)}} \tag{5.5}$$

Using the independence-from-irrelevant alternatives Lemma, specify the inverse of equation (5.3) as

$$\frac{P(j,i,z \in B)}{P(i,j,z \in B)} = \frac{P(j \in B)}{P(i \in B)} \tag{5.6}$$

Substituting equation (5.6) into equation (5.5) gives

$$P(i \in B) = \frac{1}{\sum\limits_{j \in B} \frac{P(j \in B)}{P(i \in B)}} = \frac{P(i \in B)}{\sum\limits_{j \in B} P(j \in B)}, \quad \sum\limits_{j \in B} P(j \in B) = 1 \tag{5.7}$$

This is the verification of equation (5.5). Equation (5.5) illustrates an assumption that the pairwise choices (i,j) give sufficient information to account for choices from all larger sets of alternatives. Having introduced the choice axiom and the IIA property, let us define a positive real valued function that determines a strength measure (the u-scale) by selecting an arbitrary element b of B. The strength of i, denoted by u(i) is

$$u(i) = \frac{P(i \in B)}{P(b \in B)}, \ B = (i,b) \tag{5.8}$$

The u-values have some useful properties:

$$\frac{u(i)}{u(j)} = \frac{P(i \in B)}{P(j \in B)} \tag{5.9}$$

Proof by construction:

$$\frac{u(i)}{u(j)} = \frac{P(i \in B)}{P(b \in B}) \cdot \frac{P(b \in B)}{P(j \in B)}$$

$$= \frac{P(i \in B)}{P(j \in B)}, \ B = (i,j,b) \ \text{(by cancellation)}$$

$$= \frac{P(i \in B)}{P(j \in B)}, \ B = (i,j) \quad \text{(by constant ratio rule)}$$

From equation (5.9), equation (5.5) can be rewritten as

$$P(i \in B) = \frac{1}{\sum_{j \in B} \frac{P(j \in B)}{P(i \in B)}} = \frac{u(i)}{\sum_{j \in B} u(j)} \tag{5.10}$$

Equation (5.10), referred to by Luce as the Existence Theorem, is the representation of the Strict utility model (Marschak, 1959). If a set of choice probabilities conforms to the implications of Luce's axiom, then numbers (u(i)) can be assigned to the alternatives in such a manner that these numbers reflect the choice probabilities and are unique up to multiplication by a positive constant. That is, the u's form a ratio scale of measurements.

To prove the uniqueness of the assigned u-values, assume that u(i) is defined relative to an arbitrary element b of the set B. If a new scale value, u*(i) were defined with respect to a

141

different arbitrary element d of set B, then it can be shown that

$$u^*(i) = ku(i) \qquad (5.11)$$

where k is some positive constant.

Proof:

$$u^*(i) \;=\; \frac{P(i,d)}{P(d,i)} \;=\; \frac{P(i\in B)}{P(d\in B)}$$

But

$$u(i) \;=\; \frac{P(i,b)}{P(b,i)} \;=\; \frac{P(i\in B)}{P(b\in B)}$$

Thus

$$u^*(i) \;=\; \frac{P(b\in B)}{P(d\in B)} \; u(i) = ku(i)$$

This property ensures that if all scale values are multiplied by a positive constant, one preserves the original relationships of the scale values to the choice probabilities. This invariance occurs because the choice probabilities depend on the ratio of the u's and in the ratio form $(u(i)/u(j))$, the scale constant k will cancel. This is Luce's 'invariance under uniform expansion of the choice set' which he argues is an intuitively plausible constraint. You will have realised that this is also the IIA property. This strict utility model is the least general (or most restrictive) random utility model. By utilising some more general utility function specifications in the strict utility model we can derive from this probabilistic choice model the empirical function. The more general assumptions are defined under the heading of a strong utility function, and correspond more closely to Thurstone's discriminal process.

Becker, de Groot & Marschak (1963) called a binary model a strong utility model if there exists $V_1,\ldots,V_J$ and a non-decreasing real valued function $\phi(r)$ defined for all real numbers, r, so that for every binary offered set J = (i,j),

$$P(i,j) = \phi_V(V_i - V_j); \; \phi_V(0) = 0.5 \qquad (5.12)$$

$\phi(r)$ is the distribution function (CDF) of a continuous random variable with a symmetric distribution around zero. For each alternative $i\in B$, V_i represents the value of i to the individual. Thus when faced with a choice (i,j) the individual would ideally want to select i if $V_i - V_j > 0$ and j if $V_i - V_j < 0$. However, the psychologist would say that the individual cannot calculate $V_i - V_j$ exactly because of inherent characteristics in the decision-making process (contrasted with the economist who would say that the individual is a deterministic utility maximiser, yet the analyst is unable to fully account explicitly for all relevant discriminating attributes) and hence the rule becomes:

choose i   if $V_i - V_j + \varepsilon > 0$

choose j   if $V_i - V_j + \varepsilon < 0$

The constants $V_1,\ldots,V_J$ are called <u>strong</u> utilities in contrast to the strict utilities $u_1,\ldots,u_J$ in Luce's model. Both should not be confused with the random utilities $U_1,\ldots,U_J$, which are random variables, not constants. To prove equation (5.12), define the random vector $(U_1,\ldots,U_J)$ by $U_i = V_i + \varepsilon_i$, $i = 1,\ldots,J$ where ε_i are iid random variables for all $i \neq j$ and $V_1,\ldots,V_J$ are the constants in the strong utility model. Note the equivalence of this to Thurstone's discriminal process. Then for any $J = (i,j)$

$$
\begin{aligned}
P(i;J) &= P(U_i > U_j) \\
&= P(V_i + \varepsilon_i > V_j + \varepsilon_j) \\
&= P(\varepsilon_j - \varepsilon_i < V_i - V_j) \\
&= \phi_V(V_i - V_j)
\end{aligned}
$$

This result can be used in the binary case of the strict utility model. Marschak (1959) defines the binary strict utility model as a positive-valued function u on J if

$$
P(i,j) = \frac{u_i}{u_i + u_j} = \frac{1}{1 + \dfrac{u_j}{u_i}} \tag{5.13}
$$

The only element missing in the discussion is the connection between Luce's choice axiom and Thurstone's model (Case V), both of which contain contributions to the basic choice model. Fortunately, it can be demonstrated that for the general case of multiple alternatives (equation

143

3.24) in a choice set, if random variables in the
Thurstone model are restricted to differ only in
their means (V_j's) and the ε_j's are double
exponentially distributed, not normally distributed
as assumed by Thurstone, then Luce's choice axiom
and Thurstone's Case V random utility model are
formally equivalent. The result is a basic multinomial logit model.

For pair-comparison applications, the choice
axiom is equivalent to the version of Thurstone's
theory in which the <u>differences</u> between the
discriminal processes (i.e. $(V_i + \varepsilon_i) - (V_j + \varepsilon_j)$)
have a logistic distribution. Holman & Marley
(cited in Luce & Suppes, 1965) demonstrated that for
the differences to be logistic, the separate
discriminal processes have the double exponential
distribution

$$P(V_i + \varepsilon_i \leq x) = \exp\{-\exp-[a(x - V_i) + b]\} \qquad (5.14)$$

$$(-\infty < x < \infty)$$

where a and b are arbitrary constants, a > 0. The
resulting model is equivalent to the choice axiom
for any number of alternatives. Yellott (1977)
completes the contribution by demonstrating that
the double exponential (or Weibull) distribution is
the only distribution for any number of alternatives which equivalences Thurstone's Case V model
and Luce's choice axiom. Hence we cannot estimate
a basic logit model on any other distributional
assumption for the ε_j's.

The Holman-Marley theorem is:

*if F is a distribution function of the
double exponential type
F(x) = exp (-exp -(ax+b)) (a > 0, b arbitrary)
then the Thurstone model is completely
equivalent to the Choice Axiom.*

Proof (after Yellott)

To simplify the proof for particular case
a = 1, b = 0, let us initially show that if T_F and
T_G are Thurstone (Case V) models, and F and G are
distributions of the same type (i.e.
F(x) = G(ax + b)) for all x and same pair of
constants a, b with a > 0) then T_F is completely
equivalent to T_G.

144

Suppose T_F admits the global choice set with representative utilities $V_1, V_2, \ldots, V_J$, $A = 1, \ldots, J$ then

$$P_{i \in A} = P(V_i + \varepsilon_i = \text{Max } \{V_j + \varepsilon_j | j \in A\})$$

$$= P(aV_i + a\varepsilon_i + b = \text{Max } \{aV_j + a\varepsilon_j + b | j \in A\})$$

$$= P(aV_i + \varepsilon_i^* = \text{Max } \{aV_j + \varepsilon_j^* | j \in A\}) , \; \varepsilon_j^* = a\varepsilon_j + b$$

where $P(\varepsilon_j^* \leq x) = P(a\varepsilon_j + b \leq x)$,

$$= P(\varepsilon_j \leq (x - b)/a)$$

$$= F((x - b)/a)$$

$$= G(x)$$

Hence the global choice set is admitted by T_G with representative utilities $aV_1, aV_2, \ldots, aV_J$.

Suppose the global choice set is admitted to T_G ($G(x) = \exp (\exp - x)$) with representative utilities $V_1, \ldots, V_J$. Set $V_i = \log u_i$ (an assumption justified below, in the proof, noting that u_i is small u, the strict utility). That is, u_i are unique up to a multiplicative transformation, then $\log u_i (= V_i)$ are unique up to an additive constant. Since the only issue of relevance in V_i is the ranking of V_i's and not distance apart, it does not matter whether you take logs or not. Let $\varepsilon_i = \log Y_i$ (where Y is a particular random variable with the exponential distribution function $1 - (\exp - y)$).

$$P_{i \in A} = P(V_i + \varepsilon_i = \text{Max } \{V_j + \varepsilon_j | j \in A\})$$

$$= P(\log u_i - \log Y_i = \text{Max } \{\log u_j - \log Y_j | j \in A\})$$

$$= P(u_i/Y_i = \text{Max } \{u_j/Y_j | j \in A\})$$

$$= P(Y_i/u_i = \text{Min } \{Y_j/u_j | j \in A\})$$

$$= \int_0^\infty u_i \exp (-u_i y_i) (\prod_{j \in A-i} \exp - u_j y_j) \, dy_i$$

$$= u_i / \sum_{j \in A} u_j \qquad \text{Luce's Choice Axiom} \qquad (5.15)$$

Thus the global choice set with A alternatives also satisfies the choice axiom, with u scale values $u_i = \exp V_i$. A trivial step gives us the basic choice model

$$P_{i \in A} = \exp V_i / \sum_{j \in A} \exp V_j \qquad (3.24, 5.16)$$

To show that the IIA property is an assumption underlying this model, we can follow Yellott's demonstration based on Feller's version of a theorem due to Gnedenko, and which is an intuitively more plausible proof of the contribution of Fisher & Tippet in 1928 who used a function $F^k(x) = F(x + b_k)$ to prove that the limit distribution of the normalised maximum Z_k of k iid random variables $Z_1, \ldots, Z_k$ (i.e. the limit distribution of $Z_k - b_k$ as $k \to \infty$) is the double exponential. Given the proof leading to equation (5.11), then equation (5.15) can be redefined as

$$P_{i \in A} = k\, u_i/k \sum_{j \in A} u_j = k \exp V_i/k \sum_{j \in A} \exp V_j \qquad (5.17)$$

Then

F is a distribution function that satisfies $F^k(x) = F(x + b_k)$ (i.e. for every k there exists a b_k such that $F^k(x) = F(x + b_k)$ for all x) if and only if F is a distribution of the type $F(x) = \exp(-\exp - (ax + b))$

Proof

If F is double exponential, then

$$F^k(x) = \exp(-k\exp -(ax + b))$$

$$= \exp\{-\exp - [a(x - 1/a)\log k) + b]\}$$

$$= F(x + b_k)$$

where $\quad b_k = -(1/a)\log k$

Thus, within the class of Thurstone models from which the random utility model is obtained,

146

invariance under uniform expansions (or the IIA property) implies the choice axiom. This leads to the basic choice model. We should now be in a position to discuss the IIA property in some detail.

5·3 The Independence from Irrelevant Alternatives Assumption

From Section 5.2 it is clear that models, such as the random utility model in its basic logit form, are members of the family of share models. In general terms a share model defines a market share or probability of choice of a particular alternative as the representation of the ratio of its utility to the sum of utilities of every alternative in the relevant set. Thus the logit form is consistent with the share condition:

$$P_i = \exp (V_i) / \sum_{j=1}^{J} \exp (V_j) \qquad (5.18)$$

Apart from the condition of fixed market shares for each alternative, the model permits the introduction of 'new' alternatives[1] (new in the sense that they are not included in the alternatives used in model estimation, and they may or may not be presently available), since the denominator is common to all alternatives. It is assumed that the representative utility is applicable to the new alternative. To illustrate this operation of the share model in its logit form, let

$$P_q (\ell_1 \in L) = \exp (V_{\ell 1}) / \exp[(V_{\ell 1}) + \exp (V_{\ell 2}) + \exp (V_{\ell 3})] \qquad (5.19)$$

$$P_q (\ell_2 \in L) = \exp (V_{\ell 2}) / [\exp (V_{\ell 1}) + \exp (V_{\ell 2}) + \exp (V_{\ell 3})] \qquad (5.20)$$

Then, given the choice axiom

$$\frac{P_q(\ell_1 \in L)}{P_q(\ell_2 \in L)} = \frac{\exp (V_{\ell 1})}{\exp (V_{\ell 2})} = \exp (V_{\ell 1} - V_{\ell 2}) \qquad (5.21)$$

That is, the ratio of the probability of choosing alternative ℓ_1 to the probability of choosing any

147

other (ℓ_2) is independent of the set of available alternatives. The ratio of the probabilities is only a function of the attributes of ℓ_1 and ℓ_2.

The estimatable function (assuming additivity of the attributes) becomes:

$$\frac{P_q(\ell_1 \in L)}{P_q(\ell_2 \in L)} = \exp (V_{\ell 1} - V_{\ell 2})$$

$$\exp \left[\sum_k \beta_{k\ell 1} x_{k\ell 1q} - \sum_k \beta_{k\ell 2} x_{k\ell 2q} \right]$$

An example illustrates this property. Assume that there are two alternatives in the choice set for occupant status (rent, own). The market share of each alternative is:

$$P_{rent} = \exp V_{rent} / (\exp V_{rent} + \exp V_{own}) = 2/(2 + 3) = .40 \tag{5.22a}$$

$$P_{own} = \exp V_{own} / (\exp V_{rent} + \exp V_{own}) = 3/(2 + 3) = .60 \tag{5.22b}$$

The ratio of the shares is $P_{rent}/P_{own} = .4/.6 = .66$ (5.22c)

Suppose a third alternative were introduced (e.g. 'purchase' on leasehold, not freehold), and that $\exp V_{lease} = 1$ then the new market shares become

$$P_{rent} = \exp V_{rent} / (\exp V_{rent} + \exp V_{own} + \exp V_{lease})$$

$$= 2/(2 + 3 + 1) = .33 \tag{5.23a}$$

$$P_{own} = \exp V_{own} / (\exp V_{rent} + \exp V_{own} + \exp V_{lease})$$

$$= 3/(2 + 3 + 1) = .50 \tag{5.23b}$$

$$P_{lease} = \exp V_{lease} / (\exp V_{rent} + \exp V_{own} + \exp V_{lease})$$

$$= 1/(2 + 3 + 1) = .17 \tag{5.23c}$$

In accordance with the IIA property, the share of the market obtained by the 'new' alternative from each of the other alternatives is directly proportional to their original share; i.e. P_{rent}/P_{own} initially was .66; it is now still .66 (i.e. .33/.50).

Clearly this property is valid only if the new alternative competes equally with each existing alternative. The Basic MNL model as a simply scalable model tends to overpredict the choice probabilities for alternatives which are perceived by individuals to be 'similar'. Tversky (1972) has called this the order independence property; if i is more likely than j in choice set B and A is any choice set not containing i or j, then introducing i into A would draw more choices away from each alternative in A than would adding j to A. While the property may not be logically a very plausible one for all applications, its substantial advantages in the formulation of an analytically tractable model (shown in Chapter 3) are such that providing it does not significantly distort the empirical validity of the predictions, it can be deemed a useful contribution to modelling.

There are two major problems with the existence of the IIA property:

(a)   Failure to ensure that all alternatives are distinct may lead to biased estimation of model parameters. The definition of "distinct" is complex, and revolves around an identification of the extent to which alternatives are similar/ dissimilar. The classical example is called the "red bus/blue bus" problem where the only distinguishing characteristic between two of the alternatives is colour, all other influencing dimensions being the same. With the car as the other alternative, the introduction of the 'new' blue bus alternative would be expected to lead to an adjustment in the red bus share, but not in the car's share (assuming no generated trips); however the IIA property results also in a change in the car share so that $P_{car}/P_{red\ bus}$ remains unchanged. The implication is that cross-elasticities of choice with respect to a particular attribute are invariant to the particular alternative (see equation 3.42 of Chapter 3).

(b)   Proscribed market-share changes may occur when any existing alternative is altered or the set of alternatives is changed by addition or deletion.

5·4 Procedures to Determine Violations of the IIA Property and Proposals to Remedy Violation

Two main procedures have been proposed to deal with the IIA property and its associated problems in share models. We will now outline, in historical sequence, the procedures, but would remind you that the IIA property is not always an undesirable property of share models, and that it is often a valid assumption.

Procedure A.   This procedure involves modifications of the basic multinomial logit model that reduce or eliminate the problems resulting from violation of the IIA property. These modifications result in a "structured-share" model (McFadden, 1974a; Westin, 1974) where similar alternatives in a choice set are initially modelled together and then redefined as a single (combinatory) alternative in the next stage of the structure. The probabilities of choice associated with each of the similar alternatives in the initial model represent each alternative's share of the combined market for the two initial alternatives (e.g. red bus/blue bus). The combined alternatives can be entered into the next model in a number of ways. The favoured ways are either to represent the attributes of the combined alternatives as those of the alternative having the higher choice probability (referred to as the Maximum method) or as a combination of the attributes of both alternatives weighted by their choice probabilities (known as the Cascade approach). This process is repeated until the two most dissimilar alternatives have been compared. The selection of the alternative with the highest probability is decided on an individual basis. In the Cascade approach, a problem arises when an attribute is dichotomous since it then becomes continuous (after calculating the weighted average).

This approach can be criticised for not attacking the cause of the IIA problem, namely that there is no place in the basic choice model where the relative similarity of alternatives can be defined. The type of model that has such a capability was introduced in Chapter 4 (as nested logit). Procedure B is another approach which goes beyond Procedure A in the context of the share (logit) model.

Procedure B. The emphasis is on tests to determine when the IIA property is violated and remedies in the case of violation. A study by Charles River Associates (1976) argued that

> *The independence assumption is a priori neither desirable nor undesirable, but should be accepted or rejected strictly on empirical grounds depending on the circumstances (D-104).*

Violations of IIA fall into two basic classes:

Class 1: correlation of the unobserved components of utility among alternatives (i.e. the ε_j's are not independent)

Class 2: observed and unobserved attributes of utility are not independent of one another.

In the following discussion, tests that are likely to be of relevance to the most common data configurations are outlined. When violation of the IIA property is thought to exist then the following tests should be undertaken for each individual observation:

Case 1(a) tests on residuals for a single choice set using an unbiased parameter estimate, by either estimating another data set or estimating a random subsample of the existing data set. The formula for linearly transformed residuals is (McFadden, Train & Tye, 1977: 44):

$$Y_{jq} = D_{jq} - D_{1q} \ (P_{jq})^{\frac{1}{2}} / (1 - P_{1q}), \qquad (5.24)$$

where

$$D_{jq} = (f_{jq} - P_{jq}) / (P_{jq})^{\frac{1}{2}} \qquad q = 1,\ldots,Q \text{ individuals}$$
$$j = 1,\ldots,J \text{ alternatives}$$

f_{jq} are the selections of alternatives j (i.e. = 1 if j is chosen, 0 otherwise), P_{jq} (= $P(j|A, x_q, f_q)$) are the estimated probabilities, and D_{jq} are the weighted untransformed residuals. $1 \in A$ is a fixed alternative and $j \neq 1$. The transformation is a way of adjusting for nonindependence and heteroskedasticity of the D_{jq}.

151

$(P_{jq})^{\frac{1}{2}}$ is a normalising weight. Under the hypothesis that the estimated model is correct, the residuals (D_{jq}) have, asymptotically, zero mean, unit variance and covariance $E(D_{iq}D_{jq}) = -(P_{iq}P_{jq})^{\frac{1}{2}}$. Hypothesising correctness of the estimated model (Y_{jq} are iid), if the test statistic differed significantly from zero for the mean test, the hypothesis of the model can be rejected. Similarly for the variance test, if the unit variance of Y_{jq} under the null hypothesis is true, we can accept the hypothesis if chi-square falls in the acceptance region for the chi-square test.[2]

The transformed residuals can also be used in an association test. For alternative j rank the estimated probabilities P_{jq} and identify the sign of D_{jq}. Form a contingency table (signed residual x number of column cells, the latter being an arbitrary number of cells of approximately equal number of individuals). An average probability for each cell $(\bar{P}_{jm})$ is obtained ($m = 1,\ldots,M$ cells). Defining RP_m as the number of positive residuals in the mth cell and N_m as number of positive and negative residuals, a goodness-of-fit test is

$$\chi^2 = \sum_{m=1}^{M} \frac{(RP_m - N_m \bar{P}_{jm})^2}{N_m \bar{P}_{jq}} \qquad (5.25)$$

given that under the null hypothesis, $E\left(\frac{RP_m}{N_m}\right) = \bar{P}_{jm}$.

The distribution is asymptotic, bounded by chi-square distributions with $M - 1$ and $M - k - 1$ degrees of freedom where k is the number of estimated parameters. If there are three alternatives, then this calculation is repeated for each alternative.

Case 1(b) tests on estimated coefficients to assess bias, by either rearranging data as in Case 1(a) and comparing coefficients with those of the full data set, and/or comparing estimated models which are separated according to dominance and recessiveness of an attribute in the alternative known to be independent. The likelihood-ratio test can be used for testing the hypothesis.

<u>Case 2(a) tests, based on restricted choice sets for</u>
<u>aggregation of heterogeneous market segments as a</u>
<u>result of failure to separate market segments with</u>
<u>significantly different valuations of attributes.</u>
Case 1 violation from this source can also be
tested using 1(a) and 1(b) tests.

Additional dummy variables can be introduced
into the full data set to test an hypothesis that
the valuation of a particular attribute is
different between groups. The same statistic as
used in 1(b) can be used to estimate the
significance of the between-group difference in the
value of the attribute.

<u>Case 2(b) tests based on the full data set where the</u>
<u>correlation is not due to aggregation of</u>
<u>heterogeneous market segments</u>. New data that
permits unobserved attributes to be tested as
observed attributes is required to assess dependence.

If the test suggests violation, then the
following modifications (within the logit framework)
to the model should be carried out:

(i)   improve model specification to eliminate
dependence. Individual behaviour assumptions may
be incorrect, relevant variables may be missing
(there are nonsystematic variations in unobserved
attributes across alternatives), market
segmentation may be required to overcome the lack
of an appropriate average behaviour of individuals
in a group with similar observed attributes and
facing similar choices.

(ii)   change the model estimation procedure
to account for dependence (e.g. use multinomial
probit or dogit - see Chapter 6).

(iii)   change the model itself, in particular
use the Maximum model, or Cascade model.

Remedies for Case 1(a) and (b) are the
addition of explanatory variables and the elimination of choice alternatives. In the latter
instance, McFadden's "maximum method" is proposed,
which assigns the probability between the two
dependent alternatives according to a binary logit
model separately estimated; with the probability
(ies) of the independent alternative(s) being
obtained directly from the multinomial logit model.
The difference between the probabilities of each
alternative using the maximum method and the
probabilities from a single model when independence
is assumed, is a useful test of the maximum error
that can occur if independence is assumed when it is

153

not valid. The justification for the Maximum method is well summarised by Charles River Associates:

> it is the ability to factor the unobserved attributes into two types of factors - those that are independent between modes 2 and 3 and unimportant between 1 and 2 (or 3) and those that are independent between 1 and 2 (or 3) and unimportant between 2 and 3, where 2 and 3 are the dependent modes. According to the assumptions of this model, independence holds between 1 and 2 (or 3) and 2 and 3, but not for the joint model including 1, 2 and 3 (D-131).

Remedies for Case 2 include the use of new choice alternatives to break up the correlation, converting an unobserved attribute to an observed attribute or segmenting the sample for estimation purposes to allow for any nonquantifiable biases; and modifying the estimation procedure.

Although, in principle, violation of the IID random disturbances assumption (which is related to IIA) causes inconsistent parameter and choice probability estimates, Horowitz (1980) has demonstrated how in practice the basic logit model appears to be reasonably robust against <u>moderate</u> violations of the IID assumption:

> In numerical experiments with a three-alternative model, Horowitz found that the logit model gave consistent parameter estimates (apart from an arbitrary scale factor), even when the variances of the additive disturbances differed as much as a factor of 16 and had correlation coefficients as large as 0.75. The root mean square differences between the true choice probabilities and their logit estimates were less than 0.027 when the disturbance variances differed by less than a factor of four or had correlations of less than 0.50. The corresponding maximum differences between the true and logit estimated choice probabilities were less than 0.063. ... the fact that the logit model is erroneous would not be detected in standard statistical tests. There would, therefore, be little value in using a more general and complex model in place of the (basic) logit model.

> (Horowitz, 1980: 7-8)

5·5 An Empirical Illustration of Procedure B Tests for Violation of the IIA Property

A simulated data set can be used to illustrate the use of a selected number of tests proposed for identifying whether the IIA property has been violated in a particular application. Assume a basic choice model, estimated according to the procedures presented in Chapter 3, and note that the validity of the IIA property is dependent on the specification of the representative utility of the alternatives (given that the unobserved random utility component, ε_j, is the difference between the 'true' utility and the V_j), and has nothing to do with the particular individual's choice. Within realistic data bounds, it should be possible to 'improve' on most choice model specifications to accommodate the IIA property. However, this may result in a particular model specification (with respect to representative utility and set of alternatives) which the analyst believes is inappropriate to the study in hand, necessitating another model that is unconstrained by the IIA property. The simulated data contains three alternative establishment types (detached house, townhouse and flat) for owner-occupied dwellings. These are ranked alternatives (see Chapter 4). We assume that townhouse and flat are similar and thus expect unobserved attributes of each establishment type to be correlated across types if the representative component of utility is inappropriately specified for the basic logit model. In Table 5.1, all attributes are defined initially to include only those which enter the representative utility expression for the alternative which they are directly related to. For example, we would not include in the utility expression for townhouse, the cost of owning a flat.

All alternative-specific variables take the relevant value for the particular alternative j (ASV_j), and zero otherwise. For example, 'number of persons in the household' (ASV_2) is a variable taking on value = number of persons per households for a townhouse and zero otherwise; the estimated coefficient (-.924) is interpreted to mean that there is a negative relationship between living in a

TABLE 5·1 : **The Basic Logit Model with Three Alternatives for Choice of Establishment Type**
($j = 1,2,3$. 1 = detached house, 2 = townhouse, 3 = flat)
$Q = 600$ (Σ_j assumed iid)

Explanatory Variables $\left(V_j = \sum_{k=1}^{K} \beta_k x_{kq} \right)$	Estimated Coefficients (t-statistics in brackets)		
	detached house	town-house	flat
Fortnightly repayment over 20 years ($\$$s) (GV)	-.1724 (-4.3)	-.1724 (-4.3)	-.1724 (-4.3)
Age of structure (years) (ASV_2)	-	-.0153 (-1.8)	-
Living area (square metres) (ASV_1)	1.2310 (6.8)	-	-
Number of bedrooms (ASV_1)	2.371 (2.1)	-	-
Number of persons in household (ASV_1)	3.26 (4.9)		
Number of persons in household (ASV_2)	-	-0.924 (-2.4)	-
Age of head of household (ASV_2)	-	1.721 (3.3)	-
Number of full-time workers in household (ASV_1)	0.217 (1.2)	-	-
Full-time workers in household = 1 (ASV_2)	-	0.718 (2.0)	-
Household gross income ($\leq$ $\$10,000$) ($ASV_3$)	-	-	.0092 (1.8)
Household gross income (> $\$10,000$, $\leq$ $\$18,000$) ($ASV_2$)	-	-0.0174 (-3.2)	-
House-type dummy (=1 for detached house, 0 otherwise)	4.75 (3.9)	-	-
Townhouse-type dummy (=1 for townhouse, 0 otherwise)	-	-2.16 (-2.2)	-

log likelihood at zero (L_0) = -172.0. Log likelihood at convergence (L) = -87.0. likelihood ratio index ($-2 \log \lambda$) = 170 (13 degrees of freedom);

$\rho^2 = 1 - L/L_0 = .49$; per cent correctly predicted = 72.2

townhouse and number of household members. We will not debate the merits of the particular variables *vis-a-vis* an alternative set of variables. The interpretation of the various statistics has been given in Chapter 3.

The first test proposed in Section 5.4 was the residual test. If the IIA property is not violated, then the residuals (D_{jq}) should have asymptotically zero mean, unit variance and covariance - $(P_{iq}P_{jq})^{\frac{1}{2}}$. The linearly transformed residuals (Y_{jq}) should be asymptotically independent with zero mean and unit variance. McFadden et al. (1977) claim that non-violation of IIA is implied by the number of positive residuals being higher for low-numbered cells than for high-numbered cells, given that ranking and allocation to cells is based on estimated probabilities. For example, for individual 1 on alternative 1 (house),

P_{jq} ($= P_{11}$) is .96, D_{jq} ($= D_{11}$) $= (f_{11} - P_{11})/(P_{11})^{\frac{1}{2}}$

or $(1 - .96)/(.96)^{\frac{1}{2}} = .02$,

and $Y_{11} = .02 - .02 \ (.96)^{\frac{1}{2}} \ (1-(.96)^{\frac{1}{2}})/(1-.96)$

$= .02 - .0975 = .01$.

Note that $P_{jq} = P_{1q}$ for $j = 1$, but not when $j = 2$ or 3. Thus the residual is positive. This calculation is repeated, producing the results in Table 5.2, assuming all three alternatives are in each individual's choice set.

From Table 5.2, the chi-square value for alternative 1 is 17.6 bounded by chi-squared distributions with 20 and 7 degrees of freedom. The critical (.05 level) value of χ^2 with 20 degrees of freedom is 31.4 and with 7 degrees of freedom is 14.1. Since the test statistic for house-type is 17.6, it falls between the bounds, and the test is inconclusive. Desirably the calculated χ^2 value should lie below the lower bound of the two bounding critical values.

The ambiguous result on house alternative means that we must apply further tests. It is possible that measurement errors in the observed attributes of the house alternative is the cause of this ambiguous result.

157

TABLE 5·2: Residual Tests of Association (Case 1 (a)) — House Type

	1	2	3	4	5	6	7	8	9	10	11	12	13	14	15	16	17	18	19	20	21
Number of positive residuals (RP_m)	19	23	22	21	16	14	12	10	9	8	6	6	5	5	4	3	2	2	2	1	1
Number of negative residuals (RN_m)	9	5	6	7	12	14	16	18	19	20	26	22	23	23	24	25	30	26	26	27	31
$\bar{P}_{jm}$	.97	.94	.74	.62	.60	.52	.48	.42	.26	.20	.11	.06	.10	.10	.03	.02	.02	.01	.01	.005	.005
χ^2 (equation 5·25) = 17.6	5.8	1.9	.18	.43	.070	.03	.20	.33	.32	.62	.92	2.02	.52	.52	1.08	.64	.22	.32	.32	.08	.08

$\bar{P}_{iq} = .33$

158

Another test (relevant to case 1(b)) is suitable
if it is thought that two dependent alternatives
e.g. flat and townhouse, are included in the
estimation sample. The test involves identifying
whether the estimates of the parameters with and
without one of the dependent alternatives differ
significantly. Non-violation of IIA occurs if the
difference is not statistically significant. A
subsample of individuals who chose an alternative
in the subset of dependent alternatives is obtained,
and used in the estimation of an additional model.
The test involves the comparison of the log-
likelihood at convergence associated with this
additional model and that associated with the
original model but only based on the subsample used
in the new model. In the latter the original
parameter estimates are used. The test statistic is

χ^2 = 2 [log-likelihood of conditional choice sub
sample evaluated at the total sample ML estimator
β_B minus the same evaluated at the conditional

choice subsample estimator β_A]. If the samples of
choices from A and B are not conditional but
independent, then χ^2 = 2 (log-likelihood at
convergence for sample of choice from A plus same
for B + same from pooled sample). The latter is
asymptotically distributed chi-square with degrees
of freedom equal to number of parameters.

220 of the 600 individuals in the total sample
actually chose a flat. The re-estimated model on
380 individuals who chose a home or townhouse (with
only one alternative) produced a log-likelihood at
convergence of -164, resulting in a χ^2 of 16. With
12 degrees of freedom (having only deleted the
townhouse type dummy since there are no other
ASVs), the critical value of chi-square is 21.0.
Since 16 < 21, we can accept the hypothesis that
the coefficients estimated on the subsample are the
same as those in Table 5.1. Hence we can reinstate
the third alternative and conclude nonviolation of
IIA on this test.

A final test (related to Case 2(b)) involves
introducing additional attributes such that V_j is

a function of x's associated with j = 2 or 3. An
example of such an attribute is the cost of housing,
taking the described value in the townhouse alternative and zero otherwise. Let us introduce the
variable and one other, namely cost of a flat,
taking the described value in the house and townhouse alternatives and zero otherwise. If IIA is
not violated then the estimates of the parameters of

159

the additional two attributes should not vary significantly from zero. Using the likelihood-ratio statistic given above, we can compare the log-likelihood at convergence in Table 5.1 with the same when two interactive variables are introduced. A re-estimation of the model results in a log-likelihood at convergence of -152, with 15 degrees of freedom. The test statistic is 40; the number of degrees of freedom is equal to 2, the number of parameter restrictions imposed by the null hypothesis. Thus the critical value of χ^2 with 2 degrees of freedom is 5.99. Since 40 > 5.99, the hypothesis of zero coefficients is rejected and the IIA property appears to be violated. Thus we need to look for possible causes of violation, in the specification of the original attributes in Table 5.1 Failure to identify the likely causes might require the application of an alternative technique such as multinomial probit or nested logit (the latter particularly so if there exists a choice hierarchy).

Although the illustrative example relates to a single equation and choice set, such tests (especially the one relevant to Case 1(b)) can be applied to a sequential recursive model structure.[3] The tests outlined above are only a few of the many one could consider. However they do appear to be the most useful in practice, from the points of view of testing the most likely violation sources and ease of utilisation.

NOTES — CHAPTER 5

1. It also permits the deletion of existing alternatives. The IIA assumption has a symmetry property; thus tests of violation that involve changing the number of alternatives in the choice set should include (for a well-balanced test), addition as well as deletion of alternatives.

2. The means test is as follows: The mean of Y_{jq} for each alternative will be zero under the hypothesis that the BMNL model is correct. Since the variance of these residuals is asymptotically unity, the statistics
$$\sum_{q=1}^{Q} Y_{jq}/Q$$ are asymptotically standard normal.

For the variance test, the $\chi^2 = \sum\limits_{q=1}^{Q} \sum\limits_{j \in B} D_{jq}^2$ is asymptotically distributed with $Q(J - 1) - k$ degrees of freedom.

3. The separability of choices assumption (see Chapter 4) is like the IIA assumption in that it asserts a degree of independence between decisions. For separability to be meaningful (in any sense), a tradeoff has to occur between the degree of integrity attainable by two or more decisions and the degree of satisfiability achievable by the separability assumption. If, as Smith (1975: 107) argues, all relevant attributes were included in the definition of the alternatives associated with a particular decision and these attributes included all those that are properties of the alternatives associated with another decision, then the two decisions become indistinguishable, and the separability assumption is meaningless. The ultimate worth of this assumption can only be decided in a particular empirical situation by suitable tests. One test is given below. Assume two decisions (mode choice and destination choice), and that we can observe an individual selecting one of two modes available (ml, m2) for travel to two or more common destinations. Suppose that for a pair of modes we are able to observe n_r instances of choices for the individual within two situations, each involving a different destination. (That is, $S_r = < \{m1\ m2\}, d_r > \in A$, and where $r = 1, 2$ and $d_{rm1} = d_{rm2}$). The test of the separability assumption for mode and destination choice is $P_{s1}(m1) = P_{s2}(m2)$ or the probability that choosing mode 1 is independent of destination. The likelihood ratio test, can be used to test the null hypothesis given above against the alternative $H = P_{s1}(m1) \neq P_{s2}(m2)$.

CHAPTER 6

Alternative Model Forms and Statistical Approaches

6·1 Introduction

Previous chapters have discussed the basic choice model and extensions on the assumption that the estimation technique is maximum-likelihood and that the model is a member of the nonlinear logit family. In this chapter we will examine some alternative estimation procedures and model forms. The first two are the linear probability model which requires the least squares regression technique for estimation, and the linear logit model which requires generalised least squares. Two models are then introduced which eliminate the need for making the a priori assumption of IIA as examined in Chapter 5. These are the dogit model proposed by Gaudry & Dagenais (1979) which is basically a modified logit model, and the multinomial probit model which is based on the multivariate normal probability distribution as opposed to the Weibull which was used to derive the MNL model. The final section of the chapter is concerned with the functional form of the representative component of utility given by V_j (equation 3.26) in the logit model (also dogit and probit). Recent work in this area by Gaudry & Wills (1978) using a transformation of variables known as the Box-Tukey transform is reviewed and its implications examined in the context of individual choice models.

6·2 Linear Probability Model and Least Squares Regression

Consider a situation where there are only two possible choices (e.g. choose car or public transport, vote yes or no). Furthermore instead of specifying the basic MNL choice model assume that this choice is a linear function of a set of explanatory variables. This simple choice model may then be written (in its stochastic form)

$$f_q = \beta_0 + \beta_1 X_{1q} + \ldots + \beta_K X_{Kq} + \varepsilon_q \qquad q = 1,\ldots,Q \quad (6.1)$$

where $f_q = \begin{cases} 0 \text{ if the first option is chosen,} \\ 1 \text{ if the second option is chosen,} \end{cases}$

$X_{kq} = $ the kth explanatory variable,

$\varepsilon_q = $ a stochastic error term assumed to be normally distributed with zero mean and constant variance.

This model is known as the <u>linear probability model</u> (LPM) since the estimating equation is linear and can be interpreted as describing the probability of the second option given values of the K explanatory variables. The reason for this interpretation can be seen by examining the expected value of each f_q. Because f_q can take on only two values, the probability distribution of f_q can be denoted as Prob($f_q = 1$) = P_q and Prob ($f_q = 0$) = $1 - P_q$. Hence $E(f_q) = 1(P_q) + 0(1 - P_q) = P_q$. Therefore, the expected value of f_q is simply the probability that $f_q = 1$ and so the interpretation of equation (6.1) as a probability model.

Given observations for Q individuals on the K explanatory variables and the f_q's (i.e. the choices actually made), ordinary least squares estimates of the coefficients (βs) in equation (6.1) may be obtained using standard regression techniques. Let us denote this estimated equation by

$$\hat{f}_q = \hat{\beta}_0 + \hat{\beta}_1 X_{1q} + \ldots + \hat{\beta}_K X_{Kq} \qquad q = 1,\ldots,Q \quad (6.2)$$

where a '^' over a quantity denotes an estimated value. Then $\hat{\beta}_k$ is an estimate of the change in the probability of choosing the second alternative given a unit change in X_k, and from this we can estimate the elasticity of choice with respect to variable X_k at the sample mean by multiplying $\hat{\beta}_k$ by $(\bar{X}_k/\bar{f})$ where $\bar{X}_k$ and $\bar{f}$ are the sample averages of X_k

164

and f respectively. This elasticity is an estimate of the _per cent change_ in the probability of choosing the second alternative given a one per cent change in X_k.

The major advantage of the linear probability model is its simplicity, both in estimation and interpretation. However, there are several disadvantages that, when weighed against the advantage of simplicity, makes the LPM much less satisfactory than other models which are available, one of which is the basic MNL model.

In a binary choice situation, there are several difficulties with the LPM. A specific problem stems from the fact that the statistical properties of the ordinary least squares (OLS) regression estimates of the parameters given in equation (6.2) depend upon certain assumptions about the error term ε_q. One of these assumptions is that the variance of the error terms is constant for each observation. But, the error term in the LPM does not have a constant variance, and so the OLS estimates of the regression coefficients will not be efficient (i.e. have smallest variance), although they will still be unbiased and consistent (as long as the other necessary assumptions still hold). We can see this by noting that

$$\varepsilon_q = f_q - \beta_0 - \beta_1 X_{1q} - \cdots - \beta_K X_{Kq} = f_q - \beta_0 - \sum_{k=1}^{K} \beta_k X_{kq}$$

so that the only two values that ε_q can take are:

$$\varepsilon_q = 1 - \beta_0 - \sum_{k=1}^{K} \beta_k X_{kq} \qquad \text{if } f_q = 1$$

$$\varepsilon_q = -\beta_0 - \sum_{k=1}^{K} \beta_k X_{kq} \qquad \text{if } f_q = 0$$

Now, since Prob $(f_q = 1) = P_q$
and Prob $(f_q = 0) = 1 - P_q$, and since one of the assumptions made about the error term is that it has an expected value of zero (i.e. $E(\varepsilon_q) = 0$), we know that:

$$E(\varepsilon_q) = (1 - \beta_0 - \sum_{k=1}^{K} \beta_k X_{kq}) P_q + (-\beta_0 - \sum_{k=1}^{K} \beta_k X_{kq})(1 - P_q) = 0$$

165

Solving for P_q gives

$$P_q = B_0 + \sum_{k=1}^{K} \beta_k X_{kq} \qquad (6.3)$$

and so $\quad 1 - P_q = 1 - \beta_0 - \sum_{k=1}^{K} \beta_k X_{kq}$

We may now calculate the variance of ε_q as follows:

$$\text{Var}(\varepsilon_q) = \text{E}(\varepsilon_q^2) = (1-\beta_0 - \sum_{k=1}^{K} \beta_k X_{kq})^2 P_q$$

$$+ (-\beta_0 - \sum_{k=1}^{K} \beta_k X_{kq})^2 (1-P_q)$$

$$\text{(using 6.3)} = (1-\beta_0 - \sum_{k=1}^{K} \beta_k X_{kq})^2 (\beta_0 + \sum_{k=1}^{K} \beta_k X_{kq})$$

$$+ (-\beta_0 - \sum_{k=1}^{K} \beta_k X_{kq})^2 (1-\beta_0 - \sum_{k=1}^{K} \beta_k X_{kq})$$

$$\text{(factoring)} = (1-\beta_0 - \sum_{k=1}^{K} \beta_k X_{kq})(\beta_0 + \sum_{k=1}^{K} \beta_k X_{kq}) \cdot$$

$$(1 - \beta_0 - \sum_{k=1}^{K} \beta_k X_{kq} + \beta_0 + \sum_{k=1}^{K} \beta_k X_{kq})$$

$$\text{so,} \quad \text{Var}(\varepsilon_q) = (1-\beta_0 - \sum_{k=1}^{K} \beta_k X_{kq})(\beta_0 + \sum_{k=1}^{K} \beta_k X_{kq})$$

$$= (1-P_q)P_q \qquad (6.4)$$

Now, clearly the variance of ε_q is <u>not constant</u> (a condition known as heteroskedasticity) but depends upon the individual observations. One can easily note that the variance will be larger the closer P_q is to one-half.

One possible solution to this problem of heteroskedasticity is known as <u>weighted least squares</u> (WLS). WLS in the present case requires one to divide each of the variables in equation (6.1), including the constant term, by the standard deviation of $\varepsilon_q (\sigma_q)$. This would result in a transformed model given by

166

$$\frac{f_q}{\sigma_q} = \beta_0 \frac{1}{\sigma_q} + \beta_1 \frac{X_{1q}}{\sigma_q} + \cdots + \beta_K \frac{X_{Kq}}{\sigma_q} + \frac{\varepsilon_q}{\sigma_q} \tag{6.5}$$

Since the error term in equation (6.5) has constant variance $(\mathrm{var}(\frac{\varepsilon_q}{\sigma_q}) = \frac{1}{\sigma^2} \mathrm{var}\,(\varepsilon_q) = \frac{\sigma_q^2}{\sigma_q^2} = 1)$, OLS estimation of the parameters of equation (6.5) will now be efficient (e.g. see Theil, 1971).

In the above, it would be preferable to use the actual standard deviation of ε_q, but as can be seen from equation (6.4), we would need to know each P_q whereas we only know which alternative the qth individual has chosen, not his probability of choice. Therefore, we must first estimate the standard deviation (or variance) of each ε_q, and then use these estimates as weights instead of the actual standard deviations as in equation (6.5). To do this, we simply apply OLS to the original specification (6.1) and then, using the estimated regression coefficient to calculate f_q as in equation (6.2), find a consistent estimate of the variance of ε_q by

$$\hat{\sigma}_q^2 = \hat{f}_q (1 - \hat{f}_q) \tag{6.6}$$

which uses the result (6.4) for the actual variance of ε_q and the fact that $\hat{f}_q$ is an estimate of P_q.

On the surface, then, it seems that the above WLS procedure solves one of the problems associated with the LPM, and that efficient estimates of the model's coefficients may be found. However, there is a serious problem associated with the estimation of variances using equation (6.6) which is not as easy to solve, and as we shall presently see, seriously weakens the LPM as a vehicle for estimation. This is that with the LPM, there is no guarantee that the estimated value $\hat{f}_q$ will be between 0 and 1. Any $\hat{f}_q$ outside this interval will result in a negative estimated $\hat{\sigma}_q^2$ which is, of course, nonsense. Arbitrarily setting any $\hat{\sigma}_q^2$ to .99 or .01 (say) for any observation where $\hat{f}_q$ is outside the unit interval is one solution to this problem, but not a particularly satisfactory one, since WLS may not be efficient in that case. WLS is actually only efficient asymptotically (i.e. as the sample size gets arbitrarily large) so that for relatively small samples it may be preferable to use OLS anyway.

The possibility of getting predicted $\hat{f}_q$'s outside the unit interval is disturbing for another reason; simply that, given the interpretation of f_q as a probability, it makes no sense to arrive at a predicted $\hat{f}_q$ of 1.3 or -0.4, for example. It has been suggested that a solution to this problem would be to estimate the model (6.1) subject to a restriction that $\hat{f}_q$ lie in the unit interval. This becomes a problem in nonlinear programming which we will not discuss here because, although the resulting estimated coefficients have smaller variances, they are not necessarily unbiased.

If we overlook all of the abovementioned problems with the LPM and use OLS or WLS to estimate the coefficients (βs) of the model, it would be useful to be able to test hypotheses about these coefficients. The problem here is that the usual testing procedures (e.g. t-tests) rely on the assumption that the ε_q in equation (6.1) are normally distributed which is equivalent to assuming that the f_q are normally distributed. This is not the case since f_q takes on only the values 0 or 1, and so the usual tests are not valid. Warner (1963, 1967) has developed tests which are valid asymptotically, but again, unless sample sizes are quite large, the results of such tests may be suspect. We will not pursue the issue further here.

From the above discussion, one may get the idea that the linear probability model is not to be recommended in a binary choice situation. Clearly, the problems with the model seem to far outweigh its advantage of simplicity. However, since it is quite simple to estimate the LPM using OLS, it may be used as a preliminary screening device to get a feel for the data before using one of the alternative models which have been developed.[1]

We began this section by assuming a binary choice situation for the linear probability model. However, Domencich & McFadden (1975: 75-80) have shown that if one takes the basic choice model (equation 3.24) derived earlier in Chapter 3 and makes some specific assumptions about the nature of V_j in that model, the result will be a model of the form given by the LPM. The assumptions on V_j are specifically that

$$V_{jq} = \ln \left[\sum_{k=1}^{K} \beta_k x_{jkq} \right] \tag{6.7}$$

$$0 \leq \sum_{k=1}^{K} \beta_k x_{jkq} \leq 1 \qquad (j=1,\ldots,J) \tag{6.8}$$

and

$$\sum_{j=1}^{J} \sum_{k=1}^{K} \beta_k x_{jkq} = 1 \tag{6.9}$$

Given these assumptions, insertion of equations (6.7 to 6.9) in equation (3.24) yields:

$$P_{iq} = \frac{\exp \left(\ln \left[\sum_{k=1}^{K} \beta_k x_{ikq} \right] \right)}{\sum_{j=1}^{J} \exp \left(\ln \left[\sum_{k=1}^{K} \beta_k x_{jkq} \right] \right)}$$

$$= \frac{\sum_{k=1}^{K} \beta_k x_{ikq}}{\sum_{j=1}^{J} \sum_{k=1}^{K} \beta_k x_{jkq}} = \sum_{k=1}^{K} \beta_k x_{ikq} \tag{6.10}$$

Formulation (6.10) is the LPM (6.1) with P_{iq} replacing f_q and is exactly (6.1) when we add an error term ε_q. Notice that equation (6.10) is not limited to a binary choice situation but holds for any $j = 1,\ldots,J$. However, it is difficult to use equation (6.10) (i.e. the LPM) in the multinomial case since the sum of estimated probabilities over alternatives for each individual must sum to one (equation 6.9), but this implies that the representative utility of one alternative (V_{jq}) depends upon the attributes of all other alternatives, contrary to the usual assumption of independence of tastes. Furthermore, the imposition of the inequality constraint (equation 6.8) provides a computational nonlinearity which implies that linear least squares is no longer applicable. It is also difficult to see how we would specify the dependent variable, f, in the situation of more than two alternatives. Given these problems with the LPM in general, other estimation procedures are seen as preferable, in particular the basic MNL model (3.24) with V_{jq} <u>not</u> defined as in equation (6.7).

6·3 Linear Logit Model and Weighted/ Generalised Least Squares Regression

We have seen in Chapter 3 that the basic MNL model may be estimated with Q individual observations using nonlinear maximum-likelihood techniques. For this reason, estimation of the MNL model (3.24) using maximum-likelihood methods is sometimes termed estimation of the <u>nonlinear logit</u> model. This terminology is used to differentiate this estimation procedure with estimation of what may be termed the <u>linear logit</u> model, to which we now turn.

Consider the binary choice case where the probability of choosing the first of two alternatives (P_1) is given by the (binary) logit model

$$P_{1q} = \exp V_{1q}/(\exp V_{1q} + \exp V_{2q}) \tag{6.11}$$

where V_{1q} and V_{2q} are again linear functions of the characteristics associated with alternatives 1 and 2 respectively. Equation (6.11) may be rewritten as

$$P_{1q} = 1/(1 + \exp - (V_{1q} - V_{2q})) \tag{6.12}$$

Hence

$$P_{1q} (1 + \exp - (V_{1q} - V_{2q})) = 1$$

so,

$$\exp - (V_{1q} - V_{2q}) = \frac{1 - P_{1q}}{P_{1q}}$$

and

$$\exp (V_{1q} - V_{2q}) = \frac{P_{1q}}{1 - P_{1q}}$$

Taking the natural logarithm of both sides, we get

$$V_{1q} - V_{2q} = \ln (P_{1q}/(1 - P_{1q}))$$

or, upon substituting for V's using equation (3.26) and assuming that a total of K variables, including alternative-specific constants, appear in the model

$$\ln \left(\frac{P_{1q}}{1 - P_{1q}}\right) = \sum_{k=1}^{K} \beta_k X_{kq} \qquad (6.13)$$

The left-hand side of equation (6.13) is known as the logit of the probability of choice, and it represents the logarithm of the odds that individual q will choose alternative 1.

An appeal of the logistic transformation of the dependent variable is that it transforms the problem of predicting probabilities within a $(0, 1)$ interval to the problem of predicting the odds of an alternative being chosen within the range of the entire real line $(-\infty \leftrightarrow +\infty)$.

Direct estimation of equation (6.13) is not possible. If P_{1q} (actually, f_{1q} is what we observe) is equal to either 0 or 1, then $P_{1q}/(1 - P_{1q})$ will equal zero or infinity and the logarithm of the odds is undefined. Thus the application of ordinary least squares (OLS) estimation to equation (6.13) where $P_{1q} = 1$ or 0 is inappropriate. We have two options:

(1)   Group data: this is only possible if observations are repeated for each value of an explanatory variable: OLS or weighted least squares (WLS) is used in estimation.

Defining $\hat{P}_1 = \frac{r_1}{n_1}$ where r_1 is number of replications (observations) choosing alternative 1 that are contained in the cell representing the particular value of the explanatory variable, and n_1 is the number of observations relevant to that particular cell;

then $\ln \left(\dfrac{r_1/n_1}{1 - r_1/n_1}\right) = \ln \left(\dfrac{r_1}{n_1 - r_1}\right) = \sum_{k=1}^{K} \beta_k X_k$ (6.14)

where X_k is the value of the independent variable for that cell. This equation, referred to as linear logit, can be estimated using OLS and will yield consistent parameter estimates when the number of repetitions for each of the levels of the Xs grows arbitrarily large. A large sample size is required to ensure approximation to a normal distribution when the dependent variable is of the form in equation (6.14). To accommodate the error

variance (heteroskedasticity) especially if the
sample is not large, we can apply WLS and weight each
cell by

$$n_1/(r_1(n_1 - r_1)) \quad \text{since} \quad \ln [r_1/(n_1 - r_1)] \quad \text{is}$$

approximately normally distributed with mean 0 and
variance

$$\sigma_1 = n_1/[(r_1(n_1 - r_1)]$$

This weight will assist when a small sample is used.
However, regardless of sample size, this approach is
suitable only when sufficient repetitions occur.
With extreme values or outliers the OLS and WLS
approaches perform poorly. As $r_1/n_1 \to 0$ or 1, σ_1
could be adjusted to accommodate this as in equation
(6.15):

$$\sigma_1 = \frac{(n_1 + 1)(n_1 + 2)}{n_1(r_1 + 1)(n_1 - r_1 + 1)} \tag{6.15}$$

However, for successful application of the approach,
given that heteroskedasticity and required
repetition can be accommodated, continuous explanatory variables would have to be categorised. This
can introduce bias because of the potentially
serious errors in variables problem. Fortunately
an appealing alternative is available, namely the
maximum likelihood estimation of the basic MNL model
outlined in Chapter 3.

(2)   Disaggregate data: in the majority of
consumer research applications, where there exists
more than one determinant of the choice of an
alternative from a choice set, only one choice is
associated with each set of explanatory variables.
The maximum-likelihood estimation procedure is
ideally suited to this task, and has the added
advantage of data economy (relatively small sample
sizes); for example 300 observations, with 10
explanatory variables with a choice split of 30 per
cent to 70 per cent. The data economy is due,
amongst other reasons, to the maintenance of the
decision-making unit as the unit of analysis, rather
than an aggregate unit as in the grouped case,
hence increasing the amount of variance to be
explained and maintaining maximum relevant information. The aggregation error need not, however, be
serious with grouped data. It is very much
dependent on the nature of policies being investigated - in particular the extent of the homogeneous

effect across the members of the aggregated unit of analysis (see Chapter 7 or McFadden & Reid, 1975). Because a unique maximum always exists for a logit model (McFadden, 1974), maximum-likelihood estimation is appealing. The additional cost in computer time is more than compensated for by the practical advantages of not having to group observations. This also greatly increases the flexibility of data manipulation.

The above discussion notwithstanding, we can extend the linear logit model to the case of more than two alternatives quite easily. Assuming J alternatives, we can express the logarithm of the odds of choosing any alternative compared to any base alternative (arbitrarily, alternative 1) by

$$\ln \left(\frac{P_{iq}}{P_{1q}}\right) = \sum_{k=1}^{K} \beta_{kil} X_{kq} \tag{6.16}$$

There are $J - 1$ equations of the form (6.16) with alternative 1 as a base, the parameters of which (i.e. the β_{kil}) reflect the effect of the kth explanatory variable on the choice of alternative i versus alternative 1. In order to examine other binary pairs, for example i versus j, we need only look at binary pairs (i, 1) and (j, 1) and combine them as follows.

$$\ln \left(\frac{P_{iq}}{P_{1q}}\right) + \ln \left(\frac{P_{1q}}{P_{jq}}\right) = \sum_{k=1}^{K} \beta_{kil} X_{kq} + \sum_{k=1}^{K} \beta_{k1j} X_{kq}$$

$$\ln \left(\frac{P_{iq}}{P_{1q}} \times \frac{P_{1q}}{P_{jq}}\right) = \ln \left(\frac{P_{iq}}{P_{jq}}\right) = \sum_{k=1}^{K} (\beta_{kil} + \beta_{k1j}) X_{kq} \tag{6.17}$$

Now, using the general format (6.16), we can also write this as

$$\ln \left(\frac{P_{iq}}{P_{jq}}\right) = \sum_{k=1}^{K} \beta_{kij} X_{kq} \tag{6.18}$$

and hence, $\beta_{kij} = \beta_{kil} + \beta_{k1j}$, so that $\beta_{kil} = \beta_{kij} - \beta_{k1j}$. Theil (1970: 119) has noted that β_{kil} above may be written $\beta_{kil} = \beta_{ki} - \beta_{k1}$ so that equation (6.16) may be written

$$\ln \left(\frac{P_{iq}}{P_{1q}}\right) = \sum_{k=1}^{K} (\beta_{ki} - \beta_{k1}) X_{kq} \tag{6.19}$$

173

As the above analysis shows, the linear logit model depends on analysis of the difference in response from some base alternative (in our case, alternative 1). Furthermore, we may impose initialisation constraints on β_{kl} such that $\beta_{kl} = 0$ for all k, without loss of information. Therefore, the basic model becomes

$$\ln \left(\frac{P_{iq}}{P_{lq}}\right) = \sum_{k=1}^{K} \beta_{ki} X_{kq} \qquad (6.20)$$

Adopting notation used by Wrigley (1976), let us define $\ln (P_{iq}/P_{lq})$ as $L_{il/q}$. In order to estimate the parameters of equation (6.20), we must first categorise the explanatory variables (Xs), assuming that the variables are continuously measured. For example, if there are two Xs, X_1 and X_2, we might group X_1 into ten sets and X_2 into five sets so that there are 50 possible combinations of X_1 and X_2. We may then find the frequency of occurrence of any alternative for each cell in a 10 x 5 contingency table and use these as estimates of P_{iq}'s in $L_{il/g}$. Hence we now refer to group g instead of individual q. Denoting these frequencies as $fr_{i/g}$, the estimatable version of equation (6.20) becomes

$$\tilde{L}_{il/g} = \ln \left(\frac{fr_{i/g}}{fr_{1/g}}\right) = \sum_{k=1}^{K} \beta_{ki} X_{kg} + (\tilde{L}_{il/g} - L_{il/g}) \quad (6.21)$$

where the model is specified in terms of group g instead of individual q and where the last term is an error term reflecting the fact that the observed relative frequencies only approximate the relative probabilities in equation (6.20). J - 1 equations are implied by equation (6.21).

   To illustrate the estimation procedure, suppose there is a five alternative choice scenario (alternatives numbered 0 through 4). For the 5-choice situation, we can write the following equations (ignoring the distinction between P and fr at present and dropping the subscript g):

$$\ln (P_0/P_1) = \beta_0 + \beta_{10} X_1 + \ldots + \beta_{K0} X_K$$

$$\ln (P_2/P_1) = \beta_2 + \beta_{12} X_1 + \ldots + \beta_{K2} X_K$$

$$\ln (P_3/P_1) = \beta_3 + \beta_{13}X_1 + \cdots + \beta_{K3}X_K \qquad (6.22)$$

$$\ln (P_4/P_1) = \beta_4 + \beta_{14}X_1 + \cdots + \beta_{K4}X_K$$

Although one could continue with other pairs P_0/P_2, P_0/P_3, P_0/P_4, P_2/P_3, P_2/P_4, P_3/P_4, a 'circulatory' condition guarantees sufficiency by considering only the number of equations where all response categories are different from a selected base or denominator category, arbitrarily selected in this case as alternative 1. The system of equations is constrained so that the sum of the probabilities is equal to 1 for any given group.

Some adjustments to the estimatable model are required to allow for the error introduced by grouping observations. We have already mentioned the adjustment ($\tilde{L}_g - L_g$) to account for the use of relative frequencies as estimates of probabilities. However, the error variances between cells are not constant (a requirement for ordinary least squares regression); hence an adjustment is required to remove heteroskedasticity. Theil (1970: 317) has demonstrated that these error variances take the asymptotic form:

$$1/(n_g P_g (1 - P_g))$$

Thus in estimation, given the knowledge of heteroskedasticity, the ordinary least squares estimators of $\beta_0, \beta_1 \cdots, \beta_K$ are replaced by another set of weighted least squares estimators using weights of the form:

$$w_g = n_g F_g (1 - F_g) \qquad (6.23)$$

where $\quad F_g =$ relative frequency (n_g/Q).

These weights imply that as the number of observations n_g in a cell increases, more weight is allocated to that cell in the estimation procedure. Given n_g, however, as F_g approaches 0 or 1, less weight is allocated because $\tilde{L}_g$ takes large negative or positive values and is thus highly sensitive to small changes in F_g. The system of weights thus effectively excludes a cell g in which the observed relative frequency is 0 or 1. Berkson (1953) proposed alternative working values in order to reduce information loss:

$$1/rn_g \text{ to replace } 0 \text{ when } F_g = 0$$

$$1 - 1/rn_g \text{ to replace } 1 \text{ when } F_g = 1$$

where r is the number of response categories.

So far, the model is as follows:

$$\tilde{L}_{01g} = \ell n \; (\frac{F_0}{F_1})_g = w_g \beta_0 + w_g X_{1g0} \beta_{10} + \cdots + w_g X_{Kg0} \beta_{K0}$$
$$+ (\tilde{L}_{01g} - L_{01g}),$$

(with the 0 subscript dropped for X if the X-variable is generic)

$$\tilde{L}_{21g} = \ell n \; (\frac{F_2}{F_1})_g = w_g \beta_2 + w_g X_{1g2} \beta_{12} + \cdots + w_g X_{Kg2} \beta_{K2}$$
$$+ (\tilde{L}_{21g} - L_{21g})$$

(with the 2 subscript dropped for X if X is generic)

$$\tilde{L}_{31g} = \ell n \; (\frac{F_3}{F_1})_g = w_g \beta_3 + w_g X_{1g3} + \cdots + w_g X_{Kg3} \beta_{K3}$$
$$+ (\tilde{L}_{31g} - L_{31g})$$

(with the 3 subscript dropped for X if X is generic)

$$\tilde{L}_{41g} = \ell n \; (\frac{F_4}{F_1})_g = w_g \beta_4 + w_g X_{1g4} \beta_{14} + \cdots + w_g X_{Kg4} \beta_{K4}$$
$$+ (\tilde{L}_{41g} - L_{41g})$$

(with the 4 subscript dropped for X if X is generic) and the w_g matrix is

$$n_g \begin{bmatrix} f_{0j}(1-f_{0j}) & -f_{0j}f_{2j} & -f_{0j}f_{3j} & -f_{0j}f_{4j} \\ -f_{2j}f_{0j} & f_{2j}(1-f_{2j}) & -f_{2j}f_{3j} & -f_{2j}f_{4j} \\ -f_{3j}f_{0j} & -f_{3j}f_{2j} & f_{3j}(1-f_{3j}) & -f_{3j}f_{4j} \\ -f_{4j}f_{0j} & -f_{4j}f_{2j} & -f_{4j}f_{3j} & f_{4j}(1-f_{4j}) \end{bmatrix}$$

where n_g is the number of observations in cell g
and f_{2g}, for example, is the relative frequency of
the choice of response category 2 in cell g.

The estimates of βs are obtained (in matrix
form) by <u>generalised</u> least squares (see Theil, 1971
for a more detailed explanation).

$$\hat{\underline{\beta}} = (X'w^{-1}\underline{X})^{-1}\underline{X}'w^{-1}\tilde{\underline{L}} \qquad (6.24)$$

The estimated probabilities are then given by

$$\hat{P}_{0g} = \exp \hat{L}_{0g}/(1 + \exp \hat{L}_{0g} + \exp \hat{L}_{2g} + \exp \hat{L}_{3g} + \exp \hat{L}_{4g})$$

$$\hat{P}_{1g} = 1/(1 + \exp \hat{L}_{0g} + \sum_{i=2}^{4} \exp \hat{L}_{ig})$$

$$\hat{P}_{2g} = \exp \hat{L}_{2g}/(1 + \exp \hat{L}_{0g} + \sum_{i=2}^{4} \exp \hat{L}_{ig}) \qquad (6.25)$$

$$\hat{P}_{3g} = \exp \hat{L}_{3g}/(1 + \exp \hat{L}_{0g} + \sum_{i=2}^{4} \exp \hat{L}_{ig})$$

$$\hat{P}_{4g} = \exp \hat{L}_{4g}/(1 + \exp \hat{L}_{0g} + \sum_{i=2}^{4} \exp \hat{L}_{ig})$$

where $\hat{L}_g = \hat{\beta} + \hat{\beta}_1 X_{g1} + \hat{\beta}_2 X_{g2} + \dots$ (note that the
βs are obtained from a generalised least squares
regression with weights as defined above). Since
the model is estimated using relative frequencies
as estimates of probabilities, then the output
should be interpreted as 'estimates of estimates of
probability'. A comparison between $\tilde{L}_g$, the
observed logit based on relative frequencies, and
$\hat{L}_g$, the predicted logit, appropriately weighted,
provides a basis for testing the predictive
capability of the model. That is

$$\sum_g (\tilde{L}_g - \hat{L}_g)^2 w_q \qquad (6.26)$$

is a goodness-of-fit statistic asymptotically
distributed as χ^2 with (J-K) degrees of freedom.

At this point we re-emphasise the point that
the linear logit method is inferior to nonlinear
maximum-likelihood logit, especially in situations
when some or all of the explanatory variables are
quantitative (i.e. measured on a continuous scale).

177

This is so since a loss of information as to intercell variation occurs in the grouping process. However, linear logit is quite useful in experimental situations where the Xs can be controlled by the investigator. On the assumption that the majority of situations faced by the applied choice modeller are not of an experimental nature, we leave linear logit at this point to pursue various estimation methodologies more closely related to the basic multinomial logit model (equation 3.24). An extended discussion of linear logit (or log-linear models) using contingency tables is given in Payne (1977) and Goodman (1970, 1972). Oum (1979) has recently outlined some of the implausible behavioural interpretations that are associated with many specifications of the independent variables in a linear-logit model, which adds further doubt to the value of pursuing this modelling approach.

6·4 Modified Logit (or Dogit) Model and Maximum-Likelihood Estimation

An alternative logit formulation with potentially less restrictive assumptions on the relationship between alternatives i and j is the dogit model, proposed by Gaudry & Dagenais (1979) and recently tested using both aggregate cross-sectional and time series data by Gaudry & Wills (1979). The essential model is written (ignoring q subscripts for simplicity)

$$P_i = \frac{\exp V_i + \theta_i \sum_{j=1}^{J} \exp V_j}{(1 + \sum_j \theta_j) \sum_{j=1}^{J} \exp V_j} \qquad (6.27)$$

where P_i and V_j are defined as before and θ_i is a nonnegative (i.e. $\theta_i \geq 0$) parameter associated with the ith alternative. It is easy to show (an exercise left to the reader) that P_i falls between zero and one and that $\sum_{j=1}^{J} P_j = 1$, so that equation (6.27) satisfies the simple requirements of a probability distribution. Furthermore, equation (6.27) represents the basic logit model (3.24) when all θ_i are identically equal to zero.

A potentially useful aspect of the dogit model is that it allows some pairs of alternatives to exhibit the independence from irrelevant-alternative property which we discussed in detail in Chapter 5, while other pairs may not exhibit the IIA property. In other words, the model dodges the a priori necessity of imposing IIA as basic logit does and hence the name dogit. To see this, recall that IIA requires that for alternatives i and m the ratio of P_i to P_m be independent of any other alternatives. Using equation (6.27), this ratio is

$$\frac{P_i}{P_m} = \frac{\exp V_i + \theta_i \sum_j \exp V_j}{\exp V_m + \theta_m \sum_j \exp V_j} \tag{6.28}$$

since the denominators from equation (6.27) cancel. Clearly equation (6.28) depends on all the alternatives except in special circumstances, so that generally IIA is not a property of the model.

These special cases may be derived as follows. Suppose this ratio remains constant after changing the value of one of the variables associated with some other alternative (other than i or m) or introducing (deleting) another alternative. Then, the ratio may be written

$$\frac{P_i}{P_m} = \frac{\exp V_i + \theta_i \sum_j \exp V_j^*}{\exp V_m + \theta_m \sum_j \exp V_j^*} \tag{6.29}$$

where $\sum_j \exp V_j^*$ refers to the revised representative utility expressions in the sense that either the sum is over one more (or less) alternative or one of the Xs in an existing alternative (not i or m) has been altered. Now equation (6.28) and equation (6.29) are equal if either (a) θ_i and θ_m are both zero; (b) $\theta_i/\theta_m = \exp V_i/\exp V_m$ (since the $\sum$ terms then cancel after substitution for θ_i in the denominator and a little algebra); or (c) $\sum_j \exp V_j = \sum_j \exp V_j^*$. Hence, IIA holds for any pair of alternatives for which any of the above conditons hold (particularly (a) which seems more likely to hold in practice) while for other pairs, IIA is not required to hold. The model in this respect is more flexible than the basic multinomial logit model developed previously in Chapter 3.

In their discussion of dogit, Gaudry & Dagenais simply stated the model and proceeded to examine its properties, as well as provide interpretations in terms of aggregate share models. At about the same time as their work (actually 1977), Ben-Akiva (1977a) was examining the problem of choice-set generation processes which we discussed in Chapter 4.2. One of the cases examined by Ben-Akiva provide a behavioural interpretation for the dogit model in terms of 'captivity' to an alternative, and so the dogit model is also known as the capture model.

Suppose that an individual is either captive to one of J alternatives or chooses from the complete choice set which we shall call A. Then, there are J + 1 potential choice sets given by

$$\{C\} = \{1, 2, 3, \ldots, J, A\}.$$

Now, suppose μ_i is a nonnegative parameter relating to the likelihood that the decision maker is captive to the ith alternative (recall the discussion of u-values - equation (5.8) - in Chapter 5). Furthermore, suppose we arbitrarily assign a parameter, namely the integer 1, to represent the likelihood of the decision maker choosing from A (a process which, in effect, normalises the μ_i). Then the probability that an individual is captive to choice i is $\mu_i/(1 + \Sigma_j \mu_j) = \mu_i/(1 + \mu)$, and the probability of choosing from the entire choice set A is $1/(1 + \mu)$.

Using equation (4.2) repeated here for convenience

$$P_i = \sum_C P(C) \, P(i \mid C)$$

the probability of choosing i is (assuming the probability of choosing i from the choice set A is given by the basic MNL model (3.24))

$$P_i = \frac{\mu_i}{1 + \mu} \, (1) + \frac{1}{1 + \mu} \left(\frac{\exp V_i}{\sum_j \exp V_j} \right) \tag{6.30}$$

or

$$P_i = \frac{\mu_i \sum_j \exp V_j + \exp V_i}{(1 + \mu) \sum_j \exp V_j} \tag{6.31}$$

which is exactly the same as equation (6.27) with μ_i replacing θ_i. Therefore, the θ_i in the dogit model may be interpreted as representing the degree of captivity in the choice decision in the sense that the smaller the θ_i (μ_i), the less likely individuals will be captive to alternative i.

Gaudry & Wills (1979) point out that if P_i in equation (6.30) is interpreted as a market share as opposed to a choice probability, then $\mu_i/(1 + \mu)$ may be interpreted as the share of income spent to satisfy basic needs for commodity i and so $1 - \sum_i \mu_i/(1 + \mu) = 1/(1 + \mu)$ is the share of discretionary income left over. If this left-over share is distributed among the various commodities according to a logit specification $(\exp V_i / \sum_{j=1}^{J} \exp V_j)$, the sum of basic plus discretionary expenditure on good i is given by equation (6.30). The link here between the idea of 'basic need' and captivity to an alternative is obvious.

Gaudry & Dagenais (1979) provide an alternative interpretation of the θ_i in equation (6.27) by first looking at the elasticities for dogit. Using techniques similar to those in Chapter 3, the elasticity of probability of choosing alternative i with respect to a variable related to alternative j (i.e. in V_j) can be written (for dogit)

$$E_{X_{kj}}^{P_i} = \beta_k X_{kj} \left(\frac{(\delta_{ij} + \theta_i) \exp V_j}{\exp V_i + \theta_i \sum_j \exp V_j} - \frac{\exp V_j}{\sum_j \exp V_j} \right) \quad (6.32)$$

where $\delta_{ij} = 1$ if $i = j$, 0 otherwise. These are identical to elasticities in the MNL model except for the first term in brackets (see equation 3.43). For $i = j$ (i.e. direct elasticity), this first term in brackets can be written

$$\frac{1 + \theta_i}{1 + \theta_i \left(\dfrac{\sum_j \exp V_j}{\exp V_i} \right)} \quad (6.33)$$

which is clearly less than one (the value in the logit model) since

$\sum_j \exp V_j / \exp V_i$ is always positive and greater than one. Hence, the elasticity will be smaller than if the logit case held (i.e. $\theta_i = 0$), so that θ_i is a measure of an 'income' effect which reduces the substitution effect inherent in the logit model. Gaudry & Dagenais (1979) further show that this effect is not large enough to offset completely the substitution effect and hence change the sign of the elasticity.

In the same spirit, the case of $i \neq j$ (i.e. cross elasticities), the first term in brackets of equation (6.32) is positive (zero in logit) so that the effect of dogit is to increase the cross effect as compared to the logit specification. It can also be shown that the term in brackets is always negative in this case and so alternatives must still, as in logit, act as substitutes.

Although dogit seems to provide a possible viable alternative to the MNL model which does not require the modeller to impose IIA, to our knowledge, no empirical applications of dogit in individual choice situations have been carried out at the time of writing. This is one area where we feel an examination of dogit versus nested logit and probit (to be discussed in the next section) may prove fruitful since all these techniques in some way bypass the IIA requirement of basic MNL. We eagerly await the outcome of such studies should they appear.

6·5 Multinomial Covariance Probit and Numerical Approximation Techniques

Another alternative to the MNL model is the multinomial probit (MNP) model which is more general than the MNL model yet involves considerable computational complexity. Hence, up to now, the MNL model in its various forms (BMNL, SL, NL - see Table 4.1) has been used for most individual discrete choice situations. Recent developments in algorithms used to estimate the MNP model (Lerman & Manski, 1976; Hausman & Wise, 1978; Daganzo, 1979, 1980) have made it computationally feasible. However, it is felt that, in the near future at least, developments in the nested logit (Chapter 4) model will keep logit-type estimators in the forefront of choice modelling. In this section we will outline the basic MNP model, compare it with the basic MNL model and refer briefly to the various estimation algorithms that have been suggested. Given the recent empirical evidence by Horowitz (1979, 1980) on the major sources of error in logit modelling (see also Section 4.5.1 and Appendix C), the analyst now has considerable advice on ways of reducing the errors associated with using the basic logit model, to enable continuing use of this model (or the sequential logit model if a recursive structure - see Table 4.1), rather than having to go to more complex models such as the MNP model. It is increasingly apparent that careful collection and application of disaggregate data, given a knowledge of the choice set, will reduce the major sources of error in current use of logit models (i.e. error due to omission of relevant attributes, synthesised group mean levels for attributes, and random parameter variation). Random parameter variation, a source of error that the MNP model can accommodate,[2] can be accounted for in a logit model by introducing additional variables that account for taste variations in the sampled population and/or stratifying the data set and running separate logit models of sampled subsets of the population (see Chapter 7.2).

The basic choice model in Chapter 3 was developed by using the concept of random utility. Specifically, it was assumed that the utility of the ith alternative to the qth individual, U_{iq}, was the sum of a representative component, V_{iq}, and a random component, ε_{iq} (see equation 3.3 which is repeated here).

$$U_{iq} = V_{iq} + \varepsilon_{iq} \qquad (6.34)$$

The random ε_{iq} were assumed to be independent and identically distributed (IID) as Weibull (i.e. double exponential, equation 3.14) random variates. Under this assumption and the assumption that an individual would choose that alternative yielding the largest utility, the basic MNL choice model equation (3.24) was derived.

The MNP model relaxes the assumption of IID random terms in equation (6.34) so that there may be some covariance between alternatives i and j.[3] This results in the relaxation of the IIA condition (Chapter 5). The IID assumption is relaxed by substituting the multivariate normal distribution for the Weibull as the distribution of the ε_{iq}.

To see this, let us examine the utility expression (6.34) more closely. The term V_{iq} is assumed to be linear in parameters such that

$$V_{iq} = \sum_{k=1}^{K} \beta_{kiq} X_{kiq} \text{ (see equation 3.26)}.$$ In the MNL model β_{kiq} is assumed to be constant for all individuals q so that the q subscript can be dropped from the βs. In the MNP model, however, we assume that $\beta_{kiq} = \beta_{ki} + \mu_{kq}$ so that each individual's response to the variable X_{ki} is allowed to vary around some mean response β_{ki}. The deviation terms, μ_{kq}, are assumed to be distributed normally across individuals. This leads to a revised utility expression of the form

$$U_{iq} = \sum_{k=1}^{K} \beta_{ki} X_{kiq} + (\sum_{k=1}^{K} \mu_{kq} X_{kiq} + \varepsilon_{iq}) \qquad (6.35)$$

which now has a more complex error term (in parenthesis). The utility expression for some other alternative, say alternative j, will also contain these μ_{kq} terms so that the overall error terms in the utility expressions are correlated as opposed to the independence found in the MNL model.

Along with allowing taste variation across individuals, by introducing the terms μ_{kq}, the MNP model assumes that the ε_{iq} are distributed as multivariate normal across alternatives, in particular, allowing the possibility of some covariance between alternatives. This is much more general than the basic MNL model which requires the assumption that alternatives are independent (i.e. covariances are zero). Hence, IIA is not a general property of MNP models (although it could be if one specifies all covariances to be zero - a model known as independent probit; see Hausman & Wise, 1978, for more details).

It would seem that the MNP model is to be preferred to the basic MNL model in that it allows for taste variation across consumers which the MNL does not, and that it allows for covariance between alternatives, again as the basic MNL model does not. The major reason that applied choice modellers have not embraced the MNP model as their usual estimation method is that the model is very difficult to estimate. Indeed, until recently, only binary probit was computationally feasible. The difficulty

lies in the J choice situation, where the MNP model
necessitates the evaluation of a multiple integral
of dimension J-1 which cannot be reduced to an
analytical expression. Manski & Lerman (1977) have
developed a simulation procedure (see also Albright,
Lerman & Manski, 1977). Daganzo, Bouthelier & Sheffi
(1977) suggest an approximation technique based on
work by Clark (1961) on approximating the distribution of the maximum of a set of random variables,
and Hausman & Wise (1978) discuss a maximum-
likelihood technique using a modification of an
algorithm introduced by Owen (1956) to obtain
likelihood values.

Each of these approaches has some merit and
further work may lead to an efficient algorithm for
future use. However, even if this eventuates, an
additional difficulty with the MNP model is that
there are more parameters to estimate. Not only are
there K βs, as in the MNL, but the $K(K + 1)/2$
individual elements of the covariance matrix for the
random taste parameters, μ_{kq}, and the $J(J + 1)/2$
individual elements of the covariance matrix for the
ϵs. This very quickly increases the computational
burden. For example, if J = 4 and K = 5 (not a
particularly large choice problem), there will be
5 + 10 + 15 = 30 parameters to estimate as compared
to 5 with the basic MNL (the common variance of the
ϵs need not be estimated in MNL). There is scope
to impose a priori beliefs as to whether the
covariances between alternatives are zero, thereby
reducing the number of parameters, but we are still
left with quite a few more than in the MNL model.

Fischer & Nagin (1980) have suggested that the
additional computational burden imposed by MNP is
justified on the basis of the richer information
that it provides as to the choice process. We are
not in a position to judge the general appropriateness of this assertion here; we can only contrast
this with Horowitz's conclusions given above for an
empirical comparison of basic logit and covariate
probit. However, a comparison of MNP and more
general logit models (e.g. nested logit, dogit),
would be particularly helpful in reaching a
conclusion on this matter. In the meantime, we will
concentrate in this book on the MNL model, and refer
the interested reader to the recent book by Daganzo
(1979) for more detail on the MNP model.

6·6 Functional Form — The Box-Cox and Box-Tukey Transformations

The representative component of utility, V_{iq}, was assumed to be linear in parameters such that

$$V_{iq} = \sum_{k=1}^{K} \beta_{ki} X_{kiq} \qquad (6.36)$$

The Xs are variables which relate to the utility of the ith alternative. Some of these variables may be qualitative in nature and hence not be directly measurable, so are normally entered as dummy variables (e.g. the variable is set equal to one if a certain characteristic is present, zero otherwise). Other variables may be measurable e.g. cost, time, income, etc.) and hence the investigator must choose how to enter these variables in equation (6.36). In other words, equation (6.36) would be more correctly specified as

$$V_{iq} = \sum_{k=1}^{K} \beta_{ki} f_{ki}(X_{kiq}) \qquad (6.37)$$

which is still linear in parameters but where we explicitly note that the functional form of the Xs is somewhat arbitrary. The usual practice is to enter the Xs in their absolute form so that say a cost variable will enter equation (6.37) in direct monetary terms (as opposed, for example, to logarithmic or reciprocal terms). This practice will be of no particular consequence unless estimated elasticities and/or probabilities from the estimation of a choice model are sensitive to the functional forms chosen. If theory cannot adequately tell the modeller what function form to choose for the Xs (although see Section 4.5), an investigation of the effect of different functional forms on choice model estimates seems warranted.

One class of power transformations examined by Anscombe & Tukey (1954), Tukey (1957), Box & Tidwell (1962), Box & Cox (1964), Zarembka (1974) and Spitzer (1978) is quite useful in this regard. Before proceeding to the use of this transform in the MNL model, we shall briefly outline its main features.

The basic Box-Cox transformation which results in a generalised functional form can be defined by considering a positive variable X which has been transformed such that

$$
X^{(\lambda)} = \begin{cases} (X^\lambda - 1)/\lambda & \text{if } \lambda \neq 0 \\ \ln X & \text{if } \lambda = 0 \end{cases} \tag{6.38}
$$

That is, as long as the parameter λ is nonzero, we define the transformed variable $X^{(\lambda)}$ as $(X^\lambda - 1)/\lambda$. But since it can be shown that as λ approaches zero, $(X^\lambda - 1)/\lambda$ approaches the natural logarithm of X, we define $X^{(\lambda)}$ as $\ln X$ at $\lambda = 0$ so that the transformation is continuous for all possible values of λ.

Now defining $f_{ki}(X_{kiq})$ in equation (6.37) using equation (6.38), we get

$$
V_{iq} = \sum_{k=1}^{K} \beta_{ki} X_{kiq}^{(\lambda_k)} \tag{6.39}
$$

It is not difficult to see that if $\lambda_1 = \lambda_2 = \ldots = \lambda_K = 1$, equation (6.39) reduces to the simple linear function (6.36) while if all λs are 0, a log-linear form results where all Xs enter in logarithmic form. Therefore, it appears that the usual linear and log-linear forms are simply special cases of the generalised form (6.39).

The basic Box-Cox transform given by equation (6.38) was defined for a _positive_ variable X. The question arises as to what can be done if the researcher's model contains one or more variables which take on _negative_ values. A more general transformation, named the Box-Tukey transform (apparently named by Gaudry & Wills (1978)) is defined as

$$
(X + \mu)^{(\lambda)} = \begin{cases} ((X + \mu)^\lambda - 1)/\lambda & \text{if } \lambda \neq 0 \\ \ln (X + \mu) & \text{if } \lambda = 0 \end{cases} \tag{6.40}
$$

where $X + \mu > 0$. In other words, the new parameter μ is simply a location parameter (as opposed to the power parameter λ) chosen to assure that $X + \mu$ is greater than zero for all observations. Gaudry & Wills (1978) have analysed this transform in the context of travel demand models but most empirical work has concentrated on the Box-Cox transform which is simply a special case of equation (6.40) with μ set equal to zero.

The use of the Box-Cox (or Box-Tukey) transform in choice models is reasonably straightforward although, as yet, very few investigations have chosen to consider investigating the effects of functional form on estimation results. Hensher & Johnson (1979) using disaggregate data on choice of mode to work (car vs. train) in Sydney have examined the functional form of cost and travel time as they enter a linear probability model using the Box-Cox transform with all λs constrained to be equal. Their results imply that estimated elasticities are sensitive to the value of λ chosen. Gaudry & Wills (1978) have used the Box-Tukey transform in a MNL model using aggregate data on mode of travel between city pairs in Canada with results also confirming that the functional form is important to the values of estimated elasticities.

In the basic MNL choice model, if we specify that all λs are equal in equation (6.39), the elasticities become

$$E_{X_{kj}}^{P_i} = [\delta_{ij} - P_j] \, X_{kj} \beta_k (X + \mu)^{\lambda-1} \tag{6.41}$$

where δ_{ij} is again equal to 1 if $i = j$ and 0 otherwise, and where we have included the location parameter μ from the Box-Tukey transform (6.40) since the Box-Cox transform is only a special case of this. It is clear, then, that elasticities are dependent upon the values of λ (and μ), although in some situations there may be little change in actual estimated elasticities since as λs change, so too do estimated βs because they are coefficients of a different (transformed) variable when λ is changed.

In order to determine which λ is optimal (assuming all quantitative Xs are transformed by the same λ), the MNL model is estimated using different λ values in the definition of V_{iq} and then the estimate of λ is selected which results in the maximum of the maximised likelihood functions.[4] One can then test using a likelihood-ratio criteria whether the model with optimal λ is different from the model with λ = 1 or λ = 0, the usual cases met in practice. This can be done also, with the parameter μ or for λ and μ simultaneously. The easiest way to see this is by looking at a simple example. Consider a mode of travel to work choice where the individual has the choice of either car or train as the means of travel and where the variables influencing the choice are total in-vehicle time, walk time, wait time, total in-vehicle cost and parking cost. We shall assume that the variables are generic except for parking cost which is specific to car. Further, we shall define V_{iq} using the general Box-Tukey transform (6.40) so that

$$V_{1q} = \beta_0 + \sum_{j=1}^{4} \beta_j (x_{j1} + \mu)^{(\lambda)} + \beta_5 (x_{51} + \mu)^{(\lambda)}$$

and

$$V_{2q} = \sum_{j=1}^{4} \beta_j (x_{j2} + \mu)^{(\lambda)} \qquad (6.42)$$

where 1 = car, 2 = train, X_{ji}, $j = 1,\ldots,4$, $i = 1,2$ are in-vehicle time, walk time, wait time and in-vehicle cost, X_5 is car parking cost and we have included an alternative-specific constant for the car mode (β_0 in V_{1q}).

The data used for this illustration was collected in the northern suburbs of Sydney, Australia, in 1971 and consisted of 332 observations on the variables described. Hensher & Johnson (1979) have examined a subset of the data using a Box-Cox transformation in a linear probability model and found that estimated elasticities are sensitive to functional form (i.e. choice of λ). We have estimated a basic MNL model using various values of λ and μ in the definitions of the V_{iq} (6.42). The values of the maximised log-likelihood functions at various λ, μ combinations are given in Table 6.1.

TABLE 6·1 : Values of the Maximised Log–Likelihood Functions at Various $\lambda . \mu$ Combinations

λ \ μ	.001	10	30	60	90
1.0	-151.65	-151.65	-151.65	-151.65	-151.65
0.5	-149.93	-149.68	-150.01	-150.35	-150.58
0.0	-155.50	-149.67	-149.29	-149.51	-149.97
-0.5	-164.05	-151.92	-149.54	-149.12	-149.27
-1.0	-175.30	-156.49	-150.81	*	*

* Failed to converge after 25 iterations

189

The maximum value for the log-likelihood function occurs at a value of $\lambda = -0.5$ and $\mu = 60$. To test whether this optimum value of λ and μ is statistically different from any (λ,μ) pair a chi-square test with one degree of freedom can be used. The statistic is minus two times the difference in the likelihood functions. Table 6.2 contains these calculated chi-square statistics based on the null hypothesis that the optimal values of λ and μ (i.e. -0.5 and 60) are the actual values of λ and μ. One should note that the smallest value of μ used is .001 since the Box-Tukey transform is not defined for $\mu = 0$ when some observations of X can take on zero values as they do here (e.g. parking cost).

TABLE 6·2 :   Chi – Square Statistics for Hypothesis that $\lambda = -0.5$, $\mu = 60$

λ \ μ	.001	10	30	60	90
1.0	5.06	5.06	5.06	5.06	5.06
0.5	1.62	1.12	1.78	2.46	2.92
0.0	12.76	1.10	0.34	0.78	1.70
-0.5	29.86	5.60	0.84	0.00	0.30
-1.0	52.36	14.74	3.38	*	*

* Failed to converge after 25 iterations

Since the critical points for the chi-square distribution with one degree of freedom are 6.635 at the 1 per cent level and 3.841 at the 5 per cent level, the usual specification of $\lambda = 1$ is significantly different from the optimal $\lambda = -0.5$, $\mu = 60$ at the 5 per cent level of significance. We note here that when $\lambda = 1$, μ has no effect since μ is simply a linear translation of the variables at $\lambda = 1$ and has no effect on the likelihood surface. It is useful to examine the differences in estimated elasticities arising from the various combinations of λ and μ. These are given in Table 6.3 for the direct elasticity of probability of choosing train with respect to train in-vehicle time using the sample enumeration approach discussed in Chapter 3.

Inspection of Table 6.3 suggests quite a lot of difference in the estimated elasticities for various (λ,μ) combinations. Furthermore, there is more than 25 per cent difference between the elasticity estimate at the optimal (λ,μ) point and the usual $\lambda = 1$ specification most investigators use by default. This difference most likely is due to the

TABLE 6·3 : **Estimated Direct Elasticities of Probability of Train Choice with Respect to Train In–vehicle Time**

λ \ μ	.001	10	30	60	90
1.0	-.274	-.274	-.274	-.274	-.274
0.5	-.193	-.221	-.238	-.249	-.254
0.0	-.079	-.161	-.200	-.223	-.234
-0.5	-.026	-.098	-.163	-.197	-.214
-1.0	-.101	-.040	-.128	*	*

fact that with $\lambda = 1$, the utility expression is misspecified according to the chi-square criterion and that $\lambda = -0.5$ and $\mu = 60$ more correctly specifies utility. Incorrect functional form would suggest in this example an elasticity of in-vehicle train time that was too high so that decreasing train travel time would not have such a large effect as one would expect if $\lambda = 1$ were used.

Similar results could be stated for the other direct and cross elasticities estimated for this model. Since our purpose is illustrative only, we will not present any more empirical results (see Hensher & Johnson, 1980, for further discussion).

NOTES — CHAPTER 6

1. Another use frequently made of the LPM (e.g. Struyk, 1976) is as a mechanism for comparing alternative specifications of the attribute set defined in the utility expression, where prediction is not an issue.

2. Horowitz (1980) warns the analyst that the Clark Numerical approximation method (see text) used in the probit programs developed by Daganzo and Lerman & Manski for computing choice probabilities appears capable of making substantial errors in random parameter models.

3. This assumption was partially relaxed in the nested logit model (see Table 4.1).

4. Alternatively, we may maximise the likelihood function with respect to βs and λs simultaneously a preferable approach theoretically but computationally quite burdensome (see Spitzer, 1978).

CHAPTER 7

Other Analytical and Empirical Issues

7·1 Introduction

The preceding chapters have emphasised the underlying choice theory, alternative decision structures, the range of statistical techniques, and some important tests for possible violation of a central assumption of the basic choice model. The present chapter, in contrast, is concerned with data issues. There are at least three issues of central concern in the empirical estimation and application of individual choice models; these are the aggregation issue,[1] the potential for transferring the coefficients of models in space and time, and the design of the sample and selection procedure. Experience has demonstrated that the predictive ability and cost of a model are sensitive to the nature of the data, especially its level of aggregation prior to estimation and the composition of the sample in relation to the sampled population. The three issues are discussed in the following sections of this chapter. They are closely related; for example the transferability issue is concerned with using choice models estimated on one sampled population to make predictions about other populations; the less spatially biased (for example) is the data unit the greater the likelihood, ceteris paribus, that the model is transferable to another location.

7·2 Aggregation

A major objective of choice modelling is to make aggregate conditional and extrapolative predictions[2] in order for policy makers to assess the market impact of proposed and implemented policies. Although the operative decision-making unit in choice analysis should be the individual or household, planning at a governmental level requires accurate predictions on groups of individuals, and thus some mechanism is required whereby aggregate predictions can be obtained without the loss of information required to generate reliable results. In essence the issue under consideration is the way in which individual choice behaviour can be represented in a market prediction without any predictive bias due to the way in which the actions of individuals are aggregated.

There is a sizeable literature on the aggre-gation problem and aggregation bias; however what is of particular importance in choice modelling from a prediction viewpoint is the extent to which the presence of aggregation bias contributes to errors in prediction and/or whether other dimensions of the modelling process play a more prominent role in the contribution to predictive error. In this section the aggregation problem is outlined, and particular attention is given to the nature of aggregation bias, its associated origins and alternative compen-satory measures. We also seek out the evidence on the effect of aggregation bias and conclude with a proposal for data segmentation as a desirable procedure for improving predictive capability. It should be pointed out that data segmentation is not only a way of reducing aggregation bias, it is also a way of reducing some of the other biases in modelling such as biases which exist to constrain the transferability of models and model output from one action space to another and from one time period to another. Transferability will be discussed in Section 7.3.

Suppose a policy analyst wants to use an individual choice model (of the multinomial logit form) which relates the probabilities of choosing to rent or buy a house to the costs of purchase, rent, household and personal net income etc. to predict the effect on home ownership of a system-wide increase in house prices. The simplest approach is to use the average sample values of the independent variables (with respect to study area) to predict the "before" and "after" aggregate occupant-status split. Unfortunately the approach will, in general, lead to erroneous predictions even if the model being used is the correct one for the population being studied. In the words of Green:

> *a part of the information available for the*
> *solution of a problem is sacrificed for the*

purpose of making the problem more easily manageable. (1969: 3)

The correct approach is to use the values of the independent variables that are directly relevant to each individual in the affected population, to predict the individual probabilities, and then to sum these probabilities. The predictions obtained by the individual disaggregative approach (referred to later in this section as the enumeration method) will be more accurate than those obtained by the aggregate approach (conveniently referred to as the naive aggregation method) because the average of a nonlinear function is not equal to the function evaluated at the average of the explanatory variables. The difference between the predictions obtained by the enumeration method and the naive method is referred to as the aggregation bias. Hence this term has a well-defined meaning and is not to be interpreted as the sole source of error due to aggregation. Other sources of error (in particular level of measurement of variables) are discussed later in this section.

The example above is an illustration of one form of aggregation error, which is due to nonlinearity of the choice function. Even if the enumeration approach is used, it is often the case that the representative utility condition does not hold across the population under study and that it is desirable to segment the population on the basis of the criterion variable and/or other variables which may or may not be independent variables (for an example based on the dependent variable, see Reid, 1978). This approach is developed in detail below. However, it is important to point out that the issue of variance in representative utility can also be resolved in part by appropriate redefinition of variables, in particular the specification of a composite variable; for example the ratio of establishment costs to household net income.

It is important to recognise that the aggregation problem is inherent in the prediction problem (i.e. a desire to use a shortcut method to make aggregate predictions), and is not a problem which arises because of the individual choice modelling approach. Aggregate modelling approaches merely "sweep the problem under the rug", reducing variance as well as relevance.

Let us conclude this introduction to aggregation with an empirical illustration. Assume that the correctly specified model for choice of occupant status of a given establishment type (say

195

detached single family house) is

$$\ln \left[\frac{P \text{ (owning)}}{P \text{ (renting)}} \mid \text{location} \right] = 0.64 - 0.016$$

$$\left[\frac{\text{perceived purchase / net household}}{\text{price of house} \qquad \text{income}} \right]$$

$$+ \ 0.042 \ [\text{owners} \qquad - \ 0.012 \ [\text{size of}$$
$$\text{accessible savings}] \qquad \text{household}]$$

All independent variables are defined on an equivalent weekly basis in the estimation of the model. Assume that all individuals in the population under study face an average purchase price of a house in the given chosen location of $50,000 (equivalent to approximately $77 repayment per week over 25 years), an average net household income of $6,000 (equivalent to $115 per week), an average household size of 3 persons, and an average level of accessible savings equivalent to (over the life of the loan) $30 per week. The average probability of owning a house in the chosen location is 0.86. Furthermore, now assume that half of the sample are under 25 years old and the remaining individuals are over 35 years old. The level of income for the young persons is $100 per week, their household size is 2 persons, and their accessible savings is $10 per week. Similarly, the older people have an income of $130 per week, a household size of 4, and an average level of weekly savings of $50.

For the young individuals, the probability of owning a house in a chosen location is .74, and the corresponding probability for an older person is .89. The true occupant status split for the population is 81.5%, in contrast to the 86% estimated proportion of home ownership obtained by the naive aggregation method. This is summarised in Figure 7.1, using a convenient graphical representation proposed by Charles River Associates (1976).

7.2.1 Aggregation Error

There are a number of levels of aggregation error. The levels of particular interest are:

(1)   the use of group and intergroup averages in the definition of the magnitudes of explanatory variables for each individual;

196

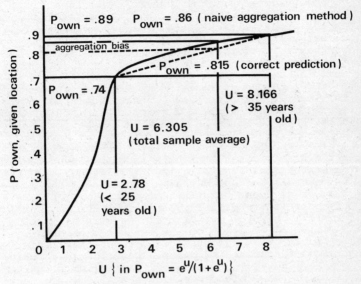

FIGURE 7·1 :
Aggregation Bias

P_{own} = .89 P_{own} = .86 (naive aggregation method)

aggregation bias

P_{own} = .815 (correct prediction)

P_{own} = .74

P_{own} = .74

U = 8.166
(> 35 years old)

U = 6.305
(total sample average)

U = 2.78
(< 25 years old)

P (own, given location)

$U \left\{ \text{in } P_{own} = e^{u}/(1+e^{u}) \right\}$

(2)   the use, after estimation, of the average
        level of a variable (associated with all
        individuals in a sample) in obtaining
        the average probability of choice, both
        before and after a policy change, and in
        the calculation of the elasticities of
        choice.

Both aggregation errors may appear, even though
the individual is the unit of analysis and not the
group. With group data definition, especially for
variables associated with the nonchosen alternatives,
the demarcation line is rather dubious. Error type
(1) has been less researched than error type (2)
(see Horowitz, 1980; and Talvitie, 1980 for recent
evidence); although it can be concluded on the
basis of research by McFadden & Reid (1975) that,
with a random sample, if a policy has a homogeneous
effect within a group, then the aggregation error
when using group estimates of variables is minimal.
There is still a need for research into the significance of homogeneous-effect policies vs.
heterogenous-effect policies at the group level.
In addition there is a need to determine the
relationship between the within group variance of

197

an attribute, a number of easily determined
causal-associates, and the extent of predictive
error.

Even if the average group value associated with
an independent variable is a reliable input from
the aggregation bias viewpoint in the calculation of
choice probabilities (because the function is
linear), there is still the possibility of
substantial error as a result of the 'internal
structure' of a variable (see Section 4.5.1). For
example, the use of the average income of a
particular type of individual as the definition of
the level for an individual contained in that type
set is a common source of error. Evidence suggests
that there is often as much within-type variance as
between-type variance. In addition, we have an
unclear knowledge of the relationship between the
actual level of an attribute and that level of
relevance in influencing individual behaviour. It
is generally accepted that an individual's perception of an event or attribute is the appropriate
dimension for explaining behaviour; as it is not
possible, however, to directly measure how people
perceive a situation or the relevance of an
attribute, this is obtained by reporting. This is
assumed to reflect how people consciously perceive
reality, but is not necessarily a reliable indication of how this perception actually influences
behaviour. There is a continuing need for research
into the relationship between reported perception
and true perception (from the viewpoint of
explaining individual behaviour). Furthermore,
since policy involves changes in supply of an
objective nature, it is necessary for consistency to
'modify' the actual change in attribute levels
associated with supply strategies, so that the
prediction of resultant behaviour can be improved.
This is another major source of error which has
still to be thoroughly researched (Hensher & Dalvi,
1978; Daly, 1978).

We now examine the nature of aggregation bias
associated with error type (2) and suggest the
appropriate course to follow when using the
multinomial-logit model in assessing policy
changes. Koppelman's extensive research into
aggregation bias, has identified four properties
which hold under certain conditions (1975, 1976,
1976a):

    (a)   for any pairwise comparison of alterna-
           tives, the aggregation bias will result
           in the share of the dominant alternative

being overpredicted. Hence, in the
example above, if we were to use the
naive aggregation method, we would
overpredict home ownership levels;

(b)   the aggregation bias will be greater,
ceteris paribus, when the mean representative utility difference falls in the
tails of the logit function;

(c)   the aggregation bias will increase,
ceteris paribus, with an increase in the
variability of representative utility;

(d)   the aggregation bias will, in general,
remain with all sample sizes.

In practice, Koppelman points out that the magnitude
of these biases are not large when compared to
other sources of error in model estimation although
the evidence is currently limited to a handful of
studies.
    Reid (1978) has recently reported empirical
results which suggest that because Koppelman's
findings are based on a very specific empirical
issue, the magnitudes of bias should not be
generalised. Reid indicates that the bias is likely
to increase significantly with the size of the
aggregate unit; hence reopening the debate on the
relative magnitudes of alternative sources of
error. Horowitz (1980 and Appendix C) has recently
summarised the major sources of error.

7·2·2 Accounting for Aggregation Error

    To overcome this aggregation bias, when using
a nonlinear choice model like the logit model, an
appropriate aggregation procedure is the sample
enumeration method (Hensher, Smith & Hooper, 1978;
Hensher & Stopher, 1979). This approach involves:

(i)   predicting the behaviour of each
individual in a sample drawn from the
population and taking the average of
those predictions;

(ii)   predicting the after behaviour for
each individual and taking the average;
and

(iii) identifying the differences between
those average predictions to obtain
the aggregate policy effect.

Every individual in the sample is assumed to be
representative for a part of the sampled population;
and the variation within the sampled population is

reflected in the sample variability. If the sample is random, the random sample enumeration method assigns a unit weight to each observation. Where the sample is nonrandom (e.g. stratified or choice-based - see Section 7.4) a weight is assigned that modifies the role of a particular observation according to its representativeness in the sampled population. This weight is defined as the ratio of observation incidence in the sampled population and the sample.

Adopting the enumeration method as the correct procedure for obtaining market shares from the sum of individual choices, a useful (although linear) measure of aggregation error is the percentage root mean square (RMS) of choice shares, given as

$$\text{RMSE} \;=\; [\; \sum_{j=1}^{J} \; ((\hat{P}_j - P_j)/P_j)^2 \; P_j]^{\frac{1}{2}}$$

where $\hat{P}_j$ = the aggregate share of alternative j estimated by the tested method
P_j = aggregate share obtained by the enumeration method.

This procedure consists of delaying aggregation to the last possible moment, by aggregating the results of the model application rather than the model itself.

The method of measurement of the independent variables in the analysis phase should comply with measurement in the model application phase. It is frequently not possible, however, to determine the 'after' level of an attribute at the individual level, only at the group level. A substantial amount of work is required to generate individual-specific levels (Hensher, 1979a). High variation in the representative utility across the individuals in the sample may occur, by using either group or truly-individual specific magnitudes of attributes in the estimation of the choice model. Some adjustment for aggregation bias is desirable, if it will reduce predictive error, even when only average (across sample) levels of attributes are available in the 'after' situation. This would apply both when assessing the after effect of a policy change, and when obtaining estimates of elasticity of choice. In the case of the latter, a weighted aggregate elasticity of choice should be calculated for the sample, to account for the variation in the probability of choice in the sample; initially the elasticity of choice at the individual level

200

should be calculated and then weights applied to obtain the aggregate elasticity (see Chapter 3). Experience suggests errors are of the order of 20 per cent (upwards) if a direct aggregate elasticity is calculated using the average sample levels.

Sampling randomly from the empirical distribution and forming the sample expectation, as an approximation to the population expectation, is the most flexible approach for aggregate forecasting from individual-choice models. When such an option is not possible, we are left with three other approaches (McFadden, 1976a):

(a) approximate the empirical distribution with a mathematical distribution for which the expectation can be performed analytically (McFadden & Reid, 1975), possibly after transformation of variables (Westin, 1974). Westin's procedure has not been worked out when more than one alternative to the chosen exists;

(b) approximate the empirical distribution by a histogram. Then each cell in the histogram corresponds to a relatively homogeneous market segment, and the expectation is the sum of these market segments. The finer the segmentation structure, the more accurate the segmentation. Essentially, this approach seeks to group the data into market segments so that the variance of representative utility is minimised within any group and maximised across groups (see Section 7.2.3). Reducing the variance within any segment should reduce the aggregation bias that results when the model is applied to the means of the independent variables for that market segment. Aggregate choice share predictions are obtained by taking a weighted average of the probabilities of choosing a particular alternative for various market segments, where the weights are the segments' shares of all alternatives. This approach is favoured together with the sample enumeration method, although it does require additional data in order to determine market segments. It is a realistic compromise given the difficulties of sample enumeration in the 'after' situation;

(c) approximate the empirical distribution using Taylor series expansions in terms of statistical moments, so that the aggregate shares are given as functions of choice probabilities at the average arguments and moments of the distribution of explanatory variables.

Talvitie (1973) used this 'corrected average' approach. This method requires information on the moments of the distribution of explanatory variables which are usually not readily available. Truncating the series after the third term produces the expression:

$$\bar{P}(A) = P(A) \left[1 + var (Y) (1 - P(A)) (\tfrac{1}{2} - P(A)) \right] \qquad (7.1)$$

where var (Y) is the sample variance of the values of the representative utility;

$$var (Y) = (1/Q) \cdot \sum_{q=1}^{Q} (Y_q - \bar{Y})^2 \qquad (7.2)$$

$\bar{P}(A)$ is the average of the individual probabilities. $P(A)$ is the function probability evaluated at the mean value of Y, i.e. $\bar{Y}$; the mean representative utility for the population. The correction term depends jointly on the sample variance of representative utility and the value of the share predicted by the naive aggregation method. The appeal of this approach is diminished when one attempts to compute var (Y), either for the estimated model's sample or the application sample. With n variables in the representative utility function there are potentially $(n^2 + n)/2$ variance-covariance terms in computing var (Y). Even though many of the terms are zero, there are still many to calculate. To estimate the elements of Z in var (Y) = $\underline{\alpha}'$ Z $\underline{\alpha}$, the source of sample variances and covariances, is more work than computing $\bar{P}(A)$ using the random sample enumeration method.

Research by Charles River Associates (1976) however has shown that in a significant number of cases, the variance of the log odds function was relatively close to unity. The variance of the log odds function must be constrained to be between zero and unity to meet the condition that the estimated market share changes, in a consistent fashion, with the change in the level of an attribute. It is now reasonable to approximate var (Y) to unity, and remove the burdensome task of calculating var (Y). This gives:

$$\bar{P}(A) = P(A) \left[1 + (1 - P(A)) (\tfrac{1}{2} - P(A)) \right] \qquad (7.3)$$

This approach seems to be the only alternative to the sample enumeration method and market segmentation, although it is regarded as a poor approximation.[3] By grouping similar values of the

202

independent variables together by segmentation, the variances and covariances within each group are reduced to levels significantly less than the entire population. Evidence from a study by the New York State Department of Transportation Planning Research Bureau suggests that the series 'correction' estimates deteriorate in accuracy markedly as the standard deviation increases for values of the mean away from zero. For example, with a mean of unity and standard deviation of zero, the error in applying the series correction is zero; for a mean of 4.0 and a standard deviation of 2, the error in applying the series correction is .44. The discussion of approach (b) above as a way of reducing aggregation error in prediction made no distinction between segmentation prior to estimation and post estimation (even though as an approximation method we usually mean postestimation segmentation). While priorestimation segmentation is generally preferable where the coefficients of explanatory variables are known to differ significantly between groups of individuals, it is often not feasible, for cost and data availability reasons, to develop separate segment models. Before presenting the ex ante segmentation approach in Section 7.2.3, we introduce a final postestimation procedure for obtaining aggregate predictions from individual data which is possibly the 'best' (in the sense of error minimising) approximation method to the enumeration approach. This approach assumes that individual-specific data observations are available to calculate the cell average values.

A recent study by Reid (1978) argues that the classification of the sample based on the scales of the total utility of the explanatory attributes in each alternative in the choice set is a more efficient approximation approach in reducing error than segmentation by individual variables provided the model is simply scalable.[4] A major advantage of this approach, if empirically valid, is that we have a systematic method of selecting the type and number of classification attributes; this advantage is reinforced by the evidence that the size of the aggregation unit has an influence on the variance of each explanatory variable.

Thus, because the information used in the prediction of each individual's choice is contained in the utility scales of the attributes of the J alternatives of choice, then segmentation or cross-classification between the utilities gives the full-scale variances and between-scale covariances. This approach describes the full distribution of individual choice attributes in an aggregate prediction sample. Reid states that

> *Regardless of scale complexity, this procedure bypasses those individual variable cross-classification trade-offs, which do not change the scale values. Thus, the procedure requires fewer classes. Classification on the total utility includes the variances of the minor variables, not just the variances of the limited number of interactions feasible in classification by a subset of model variables. This further increases its efficiency. To define relatively homogeneous classes of utility combinations across (alternatives) is to probe the essence of the classification approach: the grouping of individuals with uniform choice situations. Since the procedure operates on the utility scales, it is termed the utility scale classification method of aggregation.*

(Reid, 1978: 61)

Since utility is a continuous dimension, a criterion has to be defined for the threshold for classification; that is, we need to approximate the utility distribution by a histogram (like in (b) above), where each utility cell corresponds to a relatively homogeneous market segment. Reid suggests that this be accomplished by successive stratification of an aggregate sample about the median or mean values of pairwise utility differences. Commencing with the largest variance in utility difference, all utility pairs were examined, further subdividing the initial pairs if the variances in resulting classes are still large. The stopping rule relates to the requirement for a desired level of accuracy. This is a complex issue, to which we refer the reader to Reid's paper for details.

In concluding, two points need to be stated. Firstly, Reid's empirical evidence indicates that for utility class cells, varying from 2 to 8, the percentage error (using the RMSE formula) lies between 6.4 and 0.5 per cent. This suggests a major improvement on all other approximation methods. Secondly, this approximation method is particularly suited to the identification of aggregate market share predictions after a policy change, provided the analyst has sufficient information on the policy variable to enable calculation of at least the

average (class cell) value after the change. Thus
this is an improvement over other approximation
methods in accommodating the problem of consistency
between the before and after (class mean in this
method) levels of a policy variable. This is not,
however, a substitute for the enumeration method,
if data, programmes and cost constraints are not
binding, despite the low levels of error in Reid's
case study. For long-term forecasting, where the
change in levels of all variables occur, the
enumeration method is likely to be difficult to
apply (how do we identify the future levels of
variables for a particular representative individual?); hence the utility classification approach
is more likely to be operational - it is relatively
easier to obtain future levels for classes of
representative individuals. This might be the main
strength of this approach in its bid as the
operational procedure for aggregate forecasting with
disaggregate models. Reid's study concentrated on
aggregate prediction under a nonpolicy change
environment with the emphasis on internal predictive
accuracy. Further analysis, considering the
aggregate predictions after policy changes (with
comparison of all methods including enumeration
with the actual shares) is required before we could
assert any firm conclusions on the true predictive
performance of the various methods.

7·2·3 Market (Consumer) Segmentation

Market segmentation[5] as a procedure aimed at
identifying homogeneous groupings of the population
(with respect to an issue) has possibilities for
reducing the errors of aggregation. Group
prediction has been proposed as a means of reducing
the naive aggregation error; furthermore
aggregation by market segmentation is also central
to the postmodel aggregation processes referred to
above, where the identification of appropriate
segments can reduce substantially the required
sample sizes for accurate prediction. The
literature on market segmentation has been
exhaustively reviewed by Dobson (1979), and the
general idea of segmentation discussed elsewhere
by Hensher (1976).
    The important contribution of segmentation as
applied in the context of individual choice models
is the reduction in the variability of the utility
expression by systematic procedures. When maximal
detail is maintained in the data set (because the
individual is the unit of analysis rather than the

group) then there is a substantial amount of variance to be explained. Rather than group or aggregate prior to estimation, as is so frequently done, it is preferable to segment and estimate separate individual choice models. By doing so, the total variance in existence is able to be properly accounted for (although not necessarily 'explained') and a more realistic representation of the heterogeneous population is obtained.

Since the analyst may have some special interest in some of the market segments per se (e.g. low income households with one earner and many children), the segmentation approach allows him to observe the effect of various policies on each of the segments. Thus, in addition to knowing the total predicted effect of a proposed policy, we can ascertain the incidence of the policy on various members of the population. If the sole purpose of analysis is forecasting, then while market segmentation allows for the testing of statistical behavioural differences, if a subsequent testing to determine whether the differences are important enough to affect forecasting accuracy yields no improvement, segmentation is not worth the additional effort and cost.

This question of market segmentation has been associated with two schools of thought: the 'behaviourists' who are concerned with consumer differences, as such differences reflect generalisations about behavioural differences, and the 'normatives' who assume immediately that differences in the behaviour of segments exist and ask not why they exist, but how the differences can be exploited to improve the individuals' or the firms' marketing posture.

In either instance the emphasis is on deriving homogeneous classes of consumers with respect to various aspects of their behaviour, their social and economic characteristics, and other factors thought to be relevant to segmentation. The basic difference between the two schools is fundamental in seeking to decide whether in fact a grouping on the basis of a selected set of characteristics is going to assist in providing an improved under-standing of behaviour, and thus increased predictive capability. A normative strategy would involve, for example, undertaking a survey to assist in identifying improvements to the housing system and segmenting by income, developing response curves for each income level. For the high income groups one might provide relatively large and/or expensively built facilities and for the low income earners one might provide less expensive and smaller facilities. This normative approach assumes a basis for grouping, and that income is necessarily an appropriate segmentation variable in identification of 'homogeneous' groups. This need not be so, given the issue, and in fact a priori stratification of this type need not necessarily yield the same groupings as a more behavioural systematic segmentation procedure.

The behaviourists' approach is preferred as a framework in which we can seek to identify consumer differences through understanding the relationship between present housing patterns and various socioeconomic characteristics of the occupants, and having employed the systematic segmentation procedure, then use the resultant grouping in identification of the projects which will assist in achieving an externally determined objective. The aim is not to change individuals' preferences in order to 'sell' a service, but rather to identify variations in individuals' preferences, and then group individuals in a systematic manner so that we can more accurately identify the types of services that individuals will respond to and thus change our services.

There are a number of examples in the literature of studies which have adopted a behaviourist approach, but which are based on a priori stratification (Wilkie, 1971; Lovelock, 1975) and very few examples of studies which have attempted any systematic segmentation, where the only a priori stratification relates to the range of variables selected for the analysis of relationship between the criterion variable and the explanatory variables (e.g. Dobson & Nicolaidis, 1974). The state of the art in market segmentation as applied to public sector issues is rather crude, limited essentially to initial subdivisions of the universe lacking any necessarily systematic procedure in a framework of general applicability to the gamut of relevant matters (Hensher, 1976a). In order for meaningful market segments to be developed, we need to satisfy three criteria (Lovelock, 1975):

(1) measurability - the degree to which information exists or can be obtained on the specific consumer characteristics of interest;

(2) accessibility - the extent to which policy makers can identify and effectively focus its marketing efforts on chosen segments;

207

(3)   substantiality - the degree to which
      the segments are large enough to
      merit separate attention.

Wilkie (1971) argues that segments should be
chosen which are useful as correlates of behaviour
and which can be related to strategic considerations.
Since variables are the things that account for the
differences among behavioural groups, then we must
investigate the structure of markets through a
consideration of the role of variables. That is,
the effectiveness of a study of choice depends to
no small degree on the extent to which the finer
details of the structure of a market are known.
More specifically, since the market is composed of
individuals, it is desirable to be able to describe,
in terms of a range of variable types (socioeconomic,
environmental, attitudinal etc.) the various
subgroups of the market which are at different
usage levels. By investigating the interactions and
the causalities we should be able to identify each
submarket with the right degree of emphasis.
The research problem of characterising these
different groups of users is even more complex than
it may first appear to be. Suppose, for example,
that we have examined a large number of
socioeconomic and attitudinal variables to see if
any of them relate to the occupant status of
residential dwellings. Suppose that out of a large
number of different measurements taken on each
respondent, such as age, taste, preference, etc.,
only one variable seems to be related to occupant
status: the income level of the respondent.
Through conventional cross-tabulation analyses
(Figure 7.2) we might find that although the
propensity to own averages .4 in the overall population, this total market can be split according to
income into two groups which differ significantly in
their ownership propensity: a low-income group
averaging .3, and a high-income group averaging .6.
This is an important finding and we may conclude
that we have isolated a market, the high income
groups, and solved a research problem. But have we?
Will a policy focused on the high income group
which disregards the low income consumer represent
the best allocation of housing resources? Possibly,
but there may well be a market, hidden within the
low income group, which is being ignored. For
example, suppose that we could reconsider the
possibilities of predicting occupancy status, but
studying only the responses of the low income,
supposedly low ownership group. If we search the

208

FIGURE 7·2:

The Hidden Market

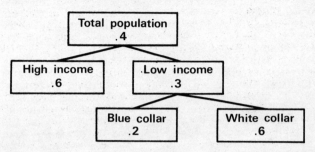

socioeconomic and attitudinal measurements in this
group, we might find that in contrast with the
total population in which only income can predict
occupancy status, occupation of the individual can
be used to split this subgroup into two smaller
groups which differ in their propensity to own: a
blue collar group with very low ownership (.2), and
a white collar group with a very high ownership (.6).
Because the ownership levels of these two, 'sub-sub',
groups average out, the low income group to which
they both belong seems to be an uninteresting, low
ownership group. But the low income group is
actually not at all homogeneous in its ownership
level. Concealed beneath an apparently low average
ownership is a subgroup in which ownership is as
high as in the primary (high income) market.

Missing important markets may be the
consequence of the researcher's method for seeking
significant subgroups. In searching through the
total population for measurements which will
distinguish the owners from the nonowners, the
researcher is really considering the averaged
responses of what may be a highly divergent group.
It is quite possible that response tendencies in
one subgroup of this population are opposed to and
act to average out response tendencies in other
subgroups.

In the analysis of data, interactions are
commonly ignored. When a large number of explanatory variables are involved, and especially when
the data deals with behaviour, this assumption is
probably a very risky one. There are two basic
reasons why the usual additive assumptions are
unwarranted in this type of situation. The first is
that we already know about many cases of powerful

209

interaction. For example, education increases a
man's income more than it does a woman's. In the
area of housing we would expect a high income to
increase an individual's propensity to own, but the
income-effect will be different for someone with a
large family than for someone with a small family.
So the real world is full of interactions. The
second reason for questioning the simple additive
assumption is that the variables we use are often
only proxies, and several of these may jointly
represent a theoretical construct. That is, the
variables we are using may have to interact to
produce a single theoretical construct which is a
really important factor in explaining behaviour.
An example of this is the concept of accessibility.
Although this is often arbitrarily created from
several components before analysis begins, it is in
fact a set of interactions between travel time and
the availability of various types of activities.

Interaction and intercorrelation between
explanatory variables should be carefully
distinguished. Figure 7.3 shows three cases which
help to clarify the distinction. The examples are
real, but very exaggerated. In Figure 7.3(a) the
explanatory factors are correlated with each other,
but do not interact. A simple relation between
income and propensity to own an establishment would
exaggerate the effect of income on ownership, by
not allowing for the fact that high income people
also have a higher education, which also tends to
increase their likelihood of owning. However, the
effect of income on ownership is the same for both
low and high education people. A multiple
regression with a dummy variable for education
would handle this situation.

In the second case it is assumed that there is
no correlation between income and size of family.
But people with no children have a higher marginal
propensity to own than those with children. A
simple relation between the propensity to own and
income becomes a weighted compromise between two
different income effects. A multiple correlation
would not help, since it would show no effect from
having no children, and give the same average
income effect. Only a separate analysis for
childless and nonchildless individuals would
indicate the true state of things.

In the final case not only do families without
children have a greater marginal propensity to own,
they also tend to have higher incomes. Multiple
correlation is again inadequate. It will give an
income effect and a family size effect, but these

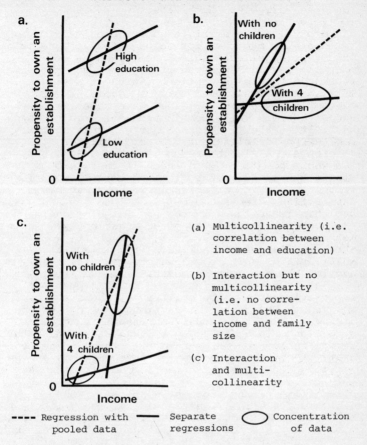

FIGURE 7·3 :

Interaction and Intercorrelation

a. [graph: Propensity to own an establishment vs Income, with "High education" and "Low education" data concentrations]

b. [graph: Propensity to own an establishment vs Income, with "With no children" and "With 4 children" data concentrations]

c. [graph: Propensity to own an establishment vs Income, with "With no children" and "With 4 children" data concentrations]

(a) Multicollinearity (i.e. correlation between income and education)

(b) Interaction but no multicollinearity (i.e. no correlation between income and family size

(c) Interaction and multicollinearity

---- Regression with pooled data   ──── Separate regressions   ◯ Concentration of data

will not accurately represent the true situation. In both this case and the preceding one, a procedure is needed to uncover these interactions and to deal with them adequately. The problem is, of course, compounded by the fact that real-world interactions will often be more complex than these.

The problems of logical priorities and chains of causation are very much related to interaction (see Appendix B). The idea of the contextual or environmental effect illustrates this clearly. The way in which an environmental factor influences behaviour may depend on other environmental factors

— on the individual's characteristics, or on both.
Thus, there may be different levels of construction.
In considering a decision-making process, not only
must the variables which directly affect an
individual's decision be considered, but also other
factors which may determine how these more
immediately important variables affect the decisions.
This type of effect is essentially interactive.

Interactions are usually ignored for the simple
reason that this assumption results in a very
efficient analysis procedure and avoids a great deal
of complexity. However, they have sometimes been
accounted for. Also combinations of predictors can
be built at the first stage, or separate analyses
can be run for different groups. Analysis for
subgroups can also be rerun after an analysis for
the whole population, to check if these groups are
significantly different from the total population.
If the number of variables is reduced, then all
interaction effects can be built into the analysis,
but this leaves us with the problem of reducing
the number of variables, often drastically. Another
method which has been used is to look at two- and
three-way tables of residuals from an additive
multivariate analysis. However, this is usually a
complex and expensive process.

All these approaches require that possible
interaction effects be built in at the start of the
analysis. Where the interactions are complex and
unknown, this is obviously an unsatisfactory
situation. In order fully to understand the nature
of the influences on behaviour, a large number of
explanatory variables must be investigated, and an
analysis technique which can account for interaction
effects is essential. Models which ignore the
possibility of interaction, especially when
behaviour is being investigated, are very likely to
be misspecified, and thus to give misleading results.
'Hidden markets' can be isolated by procedures such
as the automatic interaction detector (Sonquist,
Baker & Morgan, 1971). The general issue of
structure (or functional form) and specification of
the form of variables is outlined in Appendix B.
A useful overview of the range of statistical
classification techniques (e.g. cluster analysis,
factor analysis, latent structure models,
multidimensional scaling, and AID) is given in
O'Muircheartaigh & Payne (1977).

7·3 Transferability of Model Parameters[6]

By developing a model at the level of the
decision-making unit, it is thought that one has the
greatest chance of transferring a model estimated
in one location (on a particular group for a
particular purpose) to another location (on a
different group etc.). The basis for this belief
is that behavioural decision processes are aspatial;
that is, regularities in behaviour of individuals
would allow a single model estimated in one place
at one time to be used in applications in other
places at other times, thereby making the
estimation of new models unnecessary. If transferability of a model estimated on Sydney data to
Melbourne is possible, then we have a very good case
for individual choice models. The savings in
resources (especially data and computer time)
would be enormous. What is the evidence and
arguments on the mechanism of transferability? In
this section we outline the nature of the
transferability issue and propose a number of ways
in which estimated models can be used in contexts
different in a particular dimension to the
estimation context.[7] Likely sources of problems in
transferability are violation of the assumption
that all individuals share a common representative
utility function, differences in sampling
procedures (affecting βs), differences in estimation
techniques and sample size, and true behavioural
differences.

While we have good evidence that representative
utility is different for different issues (e.g.
journey to work vs. journey to shops), it is not
clear that representative utilities for activities
with a common purpose vary across space. In the
housing context, for example, there is no evidence
at all; however, it does seem as though spatial
and temporal transferability are both desirable for
all types of housing decisions under consideration.
There are two main types of 'spatial' errors which
may be due to violation of the assumption that all
individuals in the sample share a common
representative utility. These are:

(a)   all individuals in space X (e.g. city
        X) are assumed to share a common
        representative utility, and all
        individuals in space Y (e.g. city Y)
        are assumed to share a common

representative utility, which is
different to that of individuals in
space X;
(b)   all individuals in space X or space Y
share a common representative utility.
This is actually an aggregation
misspecification, even if similar in
origin to the transferability problem.

There is some evidence to suggest that error
associated with incorrectly assuming a common
representative utility for all members of a group is
less than error that occurs when a model estimted on
one group is applied to another group which has a
representative utility different from the first
group (Charles River Associates, 1978).
The only known evidence on temporal transferability, for a given space, is given in two studies
of transport mode choice; one in the Sydney region,
using the logit model for 1971 and 1973 (Hensher &
Johnson, 1977) and the other in Tel-Aviv, also
using a basic logit model for 1972 and 1976 (Silman,
1979). There is very strong evidence in these
studies, to support strong transferability powers
over short-range planning periods (see also the
comments in Section 9.6).
A related issue to transferability of the
estimated model is the requirement for additional
data. Hopefully it will be possible to collect a
limited data set for application in another context
rather than a full scale data exercise. It is the
combination of model transferability and limited
data augmentation that provides the strong support
for individual choice models.
A number of procedures have been proposed for
transferring models in space (Atherton & Ben-Akiva,
1976). The main considerations relate to the
estimates of the parameters, in particular the bias
constants, and the levels of the independent
variables. The five main procedures investigated to
date are:

(1)   the 'do-nothing' case, which is a default
option if data is not available from the application
site. Even though individual choice models come
close to neutralising the effect of space on the
consistency of consumer behaviour, it is reasoned
that the consistency condition is a necessary but
not sufficient condition for direct transferability.
The further condition that similar circumstances are
maintained is in practice difficult to attain;
(2)   adjustment of the alternative-specific
constant terms using aggregate data of behaviour,

on the grounds that there is no theoretical basis
for transferring terms which account for all the
dimensions not explicitly explained by the model.
In many situations data is available on the aggregate population shares of the alternatives in the
choice set together with data on the population
averages of the explanatory variables. Procedure
two involves using the alternative-specific
constants to adjust the model so that the original
model accurately predicts the new shares of each
alternative. The plausibility of this 'convenience
approach' is diminished when the naive aggregation
method is used, for all the reasons outlined in
Section 7.2 and if the assumption of complete
transferability of the coefficients of the
independent variables does not hold;
    (3)   enrichment by re-estimation of the
coefficients with a small disaggregate sample
(Cosslett, 1978, 1980). The specification of the
original model is assumed to be appropriate in the
new location, although with a small sample (between
50 and 200 observations) estimation difficulties
may arise, in particular large biases and standard
deviations. If this approach is used, the sample
size should be incrementally increased to test for
'size effects';
    (4)   re-estimation of the constant terms and
estimation of a scalar to weight all other
coefficients so that the ratios between them are
unchanged, i.e. the marginal rate of substitution
between pairs of attributes is unchanged to reflect
the assumption that the relative values associated
with variables are invariant across space even
though the level of importance associated with the
variables may differ across space;
    (5)   Bayesian updating using the original
coefficients (procedure 1) and the coefficients
resulting from the small disaggregate sample
(procedure 3). This approach can be used for both
transferability over space and transferability over
time, with the small disaggregate sample being
used to obtain additional information in the new
space and/or new time for updating the original
model estimated on a large (and more statistically
reliable) sample. The only information required
to update a model with a second sample are the
parameter estimates for the models from each of the
two data sets and the variance-covariance matrices
for the parameter estimates. The formula for a
single-parameter model is (Raiffa & Schlaifer,
1961):

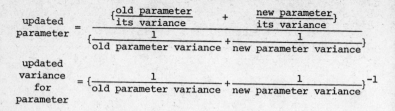

$$\text{updated parameter} = \frac{\left\{\dfrac{\text{old parameter}}{\text{its variance}} + \dfrac{\text{new parameter}}{\text{its variance}}\right\}}{\left\{\dfrac{1}{\text{old parameter variance}} + \dfrac{1}{\text{new parameter variance}}\right\}}$$

$$\text{updated variance for parameter} = \left\{\frac{1}{\text{old parameter variance}} + \frac{1}{\text{new parameter variance}}\right\}^{-1}$$

A normal distribution for each coefficient is assumed. Daganzo (1979) has shown that for large values of Q and Q' (the update sample) the updated parameter and its variance are approximately equal to the maximum-likelihood estimates that would have resulted from estimation with the combined data set. We have not discussed optimal updating; that is how to design the update sample to minimise the magnitude of the updated variance. This is beyond the scope of this book (see Daganzo, 1978).

The use of a small disaggregate data set in updating models raises the important issue of sample design.[8] Research by Manski & Lerman (1977a) and Cosslett (1978) has demonstrated the viability of nonrandom sampling methods, specifically 'choice-based' sampling for individual choice modelling. The sample can be selected to ensure that each of the alternatives in the choice set is represented by sufficient sample points. This is clearly important in situations where some alternatives form a relatively small proportion of a random sample. In the future such alternatives may be a greater proportion of any fully random sample and hence it is important to capture the utility of minor alternatives. Choice-based sampling is a relatively cost-effective procedure since it permits cost savings in the process of generating a sample of a population by sampling individuals when they are carrying out the activity of concern for the choice model under development. The sampling method should not be confused with the survey procedure, which is concerned with the technique used to administer the survey itself to the selected sample. Home interviews may still be required if the data to be collected is extensive, however with choice-based sampling the number of effective interviews required is somewhat less than 'the random sample size'.

Choice-based samples do, however, require adjusting for use in estimating individual choice models. Manski & Lerman (1977a) have shown that a simple weighting process of each data point yields consistent and asymptotically efficient estimators in the logit model. The weight for each observation is the ratio of the fraction of the total population choosing alternative i (H*) to the fraction of the total population observed in the choice-based sample choosing alternative i (H) (see Section 7.4. for more details).

McFadden (1979) has shown that it is possible to avoid the weighting procedure prior to estimation, and to compensate after estimation provided the alternatives in the choice set are ranked (see Chapter 4.5 for definitions of ranked and unranked alternatives). If the full set of alternative-specific constants are included in a choice model and the conditional logit model characterises choice, then only the alternative-specific constants are inconsistent if weighting is not carried out prior to estimation using a choice-based sample. The maximum-likelihood estimation may then be applied to the unweighted data, and the correct estimates of the alternative-specific constants can be recovered from the equation

$$Y_i^* = \hat{Y} - \delta_i \qquad (7.4)$$

where

Y_i^* = the correct estimate of the alternative-specific constant for alternative i

$\hat{Y}_i$ = the estimated value of the alternative-specific constant for alternative i

δ_i = $\ln (H*(i)/H(i))$

Whatever the survey procedure used, choice-based sampling offers major cost savings over simple random sampling or systematic sampling, provided[9] that the overall population values of the choice proportions are known or obtainable without great expense.

In concluding this section on transferability and updating, an example, using choice-based sampling, will be useful to illustrate some of the points. It should be pointed out that little use has been made to date of the transferability and updating procedures and thus any points raised are subject to empirical verification as to their appropriateness. Existing empirical studies by Atherton & Ben-Akiva (1976), Watson & Westin (1975), Talvitie & Kirschner (1978) and Charles River

Associates (1978) are somewhat inconclusive. One of the real problems is the suitability of the range of explanatory variables in the estimated model when applied to another context. It appears that nonavailable variables might explain much of the poor performance. One point is certain. If models are to be transferred then it is even more necessary to spend more effort in verifying and refining the data; and that aggregate data tends, if anything, to reduce predictive performance. Theoretically, the arguments are realistic.

Assume a choice-based sample in which 40 per cent of the observations related to establishment owners and 60 per cent related to establishment renters. Furthermore, suppose the actual ratio of ownership to renting in the study area is 70/30. The weights required are:

weight for owner observations $= \dfrac{\text{\% in population owning}}{\text{\% in choice-based sample owning}} = \dfrac{70\%}{40\%} = 1.75$

weight for renter observations $= \dfrac{\text{\% in population renting}}{\text{\% in choice-based sample renting}} = \dfrac{30\%}{60\%} = 0.5$

For this sample, an individual choice model was initially estimated, producing the following empirical relationship

$U_{own} = 0.6$ (Income), and a variance of .09 for the estimate of the parameter. Using procedure 5 (Bayesian updating), a choice-based sample was drawn and a model estimated for the new space, producing the empirical relationship

$U_{own} = 0.5$ (Income) and a corresponding variance of .2. Applying the updating formula given above, we obtain the following:

updated parameter $= \dfrac{\left\{ \dfrac{.6}{.09} + \dfrac{.5}{.2} \right\}}{\left\{ \dfrac{1}{.09} + \dfrac{1}{.2} \right\}} = (6.66 + 2.5)/(11.11 + 5) = .569$

updated variance $= \left\{ \dfrac{1}{.09} + \dfrac{1}{.2} \right\}^{-1} = .062$

Hence the updated transferred model is

$U_{own} = .569$ (Income) with a variance of .062.

Suppose we want to update using another procedure, such as procedure 4. To simplify, assume only two alternatives - occupant ownership and occupant renting. The single adjusted occupant-status specific constant and the coefficient scalar could be calculated using a weighted linear regression.[10] The observations might be each individual weighted by his representativeness in the population, or they might be market segments previously constructed. The dependent (choice) variable is defined by (ownership share/renting share)$_i$ for either the ith market segment or the ith individual. The independent variables are a constant (e.g. ownership specific bias constant) and the vector of original model coefficients (α) for variables other than the constant and the vector of average values of the independent variables (X_i) for the ith group. α and X_i are combined to define

$$V_i = \underline{\alpha}'\underline{X}_i .$$

All variables, including the dependent variable and the constant, on the observations in the regression are weighted prior to estimation by their segment or random representative shares. The constant estimated will be that appropriate for the updated model, and the coefficient of V will be the scalar to be multiplied by the coefficients to obtain the updated coefficients of the 'nonconstant' independent variables. When more than two alternatives are contained in the choice set, then we have ($\frac{1}{2}$)J(J-1) possible dependent variables, where J is the number of alternatives. Since ($\frac{1}{2}$)J(J-1) different values of the scalar are possible, we can either use the average of the values in the updated model or take a number of values and use them as one parameter in sensitivity analysis. A similar averaging approach can be applied to the alternative-specific constants, except that a sign change must be accounted for in averaging all model estimates where the particular alternative is included as the denominator of the binary model.

To investigate the transferability of the (adjusted) parameters of a basic logit model in a specific context (choice of mode of transport for the journey to work), we prepared two data sets containing independent variables, identically measured and specified (see Galbraith, 1979 for more details). The study areas are the northern suburbs (N) of Sydney (relatively wealthy) and the south western suburbs (SW) of Sydney (relatively poor).

The samples are random within the sampled population of commuters who have access to a car. The sample sizes are respectively 332 and 243.

The aim is to transfer the (adjusted) parameters of the northern suburbs model to the southwestern suburbs, and to compare the models with a model estimated on the SW data set. Procedures 4 (scaling) and 5 (Bayesian updating) are proposed. By constraining the coefficients of the SW model to equal northern suburbs coefficients (as unadjusted, scaled and Bayesian updated) and estimating the model on the local data, we can obtain the log-likelihood at convergence. A comparison of the restricted and unrestricted log-likelihood function values at convergence provides one basis for assessing the transferability potential of adjusted model parameters. The results are summarised in Table 7.1.

The Bayesian updating procedure performed better than the 'no update' model, but not as well as the unrestricted model. The ρ^2 decreased when the scaling update was applied. The problem with the scaling approach is that it is based on the assumption that if the weightings applied to variables by individuals differ in different areas, then it is only the absolute levels that vary; the marginal rates of substitution between the variables remain invariant. While this may or may not be a realistic hypothesis, the problem in practice is that the pairs of coefficients do not all differ in the same direction, so that when a single scaling factor is applied, some coefficients in the model benefit (that is, become closer to the unrestricted value), while others do not. Thus, it is possible for the scaling update procedure to decrease the fit of a model in the new area. Given this fundamental weakness of the scaling approach, a better alternative might be to simply re-estimate a new constant and leave the other coefficients at their base levels.

In the scaling update model, the calculated χ^2 value is large, such that the null hypothesis of statistical transferability is rejected. Applying the Bayesian update procedure produced a calculated χ^2 value of 15.1 which is only marginally greater than the critical value of 12.6. At the 99 per cent confidence level, the null hypothesis that the model is not significantly different could not be rejected. This provides some measure of the statistical similarity of the Bayesian updated transfer model and the unrestricted southwestern model.

TABLE 7·1: An Empirical Assessment of the Potential for Transferability of Adjusted Model Parameters

Explanatory Variables	Northern Suburbs (N) Model (Q = 332) (t-statistics in brackets)	Unrestricted Model	South Western Suburbs (SW) (Q = 243) Restricted (No update)	Restricted (Scaled) Model (Scale = 1.6071)	Restricted (Bayesian Update) Model
ASC - Car	-1.09 (3.62)	-2.731 (3.3)	-1.09 (3.6)	-1.039	-1.283
Invehicle Time	-0.020 (3.19)	-0.0135 (1.1)	-0.020 (3.1)	-0.0323	-0.0177
Out-of-vehicle Time	-0.041 (2.1)	-0.136 (4.7)	-0.041 (2.1)	-0.0669	-0.0580
Invehicle Cost - Car ÷ Income	-0.093 (4.6)	-0.323 (3.7)	-0.093 (4.6)	-0.149	-0.106
Out-of-vehicle Cost Car ÷ Income	-0.125 (2.6)	0.1178 (0.3)	-0.125 (2.6)	-0.202	-0.122
Total Cost - Rail ÷ Income	-0.169 (4.7)	-0.334 (3.4)	-0.169 (4.7)	-0.273	-0.189
Car competition Effect - Car ÷ Income	-1.34 (3.7)	-1.73 (2.8)	-1.34 (3.7)	-2.154	-1.44
log - likelihood at L(0)		-96.54	-96.54	-96.54	-96.54
log - likelihood at L(β)		-50.56		-67.46	-58.10
L_1 = log - likelihood at L(β) (SW sample, transferred βs)			-61.48	-67.46	-58.10
L_2 = log - likelihood at L(β) (SW sample, SW βs)			-50.56	-50.56	-50.56
Calculated χ^2 = $-2(L_2-L_1)$			21.8	33.8	15.1
Critical χ^2			12.6	12.6	12.6
rho-squared (ρ^2) = $1-(L_1/L_0)$		.48	.36	.29	.39

In summary, the Bayesian updating approach performs quite well when judged using statistical criteria relating to the difference between the transfer model and the unrestricted model estimated on the full southwestern data set. However, this is not surprising, since by definition, the Bayesian approach offers a direct compromise between the two models. In practice, however, the benefits resulting from a Bayesian update are likely to be less pronounced than indicated here (where the update sample is the full sample), unless the estimated coefficients of the small sample have small standard errors. If on the other hand, these estimates are unreliable (reflected in large standard errors due for example, to the collection of only a very small sample) then the updated coefficients will be based primarily on the original transfer model coefficients, and the benefits from updating would be marginal.

7·4 Sample Design and Data Collection

In previous sections of the book, whenever we have introduced data to illustrate the application of a model, no assumptions were stated as to the sampling rule adopted in generating the data, nor the nature and extent of known or possible sources of sampling error that may have significant impacts on estimation and/or prediction error. Sufficient theoretical and empirical research has now been undertaken to postulate that a (if not the) major source of estimation and prediction error is attributable to "poor" data (see Appendix C); the latter being interpreted to include the definition, specification and measurement of the variables in the utility expressions for each alternative, and the design of the sample.

In this section we discuss sample design, and adopt a broad interpretation of this notion, viewing it as the mechanism for linking an estimable choice model to the empirical environment. As such, we include such issues as sources of sampling error, alternative sample designs, the domain(s) of alternative designs, the implications of sample design on model estimation, and the relationship between sampling method and survey procedure. An important inference can be drawn from this broad interpretation of sample design, that the modeller should give a considerable amount of attention to the early stages of the empirical design of a study

and not view data collection as unrewarding relative
to the finer scientific pursuits of model
construction. Far too often data is provided from
an external source with the result that little is
known about the sample design, the sources of error,
and survey procedure. A 'good' model, cannot
perform satisfactorily with 'poor' data. Economists,
in particular, have been disinclined, until recent
years, to generate and record their own data,
relying heavily instead on published statistics.[11]
Since the sample design is a conditioning agent on
the model's output then it is essential that we
identify the range of designs and their implications
for individual choice modelling. This need is
reinforced by the possibility to reduce costs of
data collection when more complex designs are
adopted.

At the outset the reader is warned that there
are considerable difficulties entailed in taking the
theory of sample design, as developed in a formal
ideal environment and applying it to a real-world
environment; approximations (given the state of the
art) abound with the best of intentions; the
discussion below reflects this. One of the most
vexing issues is the identification of the universe
when a nonrandom sample is to be used, and thus the
ensuing problem of applying the estimated model to
forecast the impact of a policy change. Before
discussing the main issues in sample design, it is
necessary to introduce some of the terminology that
is specific to survey sampling and data collection
and which needs precise definition. Additional
definitions will be introduced at the appropriate
place in the text.

A sample is a representative subset of the
population; however because it is usually not
possible to obtain a sample of dissimilar observations which is completely representative, rules of
sampling have to be established. Even with these
rules we still have sampling errors. It is
particularly important that we know the nature and
extent of sampling errors so that the empirical
results can be qualified; so that, for example,
forecasts based on a model estimated on data with a
particular known sampling error are not generalised.
There is always a sampling error in any sample;
the term 'random sampling error' is often used to
refer to the use of a sample to represent a
population. Random sampling error is not to be
confused with sample bias, the latter error
associated with 'bad' sampling, due to an incorrect
sampling frame, insufficient control of sampling, or

excessive nonresponse, for example. Such bias does not always exist in a sample: it can be avoided. A sampling frame is a basic list which unambiguously defines every element in the population from which a sample is to be drawn. The existence of a sampling frame is essential to the process of sampling. For purposes of exposition, let us refer to bias as consistent sampling error; and the error due to chance differences between those members of the population who are surveyed and those who are not as random sampling error.

Applied discrete choice modelling involves model estimation and model prediction (or application). It is useful to discuss sources of error separately for each modelling phase. For completeness, nonsampling sources of error are also presented; this helps in emphasising the sample design-related errors. There are three major sources of error in model estimation; each of which can be difficult to separate out in an analysis of errors:

(1) Specification error. This results from the simplifying process associated with the construction of models, and represents a misspecification due to one or more of omitted structure, cross-sectional preference variation or instrumental variables (Manski, 1973). Omitted structure is associated with excluded relevant variables, due to measurement problems and/or improper model hypothesis; cross-sectional preference variation is associated with the existence of noninvariant functional form of the utility expression across the sampled population; and instrumental variables is associated with the use of inappropriate surrogates in the model for variables that have a significant effect on the choice process. Specification error has already been discussed as a source of the explanation of the violation of the independence-from-irrelevant alternative property (Chapter 5). Specification error can influence the magnitude of alternative-specific constants; however it is not the only factor that may affect these constants. We have already seen in Section 7.3 that sample design can affect the constants.

(2) Measurement error. This error is primarily associated with errors made in the measurement of variables, and is in part related to imperfect information (see Section 4.5.1). Since the dependent variable is quantal, we have no measurement error from this variable although

specification error is possible if the alternatives are not well defined. An example of measurement error is where an individual is asked to indicate the income group that his/her income belongs to, with a resultant allocation to a group above the correct one.

(3) <u>Sampling error - consistent sampling error (or bias)</u>. There are many sources of bias in sampling; however the most common ways in which bias may occur include:

(a) deliberate selection of a 'representative' sample or an 'average' sample;

(b) sampling on the basis of an attribute that is correlated with one or more properties of the observational unit; the most common instance being the use of the telephone directory as the sampling frame if the analyst is interested in the incidence of telephone availability;

(c) selection of a random sample in which the random selection process is not strictly adhered to; a frequent application being the elimination of households which have an 'enter at your own risk - vicious dog' sign on the gate; especially if the survey related to attitudes on security;

(d) the substitution of additional members of the population when difficulties are encountered in sampling the original sample observation; for example the selection of the house next door after two call backs on selected home, can result in overrepresentation of households with a higher incidence of being at home.

(e) nonresponse, associated with no reply and nonsubstitution of a household.

Minimisation of bias means avoidance of the various sources of bias. Bias may occur in many stages of the survey task, in addition to that in the sample selection process. Specification and measurement error are other forms of bias. In general, bias should be minimised, although a circumstance exists where it is tolerated. This occurs where, from a series of surveys, we are interested in the changes that are occurring in a particular attribute; and provided a constant bias exists across the surveys, then we can tolerate this situation.

225

(4) Sampling error - random sampling error.
Random sampling error (rse) is, all other things
being constant, approximately proportional to the
inverse of the square root of the sample size. The
task is to select a sample in such a way as to
ensure that the rse is sufficiently small to permit
the achievement of a desired level of accuracy.
Thus rse is a function of both the sample size and
the variance of the units in the population. One
way of reducing the size of the rse, without
introducing any consistent sampling error, is to
impose restrictions on the fully random sample which
reduce that part of the variance of the observations
which contributes to sampling error. The consequence is also a reduced sample size, for a given
level of accuracy. Market segmentation (Section
7.2) is an example of such a restriction. Sample
design is primarily concerned with the types of
restrictions (on a full random sample) and the
implications this has on the estimation and application of individual choice models. Random samples
are costly to collect; fortunately there is often
no necessity to draw random samples; and provided
that the analyst is aware of the implications of
alternative sample designs, then accuracy can be
maintained at a desired level for a lower cost
outlay by the adoption of other designs. Furthermore, in many empirical investigations a random
sample provides much redundant data. For example if
an analyst is interested in modelling the choice
between renting private and government flats, then
the sampling frame should only contain current
renters of both types of establishments; there is
no value in sampling randomly from all establishment
and occupant statuses. An important point,
however, is that often the analyst has inadequate
information, prior to the survey phase, to identify
the relevant population from which to draw the
appropriate sample. This is one of the major
practical problems which results often in the
selection of a random sample, and then the removal
of much of the data (at a considerable expense) at
the model estimation stage; or the screening of
potential respondents and the drawing of sample
points during the stage of fieldwork.

What are the range of restrictions, or sample
designs? While the range is very large in general,
for individual choice modelling it is convenient to
classify designs as being fully random, stratified
(exogenous) and stratified choice-based or
endogenous.[12] Since each design has an influence

on the variance in the units of population, and each unit is defined in terms of a set of explanatory variables on a set of alternatives, socioeconomic attributes and a choice outcome, then it is likely that the parameter estimates might be influenced by the sample design. Different sample designs might affect the attribute distribution and the choice probabilities. We have to decide if there is an influence, and if there is, whether or not the estimation procedure associated with the basic choice model in Chapter 3 needs modification or whether postestimation adjustments can accommodate the influence of design. This is the central issue of this section.

Although we have not defined probability up to this point, in the context of individual choice modelling as presented in this book (i.e. predominantly the economist's perspective) the probability notion refers to a sampling probability that the individual who has completed a single choice will be selected by the analyst.[13] Thus 'probability' refers to the analyst's sampling probability of selecting an individual who is assumed to have a constant (1, 0) choice, and is thus a relative frequency notion. Hence, varying the sampling rule might affect the likelihood of an observation.

A fully random sample (frs) involves selecting individuals at random such that each has an equal probability of being selected. Relatively large sample sizes are often required in order to achieve the required statistical validity, that is, to ensure that the proper proportions of choosers of each alternative is obtained as well as the distributions of the attribute levels. It is usually assumed that if the sample size is adequate to estimate the mean value within satisfactory limits (the distribution of the mean values of the distributions assumed to be normally distributed), it is also large enough to represent the other moments of the distribution (i.e. variance, covariance).

To attain the desired level of reliability of the survey data in a frs, the size of the sample must be determined so that the specified probability that the percentage of the sample (P) deviates from the unknown percentage of the population $(\bar{P})$ is less than a predetermined quantity (ϕ). This involves establishing the maximum deviation between P and $\bar{P}$, which the analyst is prepared to accept; and establishing the probability of such a deviation being maintained within the specified limits. The system of equations to solve is:

$$(P - \bar{P}) \leqslant \phi \tag{7.5}$$

$$\text{Prob } ((P - \bar{P}) \leqslant \phi) = \alpha \tag{7.6}$$

Solving equations (7.5) and (7.6) in the case of a Bernoullian sample, gives[14]

$$Q = \frac{Q^* R^2 \bar{P}(1-\bar{P})}{(Q^*-1)\phi^2 + R^2 \bar{P}(1-\bar{P})} \tag{7.7}$$

where

Q = unknown size of sample

Q^* = size of the population

R = a measure of the reliability of the results. R takes on one of three values (R = 1, 2, 3), increasing in value if greater reliability is required.

ϕ = maximum deviation between P and $\bar{P}$

This formula is also relevant for subsets of the population when a sample of randomly selected individuals is required.

The majority of the more specialised sample designs which impose restrictions on simple random sampling belong to the family of stratified samples which use exogenous (to the model) criteria for stratification. In a stratified (exogenous) sample, the population is divided into groups based on one or more attributes, and each group is sampled with either a constant or varying sample fraction, and with the option of additional (multistage) stratification within each previous population group. A variable sampling fraction means that the strata (or groups) are sampled randomly but at different rates in such a way that the strata which are of more importance, or are more variable, are sampled more intensively. This usually requires that survey results are weighted correctly before being combined to yield a total result for the entire population; however, it is demonstrated below that stratified samples do not require weighting if the estimation procedure of Chapter 3 is used with the basic choice model. An example of a multistage stratified sample design is cluster sampling, which

involves the grouping of the total population into
clusters where each cluster can be considered to be
a natural unit of the population. It is often
argued, for example, that individuals living in
households in the same street or suburb display more
similar behaviour than individuals living in
different streets or suburbs, given a particular
issue. The clusters are then sampled at random,
and the units within the cluster are either selected
with certainty or sampled at a high rate (with a
constant or variable sampling fraction). This
particular sampling rule is popular with real world
survey research organisations when faced with a
limited budget for data collection, since it helps
to minimise the amount of interviewer time in moving
between interviews. Up to 50% of fieldwork costs
are attributed to such movement.

Let us formalise the class of stratified
sampling rules in the context of the basic choice
model (and any other discrete choice model which is
estimated by the maximum likelihood estimation
technique (Lerman & Manski, 1978a)). A useful
starting point is the likelihood of observation
formulation for a fully random sample, which is a
special case of the stratified sample (i.e. a single
stratum).

Given the interpretation of probability as a
relative frequency, then the basic probabilistic
assumption underlying the discrete choice model is
that the frequency distribution of choices (i) and
attribute matrices (x) in the actual population can
be characterised by a generalised probability
density (Lerman & Manski, 1978)[15]

$$f(i,x) \equiv P(i|x)p(x) \qquad (7.8)$$

defined over the choice set (A) and the complete
attribute space (S) (i.e. $(i,x) \in AxS$) and where
$P(i|x)$ is the choice model predicting the probability that i is selected given x (equation 3.24)
and $p(x)$ is the marginal generalised probability
density of x in the population. Given that the
choice probabilities $(P(i|x))$ have the multinomial
logit form, then the choice probability can be
written as $P(i|x,\beta^*)$, where β^* is a vector of
unknown parameters.

The analyst can draw observations of (i,x) pairs
from A x S according to one of various sampling
rules; and having done so, has to determine how β^*
may be estimated. Assume that we can partition the
set A x S into B mutually exclusive and collectively
exhaustive subsets $(A \times S)_b$, b = 1,...,B. A set of

variable or constant sampling fractions H_b are selected, and a sample size Q such that

$\sum_{b=1}^{B} H_b = 1$ and $Q_b = H_b \cdot Q$, where for each stratum a

total of Q_b individuals are independently drawn from Q_b^*, the subpopulation of Q* defined by $Q_b^* = (q^* \in Q^* : (i_{q^*}, x_{q^*}) \in (AxS)_b)$. For each sampled individual (q), the associated choice-attribute pair (i_q, x_q) is observed, for $q = 1, \ldots, Q$ and $b = 1, \ldots, B$.

The initial stage in the identification of the estimates of the unknown parameters is to define the likelihood of a (stratified) sample. The likelihood of an individual drawn independently from a stratified sample is the product of the probability that the stratum $(A \times S)_b$ of membership is selected (i.e. H_b) and the conditional likelihood of selecting the (i,x) pair out of this membership stratum. The latter is $f(i_q, x_q)/H_b^*$, where H_b^* is the population (as distinct from sample) fraction (i.e. fraction of Q* who are members of Q_b^*). Manski & McFadden (1980) show that H_b^* is equal to

$$\int_{(AxS)_b} f(i,x)d(i,x) \qquad (7.9)$$

i.e. the integral of the joint distribution f(i,x) over the subset $(A \times S)_b$. Thus, the likelihood of the sample is

$$L = \prod_{b=1}^{B} \prod_{q=1}^{Q_b} \frac{f(i_q, x_q)}{\int_{(AxS)_b} f(i,x)d(i,x)} \cdot H_b \quad \text{or}$$

$$\prod_{b=1}^{B} \prod_{q=1}^{Q_b} \frac{P(i_q | x_q)p(x_q)}{\int_{(AxS)_b} P(i|x)p(x)d(i,x)} \cdot H_b \qquad (7.10)$$

Clearly, for a fully random sample the denominator of equation (7.10) is unity, and so is H_b. Hence the sample likelihood function is a special (limiting) case:

$$L_{frs} = \prod_{q=1}^{Q} P(i_q | x_q)p(x_q) \qquad (7.11)$$

230

which is similar to equation (7.8) and compatible with equation (3.28).

The sample likelihood functions for stratified exogenous and endogenous sample designs are restrictions imposed on the random sample or modifications of equation (7.10). For an exogenous sample design, $(A \times S)_b = A \times S_b$ (i.e. the pair (i,x) is included in stratum $(A \times S)_b$ if and only if $x \in S_b$ and i (i.e. choice) is not a criterion of stratification).[16] Hence the denominator of equation equation (7.10) becomes $\int_{S_b} p(x) dx$, resulting in equation (7.12)

$$L_{exs} = \prod_{b=1}^{B} \prod_{q=1}^{Q_b} \frac{P(i_q|x_q)p(x_q) H_b}{\int_{S_b} p(x) dx} \qquad (7.12)$$

The analyst has control only of the sampling fraction and the criteria for defining strata (S). He still has to somehow determine the other influences on the attribute distribution (i.e. $p(x_q)/\int_{S_b} p(x) dx$). Since the within-stratum sampling is fully random, the analyst has no control over this aspect of data collection. Hence there is no way of ensuring in advance the full identities of the individuals drawn from within each strata, other than the stratum identity.

When the sample strata criterion relates to the choices available, rather than exogenous variables, then a different partitioning rule applies. For an endogenous (or choice-based) sample design $(A \times S)_b = A_b \times S$ (i.e. the pair (i,x) is included in stratum $(A \times S)_b$ if and only if $i \in A_b$).[17] Hence the denominator of equation (7.10) becomes

$$\int_S (\sum_{i \in A_b} P(i|x)) p(x) dx$$

resulting in equation (7.13)

$$L_{ens} = \prod_{b=1}^{B} \prod_{q=1}^{Q_b} \frac{P(i_q|x_q)p(x_q) H_b}{\int_S P(i|x)p(x) dx} \qquad (7.13)$$

231

Endogenous sampling enables control over the frequency distribution of chosen alternatives in the sample, this being particularly useful where certain known current and/or future alternatives are a small proportion of the population choices such that random or exogenous sampling can result in an inadequate number of sample points on these alternatives and thus limited confidence in the precision of the estimated parameters. When the alternatives in the choice set define the strata, then equation (7.13) can be simplified as equation (7.14).

$$L_{cs} = \prod_{i \in A} \prod_{q=1}^{Q_b} \frac{P(i|x_q)p(x_q) \, H_b}{\int_S P(i|x)p(x)dx} \qquad (7.14)$$

The next task is to identify suitable maximum-likelihood estimators for the alternative stratified sample designs. The state of the art in this area is somewhat recent in origin, and as such the discussion below is partly tentative. Manski & McFadden (1980) have undertaken an extensive investigation of this area, which is far too complex for an introductory book on applied discrete choice modelling. The discussion on estimators is no more than a summary of what is relevant for the analyst in the use of individual choice models. All proofs are given elsewhere (Manski & Lerman, 1977a; Manski & McFadden, 1980; McFadden, 1979; Lerman & Manski, 1978a).

Before we can estimate the choice model and hence empirically identify $P(i|x_q)$, we need to have some description of the attribute distribution, suitable for each sample design. On this issue, Lerman & Manski (1978) state:

> Because the attribute distribution simply
> describes the existing ... environment
> and is not derived from any causal model,
> it is generally assumed in discrete choice
> analysis that one knows little, if anything,
> about the form of p(x) a priori. In
> particular, unlike the behaviourally
> derived choice probabilities, the attribute
> density is usually not specified to be a
> member of any parametric family. Thus,
> learning the attribute distribution means
> learning the whole distribution function,
> not merely some parameters characterizing
> this function.   (1978: 19)

Two general approaches to using stratified samples to estimate the distribution of attributes in the population are:

(1)   constraining the sample design such that the fraction of individuals in each stratum equals the corresponding population fraction, i.e. $H_b = H_b^*$

(2)   using simple probability statements to solve for the population attribute distribution as a weighted sum of the attribute distributions within the strata. The weights are H_b^*

Both approaches require an a priori knowledge of the share of the population in each stratum; and provided this is the situation then no knowledge of the choice process is required (Lerman & Manski, 1978: 22). Herein lies the major problem - how does one identify population shares (H_b^*) in each stratum?[18]

Three alternative procedures are available for obtaining a true or approximate population total and subpopulation shares. The selection among the alternative approaches is primarily an empirical issue, although the cost of obtaining the required data is an important consideration. The first procedure can be called the 'census approach', since it involves the direct measurement of population levels from an existing data source (or possibly a data source that is currently being prepared for uses other than or in addition to choice modelling). This approach is suitable when the data required for choice modelling is compatible with the date of the external data source or can be easily updated (or backdated). Such data would come primarily from the census or from stock types of data regularly collected by government organisations. Examples of the latter are motor vehicle registrations, records of government housing authorities on government housing, water board records on residences, labour department unemployment statistics, irregular bureau of statistics population surveys on size and composition of various industries, health authority records on incidence of various diseases. A word of warning is required, since many of the examples might not lead to sufficient detail to permit the determination of subpopulation sizes. Often the analyst must take this into account and check out the information content of such data sources before defining the stratum criteria. A considerable amount of time, money and effort can go into this phase of modelling; in general the rewards make this stage well worthwhile. A common problem is that we know the row and column totals in a multiple stratification yet have no control of the substrata. An example is given in the footnote[19] of use of an approximation method developed by Yates (and used by Stopher & Meyburg, 1979) to obtain these substrata totals.

A second procedure involves an 'auxiliary random sample'. Since the sample distribution of (i,x) pairs is a consistent estimator of the population distribution $f(i,x)$, then it follows that for any stratification $(A \times S)_b$, $b = 1,...,B$, the fraction of the random sample who belong to each stratum is a consistent estimate of H_b^*. This random sample would emphasise obtaining information on a few socio-demographic dimensions only, and is not too costly, in comparison to a full survey required for choice modelling. Use of the telephone for obtaining such data is discouraged since many individuals are not listed in telephone directories. This approach provides the substrata totals directly and avoids the laborious approximation method.

The third approach, proposed by Lerman & Manski (1978, 1978a) is referred to as the 'post stratification solution', which involves solving a set of linear equations. The best way to present this approach is with an example. Suppose the population is a set of residents in a metropolitan area, and that we want to stratify by three establishment types (detached house, townhouse, flat) using knowledge of population means on various attributes. Define $v(x)$ to be any vector valued function of x. We can state the identity

$$g(x) = \sum_{b=1}^{B} g(x|b) \, H_b^* \qquad (7.15)$$

i.e. the cumulative distribution of attributes in the population is equal to the product (summed across all stratum) of the cumulative distribution of attributes in the bth subpopulation and the population sampling fraction associated with the bth subpopulation. It follows that

$$E(v) = \sum_{b=1}^{B} E(v|b) \, H_b^* \qquad (7.15a)$$

For known values of $E(v)$ and $E(v|b)$, and that

$$\sum_{b=1}^{B} H^*_b = 1,$$

and the v-vector has at least one less than the number of alternatives in the choice set, then we can solve a set of equations to obtain the H^*_b values.

Suppose we are able, from published sources, to obtain information to calculate the mean values for two attributes (household income and number of children) associated with each establishment type (and hence a choice-based stratification), and overall:

```
detached house = $34,000 and 2.8 children
town house     = $20,000 and 1.6 children
flat           = $12,000 and 1.2 children
overall        = $22,600 and 1.9 children.
```

Then the equations to solve are:

$$22600 = 34000\, F_1 + 20000\, F_2 + 12000\, F_3$$
$$1.9 = 2.8\, F_1 + 1.6\, F_2 + 1.2\, F_3$$
$$1 = F_1 + F_2 + F_3.$$

The solution gives $F_1 = .3$, $F_2 = .5$ and $F_3 = .2$.

This method becomes more complicated as the number of attributes and alternatives increases, although there are standard computer programs available to solve a set of simultaneous equations. The main disadvantage of this approach is that a stratified sample has to be drawn initially, and thus we cannot use the knowledge of H^* (i.e. H^*_1, H^*_2,...,H^*_b,...,H^*_B) in selecting the sample composition H^*_b. The previous procedures are in general more appealing.

Estimation using each sample design involves solution of one of the equations (7.11), (7.12) or (7.14).[20] We need not comment on the fully random sample design since the procedure outlined in Chapter 3 assumes such a design. Furthermore, Manski & Lerman (1977a) and Manski & McFadden (1980) have shown that for exogenous samples the application of maximum-likelihood estimation is the same as that for a fully random sample:

It is only in exogenous samples that the
terms $\sum_{(A \times S)_{ix}} P(j \,|\, y, \beta)\, p(y),\ b \in B$

reduce to expressions not involving β.

> *Hence it is only in such samples that*
> *the likelihood function kernel takes*
> *the simple form P(i|x,β).*
> *simplification differentiates the*
> *parameter estimation problem in*
> *exogenous samples from that encountered*
> *under all other stratified sampling*
> *rules.*
>
> (Manski & McFadden, 1980: 52-53)

This leaves us with the final sample design, choice-based sampling (equation 7.14). The aim is to use the choice-based sampling likelihood to obtain estimates of β.[21] The integral in the denominator of equation (7.14) makes maximum-likelihood estimation complex. Manski & Lerman developed the first tractable estimator with desirable statistical properties; however their estimator is dependent on knowing H_b^* $(=\int_S P(i|x,\beta^*)p(x)dx)$.

The selection of an estimator for choice-based sampling is primarily dependent on the knowledge of H_b^* and $p(x)$. Table 7.2 presents the estimators proposed by Manski & McFadden when H_b^* and $p(x)$ are known and unknown.

The special case of using the exogenous sampling estimator (in a multinomial logit context) when a choice based sample is drawn was discussed in Section 7.3. Since in many applications we do not have ranked alternatives, then recourse has to be made to one of the estimators in Table 7.2. Current practice applies the estimator for H_b^* known and $p(x)$ unknown. It is a simple programming change to weight the log of $P(i_q|x,\beta)$ by H_{iq}^*/H_{iq}. This concludes the discussion on sources of estimation error. Sources of prediction error can be covered in less space, since many such sources have already been introduced in other sections of this chapter and earlier chapters.

Measurement error in prediction is associated with the estimated or measured values of the explanatory variables and can arise for a number of reasons; for example, the use of calculated levels of variables for predicting the effect of a change in a variable's level on choice outcome in a model estimated on reported perceived data (see Sections 4.5.1 and 7.2.2). This is a very common problem because in practice the 'equivalent' reported perceived levels associated with the new situation are usually not known. This can have important implications on the reliability of elasticity of choice estimates.

TABLE 7·2 : Choice-Based Sample Design Maximum-Likelihood Estimators Under Alternative Assumptions (on H_b^* and $p(x)$)

H_b^* is the population fraction, i.e. fraction of Q^* who are members of Q_b^*; $p(x)$ is the marginal distribution of attributes; $H_b^* = \int f(i,x)\,dx$; $p(x) = \sum_{i \in A} f(i,x)$ [22]

	p(x) known	p(x) unknown (i.e. $\tilde{p}(x)$)
H_b^* known	$$\max_{\beta \in \underline{\beta}_0} \left\{ \sum_{q=1}^{Q} \ln P(i_q|x_q,\beta) - \sum_{q=1}^{Q} \ln \sum_{S} P(i_q|x,\beta)p(x) \right\}$$ $\underline{\beta}_0$ is the constrained parameter space thus requiring a complicated set of constraint equations. Manski & Lerman (1977a) show that a tractable approximation to the constraint equations which does not involve the distribution $p(x)$ can be used. It is simpler although less efficient and is the formulation given for $p(x)$ unknown and H_b^* known	$$\max_{\beta \in \underline{\beta}} \sum_{q=1}^{Q} \frac{H^*(i_q)}{H(i_q)} \ln P(i_q|x,\beta)$$ This is the **weighted exogenous sampling maximum-likelihood estimator**.
H_b^* unknown (i.e. $\tilde{H}^*$)	$$\max_{\beta \in \underline{\beta}} \sum_{q=1}^{Q} \ln P(i_q|x_q,\beta) - \sum_{q=1}^{Q} \ln \sum_{S} P(i_q|x,\beta)p(x)$$	$$\max_{\substack{(\tilde{\beta},\tilde{H}^*) \\ \in \underline{\beta} \times \Pi}} \frac{1}{Q} \sum_{q=1}^{Q} \ln \frac{P(i_q|x,\beta)\,\dfrac{H^*(i_q)}{H(i_q)}}{\sum_{j \in A} P(j|x_q,\beta)\,\dfrac{H^*(j)}{H(j)}}$$ $\underline{\beta}$ is full parameter space. A unique maximum is not guaranteed for an MNL model with ASCs.

Source: Manski & McFadden (1980)

237

Specification error results from the misspecification of the initial model and its application to a new or modified data set. This issue has been partly covered in the previous section on transferability. However, an inadequate or incorrect hypothesis of the model or inadequate sample size can contribute to specification error. Such issues as the functional form of the utility expression, the form of the explanatory variables (generic vs. alternative-specific, polynomial or order one), and the definition of alternatives can all be major sources of error. Inadequate sample size can prevent the correct application of asymptotic measures of significance, and biased parameter estimates due to an unsuitable representation of the range and distribution of the attributes being used in the model. The prediction of group response is influenced by sample size, and is a point that has to be taken into account in the initial sample design.

Aggregation error has already been dealt with in Section 7.2. This leaves sampling error in prediction. Even if we had no measurement, specification or structural error, the predictive accuracy of a model is influenced by the quality of the sample. Poor predictions can result from inaccurate information required in converting the sample predictions to population predictions (this clearly requires knowledge of the sample design, the sampling frame and the date of sample data compared to the date of population application). It can be associated with the sample size which can influence the level of accuracy for representing the attribute distribution. We cannot add any more commentary on the mapping of a sample into a population than has been given earlier in this section; we will concentrate on the influence of sample size, something which the analyst can control (subject to budget constraints). It is often stated that sample size can be varied to suit the degree of predictive precision required, all other things being constant.[23] This is influenced by the sensitivity of the model with respect to each of the attributes and the attribute distribution.

An 'acceptable' error can be defined in absolute or relative terms and assigned a likelihood of occurrence. In a logit model context, the function tends to reduce the size of the error in the attributes as a function of the estimated probability at which the error takes place, since the relationship is nonlinear. Stoner (1977) has shown that the confidence limits associated with a given sample size are dependent on the distribution of the error in the prediction of the probability of choice associated with a given attribute distribution. Two conclusions emerge:

(1) For the effect of a constant error in the linear terms on the absolute error in the probability of choice, the absolute error is greatest at the midpoint of the function and decreases towards the asymptotes. The y-axis is the absolute error in prediction of P, the x-axis is the value of P.

(2) For the effect of a constant error in the linear terms on the proportional error in P, a decreasing relationship exists, and indicates that even though the absolute error is decreasing with a decreasing expected probability, the proportional error is increasing. The y-axis is the proportional error in the prediction of P, x-axis is the value of P. For example, if a relatively low level of housing service is being evaluated, involving a low percentage of low-quality housing respondents, then the sample size would need to be much larger if the concern was with proportional error than absolute error.

It appears that one of the most important determinants of sample size is the attribute distribution, and its degree of deviation from a normal distribution. Security in sample size selection is given in the confidence limits (based on a normal distribution assumption and asymptotic measures). If nonnormality exists (which is frequently the case), then the sample variance is more variable from sample to sample, making prediction (application) less reliable in terms of the interpretation of conventional measures of confidence. Cochran (1964) indicates that sample variance is mainly a function of the fourth moment, known as kurtosis measure; and that a simple formula can be provided to determine the increase in sample size to accommodate nonnormality. The formula (equation 7.16) is

$$\frac{1}{4} \left[\frac{Q(k + 2) - k}{Q} \right]^2 \qquad (7.16)$$

where k is the measure of kurtosis. The variance of the population is inflated by normality by the square root of equation (7.16). Hensher, McLeod & Stanley (1975) used the kurtosis measure to identify the degree to which alternative specifications of attributes influenced the distribution of each attribute across the sample, away from normality (Table 7.3). The value of k for the normal distribution is .263. With the exception of the convenience attribute, the percentile coefficient of kurtosis indicates similar deviations from normality on a single attribute basis. Both specifications require sample sizes larger than required if the single normality assumption were valid. This example suggests that there is a great deal of scope in influencing sample size via the specification and measurement of independent variables. Stoner (1977) found that the disaggregation of a single variable 'travel time' into component time variables (wait, walk, invehicle) reduces sampling requirements.

TABLE 7·3 : Percentile Coefficient of Kurtosis (k)

I_t^P	I_t^{SN}	I_c^P	I_c^{SN}	I_{cm}^P	I_{cm}^{SN}	I_{cn}^P	I_{cn}^{SN}
.267	.307	.120	.195	.526	.518	.106	.274

Notes: I^P is constrained points allocation to indicate relative importance of an attribute.

I^{SN} is unconstrained points allocation using a separate scale, (1 to 100) for each attribute.

t = travel time, c = travel cost, cm = travel comfort, cn = travel convenience

Within each stratum (or overall if a fully random sample), the formula given in equation (7.7) can be used to determine the sample size, given a finite population, since all stratum are randomly sampled. Formula (7.16) can be used to adjust the sample size in a stratum if nonnormality is shown to exist on the kurtosis measure. R in equation (7.7) is the t-value at the selected level of confidence. In general it can be shown that the required randomly drawn sample sizes do increase as the proportions in each choice alternative approach equality (and allowable error should decrease), and hence the analyst should consider a choice-based sample with appropriate weighting.[24] With a choice-based sample there is more scope for adjusting sample sizes while still keeping the size manageable on a cost basis. Once again the attribute distribution is the main influence on the final size. The analyst must still conduct the sample tests for nonnormality and adjust the substrata sample sizes accordingly. In all the discussion we are assuming that selection within a substratum is truly random, however in practice it may be difficult to ensure this is so; and since the analyst cannot control the identities of the individuals then drawn, he must conduct tests on the attribute distribution to identify deviations from normality.

To conclude this discussion on sample size for 'precision of predictions', the main factors that affect sample size and which are model-related include the complexity of the model form, the sensitivity of the model, the size of the population variance of the attributes, the range of alternatives being evaluated and the required reliability of the estimates. Stoner's empirical study shows that reliable estimates can be obtained from very small samples (≈ 200) when the model is insensitive to relative alternative attribute differences, the actual attribute variances are small or are reduced through stratification or classification, or only relative measures of choice probability are required. If these findings can be confirmed in other empirical research then this will provide the practitioner with a degree of confidence in estimating and applying models on small data sets.

Although the approaches outlined above have operational merits, there are still many issues not yet clarified. To conclude this section, we list a range of issues that the analyst should be aware of, and which require contact with the continuing literature on basic research in this area to monitor resolution of these outstanding concerns:

(1) the procedures outlined assume maximum-likelihood estimation and should not be applied to other estimation procedures without careful scrutiny.

(2) the 'best' sample design on the classical criterion of minimising the variance of parameter estimates depends on the true parameter values, which are a priori unknown.

241

(3)   for choice-based sampling we assume
      that known distributions are known
      with complete certainty, yet in
      practice only estimates of the
      attribute distribution p(x) or H are
      available. The extent of error is
      unknown.

(4)   Homogeneous sample designs were
      assumed above; however if mixed
      designs are used then the likelihood
      functions associated with each design
      have to be summed and then maximised.
      All attributes will then have to be
      weighted by H_b^*/H_b if at least one
      subsample is not exogenous.

(5)   All the attributes have been assumed
      to be exogenous; however it is often
      more appropriate to include some
      attributes as endogenous. Although
      the early discussion on measurement
      error in estimation indicated one
      source to be instrumental variables,
      the argument can also work in
      reverse. If a reversal is more
      consistent with a behavioural
      relationship (i.e. a two-way causality)
      then it may happen that the
      distribution of this attribute as an
      instrumental specification is closer
      to a normal distribution and assists
      in keeping the sample size down for
      a given level of predictive precision.
      It could however require an increased
      sample size. This is an empirical
      issue relevant to a particular study.
      Some studies have shown that
      particular attributes, if improperly
      specified or measured can be a major
      contributor to the need for increasing
      sample size; hence careful
      consideration should be given to this
      issue, in the interests of minimising
      model estimation and prediction error
      and in cost savings.

(6)   We have assumed that missing data is
      not a problem. In practice this is a
      real issue which is usually 'resolved'
      by the analyst providing the 'missing
      information', deleting the
      observation entirely, or (and less
      often) specifying a model structure
      to accommodate incomplete information,

given that the latter is no more
than a specification bias. This
is discussed in the next chapter.
However, when the analyst provides
the data it is very difficult to
assess the possible additional
error. The tests available are
distributional, but do not guide us
to the 'correct' distribution, only
the relationship between the
empirical distribution and some
statistical criterion for 'acceptance'.

Finally we have not discussed survey procedures
per se, except insofar as it is of relevance to
sample design. This is an extensive area in its
own right. The reader is strongly advised to
consult any one of the many texts on survey
procedures (e.g. Stopher & Meyburg, 1979), since the
procedure used may well influence the sample
design as well as the sample design influence the
survey procedure.

7·5 Valuation of Attributes

Individual choice models prove a useful framework for obtaining empirical estimates of the
monetary-equivalences of attributes. Assuming
that one of the explanatory variables is expressed
in monetary units (e.g. travel cost, house price
per unit of time) then the value of an attribute
can be determined. Since the models are concerned
with choices at the level of the decision-making
unit, then we can observe tradeoffs that individuals
make in terms of the attributes influencing the
decision being modelled. Thus we have a means of
determining, at the margin, the rate at which one
attribute is traded for another in arriving at the
selection of a particular alternative in the choice
set.
Many of the determinants of consumer choices
do not have a value that is identifiable in the
units in which commodities are exchanged in the
market. Such values (or shadow prices) are
particularly useful in cost-benefit studies, where
single indices of generalised cost or benefit are
required (Williams, 1977). Although there is an
active debate in the literature on the merits and
demerits of combining the dimensions of choice and
impact into single monetary indices of benefits and
costs, nevertheless the practice is likely to

continue and hence we need ways of determining the value of a choice-related attribute which is not usually expressed in the common units of market exchange. Typical examples of user-related specific or abstract attributes are travel time, comfort of a house, and quality of a neighbourhood. Abstract attributes, such as the latter two examples, would require more definition before they could be of value to planners; essentially a metric would have to be determined that is in policy sensitive units (PSUs) before useful shadow pricing can be undertaken.

The theoretical literature on the valuation of attributes is extensive, while the empirical evidence is limited to a few areas such as transport, housing and recreation. An exhaustive review of theory and practice is outlined in Hensher & Dalvi (1978) and Bruzelius (1979). Theoretically, the values that individuals place on a particular attribute should be equal at the margin at all times. However, because of constraints in the real world which distort the theoretical uniformity, we need to be very careful in the empirical valuation of attributes. Populations will have to be segmented for empirical valuation in a way which accounts for the greatest between-segment variation in constraints and least within-segment variation in constraints. The identification of constraints becomes a major issue in the empirical valuation of attributes (Hensher & Dalvi, 1978).

Alternative individual-choice modelling formulations have been proposed for the valuation of attributes, although all approaches can be derived from the same theory. The main difference is in the amount of information provided for the identification of the tradeoff margin. The alternative approaches are well documented elsewhere (Hensher & Dalvi, 1978).

The derivation of shadow prices from an individual choice model using a logit function and a linear-additive preference function is outlined below. Assume only two attributes, 'a' and 'c', where 'a' is the attribute to be valued and 'c' is the attribute 'cost'. Let f be a real-valued utility function such that $U = f(a,c)$, and 'a' and 'c' are expressed as a function of differences of levels of attributes pertaining to the alternatives (1 and 2) in the choice set.

To value one attribute in terms of another, we can argue that for a utility-maximising consumer he would tradeoff alternative bundles of levels of a common set of attributes by assessing their

contribution to his utility. Hence to maximise
utility, we have to set dU/da = 0. It follows that

$$\frac{dU}{da} = \frac{\partial U}{\partial(a_1-a_2)} \cdot \frac{d(a_1-a_2)}{da} + \frac{\partial U}{\partial(c_1-c_2)} \cdot \frac{d(c_1-c_2)}{da}$$

$$\frac{\partial U}{\partial(a_1-a_2)} = \beta_1 \quad ; \quad \frac{\partial U}{\partial(c_1-c_2)} = \beta_2 \qquad (7.17)$$

For maximum utility, dU/da = 0
Thus $\beta_1 \, d(a_1-a_2) + \beta_2 \, d(c_1-c_2) = 0$;

$$\frac{\beta_1}{\beta_2} = -\frac{d(c_1-c_2)/da}{d(a_1-a_2)/da} = -\frac{d(c_1-c_2)}{d(a_1-a_2)} \qquad (7.18)$$

The ratio of the coefficients of attribute 'a' and
attribute 'c' (the cost variable) respectively give
the value of the ratio of the change in cost
difference with respect to a change in difference in
levels of attribute 'a' between the two alternatives.
Formally, the value of a particular attribute
(saving) is equivalent to the amount of money an
individual is willing to outlay in order to save a
unit of the particular attribute, ceteris paribus.
The empirical validity of the obtained value is very
much dependent on the validity of the ceteris
paribus condition, and has been an issue of
considerable debate (Hensher & Dalvi, 1978).
Nevertheless, the approach is basically sound, but
needs careful use in empirical investigations and
particularly in application.

7·6 The Influence of Discontinuities or Thresholds in Individual Behaviour

While work has continued on the development of
multinomial logit and multinomial probit models,
along the lines outlined in Chapters 3 to 5, other
model structures have also been considered that are
based upon different assumptions of the choice
process of individuals, although still basically
utility-maximising procedures. A principal
departure from the established formulation of the
logit model is the consideration that the individual
does not react in a continuous fashion to attribute
changes, but rather that he reacts only when the
changes are sufficiently large to cross a threshold.
This threshold may be a threshold of awareness or a
threshold of acceptability. In addition, thresholds

245

may not be fully compensatory. In this book we are interested in the possibility of improving the choice model developed in earlier chapters by the introduction of assumptions related to choice behaviour which may be more plausible in particular circumstances. Some alternative assumptions are briefly introduced in this section.

The existence of perceptible thresholds has been acknowledged in the literature for many years, and was formalised some time ago by Weber (1820) in psychology and Georgescu-Roegen (1936, 1958) in economics. Georgescu-Roegen introduced the notion of the threshold of insensitivity into the theory of consumer behaviour over forty years ago (Georgescu-Roegen, 1936), suggesting that a choice will be considered only when the positive range or threshold of insensitivity is overcome. It has its origins in psychophysics and the general theory of signal detection (see Swets, 1967), dealing with relations between experienced intensity and physical intensity based on Weber's Law which sought to answer the question of how much intensities of stimulation must differ before the difference can be noticed. Simon (1957) formalised the threshold notion in his definition of the individual as a satisficer not a maximiser; he hypothesised that an individual seeks to achieve a minimum acceptable utility and does not seek to achieve a higher utility once this minimum is achieved. Devletoglou (1968, 1971) extended Simon's hypothesis in a theory in which stimulation is normally capable of eliciting reportable human responses only if a certain threshold or positive range of insensitivity/indifference is first overcome.

Satisficing entails model structure which requires less than perfect maximisation of a utility function under constraints. Such structures are referred to as bounded rationality models (March, 1978). The individual considers only a small subset of alternatives at any time. If, in the subset there is a 'satisfactory' alternative, i.e. an alternative i such that $U_k(s_k(i))=1$ for every k ($1 \leqslant k \leqslant K$), where k are attributes used in evaluating the ith alternative, the alternative is selected. If there is no selection, the individual commences a process of information-acquisition with a time limit in mind. If within the allocated time period a 'satisfactory' alternative is identified, then it is selected and the search process stops. If the search period ends without a selection the individual reduces the aspiration level and the process continues. There is a growing literature on this intuitively appealing approach (e.g. Radner, 1975; Williams & Ortuzar, 1979; and Richardson, 1978).

Formulating the choice process in this way does have some possible connection with the process outlined in Chapter 4. If we were to assume that the search process is a series of decision stages, as represented by a sequential recursive structure which is genuine in contrast to an approximation of a simultaneous structure, then together with the debate on the generation of alternatives, we can constrain each model to evaluate a set of alternatives available (in the individual's perceptual selection space) during a predefined search period. One of the alternatives could be the base, with attribute levels reflecting the aspiration level such that if the utility associated with each of the other alternatives evaluated during that period did not exceed the utility associated with the base alternative, the second decision stage is commenced with the base being either modified or left unchanged. A utility index obtained from a previous period could be used in the next search period to represent the 'experience' of the previous period (Johnson & Hensher, 1980).

Implicit in the discussion of the bounded rationality model is the assumption that all attributes associated with the alternatives are compensatory. This assumption also applies to the basic choice model. Compensatory models allow offsetting changes in one or more attributes to compensate for a change in a particular attribute (implying simultaneous consideration of all attributes). In contrast noncompensatory models do not permit tradeoffs between attributes - comparisons being made on an attribute-by-attribute basis (i.e. sequential consideration of each attribute). Mixed models might also be considered where individuals use a sequential noncompensatory approach in narrowing the alternatives down to a feasible set and then use a simultaneous compensatory approach for selecting an alternative from the feasible set (see Gensch & Svestka, 1978).

One noncompensatory model structure of particular interest is the Elimination-by-Aspects (EBA) model proposed by Tversky (1972). This model postulates a hierarchy of attributes (aspects), each of which must meet a threshold value in an alternative, in order for that alternative to be considered or chosen:

*According to this model each alternative
consists of a set of aspects, each of
which possesses a scale value. The
selection of an aspect eliminates all the
alternatives that do not include the
selected aspect, and the process continues
until only one alternative remains.
Consider the choice of a new car, for
example. The first aspect selected may
be automatic transmission: this will
eliminate all cars that do not have this
feature. Given the remaining alternatives,
another aspect, say a $4,000 price limit,
is selected, and all cars whose price
exceeds this limit are excluded. The
process continues until all cars but one
are eliminated. This differs from the
lexicographic model[25] in that here no
final prior ordering of the aspects (or
attributes) is assumed, and the choice
process in inherently probabilistic.*

                           (Sattah & Tversky, 1976)

The difference between this model and the basic
choice model can be used to illustrate a situation
where the IIA property is violated. Assume a
mapping of aspects (or attributes) such that for
$i \in G$, $i^1 = (x_1, x_2 \ldots)$. For any $A \subseteq G$, denote

$$A^1 = (x_1 | x_1 \in i^1 \text{ for some } i \in A)$$

$$A_0 = (x_1 | x_1 \in i^1 \text{ for all } i \in A)$$

$$A_{x_1} = (i | i \in A \text{ and } x_1 \in i^1)$$

Then a structure of choice probability satisfies
the EBA model if and only if there exists a utility
function on $G^1 - G^0$ such that for all $i \subseteq A \subseteq G$

$$P_{i \in A} = \frac{\displaystyle\sum_{x_1 \in i^1 - A_0} U(x_1) \, P_{i \in A x_1}}{\displaystyle\sum_{x_2 \in A^1 - A_0} U(x_2)} \tag{7.19}$$

Aspects common to all alternatives are excluded in
the elimination process. When all pairs of
alternatives are aspect-use disjoint (i.e. $i^1 \cap j^1 = \emptyset$

for all i∈G, j∈G), equation (7.19) reduces to
equation (5.15), the Choice-Axiom, and hence
equation (3.24). Suppose we have a choice set
containing three alternatives, $A = (a_1, a_2, a_3)$ where
a_1 and a_2 are very similar. If the individual is
indifferent to all pairs of alternatives then all
binary probabilities are 0.5. The choice axiom
implies choice probabilities of .33 for all three
alternatives. The EBA model is compatible with
the values $P_{a_1 \in A} = .25$, $P_{a_2 \in A} = .25$ and $P_{a_3 \in A} = .5$,
which are more in agreement with experience and
intuition.

The alternative ways of representing the choice
process are to varying degrees complementary. There
is no such thing as the 'best' model. This is a
reflection of the variability in the population
with respect to the manner in which attributes are
evaluated in the determination of a preference/choice
ranking of alternatives. Hence we require a
procedure for determining an appropriate assumption
on attribute integration in the choice process, thus
adding a further complexity to the choice set
generation process (see Chapter 4.2).

Besides the work on the EBA model, a number of
isolated studies have been completed in recent
years, all concerned with various facets of thresholds in choice. Uhler & Cragg (1969) and Dagenais
(1969, 1975) have developed threshold choice models
for the purchase of private cars; Hensher & Goodwin
(see Hensher & Dalvi, 1978, Ch. 1) and Blase (1979)
have explored the influence of habit on the tradeoff
between the generalised costs of alternative modes;
and Krishnan (1977) has recently tested a modified
logit model incorporating consideration of 'just-
noticeable differences' on traveller's choice of
mode for accessing commuter-rail services. Williams
& Ortuzar (1979) have recently investigated the
possibility of integrating behavioural constructs
such as habit, threshold and limited information
into the random utility theoretic framework so that
the logit and probit models might be sensitive to
such influences. Krishnan's contribution is most
relevant to developments of operational individual-
choice models using the multinomial logit
formulation, in that he takes the theory of
threshold choice and hypothesises the role of
thresholds in the utility-maximising framework
underlying the logit model. He hypothesises that:

> *the 'satisficer' would ... become a*
> *utility maximiser when a sufficiently*
> *more attractive alternative is made*
> *available to him.*

Krishnan builds the threshold constraint directly into the utility-maximisation theory underlying the derivation of the estimable model. The only concern with his approach appears to be the difficulty of defining the empirical level of 'just-noticeable differences across the sample.

The 'just-noticeable difference' (jnd) concept is built into Krishnan's logit model to overcome the present restrictive assumption that the probability of attaining a state of indifference (when two utilities are equal) is zero. To quote Krishnan (1977: 4):

> *experiments in psychophysics ... show*
> *that the probability of indifference is*
> *not necessarily zero. In fact, when*
> *two stimuli are similar, the*
> *experiments ... have demonstrated that*
> *there is a finite probability of confusion*
> *between them.*

Quandt (1956) in a relatively neglected paper had demonstrated this in economics with an indifference surface comprising probability bands of indifference around levels of utility. Leibenstein (1976) has recently proposed a theory of inert areas based on a common set of experiences in which it is possible to improve a situation in some respects, yet it is not worth the effort to do so. The action required to move from a lower to a higher utility level involves a utility cost that is not compensated for by the gain in utility. This effect is analogous to the threshold concept, suggesting a net utility band of indifference. Goodwin's notion of an effort variable (Hensher & McLeod, 1977) has relevance here, since it adds an additional dimension to the generalised cost of alternatives. For example, not only is x minutes of walk time equal to 2x minutes of invehicle time (from a disutility viewpoint), but the relationship between effort in walking (defined in k/calories per minute) and effort in invehicle travel is not proportionately the same, making the traditional generalised cost tradeoff approach in transport appraisal deficient in a likely important dimension.

Krishnan's new probability conditions are:

$$\text{Prob}(\varepsilon_1 - \varepsilon_2 > V_1 - V_2 + \delta) = \text{Prob}(A_1 > A_2) = \text{Prob}(U_1 > U_2 + \delta)$$

$$(7.20)$$

$$\text{Prob}(\varepsilon_1 - \varepsilon_2 < V_1 - V_2 - \delta) = \text{Prob}(A_2 > A_1) = \text{Prob}(U_2 > U_1 + \delta)$$

$$(7.21)$$

$$\text{Prob}(V_2 - V_1 - \delta \leq \varepsilon_1 - \varepsilon_2 \leq V_2 - V_1 + \delta) = \text{Prob}(A_1 \sim A_2)$$

$$= \text{Prob}(|U_1 - U_2| \leq \delta) \qquad (7.22)$$

where δ is the 'minimum perceivable difference'. The probability distributions for the logit formulation become:

$$P_1 = 1/[1 + \alpha \exp\{\beta(\delta + V_2 - V_1)\}] \qquad (7.23)$$

$$P_2 = 1/[1 + \alpha \exp\{\beta(\delta + V_1 - V_2)\}] \qquad (7.24)$$

$$P_{12} = [\alpha^2 \exp(2\beta\delta) - 1] P_1 P_2, \text{ where } P_{12} = 1 - (P_1 + P_2) \qquad (7.25)$$

If indifference exists, then A_1 and A_2 will be chosen randomly with probabilities θ and $(1 - \theta)$ respectively; hence the overall probabilities of choosing A_1 and A_2 are:

$$P_1 + \theta P_{12} \text{ or } P_1 [1 + \theta\{\exp(2\delta) - 1\} P_2] \qquad (7.26)$$

and

$$P_2 + (1-\theta)P_{12} \text{ or } P_2 [1 + (1-\theta)\{\exp(2\delta) - 1\} P_1] \qquad (7.27)$$

Minus log of the likelihood is then minimised subject to the minimum perceivable difference being greater than or equal to zero, and within the range zero to unity. The empirical results (see Krishnan) suggest biased results using the unconstrained logit model ($\delta = 0$) when the utility difference does not exceed the minimum perceivable difference.

If the thresholds of individuals are distributed through the population on a Weibull or normal distribution, the results, in aggregate, may not look too different from the modelling point of view from the type of process modelled by the logit model. The principal difference might occur in the use of such models for forecasting, where the logit model may overpredict changes in choice compared with reality and the threshold logit model. This

251

is particularly likely to be true where the changes in factors affecting choice are small.

This approach has important implications for choice-set determination, since it is conceivable (in the light of no evidence at present) that many physically existing 'alternatives' in space and time which individuals indicate are not presently valid alternatives (because assessment is based on levels of attributes of alternatives) may, in fact, be within the band of indifferences (when we also include the effort idea of Leibenstein), rather than be totally at odds on all attributes with the chosen alternative. Krishnan's model could be usefully extended to include a maximum perceivable difference, beyond which an alternative is not relevant, and the probability of its being chosen is zero. In a sense, Tversky's Elimination-by-Aspects approach is consistent with this direction of thought. The ideas briefly introduced in this section provide a contrast with the potentially more restrictive assumptions on choice behaviour in the models outlined in previous chapters. This serves to inform the reader about possible approaches to improving the behavioural base of the discrete choice models. The paper by Williams & Ortuzar (1979) is an important contribution to this task.

NOTES — CHAPTER 7

1. The discussion of aggregation is limited to issues directly relevant to the estimation and application of <u>discrete</u> choice models. There are a number of other aggregation concerns of relevance in other contexts. For example, where choice is continuous (e.g. housing prices, or number of cars owned per household per zone), an important contribution to bias due to using aggregate data occurs when the dependent variable (DV) is used as the basis for aggregate classification. This tends to produce correlation between the independent variables (IV) and the error term and thus create a type of simultaneity basis. Smith & Campbell (1978) call this 'pure' aggregation bias. The result is that the absolute value of parameter estimates are biased upwards. Feige & Watts (1972) also put forward this view. Assume a perfectly specified model $Y=\alpha+\beta X + \varepsilon$, where means ($\bar{Y}_i$, $\bar{X}_i$) calculated

from data classified into intervals according to the value of the dependent variable Y are used. That is, aggregate values for DV and IV were calculated. As the number of observations in each interval increases, X_i approaches the conditional expectation $E(\bar{X}|\bar{Y})$. Thus the explanatory variable X_i will not be independent of the regression error term, and parameter bias will result. Aggregation by census collectors district or zone is implicitly based on classifications of the dependent variable (e.g. number of trips by mode m for purpose p from zone i). The way we can overcome this when we only have aggregate data and we want to test microrelationships is by treating the particular IV of concern as an endogenous variable and run a two-stage least squares regression (i.e. $X=f(Z)$, $Y=F(X)$); a reduced form estimate of X is used as an IV in estimation of Y rather than X itself (Theil, 1971). This is a way of breaking down the correlation and hopefully improving causal relationships in the model. This produces, on the basis of evidence in Smith & Campbell (1978) for income elasticity of housing demand, results consistent with that using disaggregate data. Otherwise the elasticities are 70% higher.

2. Extrapolative predictions are forecasts made from a model which assumes that the anticipation of future effects is a direct extrapolation from past behaviour. Conditional predictions are predictions obtained from models which imply more definite statements about the future, based upon knowledge (and hopefully understanding) of how changes in the environment will shape the future. There is a hope that in the future, all models will be causal and capable of producing conditional predictions.

3. Talvitie's correction is truncated and the explanatory variables are assumed to be truly independent (i.e. covariance is zero). Studies have shown this approach to be inaccurate; especially when the estimated variance of the utility function is large or the distribution deviates substantially from a normal one. Reid (1978) presents evidence that indicates a 121 per cent error, compared to a zero error enumeration approach.

253

4. The logit model is simply scalable. The reason why the utility classification method is not appropriate for nonsimply scalable models (such as multinomial covariate probit) is because it does not distinguish the joint distributions of all attributes in the model. In logit models only the variances of the utility scale are required, greatly simplifying the empirical aggregate prediction. Bouthelier & Daganzo (1979) discuss a suitable procedure for covariate probit, which uses covariance procedures, suitable when unique within-alternative distributions of attribute values occur. In general, individual attribute cross-classification as discussed in the text would be appropriate; although there is no systematic guidance on the appropriate segmentation attributes.

5. The choice models presented in this book study homogeneous aggregates of consumers, not the individual per se. Thus the aggregation issue revolves around the compliance with the homogeneity assumption. Market segmentation is a way of accommodating this assumption to a significant degree.

6. There are a number of levels (in a hierarchy) at which the issue of transferability can be discussed. Hansen (1980) has suggested a 4-level hierarchy; level 1 (the most general) related to the transferability of broad behavioural postulates such as utility maximisation; level 2 is the transferability of mathematical model class; level 3 involves the transferability of specific model form; and level 4 (the least general) is related to the transferability of model coefficients. There is an assumed conditional hierarchy with a less general level being conditional on the previous more general level. This section concentrates on level 4.

7. The practical concern relates to the extent to which differences in choice settings have to exist before useful predictive power is lost.

8. See Section 7.4 for a more detailed discussion on sample design. Since sample design has to be considered in transferring models, it is briefly discussed here.

9. The term 'provided' is used here, even though in the next section it is pointed out that estimation is feasible without knowledge of the population proportions.

10. This procedure is similar to that undertaken to estimate population values in sample survey when we have supplementary information. This requires knowing the value of the supplementary variate for every individual in the population. The regression of $y=f(x)$ results in an estimate of the parameter of x (i.e. $\hat{\beta}$). This is then used to adjust the sample results for any discrepancy between the mean size of the individuals in the sample and that for the population; i.e. $y+\beta\,(\bar{X}-\bar{x})$.

11. One commentator (an economist) has remarked *'...But economists go down to the library and look up what the Commerce Department and the Bureau of Labour Statistics and the Federal Reserve have chosen to make available. Only a handful of exceptions come to mind -- Katona, Cyert, March. These days the best economists don't even look at second-hand data; they get them on magnetic tape and let the computer look at them. Economists have voluntarily set for themselves the limits on data collection faced by students of ancient history. The historian cannot question living men and women because the ones he or she is interested in are dead; the economist voluntarily chooses not to question the living people he or she is allegedly trying to prescribe for.'* (Bergman, 1978: 8).

12. Mixed designs can also occur, although we will not discuss them.

13. This interpretation can be contrasted with another meaning, more common in psychology, that refers to a true probability of choice (degree of confirmation) by an individual, where an individual's choices vary over repeated trials.

14. An empirical example of sample size determination for a fully random sample is given here. From airphotographs 7208 household units were obtained as the population (after allowing for household

255

units per dwelling, including blocks of flats).
The value of P is unknown. Assume the most
unfavourable case ($\bar{P}$ = 50%) and three other
cases, $\bar{P}$ = 60%, 70% and 80%, for two values of
R(= 2,3). The value of P is required which
will deviate from $\bar{P}$ in the sample by less than
5% (ϕ = .05). The table of varying fully
random sample sizes for different values of
$\bar{P}$ and R is

	R = 2	R = 3
$\bar{P}$ = 50%	Q = 378	Q = 800
$\bar{P}$ = 60%	Q = 363	Q = 769
$\bar{P}$ = 70%	Q = 320	Q = 683
$\bar{P}$ = 80%	Q = 230	Q = 530

Thus, for example,
if $\bar{P}$ is 60% and
R is 2, with 363
household units
we can locate the
percentage of
households which fulfil our objective, with a
margin of error of less than 5%.

15. This equation may be intuitively more plausible
if we rearrange it and define P(i|x) in terms
of the other elements. Thus P(i|x) = f(i|x)/p(x)
which is simply the conditional probability of
i given x.

16. That is, the analyst selects individuals and
observes their choices.

17. That is, the analyst selects alternatives and
observes individuals choosing them.

18. This is where census data is particularly
useful, and why it is desirable to define a
study area that can take advantage of the
census information. In particular, if the
analyst wishes to divide his population up
on a geographic basis, then he should ensure
that the spatial unit is a simple sum of
census collection districts.

19. For example, suppose we wish to select 1000
individuals from a population classified into
two sets of four strata for which substrata
totals are unknown. The correct strata totals
are known to be 120, 280, 350, 250 for each
set. After a sample of 1125 units has been
drawn, the numbers are:

Strata B	Strata A				Total	Required
	1	2	3	4		
1	37	40	35	8	120	120
2	39	140	82	56	317	280
3	45	97	173	93	408	350
4	8	40	86	146	280	250
.Total	129	317	376	303	1125	1000
Required	120	280	350	250	1000	-

We have an excess of individuals sampled in
every stratum, except 1B. A procedure of
approximation can be used to obtain the
'correct' substrata totals:

(a)   reduce each figure by deducting
excesses in proportion to number of individuals
in substrata of each row (B).
B1 = 0, B2 = 37, B3 = 58, B4 = 30, A1 = 9,
A2 = 37, A3 = 26, A4 = 53. Deduct the
following values: 0 for A1B1, A2B1, A3B1,
A4B1; 5(= 39 x 37)/317) for A1B2,
16(=(140 x 37)/317) for A2B2, 10 for A3B2,
6 for A4B2 etc. The row totals from this
calculation are 0, 37, 58 and 30.

(b)   total the columns and show deficits
in each colum:
A1 = 12 (5 + 6 + 1), A2 = 34 (16 + 14 + 4),
A3 = 44, A5 = 35. The required deficits are
9 (i.e. 129 - 120), 37 (317 - 280), 266 and
53. The deficits are wrong by +3, -3, +18, -18.

(c)   Again distribute these excesses, with
signs reversed in the same way as before but
on the columns, i.e. deduct excesses in
proportion to number of individuals in
substrata of each column.

	A1	A2	A3	A4	
B1	0	0	0	0	0
B2	-1	+2	-4	+3	0
B3	2	+1	-9	+9	-4
B4	0	0	-5	+9	+4

e.g.
$$- 1 = (\frac{5}{12}) \times - 3$$
$$- 2 = (\frac{6}{12}) \times - 3$$
$$- 9 = (\frac{25}{44}) \times -18$$

(d)   We now have to rebalance rows B3 and
B4 by same process.

	A1	A2	A3	A4	
B3	0	+1	+2	+1	+4
B4	0	-1	-1	-2	-4
			(-2)	(-1)	
	0	0	+1	-1	

e.g.
$$+ 2 = (\frac{9}{18}) \ (-4)$$
$$18 = (-4)+(-9)+(-5)$$

257

(e)   Finally, we make an adjustment to columns A3 and A4 to eradicate the imbalances.

(f)   Now the substrata totals are as:

	A1	A2	A3	A4	$\sum$
B1	37	40	35	8	120
B2	35	122	76	47	280
B3	41	81	155	73	350
B4	7	37	84	122	250
$\sum$	120	280	350	250	1000

This process is tedious and cannot be guaranteed to converge.

20. The discussion is confined to estimation using the maximum-likelihood method. The conclusions do not necessarily hold for other methods.

21. In equation (7.14), $P(i|x_q)$ and $P(i|x)$ can be rewritten as $P(i|x_q, \beta^*)$ and $P(i|x, \beta^*)$.

22. Equation (7.8) is specified for an exogenous sample; however for a choice-based sample, it could be specified as $f(i,x) = g(x|i)H_b^*$. We however are interested in analysing choice data, and not imposing any assumption as to prior knowledge, allowing specification of $g(x|i)$ as is done in discriminant analysis. Hence in maintaining equation (7.8), given the interest in $p(i|x)$, we need to allow for the possible error in estimation: the estimators in Table 7.2 are designed to handle this concern.

23. For a random sample, the absolute error is given in equation (7.7) as ϕ.

24. Cosslett (1979) (also cited in Lerman & Manski, 1978: 40) recommends that where H* is not known, and a choice-based sample is to be drawn H_b should be close to $1/J$ where J is the number of alternatives in the choice set. When H* is known, it appears optimal to oversample the 'rare' alternative, setting $H_b > 1/J$ if $H_b^* < 1/J$.

25. Lexicographic (or power) models imply the following: given a set of alternatives
$x = (x_1, x_2, \ldots, x_j, \ldots, x_m)$,

$(x_1^1, x_2^1 \ldots, x_j^1 \ldots x_m^1)$ we initially order the attributes in terms of importance. Let x_1 be the most important, through to x_m as the least important. Then $x \geqslant x^1$ if and only if $U(x_j) = U(x_j^1)$ for all $j (j = 1, 2, \ldots, m)$ or else the smallest for which $U(x_j) \neq U(x_j^1)$ has $U(x_j) > U(x_j^1)$. That is, preferences are based on the evaluation of alternatives on the most important attribute(s). Lexicographic choice models are deterministic.

CHAPTER 8

Simultaneous Equation Models

8·1 Introduction

Throughout Chapters 3 to 7 it has been assumed that the variables which influence the probability of choice (i.e. the Xs in V_{iq}) are all <u>exogenous</u> or, in other words, are variables whose values are determined independently of the choice process. This assumption in single equation models is analogous to single equation models in regression analysis. In this chapter choice situations are examined in which one or more attributes affecting choice are themselves <u>endogenous</u>, giving rise to a simultaneous equation model system as opposed to a single equation choice model.

These simultaneous equation models range from simple situations where two or more dependent (endogenous) variables in the model are qualitative (e.g. Schmidt & Strauss, 1975), to more complex situations where the analyst is faced with a simultaneous structure containing one or more latent (i.e. partially or wholly unobservable) endogenous variables (Heckman, 1978; Westin & Gillen, 1978).

The concept of endogenous attributes is introduced in Section 8.2. together with descriptions of a range of models proposed in different situations. Heckman's (1979) analysis of sample selectivity bias is introduced in Section 8.3 as a useful construct in situations where some observations are not observable on the endogenous attribute. The final section of the chapter presents a case study to illustrate more fully the principles introduced.

8·2 Endogenous Attributes

Consider a situation where individual q is faced with the choice of J alternatives from choice set A and that the variables which affect his choice contain among them the outcome of another choice, say of $J*$ alternatives from choice set A*. An example, investigated by Schmidt & Strauss (1975), is the choice of occupation and industry of employment, where the choice of occupation is assumed to depend upon, among other things, choice of industry and choice of industry depends upon occupation. Hence, the model is a simultaneous choice situation and can be modelled as such. Although this is similar to a purely simultaneous decision structure as discussed in Chapter 4, the effect that one choice has on the other can be estimated, and hence we can treat the problem as a set of simultaneous equations. To see this, assume that decisions are made according to the basic MNL model and denote the two choices considered as Y and Z.

The model can be written, for ease of exposition as (see Section 6.3):

$$\ln \left(\frac{P(Y=i|Z)}{P(Y=1|Z)} \right)_q = \sum_{k=1}^{K_1} \beta_{ik} X_{ikq} + \sum_{j=2}^{J*} \alpha_{ij} Z^*_{jq} \qquad (8.1)$$

$$(i = 2,\ldots,J)$$

$$\ln \left(\frac{P(Z=i|Y)}{P(Z=1|Y)} \right)_q \doteq \sum_{k=1}^{K_2} \gamma_{ik} X^*_{ikq} + \sum_{j=2}^{J} \alpha_{ji} Y^*_{jq} \qquad (8.2)$$

$$(i = 2,\ldots,J*)$$

where $Y = 1$ and $Z = 1$ are arbitrarily chosen as the bases for the two equations. There are K_1 exogenous variables affecting choice of Y, K_2 exogenous variables affecting choice of Z, and Z^*_{jq} and Y^*_{jq} are dummy variables such that

$$Z^*_{jq} = \begin{cases} 1 & \text{if } Z_q = j \qquad (j = 2,\ldots,J*) \\ 0 & \text{otherwise} \end{cases}$$

$$(8.3)$$

$$Y^*_{jq} = \begin{cases} 1 & \text{if } Y_q = j \qquad (j = 2,\ldots,J) \\ 0 & \text{otherwise} \end{cases}$$

The parameters β_{ik} and γ_{ik} are the usual
coefficients of exogenous variables in the MNL model
and are interpreted as the effects of the variables
in question on the choice of alternative i as
compared to the base alternative. The α_{ij} are also
parameters which must be estimated and require
comment. In particular, note that equality of these
coefficients has been imposed in the two equations.
This 'symmetry' condition, which has been shown to
be necessary for this model by Schmidt & Strauss
(1975: 746), implies that if the occurrence of
say Y = 2 makes Z = 3 more likely (α_{23} > 0 in 8.2),
then the converse is also necessarily true
(α_{23} > 0 in 8.1).
To estimate the parameters in this model, the
likelihood function formulated for the joint
probabilities of various combinations of alternatives must be specified. Schmidt & Strauss (1975)
state that the algebra involved is very tedious
but that the joint probabilities turn out to be

$$P(Y_q=1,\ Z_q=1) = 1/\Delta_q \tag{8.4a}$$

$$P(Y_q=1,\ Z_q=j) = \exp\ (V^*_{jq})/\Delta_q \quad j=2,\ldots,J^* \tag{8.4b}$$

$$P(Y_q=i,\ Z_q=1) = \exp\ (V_{iq})/\Delta_q \quad i=2,\ldots,J \tag{8.4c}$$

$$P(Y_q=i,\ Z_q=j) = \exp\ (V_{iq}+V^*_{jq}+\alpha_{ij})/\Delta_q \tag{8.4d}$$

$$i=2,\ldots,J$$
$$j=2,\ldots,J^*$$

$$\text{where } V_{iq} = \sum_{k=1}^{K_1} \beta_{ik}X_{ikq} \ , \ V^*_{jq} = \sum_{k=1}^{K_2} \gamma_{jk}X^*_{jkq} \quad \text{and}$$

$$\Delta_q = 1 + \sum_{i=2}^{J} \exp\ (V_{iq}) + \sum_{j=2}^{J^*} \exp\ (V^*_{jq})$$

$$+ \sum_{i=2}^{J} \sum_{j=2}^{J^*} \exp\ (V_{iq} + V^*_{jq} + \alpha_{ij}) \tag{8.5}$$

Given the probabilities from equations (8.4), the
likelihood function to be maximised is given by

$$L = \prod_{i=1}^{J} \prod_{j=1}^{J^*} \prod_{q=1}^{Q} P(Y_q=i,\ Z_q=j) \tag{8.6}$$

Numerical methods are used to obtain a solution of equation (8.6) as discussed in previous chapters. An important point to note about this model is that the choice framework is defined in terms of a base alternative which means that the coefficient of the variables affecting the probability of choosing this base are set to zero (note that the indexes i and j in equation (8.1) and equation (8.2) range from 2 since alternatives Y = 1 and Z = 1 are the two arbitrarily chosen bases). If we do not do this, we cannot begin by defining equations (8.1) and (8.2) and are faced in this case with a purely simultaneous choice model as described in Chapter 4. Hence, the assumption of base alternatives has allowed the development of the model discussed here.

The above analysis considered a situation where there were two endogenous choices. Similar models could be developed for more than two choices but the likelihood functions in these cases become more complex as the number of choices increase. Since there is nothing essentially different in the multichoice case we leave this model and move on to more complex endogenous attribute situations.

In particular, consider a case where individual q faces a choice of one of two alternatives (i.e. binary choice) and that among the variables affecting this choice is a continuous endogenous variable. Such a model, termed a mixed-logit model, has been used by Schmidt & Strauss (1976) to examine the relationship between choice of union membership and earnings. The model takes the form

$$\ln \left(\frac{P(Y=1|Z)}{P(Y=0|Z)} \right)_q = \sum_{k=1}^{K_1} \beta_k X_{kq} + \alpha Z_q \qquad (8.7)$$

$$Z_q | Y_q \sim N \left(\sum_{k=1}^{K_2} \gamma_k X^*_{kq} + \delta Y_q , \sigma^2 \right) \qquad (8.8)$$

where equation (8.7) is essentially the same as equation (8.1) except that the endogenous attribute, Z_q, is now continuous and equation (8.8) implies that the conditional (on choice Y_q) distribution of the continuous attribute is a normal random variable with mean equal to a linear function of exogenous X*s and endogenous Y_q and variance equal to σ^2. Olsen (1978) has shown that in much the same way as in the previous model, there is a necessary 'symmetry' condition for equations (8.7) and (8.8), namely that $\alpha\sigma^2 = \delta$ so that if the effect of Z_q on Y is positive, the converse is also true. Hence, in the estimation to be described next, this condition should be imposed.

To estimate the parameters of the model (8.7 - 8.8) the joint density of Y and Z must be obtained similar to equation (8.4) for the discrete endogenous attribute model. Using the notation $f( )$ to refer to a density (marginal, joint or conditional), then from equation (8.7)

$$\frac{P(Y_q=1|Z_q)}{P(Y_q=0|Z_q)} = \frac{f(Y_q=1,Z_q)/f(Z_q)}{f(Y_q=0,Z_q)/f(Z_q)} = \frac{f(Y_q=1,Z_q)}{f(Y_q=0,Z_q)} \qquad (8.9)$$

$$= \exp(V_q + \alpha Z_q)$$

where the definition of conditional probability is used as the ratio of joint probability to the marginal probability of the conditioning variable; V_q is as defined above. The marginal probability of Y_q is

$$P(Y_q=i) = \frac{f(Y_q=i,Z_q)}{f(Z_q|Y_q=i)} \quad , \quad (i = 0,1) \qquad (8.10)$$

Now, since $P(Y_q = 0) + P(Y_q = 1) = 1$, then from equation (8.10)

$$\frac{f(Y_q=0,Z_q)}{f(Z_q|Y_q=0)} + \frac{f(Y_q=1,Z_q)}{f(Z_q|Y_q=1)} = 1 \qquad (8.11)$$

From equation (8.9), since $f(Y_q=1, Z_q)$ $= f(Y_q = 0, Z_q) \cdot \exp(V_q + \alpha Z_q)$; then substitution of this into equation (8.11) and factoring out $f(Y_q = 0, Z_q)$ leaves

$$f(Y_q=0,Z_q) \left(\frac{1}{f(Z_q|Y_q=0)} + \frac{\exp(V_q+\alpha Z_q)}{f(Z_q Y_q=1)} \right) = 1 \qquad (8.12)$$

or, upon solving for $f(Y_q = 0, Z_q)$ (i.e. the required joint density),

265

$$f(Y_q=0, Z_q) = \frac{f(Z_q|Y_q=0)f(Z_q|Y_q=1)}{f(Z_q|Y_q=1) + \exp(V_q+\alpha Z_q) f(Z_q|Y_q=0)} \qquad (8.13)$$

Furthermore, the other joint density of interest is given by (using equations (8.9) and (8.13)),

$$f(Y_q=1, Z_q) = \exp(V_q+\alpha Z_q) f(Y_q=0, Z_q) \qquad (8.14)$$

For operational purposes, we can then substitute into equations (8.13) and (8.14) normal conditional densities for $f(Z_q|Y_q = i)$ using equation (8.8) noting that for $Y_q = 1$ the exponent of the normal density contains $(Z_q - V_q^* - \delta)^2$ whereas for $Y_q = 0$, the argument is $(Z_q - V_q^*)^2$ where V_q^* is as before.[1] The likelihood function is then defined as

$$L = \prod_{i=0}^{1} \prod_{q=1}^{Q} f(Y_q = i, Z_q)^{g_i} \qquad (8.15)$$

where g_i = 1 if individual q actually chose alternative i and g_i = 0 otherwise. This model with continuous endogenous attributes can be extended to situations of more than one continuous endogenous attribute and where the choice sets are of size J instead of two as above. Details are contained in a paper by Schmidt & Strauss (1974).

Other models with jointly determined qualitative and continuous endogenous variables have been developed which attempt to improve on the models already discussed in a number of ways. Schmidt (1978) has developed a model not unlike (8.7) - (8.8) except that the choice is a function of the difference in conditional values of Z_q (i.e. $(Z_q|Y_q = 1) - (Z_q|Y_q = 0)$) instead of just Z_q. He has proceeded to derive a simple consistent estimator along with an asymptotically efficient two-step estimator, and has illustrated the use of the model by investigating the probability of an individual belonging to a union as a function of (among other things) the union-nonunion earnings differential where earnings is an endogenous variable. The interested reader can consult Schmidt's paper for the relevant detail.

Another approach to this problem has been presented by Heckman (1976, 1978). However, his work is different in that it is based on the premise that some variable which reflects sentiment for or against a particular choice is unobservable (or latent). There are a number of situations in which this can arise and so we devote the next section to discussing Heckman-type models.

8·3 Incomplete Information, Sample Separation and Sample Selectivity Bias

8·3·1 Latent Endogenous Variables

Heckman (1978) approaches the discrete endogenous variable problem by assuming that they are generated by continuous latent (i.e. unobservable) variables crossing thresholds. His model is outlined here together with some situations in which it is applicable, in particular in cases of sample separation and sample selectivity (defined explicitly later in this section). Then, in Section 8.4, an application due to Westin & Gillen (1978) is outlined in detail which serves to illustrate the concepts introduced.

Consider a model with one continuous endogenous variable, Y_1, and one latent endogenous variable, Y_2^*, such that

$$Y_{1q} = V_{1q} + \alpha_1 d_q + \gamma_1 Y_{2q}^* + u_{1q}$$

$$Y_{2q}^* = V_{2q} + \alpha_2 d_q + \gamma_2 Y_{1q} + u_{2q} \qquad (8.16)$$

where V_{1q} and V_{2q} are linear functions of K_1 and K_2 exogenous variables respectively, d_q is a dummy variable defined as

$$d_q = \begin{cases} 1 & \text{if } Y_{2q}^* > 0 \\ 0 & \text{otherwise}^2 \end{cases}$$

and u_{1q}, u_{2q} are error terms assumed to be distributed as bivariate normal with mean zero, variance σ_{jj} ($j = 1, 2$) and covariance σ_{12} for a given individual but zero across individuals.

System (8.16) may be written in semi-reduced form (i.e. by solving equation (8.16) for Y_{1q} and

Y_{2q}^* in terms of V and d) as

$$Y_{1q} = V_{1q}^* + V_{2q}^* + \Pi_1 d_q + u_{1q}^*$$

$$Y_{2q}^* = V_{1q}^{**} + V_{2q}^{**} + \Pi_2 d_q + u_{2q}^* \tag{8.17}$$

where V_{iq}^*, V_{iq}^{**} are linear functions of exogenous variables but where the coefficients of the variables are functions of the coefficients in equation (8.16) as is usually the case in reduced forms. The parameters Π_1 and Π_2 are given by (Heckman, 1978: 935).

$$\Pi_1 = \frac{\alpha_1 + \gamma_1 \alpha_2}{1 - \gamma_1 \gamma_2}$$

$$\Pi_2 = \frac{\gamma_2 \alpha_1 + \alpha_2}{1 - \gamma_1 \gamma_2} \tag{8.18}$$

Furthermore, the error terms u_{1q}^* and u_{2q}^* are bivariate normally distributed with variances w_{11} and w_{22} and covariance w_{12}. To obtain the true reduced form, assume that the conditional probability that $d_q = 1$ (given the exogenous variables in V_{1q}^* and V_{2q}^*) exists and equals P_q. Then, the true reduced forms are

$$Y_{1q} = V_{1q}^* + V_{2q}^* + \Pi_1 P_q + u_{iq}^* + \Pi_1 (d_q - P_q) \tag{8.19}$$

$$Y_{2q}^* = V_{iq}^{**} + V_{2q}^{**} + \Pi_2 P_q + u_{2q}^* + \Pi_2 (d_q - P_q)$$

Notice that the error terms are a combination of correlated continuous and discrete random variables. Heckman (1978: 936-937) proves that for the model (8.19) to be defined, a necessary and sufficient conditions is for $\Pi_2 = 0$ (or $\gamma_2 \alpha_1 + \alpha_2 = 0$ from equation 8.18)). This makes sense in that this condition means that the probability that $d_q = 1$ is not a determinant of that event (i.e. $Y_{2q}^* > 0$). Given this condition, the second equation of (8.19) is a problem in binary choice analysis since all we are left with is

$$Y^*_{2q} = V^{**}_{1q} + V^{**}_{2q} + u^*_{2q} \qquad (8.20)$$

where u^*_{2q} is a normal random variable and Y^*_{2q} is not observed (i.e. what we do observe is d_q). The parameters in V^{**}_{1q} and V^{**}_{2q}, normalised by $(w_{22})^{\frac{1}{2}}$, are estimated in Heckman's formulation, using binary (independent) probit analysis.

The more difficult estimation task arises in the estimation of parameters of the first equation of (8.19). Notice that the conditional expectation of Y_{1q} given d_q and the Xs in V^*_{1q} is given by

$$E\,(Y_{1q}|d_q\,,\, Xs) = V^*_{1q} + V^*_{2q} + \Pi_1 d_q + E\,(u^*_{1q}|d_q,\, Xs)$$
$$(8.21)$$

Least squares regression could be used if the last conditional expectation (i.e. that of the error term) is zero. However, using a result from Johnson & Kotz (1972), it can be shown that

$$E\,(u^*_{1q}|d_q\,,\, Xs) = \frac{w_{12}}{(w_{22})^{\frac{1}{2}}}(\lambda_q d_q + \tilde{\lambda}_q(1-d_q)) \qquad (8.22)$$

where $\lambda_q = \phi(C_q)/[1-\Phi(C_q)]$, $C_q = -(\tilde{V}^{**}_{1q} + \tilde{V}^{**}_{2q})$,

$\tilde{V}^{**}_{1q}$ denotes the V^{**}_{1q} with parameters normalised by $(w_{22})^{\frac{1}{2}}$, ϕ and Φ refer to the density and distribution function of a standard normal random variable (a random variable with mean 0 and standard deviation 1), and where

$$\tilde{\lambda}_q = -\lambda_q\, [\frac{\Phi(-C_q)}{\Phi(C_q)}] \qquad (8.23)$$

Now, if we knew the value of λ_q and $\tilde{\lambda}_q$ in equation (8.22), this variable could be used as an additional regressor in equation (8.21) and least squares could be used to estimate the parameters of V^*_{1q}, V^*_{2q}, and $w_{12}/(w_{22})^{\frac{1}{2}}$. But, since we can estimate the normalised parameters in equation (8.20) by probit, C_q can be estimated and hence λ_q and $\tilde{\lambda}_q$. Therefore these estimates of λ_q and $\tilde{\lambda}_q$ can be used in equation (8.22) to estimate the parameters in equation (8.21). It has been shown (Heckman, 1978) that these estimates are consistent.

So far, we have only shown how one may consistently estimate some of the reduced form parameters in equation (8.17). We could continue Heckman's analysis by deriving an estimator for w_{11} and then describe how estimates of the structural parameters in equation (8.16) are obtained from these reduced form parameter estimates. We could further describe an asymptotically efficient estimator proposed by Heckman (1978). However, the basic idea behind Heckman's procedure is evident from what is discussed above so that we turn now to some situations in which this sort of methodology may prove particularly useful to the discrete choice modeller. The interested reader is referred to Heckman's excellent 1978 article for more complete detail concerning the above model and several other related simultaneous equation models.

8·3·2 Sample Selectivity Bias[3]

Consider a situation where the investigator has a set of Q observations available with which to attempt the estimation of some behavioural relationships but that some of the observations have some data missing. An example will help to illustrate this. In research into married women in the labour market, the fact that women at home are not working and thus receive no wage implies that estimates of the determinants of the wage for married women must be based on a nonrandom sample of working women, the only group for whom wage data is available. This type of situation has been examined by Heckman (1979) in the general context of sample selectivity bias which he discusses as an ordinary specification error that arises because of missing data. The analysis of this problem is very closely related to the Heckman model with latent endogenous variables discussed in the immediately preceding paragraphs.

As before, let us look at a 2-equation model since there is essentially nothing new in the multiequation case (except more algebra). Suppose the model is

$$Y_{1q} = \sum_{k=1}^{K_1} \beta_{1k} X_{1kq} + u_{1q}$$

$$Y_{2q} = \sum_{k=1}^{K_2} \beta_{2k} X_{2kq} + u_{2q} \qquad (8.24)$$

where u_{iq} has mean zero and variance σ_{ii} and covariance (for an individual q) equal to σ_{12}.

Now, suppose that there is some data missing in Y_1. If one attempts to estimate the first equation of (8.24) by least squares regression using only those observations for which data is not missing (say the first $Q_1 < Q$), then the estimated βs will be unbiased only if the conditional expectation of u_{1q} given the sample selection rule is zero. In other words, the conditional expectation of Y_{1q}, given by,

$$\begin{aligned}
&E\,(Y_{1q} | X_1 s, \text{ sample selection}) \\
&\qquad\qquad\qquad \text{rule} \\
&= \sum_{k=1}^{K_1} \beta_{1k} X_{1kq} + E\,(u_{1q} | Xs, \text{ sample }) \qquad (8.25) \\
&\qquad\qquad\qquad\qquad\qquad\qquad \text{selection rule}
\end{aligned}$$

must be such that the last term on the right is zero. In general, this will not be the case.

For example, suppose for the married women in the labour force example mentioned above, that Y_{1q} (market wage) is only observable if $Y_{2q} \geq 0$ where Y_{2q} is an index of the individual's attitudes toward working and where the zero threshold is purely arbitrary. Thus

$$\begin{aligned}
&E\,(u_{1q} | Xs, \text{ sample selection}) \\
&\qquad\qquad\qquad \text{rule} \\
&= E\,(u_{1q} | Xs,\ Y_{2q} \geq 0) \\
&= E\,(u_{1q} | Xs,\ u_{2q} \geq - \sum_{k=1}^{K_2} \beta_{2k} X_{2kq}) \qquad (8.26)
\end{aligned}$$

Now, if u_{1q} and u_{2q} are independent, the conditional mean of u_{1q} is zero and so using least squares in

271

the Y_{1q} equation with Q_1 observations means only a loss in efficiency (since all information is not being used). In general, σ_{12} is not zero and so the selected sample regression depends on both X_{1kq} and X_{2kq} since the second term on the right side of equation (8.25) depends on X_{2kq}. In fact, this regression can be looked at as a regression with a variable omitted, namely the conditional expectation of u_{1q}. The estimation procedure suggested by Heckman essentially depends on formulating an approximation for this missing term and using this extra variable in the Y_1 regression. The method is very similar to the latent endogenous variable procedure just outlined.

Assuming that u_{1q} and u_{2q} are distributed as bivariate normal, we again call on a result from Johnson & Kotz (1972) and state that

$$E\left(u_{1q}\big|u_{2q} \geq -V_{2q}\right) = \frac{\sigma_{12}}{(\sigma_{22})^{\frac{1}{2}}}\,\lambda_q \tag{8.27}$$

$$E\left(u_{2q}\big|u_{2q} \geq -V_{2q}\right) = \frac{\sigma_{22}}{(\sigma_{22})^{\frac{1}{2}}}\,\lambda_q$$

where
$$V_{2q} = \sum_{k=1}^{K_2} \beta_{2k}X_{2kq}, \quad \lambda_q = \phi(C_q^*)/[1-\Phi(C_q^*)]$$

and $\quad C_q^* = -V_{2q}/(\sigma_{22})^{\frac{1}{2}}$

Hence, the conditional regression functions become

$$E\left(Y_{1q}\big|X_1s,\ Y_{2q} \geq 0\right) = V_{1q} + \frac{\sigma_{12}}{(\sigma_{22})^{\frac{1}{2}}}\,\lambda_q \tag{8.28}$$

$$E\left(Y_{2q}\big|X_2s,\ Y_{2q} \geq 0\right) = V_{2q} + \frac{\sigma_{22}}{(\sigma_{22})^{\frac{1}{2}}}\,\lambda_q$$

so that
$$Y_{1q} = V_{1q} + \frac{\sigma_{12}}{(\sigma_{22})^{\frac{1}{2}}}\,\lambda_q + u_{1q}^*$$

$$Y_{2q} = V_{2q} + \frac{\sigma_{22}}{(\sigma_{22})^{\frac{1}{2}}}\,\lambda_q + u_{2q}^* \tag{8.29}$$

272

where u^*_{1q} and u^*_{2q} are error terms whose conditional means are zero, and conditional covariances for different q are zero. Furthermore, one can show that

$$E\ (u^{*2}_{1q}|X_1s,\lambda_q,\ u_{2q} \geqslant -V_{2q}) = \sigma_{11}\ [(1-\rho^2)+\rho^2(1+C^*_q\ \lambda_q-\lambda^2_q)]$$

$$E\ (u^*_{1q}\ u^*_{2q}|X_1s,\lambda_q,\ u_{2q} \geqslant -V_{2q}) = \sigma_{12}(1+C^*_q\ \lambda_q-\lambda^2_q)$$

$$E\ (u^{*2}_{2q}|X_1s,\lambda_q,\ u_{2q} \geqslant -V_{2q}) = \sigma_{22}(1+C^*_q\ \lambda_q-\lambda^2_q) \tag{8.30}$$

where $\rho^2 = \sigma^2_{12}/\sigma_{11}\sigma_{12}$ and $0 \leqslant 1 + C^*_q\ \lambda_q-\lambda^2_q \leqslant 1$

If we knew C^*_q and thus λ_q, we could use λ_q in the first equation of (8.29) as an additional variable and estimate the equation (with Q_1 observations) using ordinary least squares. The estimates of the parameters in V_{1q} (the β_{1k}) and $\sigma_{12}/(\sigma_{22})^{\frac{1}{2}}$ will then be unbiased but inefficient (since from equation (8.30) the errors are heteroskedastic). To improve efficiency, Heckman (1976) suggests using a generalised least-squares procedure (see Section 6.2).

Since λ_q is unknown, it must be estimated. If we are faced with the case that Y_{1q} is not observed when $Y_{2q} < 0$ but we have the $X_{2k}s$ for these observations, the model can be estimated as follows:

(1) Estimate using binary (independent) probit a model of the probability that $Y_{2q} > 0$ for the whole sample of Q observations. This gives estimates of $(\beta_{2k}/(\sigma_{22})^{\frac{1}{2}})s$.

(2) From these estimates, we can consistently estimate C^*_q and hence λ_q.

(3) We can then use the estimated λ_q to estimate the parameters in

$$Y_{1q} = V_{1q} + \frac{\sigma_{12}}{(\sigma_{22})^{\frac{1}{2}}}\hat{\lambda}_q + u^*_{1q} \tag{8.31}$$

when $\hat{\lambda}_q$ is the estimated λ_q from step 2. These estimates are consistent.

273

The reader will notice that this method is essentially the same as discussed previously for latent endogenous variables proposed by Heckman (1978). The analysis could be continued with a method to consistently estimate σ_{11} and to further discuss proposals by Lee (1977, 1977a, 1978) to improve efficiency with additional steps. However, the major interest is to introduce the framework within which the problem of sample selectivity bias may be examined, especially in situations characterised by choice problems (i.e. the case of Y_{2q} above being interpreted as the choice of whether to enter the labour force or not by a married woman). There are several situations where this sort of problem may arise (such as that described in the case study in Section 9.5).

We now analyse an example from transport as a case study to illustrate the ideas introduced above.

8·4 A Case Study

The existence of endogenous attributes in travel choice models has been discussed in a casual way since the early 1970s. However, the recent contribution of Westin & Gillen (1978) marks the beginning of serious analytical application of procedures that handle endogenous attributes. Their study applies a mix of binary (independent) probit and (generalised) least-squares regression to the formulation of a commuter mode choice model with various levels of service attributes defined as endogenous. The major aim of this improved approach is to obtain consistent, although not necessarily fully efficient estimates of parameters when a priori arguments suggest the existence of simultaneity. Whilst Westin & Gillen adopt Heckman's general approach (outlined above) which uses simple binary probit (in least squares format for Westin & Gillen) and least-squares regression, the acknowledged relative inefficiency of such techniques compared to maximum-likelihood procedures led Lee (1977) to accept the equivalent staged output as initial consistent estimates of parameters and to add a further stage (two steps) which reestimated the models. Amemiya's classical proof (1973) is used to show that maximum-likelihood estimates are both consistent and asymptotically efficient (Lee, 1977a). Heckman argues that the two-stage procedure (without the maximum-likelihood two-step extension) is computationally more flexible than maximum likelihood and hence is more useful in exploratory empirical work (Heckman 1976a: 490). The extent of efficiency was not tested by Heckman; this was undertaken by Lee (1975, 1977, 1977a).

The modelling framework presented below uses Westin & Gillen's application to illustrate the essential issues. The particular empirical study on parking location and transit demand provides a convincing argument for the important role of parking constraints in the commuter mode choice decision for central city workplace trip ends, and demonstrates the weakness of the common conclusion that parking cost and availability are shown to be nonsignificant determinants of mode choice. Although we have good evidence that a significant proportion of current car commuters to the central area are heavily subsidised by their employer (in respect of the vehicle, its operating and terminal costs) (Hensher, 1979), we should not conclude that parking policy will have a negligible impact on modal usage. In the past the use of parking policy instruments has influenced the move to and continued use of public transport.

Gillen (1975, 1977, 1977a) reformulated the mode choice model to improve the specification of the parking variable, in part response to this point. However, in recognising that the main reason for misspecification of the parking variable is incomplete observation, i.e. the inability to observe the influence of parking constraints on current public transport users, Gillen together with Westin (drawing on Westin's earlier theoretical contribution on the interrelationship between discrete (mode choice) and continuous (parking location) choice, have utilised the literature on switching regression, limited dependent variables and the notions of sample separation and selectivity bias (the latter associated with incomplete observations) to reinstate the role of parking as a significant influence on commuter mode choice, as it has intuitively always been so.

The proposed model of the joint determination of parking location and mode choice is given in equations (8.32) and (8.33). A random utility framework with endogenous modal attributes is adopted:

$$I_q^* = \alpha \Pi_q^* + \sum_{k=1}^{K_1} \beta_{1k} X_{1kq} + u_q \qquad \text{Mode Choice Decision} \qquad (8.32)$$

275

$$\Pi_q^* = \gamma_0 + \gamma_1 W_q + \gamma_2 W_q^2 + \sum_{k=1}^{K_2} \beta_{2k} X_{2kq} + \epsilon_q \qquad \text{Full Parking Price Function}$$

(8.33)

An auxiliary regression equation is used in the estimation of the parking location choice (Π_q^*). X_{ikq} are various modal attributes and other variables (socioeconomic), α is an unobserved scalar, and W_q is the individual's hourly wage rate. The theoretical argument of the parking price function is not relevant in the development of the model (see Westin & Gillen, 1978: 77-85). I_q^* is an unobservable (random utility) index for the qth traveller, conditional on the endogenous attribute Π_q^*. If I_q^* is $\geqslant 0$ the commuter is assumed to select the car, otherwise the transit mode.

The use of binary probit and least-square regression techniques permits the simplest stochastic assumptions. u_q is the equivalent of the random component of the utility function and is distributed as standard normal (i.e. mean zero and unit variance); ϵ_q is normally distributed with mean zero and a positive finite variance σ^2. The endogenous attribute only appears in one of the alternatives (the car journey), we observe Π_q^* in equation (8.33) only for those Q_1 individuals who choose car.

The rule relating I_q and Π_q^* is

$$\Pi_q = \Pi_{1q}^* \quad ; \quad I_q = 1 \text{ iff } I^* \geqslant 0, \text{ otherwise } I^* \text{ is unobservable}$$

(8.34)

In words, the full parking price function (Π_q) is observable (= Π_q^*) if and only if the individual used the car ($I_q = 1$); and the individual is assumed to use the car if, and only if, the utility (representative plus random) which is unobservable is greater than or equal to zero ($I^* \geqslant 0$). The limited dependent variable is truncated normal. Incomplete observations exist which if not accounted for will result in significant bias of the estimates of the parameters, and it is in the literature on limited dependent variables (Tobin, 1958)[4] where advice on this bias is given. The notion of 'self-selectivity bias', originally proposed by Gronau (1974) and refined by many, especially Heckman, has been coined to refer to the bias attributable to the selectiveness effects on the observed attributes (both endogenous and exogenous). This relates to sample selection and the recent literature on choice-based samples, although there has been no attempt (to our knowledge) to show if appropriate choice-based sampling can assist in reducing the error due to incomplete observations.[5] An example of selectivity bias will help in appreciating its significance. In Westin & Gillen's study, the selection of <u>current</u> car travellers as the only car commuters in the sample may result in the exclusion of many travellers who have chosen to use public transport because they would experience relatively higher disutility associated with parking costs and walking times. This produces a parking selectivity bias. A more general example would be the exclusion of nonparticipants (latent demand) such as in a study of international air travel and the effects of alternative air fare structures on travel behaviour. In general, it is desirable to account for selectivity bias; however the empirical evidence to date (which is somewhat limited) does not unequivocably suggest the presence of a significant bias from this source. Given the considerable additional calculations required, only future empirical research will determine whether the benefits are nonmarginal.

So far, we have I_q^* and Π_q^* with bivariate normal distributions, with truncated dependent variables and incomplete observations. The probabilities of mode selection for the conditional and marginal cases are given in equations (8.35) and (8.36).

$$P(I_q^* \geqslant 0 \mid \Pi_q^*) = \Phi(\alpha \Pi_q^* + V_{1q}) \qquad (8.35)$$

where $$V_{1q} = \sum_{k=1}^{K_1} \beta_{1k} X_{1kq}.$$

In words; the probability that an individual will select the car, given the value of the endogenous full price parking function is a function of the relative levels of utility associated with the car and transit which is located in a utility space with

277

an assumed cumulative unvariate standard normal distribution (Φ).

$$P(I^*_q \geq 0) = \Phi \left[\frac{(\gamma_0 + \gamma_1 W_q + \gamma_2 W_q^2 + V_{2q}) + V_{1q}}{(1 + \alpha^2 \sigma^2)^{\frac{1}{2}}} \right] \quad (8.36)$$

(shortened to $\Phi(\theta_q)$)

In words; the (marginal) probability that an individual will select the car is a function of the relative levels of utility associated with the alternatives (when the full price parking function is defined on its marginal means) up to a factor of positive proportionality. $(1 + \alpha^2 \sigma^2)^{\frac{1}{2}}$ is a scaling factor, originally suggested by McFadden in a different context (McFadden & Reid, 1975). To explain the scaling factor, note that the variance-covariance matrix associated with the bivariate normal distribution of I^*_q and Π^*_q is

$$\begin{bmatrix} 1 + \alpha^2 \sigma^2 & \alpha \sigma^2 \\ \alpha \sigma^2 & \sigma^2 \end{bmatrix} \quad (8.37)$$

In the absence of endogenous attributes, since the variance of the random variable in Π^*_q is 1 and in I^*_q it is σ^2, then the variance when the two equations are combined (in an additive utility expression) is $1 + \sigma^2$; likewise the standard deviation is $(1 + \sigma^2)^{\frac{1}{2}}$. When an endogenous attribute model exists, however, we have to account for the unobserved scalar α which produces $\alpha \sigma^2$ as the covariance terms in the symmetric variance-covariance matrix. When related to the variance of I^*_q it yields $1 + \alpha^2 \sigma^2$, since we have a linear combination of two random variables (given $y = az$, then var $(y) = a^2$ var (z)). The standard deviation is $(1 + \alpha^2 \sigma^2)^{\frac{1}{2}}$. The probit model estimated on all exogenous variables (hence marginal probability) will result in estimates of the structural coefficients up to a factor of proportionality. While the marginal model is a useful contribution to the development of consistent estimates, it is of limited use in the presence of endogenous attributes except in providing initial estimates of γ_0, γ_1, γ_2 and β_{2k} for calculating the selectivity bias. The inclusion of $(1 + \alpha^2 \sigma^2)^{\frac{1}{2}}$ in the denominator is applicable only when the two stage model has a nondegenerate component (Π_q^*) and a degenerate state (binary discrete choice). As demonstrated trivially by Westin (1975: 6)

$$h(I_q = 0) = 1 - \Phi\left[\frac{\theta_q}{(1 + \alpha^2 \sigma^2)^{\frac{1}{2}}}\right] \tag{8.38}$$

from the likelihood function for $I_q = 0$ (i.e. the transit use decision), with the unobservable service variable Π_q^* integrated out

$$h(I_q=0) = 1 - \int_{-\infty}^{\infty} \Phi(\theta_q)\frac{1}{(2\Pi\sigma)^{\frac{1}{2}}} \exp\left(-(2\sigma^2)^{-1}(\Pi_q^* - \gamma_0\right.$$
$$\left. - \gamma_1 W_2 - \gamma_2 W_q^2 - V_{2q})^2\right) d\Pi_q$$

Since we have a conditional relationship between Π_q^* and I_q^*, and that I_q^* is formed on a limited set of values, then we must introduce an expression to allow for selectivity bias; that is we need a selectivity bias variable when Π_q^* is observable conditonal on the choice process that is simultaneously dependent on Π_q^*. The conditional mean of Π_q^* is given in equation (8.39)

$$E(\Pi_q^* | I_q^* \geqslant 0) = \gamma_0 + \gamma_1 W_q + \gamma_2 W_q^2 + V_{2q} + \left[\frac{\alpha\sigma^2}{(1+\alpha^2\sigma^2)^{\frac{1}{2}}} \cdot \frac{\phi(\theta_q)}{\Phi(\theta_q)}\right]$$

$$\tag{8.39}$$

derived directly from equation (8.29) above. ϕ is the univariate standard normal probability density function. The final term in equation (8.39) is dependent on the choice process. Since $\phi(\theta_q)/\Phi(\theta_q)$ and θ_q are usually unknown, we need some indirect procedure to obtain consistent estimates for <u>all</u> parameters, not just the β_{2k}s. The last term in equation (8.39) is an independent variable, which if excluded due to lack of a priori information, would give inconsistent estimates of the structural coefficients and a biased Π_q^*, since the containment of θ_q in the last term acts as an omitted independent variable correlated with the W_q's and X_{ikq}'s via θ.

Heckman's staged-procedure was essentially adopted by Westin & Gillen for obtaining consistent estimates when a priori information is absent and one has incomplete or censored samples. Essentially, equation (8.35) is estimated using probit analysis to obtain consistent estimates of parameters of all exogenous variables (i.e. the W_q's, X_{1kq}'s and X_{2kq}'s), and hence θ_q; then $\phi(\theta_q)/\Phi(\theta_q)$ is calculated for each car chooser and equation (8.39) is estimated using ordinary least squares regression to provide consistent estimates of coefficients of that equation. Next, predict mean value of Π_q^* for all (i.e. current car and current transit) travellers and re-estimate the binary probit model (equation (8.36)) to obtain consistent estimates of α and β_{1k} and hence $\hat{\theta}_q$:

$$\hat{\theta}_q = (\alpha \hat{\Pi}_q^* + V_{1q})/(1 + \alpha^2 \sigma^2)^{\frac{1}{2}}$$

The product of the estimated coefficient of $\phi(\theta_q)/\Phi(\theta_q)$ obtained from OLS ($= \alpha\sigma^2/(1+\alpha^2\sigma^2)^{\frac{1}{2}}$) that of $\hat{\Pi}^*$ ($= \alpha/(1 + \alpha^2\sigma^2)^{\frac{1}{2}}$) gives the required output for calculating the conditional variance of Π_q^* (see Heckman 1976a: 480 for details). $\phi(\hat{\theta}_q)/\Phi(\hat{\theta}_q)$ are calculated from $\hat{\theta}_q$ obtained earlier and equation (8.39) is reestimated using generalised least squares to correct for heteroskedasticity. Finally, inputting the estimate of σ^2 obtained from the generalised least squares model and the probit estimates of parameters from the final probit model, solve for estimates of all parameters in the mode choice model (equation (8.32)).

Although the final estimates (and each stage estimates) are consistent, efficiency can still be improved. Lee used such initial consistent estimates (up to the estimates of probit model prior to GLS) for estimation of a nonlinear likelihood function (Lee 1977, 1977a, 1978). He assumed that the equivalent term to the last variable in equation (8.39) was a truly exogenous variable and that remaining disturbances were homoskedastic. Since no GLS was undertaken, it is not possible to satisfactorily use Lee's study to assess the advantages of the maximum-likelihood step (referred to as two step - to avoid confusion with stages - maximum-likelihood procedure - 2S ML). Lee's most useful contribution is the same as the study by

Westin & Gillen, namely to develop a procedure to handle incomplete data and sample selectivity bias. The particular empirical results are left for the reader to pursue.

NOTES — CHAPTER 8

1. In order to impose the 'symmetry' condition described earlier, for $Y_q = 1$, the argument should be $(Z_q - V_q^* - \alpha\sigma^2)^2$.

2. The zero is an arbitrary threshold.

3. An application in this context is given in Section 9.4, as well as in Section 8.4.

4. Incomplete observations is not the only type of data bias. Spurious values and interchanged observations are two important data problems that have not been addressed by behavioural travel modellers (or econometric studies in the area of the literature cited); the only exception being a consideration of data outliers (e.g. Talvitie and Kirschner, 1978). Suggestions on handling these other biases might be sought from the literature on factorial experiments (e.g. Goldsmith & Boddy, 1978).

5. One way to proceed is to take a data set with complete observations that is also fully random to estimate the model on this data; then to eliminate the observable information on the alternative so that it becomes unobservable, and reestimate using the two-stage procedure. Then select a series of choice-based samples with and without the information on the alternative and estimate a series of models. A comparison will provide one basis for inferring any likely reduction in bias associated with incomplete observations than can occur by appropriate choice-based sampling.

CHAPTER 9

Applications

9·1 Introduction

A real test of the usefulness of discrete choice
models is in the range of meaningful applications.
While the number of applications have been
increasing significantly over the last three years,
the majority have been research oriented, often as
a case study to demonstrate the use of a concept.
However, there are signs that these modelling
procedures have a real contribution in a broader
planning context, such as their adoption as the
travel choice models for the Zuidvleugal Study in
the Netherlands (Daly, 1978a) and the Metropolitan
Adelaide Data Base Study in Australia (Office of
Director-General of Transport, 1978); as the
mechanism for obtaining estimates of allocation
preferences in a USA Federal Communications
Commission enquiry into the allocational regulatory
decisions associated with ultra high frequency (UHF)
television stations among cities in the USA
(Nelson & Noll, 1978, see case study in Section 9.3)
and by Telecom (Australia) in the identification of
the major attributes that consumers (actual and
potential) require on private automatic branch
exchanges (PABXs) so that this set of information
can be used (with other data) in the design and
promotion of future electronic PABXs (Hensher, 1979b,
1979c, Communications Research (Australia) 1979).
The objective of this chapter is to present six
applications that typify studies in the selective
areas of transport, communications, education,
recreation, child care and employment. The six
studies were selected as examples of applications
in a wide range of specialty areas and as good
examples of the use of the various concepts

presented in the earlier chapters. There are many
areas of potential application such as water
resources (excess vs. normal water consumption),
health or general insurance (yes or no and type,
given yes), industrial relations (strike vs. not
strike) and betting (winner vs. loser) (Figlewski,
1979).[1] Furthermore, there are many studies with
interesting applications within the areas of the
six illustrative studies; however, to introduce
more than one study from each area would not aid
the reader in acquiring an awareness of the role of
choice models.

9·2 A Case Study in Transport

9·2·1 Introduction

Stopher & Wilmot (1979) recently developed a
series of mode choice models for the work trip in
two municipalities on the periphery of Johannesburg
(South Africa). In addition to an extensive
analysis of alternative specifications of the
independent variables in each utility expression,
this study investigated the influence of eliminating
minor alternatives on estimation power, and applied
procedures to the final model specification to pool
the results of two random subsamples and to correct
for choice-based biases in the alternative-specific
constants (see Sections 7.3 and 7.4).

The aim of this study was to predict the
likelihood of an urban commuter selecting each of
car driver, car passenger, car pool, walk and bus,
drive and bus, motor cycle, bicycle, and walk.

9·2·2 Background

The development of individual mode choice models
for the work trip was part of a larger study
undertaken by the National Institute for Transport
and Road Research to identify ways of improving bus
services at a reasonable cost. The bus is the
major public transport mode in South Africa. The
data were obtained from two surveys; a choice-based
sample of bus commuters travelling during the time
period 0400 and 1600 hours who were given a self-
administered questionnaire (to be completed and
returned at the end of the trip), and a workplace
sample of all commuters resident in the two
municipalities who were employed in firms in the
correct geographical area (Johannesburg or local
community), the latter being randomly selected from

a business directory. The self-administered
workplace questionnaire was returned via the
employer. A large sample was drawn because of the
limited control on the stratum criterion; hence many
of the returned forms were not expected to be
relevant in the study. 778 (or 30 per cent) and 589
(or 14.6 per cent) of questionnaires were returned
for the bus and workplace surveys respectively, of
which 64 per cent of the bus questionnaires relate
to the work trip purpose.

The onboard survey included details on levels of
service of current trip by bus and one alternative
modal trip plus socioeconomic variables (income, age,
educational level, stage in the family life cycle,
car ownership and licensed drivers); the workplace
survey sought the same information except that level
of service was sought for eight alternatives. All
data used in the study is individual-specific, thus
avoiding aggregation error due to manufactured data
(see Section 4.5.1), but at the risk of bias due to
the difference between true perception and reported
perception.

The sampled population of the two municipalities
represents a moderately high income and high car
ownership group (five per cent had no car, 32 per
cent had one car, 45 per cent had two cars, 19 per
cent had three or more cars).

9·2·3 The Empirical Results

The basic (nonlinear logit) choice model was
estimated using the maximum-likelihood method. After
eliminating respondents[2] who were captive to car or
public transport, who did not provide data on at
least one alternative, and who did not provide data
on the chosen mode, the usable samples were reduced
to 345 commuters for the workplace sample and 444
for the onbus work trip sample.

A series of issues were investigated in arriving
at the final model. Let us take these one at a time.

Issue 1. The original data in the workplace
sample provided information on eight alternatives.
Since four of the alternatives (lift in car club,
motor cycle, bicycle, and walk) were used by very
few commuters and not likely to be a viable
alternative, would their removal significantly
affect the estimation power of the model? That is,
a preferable model would be one estimated on the
subsample of commuters whose choice sets contain the
predominantly-used modes. The workplace subsample
was used to test the hypothesis; the results are

285

given in columns two to five of Table 9.1 for two
different specifications of time and cost. The
coefficients do not change significantly; rather
the elimination of the four alternatives removes
the alternative-specific constants that are most
significant and of greatest magnitude. This
suggests that these four alternatives are least well
specified by the level-of-service variables.
Furthermore the lack of change in parameter
estimates implies that the class I violation of IIA
did not exist (i.e. correlation of ε_j's (see Chapter
5)).

Issue 2. A series of tests of the significance
of alternative specifications of variables were
undertaken bearing in mind that certain variables
(especially wait time and walk time) were not
separately defined for the alternative mode in the
bus sample. In columns two to five of Table 9.1 only
walk time, wait time (or the two combined) and park
time have significant coefficients at the 95 per
cent level of confidence. Although it is desirable
to disaggregate the time and cost variables
sufficiently to reflect the differing values that
individuals place on a unit of each type of time
and type of cost, data limitations prevented
disaggregation beyond three time variables and two
cost variables (column eight of Table 9.1). A test
(t score) of the difference in coefficients of walk
and wait time for the workplace sample indicated no
significant differences and thus it is reasonable
to regard walk and wait time to be homogeneous.

Surprisingly, invehicle time, parking cost and
travel cost were not significant at the 95 per cent
level. Separate models were estimated to identify
if intercorrelation amongst these variables was the
cause. These models, omitting each of the three
variables in turn and both cost variables together
had no effect on the coefficients of the remaining
variables, suggesting that intercorrelation was not
a cause of lack of significance. Thus all three
variables were, in the interim, kept in the model.
An additional variable, car competition, was
introduced as a car-driver specific variable to
account for the availability of a car. It is the
ratio of cars to licensed drivers in the household,
varying in value from one to zero. While the value
could be greater than one (i.e. more cars than
licensed drivers) it was set to a maximum value of
one. Similarly, if there are no cars, the value
was set arbitrarily to zero.

TABLE 9·1: Empirical Estimates of Parameters for Worktrip Mode Choice Models

Explanatory Variables	B̂(t-stat.)	B̂(t)	B̂(t)	B̂(t)	B̂(t) (* = not reported)	B̂(t) (* = not reported)	B̂(t) (Final model)
Walk time (mins.)	-.062 (3.3)	-.063 (2.7)	—	—	—	—	—
Wait time (mins.)	-.091 (3.2)	-.070 (2.6)	—	—	—	—	—
Walk and wait time (mins.)	—	—	-.072 (4.7)	-.066 (4.1)	-.035 (3.5)	-.037 (3.9)	-.0363 (3.7)
Invehicle time (mins.)	-.018 (1.5)	-.0062 (0.5)	-.019 (1.6)	-.0064 (0.5)	-.014 (1.4)	-.026 (2.6)	-.0203 (2.0)
Parking time (mins.)	-.051 (1.8)	-.072 (2.2)	-.050 (1.8)	-.072 (2.2)	-.065 (1.5)	-.127 (2.1)	-.0957 (1.8)
Parking cost (cents)	-.0053 (1.3)	-.0035 (0.9)	-.0052 (1.3)	-.0036 (0.9)	-.014 (3.3)	-.022 (4.4)	-.0188 (3.9)
Travel cost (cents)	-.0016 (1.1)	-.0010 (0.6)	-.0017 (1.1)	-.0009 (0.6)	-.0021 (1.4)	-.0051 (2.0)	-.0036 (1.7)
Alternative specific constant (ASC) for car passenger	-.84 (3.8)	-.90 (4.2)	-.88 (4.1)	-.91 (4.4)	*	*	-2.383 (1.9)
ASC for lift in car club	-1.98 (4.8)	—	-2.08 (5.2)	—	—	—	—
ASC for walk and bus	-0.25 (0.6)	-.45 (1.2)	-.30 (0.8)	-.45 (1.2)	*	*	-1.598 (4.4)
ASC for drive and bus	-1.23 (3.1)	-1.4 (3.7)	-1.33 (3.6)	-1.42 (4.0)	*	*	-1.536 (3.7)
ASC for motor cycle	-3.17 (7.5)	—	-3.19 (7.5)	—	—	—	—

287

ASC for bicycle	-4.52 (4.3)	-4.51 (4.3)	—	—	—	—	—
ASC for walk	-.92 (1.4)	-.76 (1.2)	—	—	—	—	—
Car driver	—	—	—	—	—	—	—
Car competition effect	—	—	—	—	3.46 (3.6)	2.83 (3.5)	3.146 (3.6)
Likelihood ratio (-2log λ) (d.f.)	317.3 (13)	316.6 (12)	166.2 (9)	166.1 (8)	171.5 (9)	186.8 (9)	
% correctly predicted (see Table 3.1)	54	54	61	61	77	78	

Source: Stopher & Wilmot (1979)

This variable is a proxy for car availability for the work trip and assumes that all household members with a driving licence have equal access to all cars. This is a statisticaly significant variable (column eight, Table 9.1), which affected the magnitude of the alternative-specific constants, not the other variables. This is a desirable result since it is assisting in explaining part of the factor set represented by the global alternative-specific constant.

Issue 3. The two data sets were pooled for the development of the final model. The pooled data was split into two random halves to test for any sample size bias and because of quadratically increasing estimation costs with increasing sample size. The results are given in columns six and seven in Table 9.1. The test for the significant differences between the coefficients for the sum of subsamples indicated that no significant differences existed.

In order to combine the two subsamples to arrive at a final model, updating is required (see Section 7.3). The general formula for updating the model parameters is (Lerman, Manski & Atherton, 1976 and Section 7.4):

$$\underline{\beta}_p = (\sum_1^{-1} + \sum_2^{-1})^{-1}(\sum_1^{-1} \underline{\beta}_1 + \sum_2^{-1} \underline{\beta}_2)$$

where $\sum_1, \sum_2$ = variance-covariance matrix of the coefficients for the first and second samples, respectively

$\underline{\beta}_1, \underline{\beta}_2$ = coefficient vectors for the first and second samples respectively

$\underline{\beta}_p$ = vector of pooled coefficients.

When the two samples are random subsamples drawn from the same parent sample (as is the situation here), then the formula reduces to $\beta_p = (\beta_1 + \beta_2)/2$ because the variance-covariance matrices of the two subsamples are statistically identical.

Using equation (7.4) the alternative-specific constants were adjusted to reflect the best estimates of current modal splits in the two communities. The preadjusted values were -1.596, -3.699 and -3.11 respectively for ASCs for car passenger, walk and bus, and drive and bus. The adjusted levels are given in the final model (Table 9.1).

The final model has recently been applied in predicting modal shares associated with a range of planning changes in bus services to the two communities.

9·3 A Case Study in Regulation and Communications

9·3·1 Introduction

One of the most novel and useful applications of discrete choice models in the basic logit format is to the identification of the allocation preferences of political decision makers and their advisers in the allocation of ultra-high frequency (UHF) television stations among cities by the Federal Communications Commission (FCC) of the USA. The FCC currently uses a computer program to identify technically and economically feasible allocations. However it is felt that since political decision makers have preferences among alternative station allocations that might not be fully accounted for if allocations responded solely to measures of the economic performance of a station and technical issues, it is desirable to determine whether and to what extent noneconomic aspects of allocation policy could be incorporated into the computer program. Nelson & Noll (1978), together with support and guidance from the FCCs UHF Task Force, undertook an extensive empirical study, designed to develop an objective, quantitative scientific mechanism for making allocational regulatory decisions. The study is still in progress, although some pilot results have been published and form the basis of this case study.

9·3·2 Background

A primary role of the USA FCC is to regulate. In this capacity, it defines and allocates rights to television broadcasters to use portions of the electromagnetic spectrum for communication purposes. Within this context, the FCC has the responsibility of allocating television channel assignments to particular localities. Currently nearly all VHF (very high frequency) channel assignments have been made and there is a desire of broadcasters to have access to the largely unused UHF spectrum.

The FCC, as the administrator of regulation, can control competition by regulations on signal reception with controls on antenna height, signal power, and signal direction of a station and the geographic spacing between them. However, the FCC

only has conventional economic criteria at its
disposal in its formulation of a set of rules. In
the belief that noneconomic criteria might also have
a significant influence on the future outcome, in
particular the allocational preferences of political
decision makers, an exploratory study was undertaken.
Opinions of "wise people" outside the FFC were
obtained, including members of Congress, principal
staff of Congressional subcommittees that oversee
FCC activities, high level government decision
makers, and some senior FCC staff. The framework
for the study is a multinomial logit model that
accommodates the allocational preferences of
individuals for commercial and noncommercial
stations on VHF and UHF spectrums in a number of
separate markets (localities).

9·3·3 The Model and Experimental Procedure

A separate model is initially developed for
each individual, with each observation being defined
in terms of successive assignments of single
stations in an allocation preference experimental
design (see below). In particular, each individual
is asked to assign a new television station to one
of four competing markets and to specify the type
restriction (commercial or noncommercial) on that
assignment.

Choice behaviour is described as the assignment
of a numerical preference score (S_i) to each of the
eight alternatives, the value of that score being
determined by the market, the current allocation of
stations to each of the markets and some
unobservable factors; the individual then selects
the assignment corresponding to the largest score.
This is analogous to the decision rule given by
equation (3.5). Formally, the model is:

$$Y_{iq} = \begin{cases} 1 & \text{iff } S_{iq} > S_{jq} \; \forall j \in J, \, i \neq j, \\ 0 & \text{otherwise} \end{cases} \qquad (9.1)$$

where $S_{iq} = \beta_t X_{mq} + \varepsilon_{tmq}$

and Y_i is an indicator of preferred assignment

   i   is the subscript denoting the market and
       type mix, i = 1,...,8

   t   is the subscript denoting type (t = 1,2)

   m   is the subscript denoting market
       (m = 1,...,4)

X_m is the vector set of explanatory variables, which includes a description of attributes of market m and the current allocation frequencies to market m (i.e. number of UHF commercial, UHF noncommercial, VHF commercial and VHF noncommercial stations)

$q(= 1,...Q)$ is number of trials (observations) per person

and

$$P_{iq} = (\exp \beta_t X_{mq} / \sum_{m=1}^{4} \sum_{t=1}^{2} \exp \beta_t, X_{m'q}) \qquad (9.2)$$

Using the theory of Chapter 3, implicit in the specification of S_{iq} is the assumption that the score S_{iq} assigned to market m is independent of scores S_{jq} for any other market $m' \neq m$, and that differences between markets are reflected only through the X_{mq} and ε_{tmq}, not through differences in the form of the function (which only differs across types). Because $S_{i(t=1)}$ and $S_{i(t=2)}$ both depend on the same factors X_m (i.e. not subscripted by t), they need not be independent. This permits station type substitution <u>within</u> the same market.

S_i can be measured in a number of ways. Nelson & Noll[1] argue that individuals cannot be expected to reveal their preference scores; fortunately the conscious assignment of numerical values is not required for the choice model:

> (The choice model) *merely requires that choices made be consistent with the assignment of numerical values in the following sense: there exists a function $U_t(\ )$ and a distribution on the random variable ε_{mt} that correctly predicts the relative frequency of outcomes Y_i as the assignment task is repeated indefinitely ... the preference scores are in a sense an artificial construct ... The scores merely provide a convenience measure of preferences among alternatives. For example, given either estimates or knowledge of the functions $U_t(\ )$,*

specific values of X_m determine expected scores S_i that rank order all alternative assignments. (notation is changed for consistency)   (Nelson & Noll, 1978)

A random sample of observations on Y_i and X_m are used in a maximum likelihood estimation to obtain estimates of β_t, t=1,2.

How is the data generated? Individuals are requested to make a sequence of station allocations among a group of four cities that differ in population and their initial allocations of stations (Table 9.2). Adopting a gaming format, the initial context is a game board with details of the existing allocation to four cities, the populations served by stations in each city and the categories of current stations (UHF, VHF for commercial and noncommercial stations).

The respondent is informed that the first three commercial VHF stations in a city will be networks, and the rest will be independents. Four VHF and many UHF tokens are then supplied and the respondent is asked to allocate additional stations using his own value allocation rule. This he/she does one allocation at a time, the process terminating either when the respondent feels that no more channels serve a useful purpose or the experimenter halts the allocation using a random-decision rule for stop time. The stopping rule reinforces the initial instruction that each assignment is to be independent of all future potential assignments. This is required for the use of statistical procedure. The experiment was repeated to generate at least 50 choices.

An important aspect of the approach is that each respondent creates some of the initial conditions for nearly all decisions, because the initial condition for the next choice includes the new allocation. This has the advantage of generating variance in the variables that measure the pattern of allocations. Population is constant during all of the allocations for each experiment with the same initial conditions.

9·3·4 The Empirical Results

An individual is given a number of trials, each trial differing in terms of the initial conditions. The number of trials times number of

293

TABLE 9·2 : An Example of Initial Conditions for Station Allocations

Market population	1 5 million		2 1½ million		3 400,000		4 100,000	
	Comm. (C)	Non Comm. (NC)	C	NC	C	NC	C	NC
VHF	3	1	3	0	2	1	2	0
UHF	1	0	1	1	1	0	0	0
TOTAL	4	1	4	1	3	1	2	0

new assignments per trial gives the number of observations per individual. $Y_{iq} = 1$ for each observation is assigned to the mix of market and type of the incremental allocation; for example if the individual allocates one of his VHF tokens to market two as noncommercial station, then Y_i (m = 2, t = 2) is assigned one, the other seven alternatives are assigned zero. Within a trial, population remains constant and number of stations can vary whereas when we begin a new trial, population can change. Three individuals, each modelled separately are used to illustrate the approach. Pooled estimates are also obtained. The three individuals are all FCC staff members.

A number of different models were assessed; the first where separate β coefficients were obtained for commercial and noncommercial stations (note that β was subscripted t, not m) for each individual; then a pooled model, and then the separate and pooled models where a distinction between VHF and UHF is made in the definition of the independent variables. All variables are exogenous. The full set of results are given in Table 9.3 A number of comments can be made on these preliminary results.

The results in Table 9.3 have a rather special interpretation. Markets have been assumed as independent with substitution permitted between types of stations within a market. Thus, for example, the number of commercial VHF stations per capita appears in both the commercial and noncommercial utility expressions as alternative-specific variables; the coefficients indicating (for individual two, say) that an additional prior

294

TABLE 9-3: Empirical Results in Station Allocation Preference Study (t-statistics in brackets)

Explanatory Variables	Individual				UHF/VHF Distinction Individual			
	1	2	3	Pooled	1	2	3	Pooled
Commercial Commercial station specific dummy	5.728 (1.68)	13.458 (3.9)	6.922 (2.5)	8.249 (5.2)	.337 (.09)	13.799 (3.96)	-3.279 (-.65)	7.25 (3.9)
No. CS	-1.640 (2.29)	-3.720 (4.8)	-1.300 (2.7)	-1.836 (6.1)	—	—	—	—
No. CS/PN	-.145 (1.5)	-.270 (3.0)	-.061 (1.1)	-.116 (2.9)	—	—	—	—
No. NCS	2.633 (1.6)	2.605 (1.5)	-1.346 (.89)	1.390 (1.92)	2.019 (1.3)	5.094 (2.7)	-2.983 (1.4)	1.759 (2.3)
No. NCS/PN	.374 (1.68)	.508 (2.6)	.003 (.02)	.220 (2.3)	.388 (1.5)	.276 (1.5)	-.122 (.65)	.197 (1.99)
No. NCS/CS	-22.348 (2.52)	-18.410 (-2.0)	3.216 (.48)	-10.732 (2.9)	-20.9 (2.3)	-23.975 (2.5)	11.281 (1.19)	-11.158 (2.9)
PN	.421 (1.9)	.513 (3.5)	.633 (3.9)	.409 (4.5)	.258 (.96)	.507 (2.8)	.521 (2.8)	.270 (2.7)
No. CSUHF	—	—	—	—	-1.463 (1.8)	-6.117 (5.9)	-1.350 (1.7)	-2.508 (6.6)
No. CSUHF/PN	—	—	—	—	-.341 (2.3)	.0001 (.01)	-.113 (1.1)	-.069 (1.35)

	(1)	(2)	(3)	(4)	(5)	(6)	(7)	(8)
No. CSVHF	—	—	—	—	-.453 (.57)	-3.375 (4.2)	.377 (4.4)	-1.063 (2.9)
No. CSVHF/PN	—	—	—	—	-.050 (.40)	-.296 (-3.7)	.016 (.17)	-.142 (3.2)
Noncommercial								
No. CS	.162 (.36)	-.347 (.78)	.669 (1.6)	.396 (1.8)	-.026 (.02)	-.888 (.52)	-1.910 (.84)	-2.698 (3.4)
No. CS/PN	-.010 (.24)	.081 (2.1)	.029 (.75)	.044 (2.1)	-.032 (.21)	-.495 (2.7)	-.243 (1.3)	-.292 (3.4)
No. NCS	-.999 (.84)	-.89 (.64)	-4.096 (3.0)	-2.356 (3.6)	—	—	—	—
No. NCS/PN	-.059 (.38)	-.472 (2.9)	-.281 (1.7)	-.285 (3.4)	—	—	—	—
No. NCS/CS	-8.814 (1.4)	-6.06 (.76)	10.610 (1.5)	3.541 (1.6)	-14.590 (1.711)	-8.758 (.92)	-2.609 (.211)	4.505 (1.1)
FN	.251 (1.51)	.092 (.79)	.355 (2.2)	.152 (1.99)	.307 (1.8)	.104 (.84)	.442 (2.7)	.186 (2.4)
No. CSUHF	—	—	—	—	-.602 (.79)	-.272 (.38)	-.827 (.99)	.341 (1.02)

TABLE 9·3 (cont.)

Explanatory Variables	Individual				UHF/VHF Distinction Individual			
	1	2	3	Pooled	1	2	3	Pooled
No. CSUHF/PN	—	—	—	—	.030 (.45)	.046 (.86)	.160 (1.8)	.045 (1.5)
No. CSVHF	—	—	—	—	-.132 (.21)	-.529 (.93)	.051 (.06)	.466 (1.6)
No. CSVHF/PN	—	—	—	—	-.081 (.95)	.112 (1.8)	-.187 (1.4)	.039 (1.1)
No. of Observations	57	111	69	237	57	111	69	237
Log likelihood	77.93	144.73	103.51	366.30	73.7	130.9	97.1	354.2
χ^2(df) - null Hypothesis	81.2 (13)	172.2 (13)	80 (13)	253 (13)	89.7 (17)	199.9 (17)	92.9 (17)	277.3 (17)

Note: The reason why commercial variables appear in noncommercial set and vice-versa expression is because interdependence is permitted on t(type); but not on m (market). Thus β_1 represents weights applied to each variable in determining the preference score for a commercial assignment. See text.

*   CS = commercial station, NCS = noncommercial station, PN = population.

allocation of one commercial VHF station per unit of the population to a particular market would decrease the preference score for a commercial VHF station in that market by .296 and increase the preference score for a noncommercial assignment by .112.

There is clear evidence to support the belief that senior bureaucrats do weigh commercial and noncommercial stations differently. A further distinction was made between VHF and UHF commercial stations, the evidence (the last four columns of Table 9.3) suggesting that the distinction is also important. A likelihood-ratio test of the hypothesis that the corresponding VHF and UHF coefficients are the same yields (with four degrees of freedom) for each respondent actual values of 10.4, 2.2 and 26.9. A comparison of coefficients of no. CS for any individual (say individual two) (= -3.720) and coefficients of no. VHF CS (= -3.375) and no. UHF CS (= -6.117) clearly demonstrates the different weights placed on these preference allocations.

The results given above illustrate the type of information that can be obtained from each individual. Upon completion of the experiments with many more individuals, Nelson & Noll will be able to use the results of the estimated models to assess if there is any uniformity of preferences across individuals, permitting the pooling of the samples (as is done in the basic choice model in Chapter 3). If sufficient differences do exist to prevent pooling, as suggested by the initial evidence, then the nature and extent of such differences will have to be investigated to identify likely error in pooling. Techniques such as covariance probit (see Section 6.5) may then be more suitable.

The usefulness of this approach will be very dependent on the ability to combine the preference allocations of each individual in order to arrive at some measure of decision maker and adviser influence, in the regulatory process, that is additional to the economic and technical considerations. If such aggregation is not possible, then the study is useful in identifying the diversity of preferences across individuals and the clear differences that exist in policy objectives between (in the present context) congressional oversight committees and the regulatory agency. The identification of the nature of conflict as well as its mere existence is a useful input into any planning process. The study could well be the forerunner of a number of studies in public choice, utilising discrete choice models in the ascertainment of the existence or nonexistence of a majority rule equilibrium. Nelson & Noll are able to demonstrate (Table 9.4) in this preliminary study that the rank order of assignment preferences (based on estimated preference functions for selected current allocations) is such that apparent differences in individual preference functions are not sufficiently large to deny agreement on frequency assignments. Their conclusion, however, is

> *Whether such results will hold for the more interesting data obtained from FCC commissioners and congressional oversight committee members remains to be seen.* (1978: 34)

9·4 A Case Study in Employment

9·4·1 Introduction

There are many empirical situations where information is not available from subsets of the population. An example is the absence of a market wage for non-working women in a study of female labour supply functions. The nonworker is a relevant part of any investigation of the influence of the market wage and hours of work on the supply of female labour. Concentrating on working women is a clear illustration of specification error. Other good examples are the exclusion of childless couples in a study of family fertility, and the exclusion of noncar commuters or nonpeak period commuters in a study of the impact of pricing congested road space.

Ross (1979), in an extensive empirical enquiry has developed market wage and hours worked functions for married women in New Zealand (1967/68), as part of a study of labour supply. The model specification involves the use of a binary logit model (of the basic choice form in Chapter 3) to estimate the probability of a woman being in the workforce; and uses this output in the construction of a regressor in each of the market wage and hours worked equations, this regressor being the mechanism for allowing for the existence of sample selectivity bias when the dependent variable is defined on only working women. This application illustrates the way in which selectivity bias is accommodated in a set of simultaneous equations when sample separation is permitted (see Section 8.3).

9·4·2 Background

In 1967/68 a very comprehensive random survey of urban working-age women was completed in New Zealand by the Society for Research on Women in New Zealand Inc. The sample was drawn from the four largest urban areas in New Zealand. Ross used a subset of the data, comprising Caucasian married women in residence with their spouses, and who were not attending an educational institution. The subsample contained 3466 observations, of which 1172 were working women. Unlike other local data sets, this data is highly disaggregate; the major deficiencies being only in the unfortunate categorisation of the important variables, 'weekly hours of work' (nine categories) and earnings (nine categories). This tended to introduce aggregation error (see Section 7.2).

With approximately 67 per cent of the sample being nonworking women, this data set is an excellent example of observations with missing data. The procedures outlined in Chapter 8 and summarised below in the context of Ross's study provide an extremely useful mechanism for accommodating incomplete observations, provided the underlying assumptions are acceptable to the analyst. While the assumptions enable internal consistency and validity in the specification of the simultaneous-equation model, they might not be suitable in a particular application. This is an empirical issue. Ross believes that the assumptions are (behaviourally) plausible for the study of female labour supply functions in New Zealand.

9·4·3 The Model

The model used by Ross is best presented in terms of the estimated functions and the sequence in which they are estimated. There are three equations; the participation-in-workforce, market wage rate and weekly hours working equations:

(a) nonlinear logit model (maximum-likelihood estimation), Q = total sample of 3466 women:

probability of labour-force participation (or working women in the sample) $= \exp V_p / (\exp V_p + \exp V_{np})$

TABLE 9·4: Rank Order of Assignment Preferences Based on Estimated Preference Functions for Selected Current Allocations*

TYPE AND MARKET (M)

	Commercial				Noncommercial			
	M A	M B	M C	M D	M A	M B	M C	M D
Current allocation								
UHF Stations	4	3	2	2	2	2	1	1
VHF Stations	4	3	3	2	2	1	1	0
Preference rank								
Subject II	4	7	3	8	5	6	2	1
Subject VII	8	6	2	4	7	5	3	1
Subject IX	8	5	2	4	7	6	3	1
Pooled sample	7	5	2	4	8	6	3	1
Majority rule	8	6	2	4	7	5	3	1
Current allocation								
UHF Stations	1	1	1	0	0	1	0	0
VHF Stations	3	3	2	2	1	0	1	0
Preference rank								
Subject II	5	6	8	1	3	4	7	2
Subject VII	3	5	4	2	6	7	8	1
Subject IX	1	5	6	3	2	4	8	7
Pooled sample	2	5	7	1	4	6	8	3
Majority rule	3	6	7	1	4	5	8	2
Current allocation								
UHF Stations	4	3	2	1	2	2	1	0
VHF Stations	4	3	2	2	1	0	0	0
Preference rank								
Subject II	7	8	6	3	5	4	2	1
Subject VII	8	7	4	2	6	5	3	1
Subject IX	8	7	4	2	6	5	3	1
Pooled sample	8	7	4	3	6	5	2	1
Majority rule	8	7	4	2	6	5	3	1
Current allocation								
UHF Stations	4	3	3	3	1	1	0	0
VHF Stations	2	2	2	2	1	1	1	1

TABLE 9·4 (cont.)

			TYPE AND MARKET (M)					
	Commercial					Noncommercial		
	M A	M B	M C	M D		M A	M B	M C	M D

Preference rank								
Subject II	5	7	6	8	3	4	1	2
Subject VII	7	5	6	8	3	4	1	2
Subject IX	6	5	7	8	2	4	1	3
Pooled sample	7	5	6	8	3	4	1	2
Majority rule	6	5	7	8	3	4	1	2

* Populations are 5 million, 1.5 million, 400 thousand, and 100 thousand in markets A, B, C and D respectively.

where V_p, V_{np} are linear additive-in-parameters functions of AGE, AGE^2, SCH, SCH^2, EXP.D, EXP^2.D, DU, AGE.SCH, AGE.SCH.D, SCH.EXP.D, AGE.DU, SCH.DU, SKILL, MED, POORHLTH, HELPPD, HELPFAM, CHCARE1, FAMSIZE, $FAMSIZE^2$, CH4, CH9, CHOTH, TRINC, SPINC (see Table 9.5 for explanation)

(b)   regression models (ordinary least squares)[3], $Q = 317$, the subset of the 1172 working women who were working away from home continuously since first starting a job:

$$E\left(w_{oq} \mid X_{oq}, h_q > 0\right) = \alpha_o + \beta_o X_{oq} + \frac{\sigma_{oh}}{(\sigma_{hh})^{\frac{1}{2}}} \cdot \lambda_q \qquad (9.3)$$

$$E\left(h_q \mid X_{hq}, h_q > 0\right) = \alpha_h + \beta_h X_{hq} + \frac{\sigma_{hh}}{(\sigma_{hh})^{\frac{1}{2}}} \cdot \lambda \qquad (9.4)$$

where w_o is the market wage, h is hours of work, X_o and X_h are vectors of attributes hypothesised to influence w_{oq} and h_q. The model assumes that only women who have w_o in excess of a reservation wage (w_r) work and they are free to choose hours of work; and that the individual's private valuation of a marginal unit of their time is just equal to their offered wage, which is assumed independent of their hours of work. Thus all we can assume is that $h_q = f(w_o - w_r)$.

The estimation task is to estimate $\alpha_o, \alpha_h, \beta_o$ and β_h for the entire population based on a sample of (317) working women only. The bias in sample selection is allowed for by the introduction of the last term in each of the w_o and h_q equations. The sample selection rule can be derived from the specification of the h_q function:

$h_q = \alpha_h + \beta_h X_{hq} + e_{hq}$, where e_{hq} is the error term; if a woman is working, $h_q > 0$; but $h_q > 0$ implies $\alpha_h + \beta_h X_{hq} + e_{hq} > 0$ and hence $e_{hq} > -(\alpha_h + \beta_h X_{hq})$.

In Chapter 8, we presented Heckman's model, which states that, assuming e_{hq} and e_{oq} to be jointly normally distributed; given

303

$$e_{hq} > -(\alpha_h + \beta_h X_{hq})$$

$$E(e_{oq}|h_q > 0) = \frac{\sigma_{oh}}{(\sigma_{hh})^{\frac{1}{2}}} \cdot \lambda_q \qquad (9.5)$$

$$E(e_{hq}|h_q > 0) = \frac{\sigma_{hh}}{(\sigma_{hh})^{\frac{1}{2}}} \cdot \lambda_q \qquad (9.6)$$

where λ_q (obtained via the logit model)[4]

$$= f\left[\frac{-(\alpha_h + \beta_h X_{hq})}{(\sigma_{hh})^{\frac{1}{2}}}\right] / \left[1 - F\left\{\frac{(-\alpha_h + \beta_h X_{hq})}{(\sigma_{hh})^{\frac{1}{2}}}\right\}\right] \qquad (9.7)$$

where f and F are the PDF and CDF functions in Chapter 3 for a <u>standard</u>[5] normal variable, Z defined as $Z_q = -(\alpha_h + \beta_h X_{hq})/(\sigma_{hh})^{\frac{1}{2}}$. Thus, given the sample selection rule ($h_q > 0$), and that

$$E(w_{oq}|X_{oq}, \text{ sample selection rule})$$
$$= \alpha_0 + \beta_o X_{oq} + E(e_{oq}| \text{ sample selection rule})$$

$$E(h_q|X_{hq}, \text{ sample selection rule})$$
$$= \alpha_h + \beta_h X_{hq} + E(e_{hq}| \text{ sample selection rule})$$

we obtain the two regression equations above. To calculate λ_q from the logit output, we feed in Z_q (obtained from the logit model as adjusted probabilities by applying for each individual the appropriate levels of X_{hq} or X_{oq} to the estimated logit model, where coefficients are standardised by $1/\sigma^{\frac{1}{2}}$).

Then λ_q is a regressor in each of the market wage and hours worked equations. The extent of sample selection bias can be obtained by noting the significance of λ and its effect on the coefficients of the other variables.

9·4·4 The Empirical Results

Since the hours worked equation is, amongst other considerations, defined as a function of the relationship between w_o and w_r, then any variable which influences the offered wage will also influence the hours-of-work decision. In addition, there can be variables in X_h that are not in X_o. The full list of variables considered by Ross and the results of selected models are summarised in Table 9.5.

Although the results of the logit model are of interest in themselves, the main aim of this study is not the determinants of labour force participation vs. nonparticipation, but the development of disaggregate wages and hours worked functions. The logit model is used to obtain an empirical estimate of sample selection bias for use as a regressor in the regression models. However, the results do provide some supporting evidence for Snyder's study (1978) with CH4, CHOTH, HELPFAM, POORHLTH, MED, SKILL and DU being strongly related to educational attainment, and age of children. Participation in the work force is strongly related to education (+ve), family cooperation in home duties (+ve), grown up (including teenage) children (+ve) and very young children (-ve). Snyder, in looking at the childbearing issue, found the wife's education and the value of her time to have an important influence on family size - with a higher education plus value of time increasing the opportunity cost of an additional child because of the greater foregone market wages. Further discussion on the logit results are given in Ross (1979); however, the reader should be able to provide much comment on the results, now that s/he has worked through Chapters 1 to 8.

The particularly interesting issue in the context of this book is the significance of sample selection bias and the contribution of λ_q in reducing such bias. The market wage equation is overall very poor statistically, the significant constant suggesting considerable specification error. λ appears (with qualification) to be significant although one is not confident in the equation as a whole to say more than this, other than that the presence of λ does not appear to have any nonmarginal impact on the other variables. The weekly hours function appears to be better

TABLE 9·5: Selected Empirical Results for the Three Models in Ross's Labour Supply Study (t–statistics in brackets)

Explanatory Variable	Logit Model (1=working) coefficient ÷$\hat{\sigma}^2$		Market Wages (dependent variable is $\ell n\ w_o$)		Weekly Hours Worked (dependent variable is estimated hours)	
	1	2	1	2	1	2
Age of woman (five yearly intervals) AGE	-.024 (4.5)	.031 (.7)	.100 (2.5)	.118 (3.0)	-2.541 (3.7)	-2.154 (3.2)
Years of formal schooling completed SCH	-.036 (1.5)	-.109 (.8)	.052 (.9)	.063 (.7)	-2.312 (2.2)	-2.172 (2.1)
Dummy variable (D)=1 if never worked or worked continuously since beginning a regular job, otherwise 0	—	—	—	—	—	—
If D=1; 0 if never worked, otherwise AGE – age at start of first regular job. EXP (yrs)	—	—	—	—	—	—
EXP.D. (years)	.658 (8.3)	-.666 (.6)	-.042 (1.3)	-.063 (2.1)	1.305 (2.3)	1.236 (2.3)
DU = 1 – D	.802 (3.5)	-2.484 (2.3)	—	—	—	—
Skill dummy = 1 if current occupation is professional, technical or managerial; 0 otherwise SKILL	.497 (4.1)	.460 (3.6)	.060 (1.0)	.062 (1.0)	1.481 (1.4)	1.688 (1.6)

Variable	(1)	(2)	(3)	(4)	(5)	(6)
Education dummy = 1 if mother of woman had any post-primary education; 0 otherwise MED	-.170 (1.9)	-.182 (2.0)	.012 (.2)	.013 (.3)	.042 (.1)	.083 (.1)
Health dummy = 1 if current or history of poor health. 0 otherwise POORHLTH	-2.148 (7.0)	-2.211 (7.5)	-.021 (.1)	-.027 (.2)	-12.600 (4.6)	-12.923 (4.8)
Paid help dummy = 1 if so; 0 otherwise HELPED	.231 (.9)	.241 (.9)	—	—	.068 (.02)	2.915 (1.1)
Family help dummy = 1 if so. 0 otherwise. HELPFAM	.669 (7.3)	.648 (6.9)	—	—	1.966 (2.4)	1.786 (2.2)
Disabled dummy = 1 if at least 1 disabled member of house needing regular attention; 0 otherwise DISABLE	-.154 (.9)	-.146 (.8)	—	—	2.863 (1.2)	2.064 (.9)
No. of preschool aged children CH4	-.980 (8.1)	-.838 (6.9)	—	—	-4.250 (1.4)	-5.830 (2.0)
No. of primary school aged children CH9	-.079 (.9)	-.022 (.2)	—	—	-2.821 (2.5)	-3.531 (3.2)

TABLE 9·5 (cont.)

Explanatory Variable	Logit Model (1=working) coefficient ÷σ²		Market Wages (dependent variable is $\ln w_o$)		Weekly Hours Worked (dependent variable is estimated hours)	
	1	2	1	2	1	2
No. of children age 10 plus CHOTH	.196 (2.1)	.171 (1.8)	—	—	-.009 (.01)	-.711 (.7)
Size of family FAMSIZE	-.040 (.5)	-.113 (.7)	—	—	-3.836 (3.1)	-4.004 (3.3)
Child care service dummy = 1 if used and satisfied during last 1 month. 0 otherwise. CHCARE 1	.083 (.8)	.055 (.5)	—	—	-5.030 (1.3)	-2.609 (.7)
Estimated hourly wage of women WAGE ($NZ per hr)	—	—	—	—	—	-4.493 (3.8)
Estimated hours worked per week per woman HOUR	—	—	—	—	—	—
Estimated weekly earnings of spouse if married SPINC	-.003 (1.5)	-.003 (1.6)	—	—	.006 (.3)	.024 (1.1)
Actual transfer income per week of family TRINC	-.042 (2.5)	-.042 (2.4)	—	—	-.484 (2.0)	-.406 (1.7)
λ	—	—	-.253 (1.8)	—	-2.995 (1.2)	-4.597 (1.8)

	(1)	(2)	(3)	(4)	(5)	(6)
SCH.DU	—	—	—	—	.013 (.1)	—
AGE^2	.039 (3.0)	.040 (1.0)	-.002 (3.1)	-.001 (1.2)	-.002 (4.1)	—
SCH^2	.061 (.9)	.074 (1.1)	-.003 (.7)	-.004 (.9)	.009 (1.3)	—
EXP^{2}D	.009 (.4)	-.005 (.2)	.0002 (.3)	.001 (1.2)	-.081 (1.0)	—
AGE.SCH	.081 (1.6)	.082 (1.6)	-.002 (.5)	-.001 (.3)	.0003 (.1)	—
AGE.EXP.D	-.043 (1.6)	-.029 (1.1)	-.001 (1.6)	-.001 (.6)	-.076 (1.0)	—
SCH.EXP.D.	-.070 (1.4)	-.081 (1.6)	.004 (1.5)	.004 (1.3)	.164 (1.8)	—
AGE.DU	—	—	—	—	.112 (3.5)	—
FAMSIZE^2	.479 (3.6)	.400 (3.0)	—	—	.006 (.5)	—

TABLE 9·5 (cont.)

	Logit Model (1=working) coefficient $\div\sigma^2$		Market Wages (dependent variable is in $\ln w_o$)		Weekly Hours Worked (dependent variable is estimated hours)	
	1	2	1	2	1	2
Working bias constant for logit; otherwise a constant	-.241 (.7)	.118 (.1)	-1.827 (3.5)	-1.937 (3.8)	78.993 (8.9)	75.472 (8.5)
Log likelihood at convergence or F	-1637	-1583	6.326	6.545	8.189	8.826
R^2			.215	.207	.405	.434
No. of observations	3466	3466	317	317	317	317

310

specified, with a considerably higher R^2 and statistically significant variables.

The major variables influencing the decision to work also influence the hours-of-work decision. Age (-ve), poor health (-ve), access to family help (+ve) and preschool age children (-ve) all have significant impact on both decisions. Interestingly, schooling and older children influence the participation decision but have little impact on the hours decision. An important finding is the nonsignificance of economic variables other than the wages of women on the hours-of-work decision. This may, in part, be due to the rather coarse empirical definition of hours worked (nine codes) or the likelihood that the explanatory power of the economic variables (SPINC, TRINC) is being absorbed in the demographic variables, and that a rather complex sub-causal structure exists on a subset of the independent variables. λ in the hours decision is negative and statistically significant. Heckman expected a positive coefficient, on the hypothesis that women who were more likely to work were also more likely to work longer hours. That is, unmeasured factors affecting the participation decision are positively correlated with unmeasured factors affecting labour supply. The negative correlation implies a backward bending supply curve. Although not reported in Table 9.5 it appears that λ overall influences the coefficients of the other variables, although in no case could the change in a coefficient be described as 'large'.

The reader is referred to Ross's original paper for more interpretation of the output. This paper provides an excellent example of the use of the theoretical and statistical approach presented in Chapter 8.

9·5 A Case Study in Recreation and Travel

9·5·1 Introduction

Most applications of discrete choice modelling in transport concern themselves with travel to work or to the shops. Brown (1979) has extended the use of choice modelling by considering recreational travel decisions in a MNL framework. His analysis is particularly useful as a case study in that it serves as an illustration of the need to consider the hierarchical structure of decisions. Furthermore, it also provides an empirical example of the estimation of sequential recursive models incorporating the concept of inclusive value or expected maximum utility (or logsum in Brown's paper) as a link between decisions (see Chapter 4).

The data used in this study were collected in a 1972 survey in Wisconsin, USA, and related to household travel over a 12 month period for the purpose of outdoor recreation. The task of developing models of recreation travel choice was undertaken by Cambridge Systematics, Inc. for the Wisconsin Department of Transportation. The modelling task was limited to frequency, duration and destination choices, modelled in that sequence. The results reported were necessarily preliminary, but serve to illustrate the usefulness of the technique in examining the recreational travel decision.

9·5·2 The Model

Recalling that with sequential recursive models, estimation is implemented in reverse order, the first choice to be considered was destination. One factor determining destination choice in a recreational context is the opportunity for various activities at different destinations. When one includes more than one variable describing the quantity of opportunities at a location (called "size" variables), the probability of choice should usually be directly proportional to these variables. Brown's work draws upon the recent discussion of this problem by Daly (1979a, 1980). He argues that in a MNL model of destination choice, the utility expression for the ith destination must be written

$$V_i = \sum_{k=1}^{K} \beta_k X_{ki} + \theta \ln \left(\sum_{\ell=1}^{L} \gamma_\ell S_{\ell i} \right) \qquad (9.8)$$

where the X_{ki} are 'nonsize' variables, $S_{\ell i}$ are size variables, βs and γs are parameters and θ is a parameter included for generality - it should be equal to one if the direct proportionality of probability to size variables is to hold.

Furthermore, one of the size variable parameters must be arbitrarily assigned a value (e.g. 1) since it can be shown that all L γs cannot be separately estimated. Also, the size coefficients (γs) should be positive so that one could replace γ_ℓ in equation (9.8) by (exp γ_ℓ) to ensure this, or leave them unconstrained as a test for appropriateness of the model. Given the definition of V_i in equation (9.8) which is nonlinear in parameters, a more complicated numerical estimation procedure must be used than is the case with the usual MNL model with linear-in-parameters V_i.

Once the destination choice model was estimated, a duration choice model is estimated using the expected maximum utility (logsum) from the destination model as an additional explanatory variable. In other words, specifying a MNL choice model, the probability of duration (= 2, 3 or 4 days) was given by

$$P_i = \frac{\exp\ (V_i^* + \alpha I_{di})}{\displaystyle\sum_{j=2}^{4} \exp\ (V_j^* + \alpha I_{dj})} \qquad (9.9)$$

where i = 2, 3 or 4 days duration, V_i^* is a linear-in-parameters function of variables affecting choice of duration, I_{di} is the logsum from the destination choice model for duration i and α is a parameter. Note in particular that if $\alpha = 0$, equation (9.9) reduces to an independent MNL choice model for duration (independent of destination choice.)

Once this model is estimated, a frequency choice model may be estimated using the logsum from this model as an argument. We shall discuss these models more fully in the next section which describes empirical results from this study. We would suggest, however, that before continuing, the reader reviews the discussion of decision linking and model hierarchy contained in Chapter 4.

9·5·3 The Empirical Results

Results from the destination choice estimation are given in Table 9.6. The dependent variable is defined as the choice of one of 15 planning regions covering the whole State of Wisconsin.

Brown concludes that these results confirm his a priori beliefs in that (1) people prefer outdoor recreation in less populated areas, hence the negative sign of population and (2) travel time is an important variable and further, that its effect is greater for families with children than without and less the longer the duration of the trip. The coefficients of the size variables which serve as a

313

TABLE 9·6 : Destination — Choice Model Results

Variable	Parameter Estimate	t-statistic
Population of destination	-.669	-4.0
No children		
Time to destination if duration = 2	-.013	-4.7
Time to destination if duration = 3	-.0082	-4.0
Time to destination if duration = 4	-.0076	-2.1
With children		
Time to destination if duration = 2	-.016	-7.9
Time to destination if duration = 3	-.012	-8.5
Time to destination if duration = 4	-.011	-4.3
SIZE VARIABLES		
Number of named lakes in region	.24	1.0
Number of swimming beaches in region	.11	1.2
Length of trout streams in region	.68	.9
Total Land Area Constrained = 1		-
Log-likelihood at zero = -972		
Log-likelihood at convergence = -876		

proxy for destination attractiveness are insignificant; their inclusion does however enhance the
performance of the model as a whole. No predictive
tests were carried out with this (or any) of the
models, since as previously mentioned, the work was
still in a preliminary stage.

The duration choice model examined hypothesised
that duration (2, 3 or 4 days) would be a function
of socioeconomic or family-related variables as well
as the logsum (expected maximum utility from all
destinations) from the destination model. After
experimentation with several variables, Brown's
best results are contained in Table 9.7.

TABLE 9·7 : Duration — Choice Model Results

Variable	Parameter Estimate	t-statistic
Logsum (inclusive value)	0.369	0.31
"Cost" (= distance x hh size)	-0.0009	2.15
No. of employed adults ⎤ Specific to	-0.23	0.86
Age of household head ⎦ duration = 4	0.033	2.68
Duration = 3 (ASC)	0.08	0.14
Duration = 4 (ASC)	-2.44	2.5
Log-likelihood at zero = - 392		
Log-likelihood at convergence = - 342		

Considerable difficulty was experienced in obtaining a model specification which adequately reflected the importance of cost on duration choice. Without such a measure, the logsum variable, necessarily increasing with duration, took on an incorrect negative sign as it acts in the same direction as the (unincluded) measure of cost. The reported model contains both a logsum and a proxy for trip cost (distance by household size) which have correct positive and negative signs respectively.

The insignificance of the logsum reinforces the intuitive belief that situational constraints govern duration decisions, particularly whether or not the trip is to be made on a long weekend or vacation. As such data did not exist, the effect could not be estimated. The influence of destination accessibility (an interpretation of the logsum variable) does not appear significant.

The final choice modelled was frequency which, because of the data, took on values of 0, 1, 2 or 3+ trips per year, per household. Brown modelled this as a basic MNL model with a logsum from the duration model (which itself contained a logsum from the destination model). The results were disappointing in that the coefficient of the logsum consistently took a negative sign. Three considerations were suggested as possible reasons for this:

(1)   the logsum for the duration model cannot be expected to perform well given the problems with the duration model;

(2)   family structure affects frequency as well as duration so that the logsum from duration will be correlated with explanatory variables in the frequency model;

(3)   the sequence of choices modelled may be inappropriate and that the correct sequence may be destination/frequency and destination/duration with duration and frequency being independent of one another.

To test this last consideration, a frequency model was estimated with the logsum from the destination choice model as an argument. It was found that it had a coefficient which was positive and highly significant giving rise to the conclusion that this was the correct modelling sequence. The final frequency model is given in Table 9.8.

The frequency variable was introduced as a surrogate for cost of trip making; the negative sign is intuitively plausible. The positive and significant coefficients associated with vacation, family size and occupation status are consistent

TABLE 9·8 : Frequency – Choice Model Results

Variable		Parameter Estimate	t-statistic
Logsum·frequency		.496	10.0
Rural residents	specific to	-.275	1.65
Vacation	frequency	.017	2.4
Unemployed head	= 0	-.18	1.0
Frequency		-2.36	16.1
Income	specific to	.00002	.7
Family Size	frequency	.42	3.6
Number of Children	= 3 plus	-.25	1.4
White collar worker		2.13	4.8

Log-likelihood at zero   = -1038
Log-likelihood at convergence = - 547

with a priori hypotheses that (1) an increasing amount of vacation travel tends to reduce the likelihood of undertaking weekend recreational trips (2) white collar workers tend to make more weekend trips than their counterparts; and (3) increasing family size increases trip making potential. The inclusive value variable, obtained from the destination choice model supports the hypothesis that the proximity of activity opportunities has a considerable influence on activity participation. This variable was weighted by frequency to represent increasing utility available for higher level frequency choices.

This case study of recreational travel serves to illustrate the use of inclusive value in sequential recursive models and also points out some of the danger that can be encountered in its use. It also highlights an application of choice modelling to an area of transport that has to a great extent been ignored by choice modellers in general. The empirical results are encouraging.

9·6 A Case Study in Education

9·6·1 Introduction

Of particular interest to those involved in higher education are questions concerning the factors which influence students' choice of school. A recent study by Punj & Staelin (1978) has examined some of these questions in the context of the choice of graduate school using data on 177 students who were selecting between two or more

Master of Business Administration (MBA) programs in the United States. Their basic interest was to find out which characteristics of the schools are considered by students and what relative influence these attributes have on the choice of school. The modelling technique used was the standard MNL model developed in Chapter 3. The authors use the results of the estimation of a model of the college-choice decision to examine possible marketing strategies for a school, since education especially in the United States, has become a particularly competitive enterprise. In our discussion of their work, we will concentrate on their data development, because they use rank-order information to increase the number of usable observations, and on their use of results to aid admissions officers in development of program marketing strategies.

9·6·2 Data and Model

Questionnaires were administered in 1975 to every student accepted into Carnegie-Mellon University's MBA program (note: where the authors are affiliated) starting Fall 1975 and in Fall 1974 to every student who actually joined Carnegie-Mellon's MBA program in Fall 1974. A total of 289 of 315 questionnaires were returned. They indicated the schools where the student had applied for admission (in order of preference), where accepted and whether they had applied for and the amount (if any) of financial aid received. Socioeconomic data were then obtained from the students' application folder and characteristics of various schools from a number of sources (see Punj & Staelin, 1978, Table 1: 592-93).

The sampling procedure was choice-based (see Chapter 7.4), with Carnegie-Mellon students being oversampled. A suitable likelihood estimator, such as that given for $p(x)$ and H_b^* known in Table 7.2 was not used, but resort was made to McFadden's proof that if the logit model contains a full set of alternative-specific constants, then the estimation procedure produces consistent estimates for all variables except the coefficients of these constants.

There were 120 schools mentioned in the 289 returned questionnaires which was far too large a choice set for the authors' purpose. They therefore narrowed attention to the 20 most frequently mentioned (where the student was actually accepted and hence had the choice of attending that school), which left 177 students with a choice set of two or

317

more alternatives. In the actual estimation of the model, Punj & Staelin used 403 observations since they used the rank-order information provided on the original questionnaires to 'explode' the data. For example, if an individual was accepted at four schools and had ranked them 1, 2, 3 and 4, then three choice sets would emerge, namely (1,2,3,4), (2,3,4) and (3,4) where the first listed alternative is taken to be the actual choice made. This explosion rule requires one to assume that the reported rank-order reflects the choice that would have been made if the student was actually faced with that choice set. The authors claim that for the major decision of graduate business school, this assumption is not unreasonable.

9·6·3 Empirical Results

Using these 403 observations, an initial MNL model was estimated with 29 variables, most of which were specified as generic except for six alternative-specific dummy variables (for Harvard, Stanford, Chicago, Wharton, MIT, and Carnegie-Mellon). Some of the variables were entered in absolute as well as squared terms to reflect the authors' belief that factors such as cost and distance from home had varying marginal effects. The number of variables was subsequently reduced (by the use of likelihood-ratio tests (see Chapter 3) to determine the significance of sets of variables) to a final model with 13 variables for use as a managerial tool. The coefficients of all 13 variables were significant (using a t-test) and had signs expected by the authors. Basically, the variables reflected costs (negative effect), availability of fellowships and loans (positive), quality of program (positive), distance from home (negative), size of entering class (negative - as expected since the sample was not purely random in that all were applicants to Carnegie-Mellon which has a relatively small MBA program and hence one would expect the sample to reflect a preference for small class size), and a positive effect of the two remaining alternative-specific dummies for Harvard and Stanford. The interested reader is referred to Table 2 of Punj & Staelin (1978: 594) for more detail on the coefficient estimates.

To illustrate the application of their results, we shall summarise the analysis of the cost and financial aid variables in the model. The coefficient of gross cost (in dollars/year) for those not applying for aid was -.000404 while for

318

those applying for aid it was -.000561. Hence, for those applying for aid, an increase in gross cost/year of $1000 results in a .561 point decrease in utility. The coefficient of loans (in dollars) was .000220 so that an increase in loans granted of $1000 would increase the utility of the school by .220 points. Hence, the authors argue that a school contemplating a future tuition increase could 'moderate' the effect of the cost increase by increasing loan availability since there would be a net decrease of .341 points/$1000 if both tuition and loans were increased by the same amount. A fellowship has an even more moderating effect (a coefficient of .000312) but its cost to the school is much greater since fellowships come from the operating budget of the school whereas loans are third party agreements. Hence, they conclude that schools would find it more useful to award loan dollars instead of fellowship dollars to moderate tuition increases.

Analysis of coefficients of other variables is similar to that described above. We turn now to their analysis of the model for prediction purposes. They used both the sample of 177 students upon which estimation of the model was based and a later sample (as of April 1976) of applicants accepted to the Carnegie-Mellon MBA program for the class entering September 1976. This second sample was particularly useful in that the data necessary for prediction were available at a time prior to the students accepting admission to a particular school. Therefore, we shall concentrate on these predictions, only briefly mentioning the predictions for the first sample of 177.

To calculate the predicted number of students choosing each school, the probabilities of choice for each school in the particular choice set for each student were calculated using the estimated model and then summed for each of the 20 schools to arrive at an estimate of the number of students who would choose that school (see the discussion of prediction success in Chapter 3). This predicted number was then compared to the actual number enrolled in each school using both an absolute deviation statistic given by

$$\sum_{j=1}^{20} | \hat{A}_j - A_j | \hat{A}_j / n \qquad (9.10)$$

and a root-mean-squared error statistic given by

$$\left(\sum_{j=1}^{20} (\hat{A}_j - A_j)^2 \, \hat{A}_j \, / \, n \right)^{\frac{1}{2}} \qquad\qquad (9.11)$$

where $\hat{A}_j$ and A_j are predicted and actual enrolments in school j, n is the total number of students in the sample (i.e. either 177 or 65) and where $\hat{A}_j/n$ is used as a weighting factor instead of A_j/n since some A_j were actually zero. These statistics were compared to a naive model which assigned the probability of choice for a student i to be $1/J_i$ where J_i is the size of i's choice set.

Results for the set of 177 students used in estimation were quite good with the MNL based predictions resulting in prediction statistics (9.9) and (9.10) about one-fifth the size of the same statistics in the naive model case. These are given in Table 9.9.

TABLE 9·9: Prediction Statistics for 177 Students Used in Estimation

Statistic	MNL Model	Naive Model
(9.10)	2.76	12.22
(9.11)	3.19	16.74

Results for the sample of 65 postestimation students are given in Table 9.10.

TABLE 9·10: Prediction Statistics for 65 Post–Estimation Students

Statistic	MNL Model	Naive Model
(9.10)	1.78	4.12
(9.11)	1.97	4.94

Although these results are not as good as the predictions for the 177 students used in estimation when one compares the MNL and naive models the authors found the absolute size of the statistics in Table 9.10 quite encouraging. As a further example of how well their model performed on this postestimation sample, if one examines their Table 5 (page 597), the MNL model predicted 32 students

would choose Carnegie-Mellon (30 actually did), 11
would choose Chicago (12 did), 5 Harvard (5 did) and
8 Wharton (6 did). These results imply that at
least in the case of applicants to a particular
program (Carnegie-Mellon's MBA Program), a MNL model
estimated in one time period (1974 and 1975) seems
to be transferable at the same school to another
time period (1976) at least for predictive purposes
(see the discussion of transferability in Chapter 7).

9·7 A Case Study in Child Care

9·7·1 Introduction

The final case study is the analysis of the
determinants of various forms of child care among
two parent families with working mothers. The study
by Robins & Spiegelman (1978) used a sample of 545
observations on two parent families in which the
mother was working and at least one child was under
13 years old. A child care survey was given to
families (apparently 4800) in the Seattle and
Denver Income Maintenance Experiment during late
1972 to early 1973. As a result of the definition
of the problems being investigated, the subset of
545 was obtained after stratifying the larger sample
on the basis of household income, ethnicity and
family status. The authors state that only low and
middle income families were included and Black and
Mexican-American families as well as families headed
by women were oversampled. They admit that this
could lead to sample selectivity bias, but because
individuals in the larger samples were randomly
assigned to a control group or an experimental group
as far as the income maintenance experiment was
concerned, they were able to test for control-
experimental differences in choice of market-
oriented child care (using a t-test for differences
between means or a t-statistic associated with a
regression model - unfortunately there are no
details on exactly what was done in the paper).
Their conclusion of no sample selectivity bias
refers only to that bias possibly caused by
experimental-control differences in their sample of
545. It still does not reflect the absence of
sample selectivity bias in general (see Chapter 8).

9·7·2 Model

Robins & Spiegelman were interested in the
determinants of choice of child care type and, in

321

particular, two child care modes that are market-oriented (as opposed to home-based or nonmarket-oriented child care). One mode was termed formal market care (e.g. day care centres) and the other market mode informal market care (e.g. babysitting). Their method of estimation was nonlinear logit as described in Chapter 3 with the coefficients of variables in V_{3q}, where 3 refers to the nonmarket mode, set equal to zero. Thus the coefficients of variables in V_{1q} and V_{2q} (1 = formal, 2 = informal) are interpreted as the difference in utility for that mode as compared to the nonmarket mode due to the particular variable in question.

The independent variables used in this single decision model were all defined to be alternative specific, in this case, specific to alternative 1 or 2. For example the variable 'earnings of mother in month prior to survey' (EARNMOTH) was specific to mode 1 and also to mode 2. In other words, EARNMOTH had a different coefficient in V_{1q} than in V_{2q}. All 17 variables were defined in this way. A list and definitions of the independent variables are in Table 9.11.

9·7·3 The Empirical Results

The basic empirical results of Robins & Spiegelman are presented in Table 9.11.

TABLE 9·11 Coefficient Estimates for Child Care Demand Study

Variable	Mode 1 coefficient	Mode 2 coefficient
1 = reside in Seattle and eligible to receive subsidy through income maintenance experiment 0 = otherwise	1.120**	.787*
1 = reside in Denver and eligible to receive subsidy through income maintenance experiment 0 = otherwise	1.383*	.470
Earning of mother in month prior to survey ($1000s)	6.311**	4.031**
Earnings of father and other family income in month prior to survey ($1000s)	.459	.416

TABLE 9·11 (cont.)

Variable	Mode 1 coefficient	Mode 2 coefficient
Hours of work per week for mother x Age Dist. of nonhead family members dummy		
Hours of work per week -		
Hours of work - none over 5	- .045	- .055
Hours of work - none under 6 or over 12	- .077*	- .077
Hours of work - none over 13 but at least 1 over 6 and 1 under 6	- .089**	- .052*
Hours of work - at least 1 over 13 and 1 under 13	- .119**	- .035
Number of children aged 0 - 4	.015	- .215
Number of children aged 5	.583	.038
Number of children aged 6 - 12	-1.201**	- .831**
Number of children aged 13 - 17	.395	-1.217**
1 = at least 1 child under 6 and 1 over 6; 0 = otherwise	2.537**	2.717**
1 = nonhead over 17 living with family; 0 = otherwise	- .102	-1.473**
1 = Black family; 0 = otherwise	1.523**	- .065
1 = Chicano family; 0 = otherwise	.744	- .033
1 = reside in Seattle; 0 = reside in Denver	.423	- .935**
Constant	-2.990*	- .365

$$\rho^2 = .274$$

* indicates significant at 10% level
** indicates significant at 5% level

Note: (Robins & Spiegelman (1978: 90) report coefficients and standard errors. We have used their indications of significance assuming that the reported standard errors in their Table 2 are incorrect. If they are correct, then some (minor) corrections to the list of significant variables must be made.)

To interpret these results, first note that if the coefficients of a variable for both modes 1 and 2 are of the same sign (e.g. earnings of mother), the effect of that variable on the third mode (nonmarket care) is of the opposite sign (e.g. the greater the earnings of mother, the less the probability of nonmarket care). In particular, the

authors seize on the coefficients of the first two
variables listed to conclude that the subsidisation
of market type child care leads to a reduction in
use of nonmarket care. Furthermore, the size of a
coefficient for one mode relative to the coefficient
of another mode for the same variables gives an
indication of the odds of using one mode over
another (e.g. the higher mother's income the greater
the odds of using formal care (mode 1) since
6.311 > 4.031). Positive coefficients clearly imply
the effect of the variable is positive for that mode
in relation to mode 3 (nonmarket care).

The authors proceed to use the results of
their estimation to predict the probabilities of
various modes under different assumptions about the
value of the independent variables. Holding the
values of all but a select set of independent
variables at their sample means, they find that
families appear to be quite sensitive to the type of
subsidy and hence price. Those not eligible for
subsidy under income maintenance were eligible for
subsidy through Federal income tax rebate which
implied a difference in price of market child care
under each subsidy. In Seattle, for example, the
predicted probability of market child care (mode 1 +
mode 2) was .40 under the income maintenance program
and only .22 under the Federal income tax subsidy
program (assuming a child care price of $5/day and
subsidy rates of .4 and .16 respectively - see their
article on page 91). This implies a price
elasticity of about -2.8, a marked sensitivity.
Similar results are examined for other variable
combinations.

The Robins-Spiegelman case study has served
to illustrate a situation where choice modelling
is appropriate but where the analyst is faced with
only measurement on socioeconomic variables for the
individuals in the sample but no information on the
characteristics of alternatives. In this case, one
designates one of the alternatives as a base and
defines all explanatory variables as specific to the
other alternatives. The MNL model then takes the
general form of

$$P_{iq} = \exp(V_{iq})/[1 + \sum_{j=2}^{J} \exp(V_{jq})] \qquad i = 2,\ldots,J$$

$$P_{1q} = 1/[1 + \sum_{j=2}^{J} \exp(V_{jq})]$$

where 1 has been arbitrarily designated as the base.
In the discussion above, the base was mode 3.

NOTES — CHAPTER 9

1. Other applications include the judge's sentencing of alcoholics (Gottschalk & Goluks, 1979), the choice of television station viewing, choice of journal subscriptions, selection of cultural activities, demand for alternative health insurance schemes (Van de Ven & Van Praag, 1979), demand for primary health care (Van der Gaag & Van de Ven, 1978), and choice of leisure activities. An annotated overview of many recent studies given in a report prepared by the authors, was not included in this book because of space limitations. Copies are available on request.

2. This is an example of a situation where use could be made of an endogenous attribute model to accommodate incomplete information, including a selectivity bias variable. However, this alternative action is not justified if complete information is available from a significant proportion of the sample. A separate issue, however, is the inclusion of an endogenous attribute in the mode choice model, regardless of level of information, if it was felt that causality is two-way for certain independent variables and mode choice. Westin & Gillen argue this is the situation for parking location and mode choice.

3. With the assumptions: the expected value of each error is zero ($E(e_{jq}) = 0$); there is a constant correlation of errors within individuals ($E(e_{oq}e_{hq}) = \sigma_{oh}$); there is no correlation of errors across individuals ($E(e_{jq}e_{jq}*) = 0$. $q \neq q*$, $j = o,h$.

4. λ is the inverse of the ratio of the ordinate to the right-tail of the standard distribution; the right-tail being the probability of labour force participation (P_p);

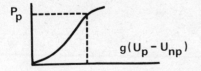

Hence in the Z_q equation, before standardising,
$$U_p = \alpha_{hp} + \beta_h X_{hq};$$
$$U_{np} = \beta_h X_{hnpq}$$

and the model is estimated with
$$(U_p - U_{np}) = (\alpha_{hp} - 0) + \beta_h(X_{hq} - X_{hnpq}).$$

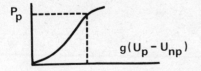

5. Standardisation of a normal variable means dividing by its standard deviation, or square root of its variance (i.e. $(\sigma_{hh})^{\frac{1}{2}}$).

CHAPTER 10

A Test Case Study

10·1 Introduction

The aim of this chapter is to introduce a computer program to estimate the coefficients of the basic MNL model (equation 3.24), and to provide suitable output such as probabilities of selecting alternatives, direct and cross elasticities of choice, and inclusive value.

In Section 10.2 the test data set is listed and described. Section 10.3 describes how the program is to be used, and a sample set of commands that may be used to estimate a model using the test data. The final section contains a listing of the output from the test case study commands.

This logit program, known as Basic Logit[1] (BLOGIT), was developed in 1979, and is an alternative to other existing programs such as MLOGIT in QUAIL4.0 (McFadden et al., 1979), XLOGIT (Manski, 1973), SLOGIT (Cambridge Systematics Inc., 1979), MLOGPROT (Hensher, 1979d), and the logit element of PROLO (Cragg & Lisco, 1968). The program was developed with flexibility as a major design criteria. The data input is uncomplicated (see Section 10.3) with the relationship between the attributes (within and between alternatives) being determined in the program itself. A wide range of data transformation options are available for the independent variables. In particular, the Box-Cox and Box-Tukey transformations (see Section 6.6), are options. The essential goodness-of-fit statistics are automatically included in the output. These are t-statistics for each independent variable, log-likelihood at zero and at convergence, rho-squared, and the prediction-success table. Subsamples of the data can be selected in a model run using any variable in the data as a

327

stratification criterion. Further details are provided in the following sections.

10·2 The Data

The test data set listed in Table 10.1 contains observations on the times and costs associated with the 1971 worktrip by car and train for 342 individual residents of suburbs located between 20 and 38 kilometres north of the Sydney Central Business District.

The data has been analysed previously by Hensher (1974) and Hensher & Johnson (1979). The data set contains a detailed set of variables defining the levels of service associated with trips where the car and train are used as the main means of transport for the greater part of the work trip (such as invehicle time, walk time, wait time, parking cost, and fare) together with socioeconomic data. We have selected out four variables for the test data set, since the sole purpose is not to estimate a well-specified model but to demonstrate how a set of data is set up and used as input into BLOGIT, and by comparing the output in Section 10.4, as a means of checking that the user is correctly using the program. The times listed are total commuter travel times to the central business district of Sydney by car and train, and costs are total travel costs for the two modes. Also listed for each observation is the actual choice made for the journey to work (1 = chosen). An interesting aspect of the data is that nine respondents neglected to indicate a time or cost for one mode so that these observations are unusable. Instead of removing these observations from the test data set, we chose to leave them in and use one of the data manipulation features of the program to eliminate them from estimations.

10·3 Using the Program

This section contains the detail required to use BLOGIT. The section begins with general information on program control (10.3.1), and then explains the three divisions of the program input commands - the general program control division (10.3.3), the data division (10.3.4), and the model division (10.3.5).

TABLE 10·1: Test Case Study Data Set

TC = Time/Car; CC = Cost/Car; TT = Time/Train; CT = Cost/Train

TC	CC	TT	CT	Choice(=1) Car	Train	TC	CC	TT	CT	Choice(=1) Car	Train
70.	50.	64.	39.	0	1	31.	25.	64.	45.	1	0
50.	230.	60.	32.	0	1	35.	50.	80.	49.	1	0
50.	70.	58.	40.	1	0	34.	77.	70.	60.	1	0
60.	108.	93.	62.	1	0	65.	50.	90.	30.	0	1
70.	60.	68.	26.	0	1	45.	60.	70.	32.	0	1
20.	32.	72.	65.	1	0	59.	37.	91.	35.	0	1
40.	30.	60.	37.	0	1	58.	55.	60.	42.	0	1
15.	8.	22.	20.	1	0	55.	99.	115.	60.	1	0
60.	60.	83.	31.	0	1	26.	28.	31.	39.	1	0
29.	20.	40.	17.	1	0	50.	80.	65.	39.	1	0
36.	30.	65.	70.	1	0	12.	12.	35.	22.	1	0
50.	30.	125.	60.	1	0	15.	12.	13.	7.	1	0
63.	35.	145.	60.	1	0	45.	50.	57.	31.	1	0
20.	30.	48.	25.	1	0	69.	57.	75.	36.	1	0
60.	40.	85.	45.	1	0	20.	30.	51.	33.	1	0
30.	20.	60.	35.	0	1	32.	44.	88.	20.	1	0
47.	60.	79.	26.	0	1	35.	30.	58.	0.	0	1
60.	72.	50.	26.	0	1	60.	52.	56.	26.	0	1
55.	40.	43.	26.	0	1	22.	28.	39.	14.	1	0
35.	80.	51.	29.	0	1	65.	65.	50.	25.	0	1
15.	30.	25.	20.	0	1	12.	16.	45.	30.	1	0
55.	50.	70.	27.	0	1	25.	60.	45.	28.	1	0
50.	50.	65.	26.	0	1	60.	60.	80.	28.	1	0
39.	25.	50.	55.	1	0	30.	48.	53.	40.	1	0
17.	20.	78.	35.	1	0	38.	56.	95.	30.	1	0
35.	56.	87.	40.	1	0	21.	30.	42.	24.	1	0
65.	55.	90.	26.	0	1	30.	54.	61.	30.	1	0
38.	40.	74.	23.	0	1	26.	20.	100.	60.	1	0
15.	15.	40.	34.	1	0	35.	60.	50.	34.	0	1
65.	130.	74.	30.	0	1	35.	65.	55.	31.	0	1
40.	80.	80.	88.	1	0	25.	50.	40.	17.	1	0
15.	35.	45.	33.	0	1	40.	40.	95.	50.	1	0
55.	82.	65.	36.	0	1	65.	60.	137.	65.	0	1
25.	36.	68.	36.	0	1	31.	40.	55.	35.	1	0
75.	72.	69.	65.	1	0	30.	50.	37.	20.	1	0
70.	60.	65.	0.	0	1	30.	50.	3.	45.	1	0
25.	60.	44.	18.	0	1	25.	30.	36.	47.	1	0
61.	50.	61.	33.	0	1	15.	10.	45.	12.	1	0
15.	36.	37.	28.	1	0	30.	22.	60.	25.	1	0
15.	44.	35.	50.	1	0	14.	25.	28.	12.	1	0
35.	36.	68.	25.	1	0	65.	94.	71.	50.	0	1
50.	60.	73.	30.	1	0	70.	25.	77.	26.	0	1
65.	120.	47.	46.	0	1	28.	20.	54.	36.	1	0
40.	60.	67.	37.	1	0	55.	30.	100.	40.	1	0
60.	56.	75.	26.	1	0	50.	35.	88.	51.	1	0
35.	56.	71.	45.	1	0	65.	75.	62.	30.	0	1
20.	24.	83.	55.	1	0	25.	20.	70.	16.	1	0

TABLE 10·1 (cont.)

TC = Time/Car;   CC = Cost/Car;   TT = Time/Train;   CT = Cost/Train

TC	CC	TT	CT	Car	Train	TC	CC	TT	CT	Car	Train
50.	40.	95.	70.	1	0	35.	75.	85.	65.	1	0
32.	25.	86.	65.	1	0	60.	40.	72.	33.	1	0
43.	60.	55.	26.	1	0	47.	55.	67.	26.	0	1
27.	40.	65.	75.	1	0	53.	72.	68.	26.	0	1
35.	30.	90.	97.	1	0	62.	92.	60.	32.	0	1
69.	55.	74.	27.	0	1	55.	76.	75.	26.	1	0
85.	92.	65.	28.	0	1	30.	50.	72.	72.	1	0
45.	70.	56.	35.	0	1	25.	15.	50.	42.	1	0
50.	75.	65.	27.	0	1	25.	30.	47.	15.	1	0
32.	99.	65.	70.	1	0	60.	68.	64.	50.	1	0
50.	70.	60.	26.	0	1	60.	30.	99.	58.	1	0
45.	52.	46.	22.	1	0	60.	110.	63.	30.	0	1
35.	30.	65.	25.	1	0	53.	60.	59.	25.	0	1
70.	100.	62.	26.	0	1	30.	50.	70.	80.	1	0
30.	40.	50.	40.	1	0	25.	25.	78.	50.	1	0
25.	40.	90.	48.	0	1	60.	30.	80.	55.	1	0
40.	80.	99.	57.	1	0	25.	30.	70.	65.	1	0
30.	42.	70.	36.	0	1	55.	60.	7.	32.	1	0
50.	50.	60.	45.	0	1	70.	70.	65.	33.	1	0
25.	32.	60.	52.	1	0	50.	50.	55.	35.	1	0
90.	70.	73.	68.	1	0	0.	0.	69.	26.	0	1
75.	61.	60.	36.	1	0	45.	50.	60.	28.	1	0
30.	50.	58.	38.	0	1	30.	64.	70.	26.	0	1
45.	50.	77.	57.	1	0	30.	64.	66.	37.	1	0
20.	40.	95.	42.	1	0	70.	60.	70.	26.	0	1
60.	99.	73.	31.	0	1	60.	53.	69.	26.	0	1
45.	99.	72.	31.	0	1	30.	40.	65.	26.	0	1
45.	99.	73.	31.	0	1	35.	50.	112.	60.	1	0
70.	50.	67.	36.	0	1	60.	60.	76.	31.	0	1
20.	50.	78.	41.	1	0	50.	40.	66.	26.	0	1
25.	70.	68.	34.	1	0	65.	60.	60.	52.	1	0
40.	50.	65.	59.	1	0	60.	60.	80.	26.	0	1
25.	20.	64.	41.	1	0	47.	56.	75.	54.	1	0
40.	50.	77.	52.	1	0	50.	99.	72.	38.	0	1
75.	72.	65.	36.	0	1	85.	40.	69.	31.	0	1
55.	50.	63.	33.	0	1	65.	50.	63.	36.	0	1
50.	70.	99.	33.	0	1	43.	60.	112.	46.	0	1
75.	60.	75.	31.	0	1	70.	99.	90.	40.	0	1
95.	70.	70.	31.	0	1	38.	30.	53.	30.	0	1
22.	20.	70.	32.	1	0	46.	136.	70.	30.	0	1
48.	100.	90.	67.	1	0	70.	84.	75.	38.	0	1

TABLE 10·1 (cont.)

TC = Time/Car ; CC = Cost/Car ; TT = Time/Train ; CT = Cost/Train

TC	CC	TT	CT	Choice Car	Choice Train	TC	CC	TT	CT	Choice Car	Choice Train
15.	26.	32.	20.	1	0	50.	75.	62.	26.	0	1
45.	36.	94.	44.	1	0	13.	37.	56.	30.	1	0
70.	59.	76.	30.	0	1	70.	60.	97.	38.	0	1
30.	40.	50.	48.	1	0	65.	15.	62.	36.	1	0
50.	10.	45.	38.	1	0	35.	40.	75.	35.	1	0
46.	180.	73.	29.	0	1	55.	30.	80.	50.	1	0
10.	20.	37.	26.	1	0	35.	30.	57.	43.	1	0
40.	114.	76.	44.	0	1	40.	40.	50.	20.	1	0
55.	80.	68.	28.	0	1	35.	52.	45.	40.	1	0
45.	72.	80.	56.	0	1	34.	40.	70.	32.	1	0
20.	20.	38.	14.	1	0	50.	143.	61.	26.	0	1
60.	60.	53.	37.	1	0	80.	99.	66.	27.	0	1
60.	99.	74.	33.	0	1	55.	120.	65.	0.	0	1
55.	68.	70.	30.	1	0	55.	55.	68.	0.	0	1
65.	90.	55.	26.	0	1	13.	15.	26.	9.	1	0
45.	68.	84.	48.	0	1	50.	30.	54.	26.	0	1
37.	60.	75.	60.	1	0	25.	30.	45.	28.	1	0
70.	148.	75.	26.	0	1	33.	32.	37.	31.	1	0
40.	80.	55.	26.	0	1	55.	68.	60.	25.	0	1
25.	20.	22.	25.	1	0	45.	60.	77.	40.	0	1
35.	25.	85.	59.	1	0	45.	78.	60.	0.	0	1
35.	45.	73.	55.	1	0	30.	48.	43.	41.	1	0
55.	40.	56.	0.	0	1	35.	40.	94.	80.	1	0
12.	9.	18.	10.	1	0	63.	72.	90.	50.	1	0
45.	40.	85.	58.	1	0	70.	60.	78.	26.	0	1
23.	30.	100.	25.	1	0	20.	20.	45.	30.	1	0
30.	25.	55.	25.	1	0	91.	48.	102.	65.	1	0
37.	30.	57.	60.	1	0	55.	80.	53.	26.	0	1
35.	20.	60.	26.	0	1	40.	30.	125.	45.	1	0
60.	60.	53.	38.	0	1	40.	60.	47.	41.	0	1
65.	68.	76.	43.	0	1	65.	150.	70.	36.	0	1
30.	50.	57.	22.	0	1	50.	150.	70.	38.	0	1
65.	85.	73.	32.	0	1	37.	40.	76.	39.	0	1
40.	145.	73.	26.	0	1	60.	50.	62.	58.	1	0
70.	50.	53.	25.	0	1	62.	68.	69.	44.	1	0
70.	75.	128.	50.	0	1	26.	20.	48.	37.	1	0
65.	40.	56.	33.	1	0	55.	75.	66.	36.	0	1
50.	68.	77.	40.	1	0	60.	60.	79.	40.	0	1
30.	50.	60.	0.	0	1	20.	20.	71.	42.	1	0
60.	152.	65.	50.	1	0	30.	30.	69.	77.	1	0
95.	75.	72.	28.	0	1	25.	30.	60.	37.	1	0

TABLE 10·1 (cont.)

TC = Time/Car ; CC = Cost/Car; TT = Time/Train ; CT = Cost/Train

TC	CC	TT	CT	Choice (=1) Car	Train	TC	CC	TT	CT	Choice (=1) Car	Train
35.	30.	69.	58.	0	1	46.	67.	77.	55.	1	0
45.	60.	40.	29.	0	1	70.	64.	60.	35.	0	1
37.	30.	71.	42.	1	0	52.	160.	80.	30.	0	1
60.	74.	75.	33.	0	1	40.	56.	60.	49.	1	0
43.	40.	50.	38.	1	0	60.	144.	66.	38.	0	1
15.	15.	50.	40.	1	0	30.	20.	59.	40.	1	0
28.	25.	90.	52.	1	0	15.	28.	48.	32.	1	0
70.	150.	62.	36.	0	1	30.	36.	32.	24.	0	1
17.	28.	73.	52.	1	0	70.	35.	67.	55.	1	0
45.	65.	60.	31.	0	1	85.	134.	67.	40.	0	1
45.	63.	71.	61.	1	0	60.	72.	60.	41.	0	1
55.	84.	68.	14.	0	1	65.	60.	65.	31.	0	1
60.	60.	82.	36.	0	1	40.	50.	91.	71.	1	0
60.	40.	72.	20.	0	1	50.	64.	70.	53.	1	0
35.	72.	72.	75.	1	0	75.	154.	60.	34.	0	1
51.	138.	62.	37.	0	1	30.	48.	60.	47.	1	0
68.	76.	62.	32.	0	1	60.	180.	64.	33.	0	1
22.	46.	77.	32.	1	0	60.	80.	75.	36.	0	1
15.	24.	20.	14.	1	0	65.	78.	70.	0.	0	1
58.	60.	82.	38.	0	1	68.	30.	65.	26.	0	1
40.	30.	70.	55.	1	0	65.	88.	76.	41.	0	1
70.	71.	81.	38.	0	1	65.	60.	73.	26.	0	1
30.	25.	43.	34.	1	0	37.	40.	57.	26.	0	1
15.	35.	38.	32.	1	0	45.	35.	65.	35.	0	1
80.	84.	67.	36.	0	1	65.	137.	73.	33.	0	1
50.	25.	68.	55.	1	0	60.	145.	54.	36.	0	1
45.	40.	65.	48.	1	0	55.	140.	74.	36.	0	1
45.	65.	80.	41.	0	1	60.	100.	50.	36.	0	1
70.	70.	83.	22.	0	1	65.	50.	100.	50.	1	0
61.	65.	57.	35.	0	1	50.	140.	85.	63.	1	0
60.	78.	75.	60.	1	0	75.	72.	63.	30.	0	1
70.	74.	57.	36.	0	1	35.	30.	48.	29.	0	1
75.	50.	76.	38.	0	1	15.	24.	28.	25.	1	0
30.	50.	42.	30.	0	1	53.	56.	42.	26.	0	1
60.	82.	80.	33.	1	0	25.	60.	65.	31.	1	0
40.	50.	80.	33.	0	1	45.	54.	67.	33.	1	0
30.	30.	75.	54.	1	0	25.	28.	48.	39.	1	0
30.	48.	85.	57.	1	0	27.	50.	52.	40.	1	0
55.	78.	78.	36.	1	0	25.	25.	63.	80.	1	0
30.	40.	72.	46.	1	0	50.	50.	80.	50.	1	0
75.	140.	80.	55.	1	0	25.	25.	39.	20.	1	0
60.	74.	72.	36.	0	1	35.	64.	95.	40.	1	0

10·3·1 Program Control Card — General Information

Nine rules apply at all times:

(1)   Unless otherwise specified, all program control inputs are in fields of four.

(2)   An 80 character card is therefore divided into 20 such fields.

(3)   A field may be: (a)   4 Alphanumeric characters (A4);   or (b)   4 character Integer (I4); or (c)   4 character Floating Point (F4.$\emptyset$);   or   (d) 4 Blanks (4X).

(4)   Program Control Commands are in fields of four or multiples thereof, and are right justified, unless otherwise specified.

(5)   Blanks, where specified, are not optional.

(6)   Block letters (e.g. VAR =) indicate the form of an optional or mandatory command on which the program will act and must be reproduced exactly, with any blanks, on the input card.

(7)   Dependent variables will be referred to as Y, and independent variables as X.   For example, Y(1) refers to the 1st dependent variable;   X(7) refers to the 7th independent variable.

(8)   A name in brackets, e.g. (NOBS) indicates the abbreviated name of a program input parameter.

(9)   Commands are formally defined as follows:

FIELD	FORMAT	DESCRIPTION	STATUS
Indicates which of the 2$\emptyset$ possible fields of four is defined	Formal input format	Either formal Command, e.g. VAR =, or information required	Either M (MANDATORY) or O (OPTIONAL)

10·3·2 Program Inputs — A General Overview

The program input commands fall into three distinct divisions:

(a)   GENERAL PROGRAM CONTROL DIVISION, which prepares the program for input from the other two divisions and stops the execution.

(b)   DATA DIVISION, which reads the data, assigns variable names, creates new variables and in general prepares data for model estimation and

(c)   MODEL DIVISION, which estimates the specified model and other related options.

10·3·3 General Program Control Division

The first command, IN, informs the program of the location of the input control cards, the data and temporary working files, and where output is to be printed.

The second command in any run is the ORIGINAL/ TEST command. This command informs the program whether the job requires full estimation (= ORIGINAL) or if input parameters are to be checked for errors with no estimation (= TEST). It also informs the program if a card follows, the 80 alphanumeric characters of which are the job name.

FORMAL DEFINITION - IN COMMAND

If you wish files to take default values:

FIELD	FORMAT	DESCRIPTION	STATUS
1	A4	IN (begin col. 1)	M

otherwise, if the program controls are not compatible with the local computer system the nondefault requirement is:

FIELD	FORMAT	DESCRIPTION	STATUS
1*	A4	(a) IN = (b) PR = (c) DA = (d) T1 = (e) T2 = (f) T3 =	0
2*	I4	(a) INPUT DEVICE No. (b) OUTPUT DEVICE No. (c) DATA DEVICE No. (d) Temporary DEVICE No. (e) Temporary DEVICE No. (f) Temporary DEVICE No.	0
3*	4X	4 Blanks	M

* There can be 6 sets of these 3 fields on the card. It is highly unlikely that the nondefault option would have to be selected.

Notes

(1) The nondefault option should only be used if one desires to use devices other than default devices.

334

(2)   To change any default device it is not
necessary to change all defaults; merely inform the
program by the appropriate command(s) of the
device(s) you wish to change from their default.
   (3)   The nondefault fields may appear in any
order on the card if you desire to use all or some
of them.
   (4)   The default numbers are:

INPUT DEVICE No. = 5, OUTPUT DEVICE No. = 6, DATA
DEVICE No. = 11, TEMPORARY DEVICE No. = 12,
TEMPORARY DEVICE No. = 13, TEMPORARY DEVICE No.
= 14, and JOB = N.

FORMAL DEFINITION - ORIGINAL/TEST COMMAND

FIELD	FORMAT	DESCRIPTION	STATUS
1-2	2A4	ORIGINAL	M
	or 2A4	TEST (Begin Col. 1)	
3-4	2A4	JOB = Y	
		(Begin Col. 1Ø)	O

Notes

   (1)   Either ORIGINAL or TEST must appear on
card beginning in Col. 1.
   (2)   TEST checks input parameters for errors —
it uses six observations and no estimation is
performed.
   (3)   JOB = Y must begin in Col. 1Ø. It is
optional and indicates that the next card contains
the job name.

10·3·4 Data Division — Overview

THE DATA

   The program expects formatted data, read by
observation, specified on a file separate from the
program control cards in card-image form.

DATA CONTROL CARDS
FIRST RECORD (CARD) - INPUT PARAMETERS

FIELDS	CONTENTS	DESCRIPTION	STATUS
1	VAR =	-	M
2	I4	No. of Independent Variables in Dataset (NVARO)	M
3	4X	4 Blanks	M
4	OBS =	-	M
5	I4	No. of observations (NOBS)	M
6	4X	4 Blanks	M
7	ALT =	-	O
8	I4	No. of Dependent Variables in Dataset (NALTY)	O
9	4X	4 Blanks	M
10	FMT =	-	O
11	I4	No. of format cards (NFMT)	O

The defaults are NALTY = 0, and NFMT = 1.

Notes

(1)   NALTY and NFMT are optional and if left out will take their respective default values.

(2)   NALTY refers to the maximum or desired number of explicitly defined dependent variables.

(3)   A variable is considered as an explicitly defined dependent variable if and only if:

(a)   It indicates which of the set of alternatives was chosen, or

(b)   An alternative was chosen, 1, or not chosen, $\emptyset$.

If inputted in integer format, it must be one of the last NALTY on each observation.

(4)   While it is not necessary to explicitly define dependent variables as such, it is advantageous to do so. This is so since the program requires, for estimation, that they be of integer form. Thus, if a variable to be used as a dependent variable in a logit model is not explicitly defined as an integer it must be transformed into integer form before estimation. While this is possible it requires an extra input card per dependent variable to be so transformed. Thus it is clearly more efficient to define the dependent variable as such an input.

(5)   While NVARO refers to the number of original explicitly defined independent variables, this set of variables can include variables which will later be transformed into independent variables.

6)   Each of NOBS observations must contain NVARO + NALTY variables.

336

SECOND CARD - FORMAT CARD

The data format is enclosed in brackets, and the program expects NFMT cards. Card image formatting is used.

THIRD CARD - EXPLICITLY DEFINED DEPENDENT VARIABLE NAMES

The program expects NALTY names, with ten names permitted per card. A name is 4 alphanumeric characters, with each name separated by 4 blanks. If all NALTY names cannot be fitted on one card, continue onto another card until all NALTY names have been specified. If the dependent variables are not explicitly defined (i.e. they are only defined by values associated with an independent variable name (see below)), then this card is not included, and on the first card ALT=0.

FOURTH CARD - INDEPENDENT VARIABLE NAMES

FIELD	FORMAT	DESCRIPTION	STATUS
1-2	2A4	Independent Variable Name	M
3	4X	4 Blanks	M
4	A4	ALT =	O
5	I4	Alternative number to which variable is specific (ASA)	O

NVARO variables must be named, with the program expecting NVARO name cards. ASA is used in logit estimation and while it is not necessary to specify an ASA for each variable on input, it is necessary to do so before estimation. An option exists (see later section) to either (i) specify the ASA of a previously unspecified variable, or (ii) respecify the ASA of a previously specified variable.

TRANSFORMATIONS

New variables, both dependent and independent, can be created using the TRAN command. Any transformation card(s) must be placed immediately after the last independent variable NAME card. The first card of the group of transformations must be the TRANSFORMATION command. This card informs the program of the number of transformations to be performed and what the new number of explicitly defined independent variables will be. Fields 1-5 of the individual transformation cards are identical to the NAME card. The TRANS command then follows on the same card.

337

FORMAL DEFINITION - TRANSFORMATION COMMAND

FIELD	FORMAT	DESCRIPTION	STATUS
1	A4	TRAN (Begin in Col. 1)	M
2	A4	SFOR	O
3	A4	MATI	O
4	A4	ONS =	O
5	I4	No. of Transformations (NTRAN) (Begin Col. 17)	M
6	A4	FN =	M
7	I4	Final number of independent variables after transformation (NVARF) excluding number of transformations where operation numbers are 24 to 29. (Begin Col. 25)	M
8	A4	FNA =	O
9	I4	Final number of transformations where operation numbers are 24 to 29. (Begin Col. 33)	O

TRAN COMMAND

TRAN N, I1, I2, VN, C1, C2,
where N = Operation number, I1 = Number of 1st
Operand, I2 = Number of 2nd Operand, VN = New
Variable Number, C1 = 1st Constant, and C2 = 2nd
Constant.

FIELD	FORMAT	DESCRIPTION	STATUS
1-5	Same as NAME		
6	4X	4 Blanks	M
7	A4	TRAN (Begin in Col. 25)	M
8	I4	N	M
9	I4	I1	M
10	I4	I2	O
11	I4	VN	O
12	F1Ø.Ø	C1 (Begin in Col. 45)	O
13	F1Ø.Ø	C2 (Begin in Col. 55)	O

The available transformations are given below. Ys
refer to dependent variables and Xs to independent
variables.

$\underline{N}$	OPERATION DEFINITION
1	$X(VN) = X(I1) + C1$
2	$X(VN) = X(I1) - C1$
3	$X(VN) = X(I1) * C1$
4	$X(VN) = X(I1) / C1$

N			DESCRIPTION
5	X(VN)	=	X(I1) ** C1
6	X(VN)	=	C1 / X(I1)
7	X(VN)	=	ℓn X(I1)
8	X(VN)	=	EXP X(I1)
9	X(VN)	=	ABS X(I1)
10	X(VN)	=	C1
11	X(VN)	=	X(I1) + X(I2)
12	X(VN)	=	X(I1) - X(I2)
13	X(VN)	=	X(I1) * X(I2)
14	X(VN	=	X(I1) / X(I2)
15	X(VN)	=	X(I1) ** X(I2)
16	X(VN)	=	Y(I1) * X(I2)
17	X(VN)	=	Y(I1) / X(I2)
18	X(VN)	=	C1 IF (X(I1).LE.C2)
		=	Ø.Ø IF (X(I1).GT.C2)
19	X(VN)	=	C1 IF (X(I1).GE.C2)
		=	Ø.Ø IF (X(I1).LT.C2)
20	X(VN)	=	C1 IF (X(I1).LE. X(I2))
		=	Ø.Ø IF (X(I1).GT. X(12))
21	X(VN)	=	C1 IF (X(I1).GE. X(I2))
		=	Ø.Ø IF (X(I1).LT. X(I2))
22	REJECT OBSERVATION IF (X(I1).LE.C1)		
23	REJECT OBSERVATION IF (X(I1).GE.C1)		
24	Y(VN)	=	Y(I1) + Y(I2)
25	Y(VN)	=	Y(I1) * Y(I2)
26	Y(VN)	=	IFIX(C1) IF (Y(I1).LE.IFIX(C2))
	ELSE Y(VN)	=	Ø
27	Y(VN)	=	IFIX(C1) IF (Y(I1).GE.IFIX(C2))
	ELSE Y(VN	=	Ø
28	Y(VN)	=	IFIX(C1) IF (Y(I1).EQ.IFIX(C2))
	ELSE Y(VN)	=	Ø
29	Y(VN)	=	IFIX(X(I1))

Notes

(1)   Operations 1-15 and 18-21 create new independent variables from independent variables and constants only.

(2)   Operations 16 and 17 create independent variables from dependent and independent variables.

(3)   Operations 22 and 23 can be used to check for bad values.

(4)   Operations 24-28 create dependent variables from dependent variables.

(5)   Operation 29 transforms an explicitly defined independent variable into an explicitly defined dependent variable.

(6)   The new variables number (VN) can be used to replace a previously defined old variable.

An original or created dependent variable may
take any integer value, but for the purposes of
model estimation the dependent variable may take
only the values 1 (if this alternative is chosen)
or Ø (if this alternative is not chosen). Thus, if
an original or created dependent variable takes
possible values other than (1, Ø) it must be
transformed via the appropriate transformations into
a series of (1, Ø) dependent variables.

Example of the creation of a dependent variable.

Suppose there are four possible alternatives —
A,B,C,D. Let 1 = A, 2 = B, 3 = C, and 4 = D, such
that if an individual chooses A, the choice is
recorded as 1; if B, the choice is recorded as 2
etc. Let the recorded value be the only original
explicitly defined dependent variable (see Section
INPUT DATASET for definition). Denote this
dependent variable as Y(1).

Then if Y(1) = 1 the individual chooses A, if
Y(1) = 2 the individual chooses B, if Y(1) = 3 the
individual chooses C, if Y(1) = 4 the individual
chooses D. Since the dependent variable Y(1) can
take values other than (1, Ø) it cannot be used for
model estimation. We require instead four (4),
(1, Ø) dependent variables. Thus we must create
four (4) new dependent variables where: Y(2) refers
to A, Y(3) refers to B, Y(4) refers to C and Y(5)
refers to D such that:

```
if Y(2) = 1, choice is A;  if = Ø, choice is not A
   Y(3) = 1, choice is B;  if = Ø, choice is not B
   Y(4) = 1, choice is C;  if = Ø, choice is not C
   Y(5) = 1, choice is D;  if = Ø, choice is not D.
```

Thus if an individual chooses:

```
A (i.e. Y(1) = 1); Y(2) = 1;  Y(3) = Ø; Y(4) = Ø;
                                         Y(5) = Ø
B (i.e. Y(1) = 2); Y(2) = Ø;  Y(3) = 1; Y(4) = Ø;
                                         Y(5) = Ø
C (i.e. Y(1) = 3); Y(2) = Ø;  Y(3) = Ø; Y(4) = 1;
                                         Y(5) = Ø
D (i.e. Y(1) = 4); Y(2) = Ø;  Y(3) = Ø; Y(4) = Ø;
                                         Y(5) = 1.
```

The above transformation would be accomplished using
OPERATION 28. Suppose you want to carry out the
following four transformations:

```
(A) Y(2) = 1 if (Y(1).EQ.1) ELSE Y(2) = Ø,
(B) Y(3) = 1 if (Y(1).EQ.2) ELSE Y(3) = Ø,
(C) Y(4) = 1 if (Y(1).EQ.3) ELSE Y(4) = Ø,
(D) Y(5) = 1 if (Y(1).EQ.4) ELSE Y(5) = Ø.
```

340

These would be accomplished as follows:

Col.	8	25-28	31-32	36	44	45-47	55-57
(A)	A	TRAN	28	1	2	1.Ø	1.Ø
(B)	B	TRAN	28	1	3	1.Ø	2.Ø
(C)	C	TRAN	28	1	4	1.Ø	3.Ø
(D)	D	TRAN	28	1	5	1.Ø	4.Ø

Thus for the purpose of model estimation you would need to inform the program via the appropriate commands (see section on MODEL COMMANDS) that the model had (4) dependent variables and these were dependent variable numbers 2, 3, 4 and 5.

It should be clear from the above that when specifying the dependent variables for a model that such variables be mutually exclusive, i.e. for all observations only one of the specified dependent variables takes the value 1 (indicating chosen) and all else takes the value Ø (indicating not chosen).

GENERATIONS

For the purpose of model estimation variables can be either (a) Alternative Specific Variables (ASV), (b) Generic Variables (GV) or (c) Alternative Specific Constants (ASC) (see Chapter 4.5). This section explains how you inform the program whether a raw variable is to be considered an ASC, an ASV or a GV and how the specified type is generated.

$$\text{Define } P_i = \exp(V_i) / \sum_{j=1}^{J} \exp(V_j)$$

$$\text{where } V_j = \sum_{k=1}^{K} \beta_{jk} X_{jk}$$

Since there are K independent variables for each of J alternatives there needs to be specified a total of J * K variables, and that J * K coefficients are required to be estimated. Let the number of coefficients to be estimated = C; and the number of ASVs, GVs and ASCs specified in a model to be respectively S, G, and A. Then C = S + G + A.

The program assumes (1) $\beta_{ik} \neq \beta_{jk}$ for some k = 1,K and (2) $\beta_{ik} = \beta_{jk}$ for some k = 1,K and the number of independent variables required to be inputted = C (the number of coefficients required to be estimated).

341

For example, suppose a model has 10 alternatives with 3 independent variables (i.e. J = 10, K = 3). If the 3 independent variables are specified as GV, then S = 0, G = 3, and A = 0 (i.e. C = 3). The program would require that 3 variables be specified only. To illustrate further how this is done we will use some examples. Assume two alternatives — car to work and bus to work — (J = 2), and two variables, time and cost (K = 2). There must be 4 independent bits of information: (1) Time specific to car; (2) Time specific to bus; (3) Cost specific to car; (4) Cost specific to bus, defined respectively as X(1), X(2), X(3) and X(4).

Example A. To estimate all variables as ASVs.

$$S = J * K, \quad G = 0, \quad A = 0,$$
$$\text{i.e. } \beta_{ik} \neq \beta_{jk} \quad \forall k = 1, K$$

now $C = S + G + A, = J * K = 2 * 2 = 4$, and

$$\beta_1 \equiv \text{TIME/CAR}; \quad \beta_2 \equiv \text{TIME/BUS}; \quad \beta_3 \equiv \text{COST/CAR};$$

$$\beta_4 \equiv \text{COST/BUS}.$$

To estimate these four (4) coefficients the program would set up a matrix, XX, of order (2 * 4) such that:

$$XX_{11} = X(1) \quad XX_{12} = \emptyset.\emptyset \quad XX_{13} = X(3) \quad XX_{14} = \emptyset.\emptyset$$
$$XX_{21} = \emptyset.\emptyset \quad XX_{22} = X(2) \quad XX_{23} = \emptyset.\emptyset \quad XX_{24} = X(4).$$

Schematically:

ALT \ BETA	1 TIME/CAR	2 TIME/BUS	3 COST/CAR	4 COST/BUS
1. CAR	X(1)	$\emptyset.\emptyset$	X(3)	$\emptyset.\emptyset$
2. BUS	$\emptyset.\emptyset$	X(2)	$\emptyset.\emptyset$	X(4)

The program is informed that a variable is an ASV, and sets up the XX matrix as follows:

When you NAME a variable (see INPUT DATASET section) you are required where appropriate to specify the alternative to which it is specific. This instruction can be seen as setting up a vector of XX values such that XX_i takes the value of the variable for the alternative specified (i.e. i = ASA) and zero elsewhere. Thus XX is a vector of order J filled with J-1 zeros and one value other than zero in the appropriate position. If an alternative has not been specified, (i.e. ASA = $\emptyset$) this is required before estimation and the GENERATION command provides this facility.

342

Thus in the example

$$XX(1) = \begin{bmatrix} X(1) \\ \emptyset.\emptyset \end{bmatrix} - TIME/CAR, \quad XX(2) = \begin{bmatrix} \emptyset.\emptyset \\ X(2) \end{bmatrix} - TIME/BUS$$

$$XX(3) = \begin{bmatrix} X(3) \\ \emptyset.\emptyset \end{bmatrix} - COST/CAR, \quad XX(4) = \begin{bmatrix} \emptyset.\emptyset \\ X(4) \end{bmatrix} - COST/BUS$$

you would inform the program that the independent variables were: 1 2 3 4, and the alternatives were: 1 2. (For explanation of this see MODEL section). Thus the specified V_j's are:

$$V_1 = \beta_1 X(1) + \beta_3 X(3) \text{ and } V_2 = \beta_2 X(2) + \beta_4 X(4)$$

Example B. To estimate all variables as GVs.

where $\beta_{ik} = \beta_{jk} \not\times k = 1, K$

$\qquad$ C = S (=0) + G (=K) + A (=0) = K = 2, and thus $\beta_1 \equiv TIME$, $\beta_2 \equiv COST$. To estimate these two coefficients the program would set up a matrix, XX, or order (2 * 2) such that:

$$XX_{11} = X(1), \quad XX_{12} = X(3), \quad XX_{21} = X(2), \quad XX_{22} = X(4)$$

Schematically:

BETA / ALT	1 TIME	2 COST
1. CAR	X(1)	X(3)
2. BUS	X(2)	X(4)

$\qquad$ The program is informed that a variable is a GV; and sets up the XX matrix as follows:
$\qquad$ In specifying a GV you require an XX vector of order J filled with less than J-1 zeros and more than one value other than zero in the appropriate positions. This is done by instructing the program to combine a given number of previously defined ASVs into a single variable. The program will place the value of each specified ASV into the appropriate position in the new XX matrix as specified by the alternative to which it was defined specific (i.e. its ASA). A GV does not necessarily have to consist of ASVs, i.e. you do not have to specify J ASVs when instructing the program to initiate a new GV. For example, suppose you specify N ASVs where N is less than J; then the program will fill

343

the XX vector of order J with J-N zeros and N values other than zero in the appropriate positions. The GENERATION command provides for creation of GVs whereby each GV is given a new variable number by the program independent of the variable number of the ASVs from which it was generated.

Thus, the example

$$XX(1) = \begin{bmatrix} X(1) \\ \emptyset.\emptyset \end{bmatrix} - TIME/CAR, \quad XX(2) = \begin{bmatrix} \emptyset.\emptyset \\ X(2) \end{bmatrix} - TIME/BUS$$

$$XX(3) = \begin{bmatrix} X(3) \\ \emptyset.\emptyset \end{bmatrix} - COST/CAR, \quad XX(4) = \begin{bmatrix} \emptyset.\emptyset \\ X(4) \end{bmatrix} - COST/BUS$$

$$XX(5) = \begin{bmatrix} X(1) \\ X(2) \end{bmatrix} - TIME, \quad XX(6) = \begin{bmatrix} X(3) \\ X(4) \end{bmatrix} - COST$$

would inform the program the independent variables are 5 and 6, and the alternatives are 1 and 2.

Thus the specified V_j's are

$$V_1 = \beta_1 X(1) + \beta_2 X(3) \text{ and } V_2 = \beta_1 X(2) + \beta_2 X(4)$$

Example C. Introduce a binary dummy variable into the DATASET.

For example DEST = $1.\emptyset$ if destination is the Central City (CBD); $\emptyset.\emptyset$ if other and assume we have already defined two additional variables, income and destination:

1. TIME/CAR=X(1) 2. TIME/BUS=X(2) 3. COST/CAR=X(3)
4. COST/BUS=X(4) 5. INCOME=X(5)   6. DEST=X(6)

Now create a 7th variable (using the appropriate TRANSFORMATION card) by weighting Destination by Income. This new variable DEST * INCOME is such that

$$DEST * INCOME = INCOME, \text{ if destination CBD}$$
$$= \emptyset.\emptyset, \text{ if other}$$

Thus INCOME is considered only if the destination is CBD. Now we have

7. DEST * INCOME=X(7)

This variable needs to be made specific to an alternative. It can be introduced into either (i) the BUS or (ii) the CAR expression. Together with an ASC, a separate variable INCOME, and a generic specification for COST, we have

$$C = S(=4) + G (=1) + A (=1) = 6,$$

where

$\beta_1 \equiv ASC/CAR, \quad \beta_2 \equiv TIME/CAR, \quad \beta_3 \equiv TIME/BUS, \quad \beta_4 \equiv COST$

344

and for (i)

$\beta_5 \equiv$ INCOME/CAR, $\beta_6 \equiv$ DEST * INCOME/CAR while for (ii)

$\beta_5 \equiv$ INCOME/BUS, $\beta_7 \equiv$ DEST * INCOME/BUS

After making the relevant GENERATIONS the XX vectors would appear as follows:

$$XX(\emptyset) = \begin{bmatrix} 1.\emptyset \\ \emptyset.\emptyset \end{bmatrix} - \text{ASC/CAR} \qquad XX(1) = \begin{bmatrix} X(1) \\ \emptyset.\emptyset \end{bmatrix} - \text{TIME/CAR}$$

$$XX(2) = \begin{bmatrix} 0.0 \\ X(2) \end{bmatrix} - \text{TIME/BUS} \qquad XX(3) = \begin{bmatrix} X(3) \\ \emptyset.\emptyset \end{bmatrix} - \text{COST/CAR}$$

$$XX(4) = \begin{bmatrix} \emptyset.\emptyset \\ X(4) \end{bmatrix} - \text{COST/BUS} \qquad XX(5) = X(5) - \text{INCOME}$$

$$XX(6) = X(6) - \text{DEST} \qquad XX(7) = X(7) - \text{DEST \& INCOME}$$

$$XX(8) = \begin{bmatrix} X(1) \\ X(2) \end{bmatrix} - \text{TIME} \qquad XX(9) = \begin{bmatrix} X(3) \\ X(4) \end{bmatrix} - \text{COST}$$

$$XX(10) = \begin{bmatrix} X(5) \\ \emptyset.\emptyset \end{bmatrix} - \text{INCOME/CAR} \qquad XX(11) = \begin{bmatrix} \emptyset.\emptyset \\ X(5) \end{bmatrix} - \text{INCOME/BUS}$$

$$XX(12) = \begin{bmatrix} X(7) \\ \emptyset.\emptyset \end{bmatrix} - \text{DEST * INCOME/CAR}$$

$$XX(13) = \begin{bmatrix} \emptyset.\emptyset \\ X(7) \end{bmatrix} - \text{DEST * INCOME/BUS}$$

and we would inform the program either

(i) Independent variables = 0, 1, 2, 9, 10, 12
and alternatives = 1, 2

where the specified V_j's are

$$V_1 = \beta_1 + \beta_2 X(1) + \beta_4 X(3) + \beta_5 X(5) + \beta_6 X(7)$$

with $V_1 \equiv \beta_1 + \beta_2 X(1) + \beta_4 X(3) + (\beta_5 + \beta_6) X(5)$

when DEST = 1, and

$$V_1 \equiv \beta_1 + \beta_2 X(1) + \beta_4 X(3) + \beta_5 X(5)$$

$$V_2 = \beta_3 X(2) + \beta_4 X(4)$$

when DEST = $\emptyset$

or (ii) Independent variables = 0, 1, 2, 9, 11, 13,

where the specified V_j's are

$$V_1 = \beta_1 + \beta_2 X(1) + \beta_4 X(3)$$

$$V_2 = \beta_3 X(2) + \beta_4 X(4) + \beta_5 X(5) + \beta_6 X(7) \text{ with}$$

$$V_2 \equiv \beta_3 X(2) + \beta_4 X(4) + (\beta_5 + \beta_6)\, X(5)$$

and when DEST = 1, and

$$V_2 \equiv \beta_3 X(2) + \beta_4 X(4) + \beta_5 X(5)$$

when DEST = $\emptyset$.

We could also use the generated XX matrix to specify the following models (at least):

	Independent Variables	Alternatives
(a)	8, 9, 10	1, 2
(b)	0, 3, 4, 8	1, 2
(c)	0, 1, 2, 3, 4, 10, 11	1, 2
(d)	0, 1, 2, 3, 4, 13	1, 2
(e)	0, 8, 9, 12	1, 2
(f)	3, 4, 5, 8	1, 2

In concluding this discussion of specification of independent variables, five questions are presented. The analyst must be able to answer these if correct use and full advantage of the program's facilities are to be accomplished.

(1) What XX variables have been specified in each model?

(2) What are the specified V_j's for each model?

(3) Which model specifies the following XX variables?

  (a) ASC/Car (b) TIME (c) COST
  (d) DEST * INCOME/CAR

(4) Which model specifies the following V_j's?

$$V_1 = \beta_1 + \beta_2 X(3) + \beta_4 X(1)$$

$$V_2 = \beta_3 X(4) + \beta_4 X(2)$$

(5) Which models cannot be estimated and why?

GENERATION COMMAND

This command allows the following options:

(1) Creation of a GENERIC variable by specifying which previously defined ASVs are to be grouped as the NAMED GENERIC variable.

(2) Creation of an ASV by specifying the ALTERNATIVE to which a previously unspecified VARIABLE is specific.

(3) Creation of a new ASV by specifying a new alternative to which a defined ASV can be considered specific. This becomes a new numbered ASV independent of the previously defined ASV.

346

(4)   As for (2) and (3) above except for
ALTERNATIVE substitute more than one ALTERNATIVE.

The first card of the group of generations must
be the GENERATION command. This command informs
the program of how many generations are to be
performed. This card is then followed by the
appropriate NAME cards.

FORMAL DEFINITION - (A) GENERATION COMMAND

FIELD	FORMAT	DESCRIPTION	STATUS
1	A4	GENE	M
2	A4	RATI	O
3	A4	ONS -	O
4	A4	ARE -	O
5	I4	Number of generations	M

(Begin 21)

(B)i GENERIC NAME CARD - OPTION 1

1-2	2A4	New Variable Name	M
3	A4	GEN (Right justified)	M
4	4X	4 Blanks	M
5	4X	4 Blanks	M
6	A4	VN =	M
7-20	I4	The numbers of each ASV you wish to group to form this GV. One number to each field	M

(B)ii GENERIC NAME CONTINUE CARD

(To be used if you wish to specify more than 14 ASVs)

1-6	6(4X)	24 Blanks	M
7-20	I4	As above (B)i	M

(Begin 25)

(Use as many of these cards as are required to
define a GENERIC in terms of its associated ASVs.)

(C) ASV NAME CARD - OPTIONS 2 and 3

1-2	2A4	New Variable Name	M
3	A4	ASV (Right justified)	M
4	I4	Original Variable Number	M
5	4X	4 Blanks	M
6	A4	ALT =	M
7	I4	Alternative Number to which variable is specified	M

(D)i ASV NAME CARD - OPTION 4

1-2	2A4	New Variable Name	M
3	A4	ASV (Right justified)	M
4	I4	Original Variable Number	M
5	4X	4 Blanks	M

6	A4	ALT =	M
7-20	I4	Alternative Numbers to	
		which variable is specified.	
		One number to each field	M

(D) ii ASV NAME CONTINUE CARD - OPTION 4

1-6	6(4X)	24 Blanks	M
7-20	I4	As (D) i	
(Begin 25)			

(Use as many of these cards as you require to
specify all the ALTERNATIVES to which you wish the
ASV made specific.)

END DATA DIVISION

To signify the end of the data division the
program is informed by means of an END card.

FORMAL DEFINITION

FIELD	FORMAT	DESCRIPTION	STATUS
1	A4	End (Begin Col. 1)	M

10·3·5 Model Division

In addition to running basic multinomial logit
estimation the program provides a number of other
features. These are:

  (a) Correlation matrix of specified variables
  (b) OLS regression
  (c) Box-Tukey multinomial logit
  (d) Restricted multinomial logit and
  (e) Multiple-correlation.

To run any of the above features requires the
following set of commands: Feature; Equation;
Option; End.

Feature indicates which of the facilities are
required, the Equation command specifies the
relevant variable numbers; Option indicates which,
if any, of the special options the analyst may
require, and End indicates the end of a feature.

To accommodate a variable number of alternatives across the observations the feature card must
have as its last command NAA, where NAA refers to
the actual number of alternative-related attributes

348

which are used to identify alternatives which are
not relevant. That is if all NAA alternative
attributes take a value of zero, the alternative is
not in the choice set for the observation. These
check-attributes must be the first NAA on the
EQUATION card after the ASCs. When each observation
has the identical set of alternatives, NAA = 0.

The Feature command allows the following
options:

1. CORR - Correlation matrix of specified variables.
The analyst has to indicate how many variables are
to appear in the matrix (NIV). To obtain a correlation matrix for all variables, NIV = 0. An
EQUATION card is not required. Drive 2 must be used.
2. OLSE - OLS regression. The number of independent
variables in the model (NIV) must be specified. The
dependent variable must not be an explicitly defined
dependent variable; since OLS requires the
dependent variable to be of floating point, not
integer, format.
3. MLOG - Normal multinomial logit estimation. The
analyst has to inform the program of the number of
independent variables (NIV), the number of dependent
variables (NDV) and NAA (= NUM 1).
4. BTTE - Box Tukey multinomial logit estimation.
(See Chapter 6.6). The analyst has to inform the
program of the number of independent variables (NIV)
and number of dependent variables (NDV). One of
four methods (NUM 1) must be specified together
with NAA (= NUM 2). Method 1 iterates lambda
through a given range conditional on the location
parameter which may be fixed or varying. Method 2
iterates the location parameter through a given
range conditional on lambda which may be fixed or
varying. Method 3 operates with given lambda and
location parameter. Method 4 determines the
maximum-likelihood estimates of lambda and location
parameter. (Note: for the current version of the
program this method is not legal.) This option
must include an option card (even if blank), to
ensure default.
5. REST - Restricted multinomial logit estimation.
Theory often suggests that the coefficients of a
relation should obey a linear restriction. This
feature allows one to incorporate the restriction in
the fitting process so that the estimated
coefficients satisfy the restriction exactly.
Linear expressions may be expressed in the form

$$r = R\beta$$

where r is a known vector of order $g < K$, g being the
number of restrictions and K the number of

independent variables, and R is a known matrix of order g x K. For example, suppose we wish to impose two restrictions of the form $\beta_3 = \beta_5$ and $2\beta_2 + \beta_5 + \beta_6 = 1$, we would let

$$r = \begin{bmatrix} 0 \\ 1 \end{bmatrix} \text{ and } R = \begin{bmatrix} 0 & 0 & 1 & 0 & -1 & 0 & \ldots \\ 0 & 2 & 0 & 0 & 1 & 1 & \ldots \end{bmatrix}$$

To use this facility, the analyst is required to inform the program of (a) the number of independent variables (K) (NIV), (b) the number of dependent variables (NDV), and (c) the number of restrictions (g) (NUM 1). The nature of the restrictions is supplied later. NAA = NUM 2.

6. <u>BRES - Restricted Box-Tukey multinomial logit estimation</u>. A combination of (4) and (5) above. The analyst is required to inform the program of

(a) Number of independent variables (NIV)
(b) Number of dependent variables (NDV)
(c) Number of restrictions (NUM 1)
(d) BTT method (NUM 2)
(e) NAA (= NUM 3).

This option must include an option card (even if blank) to ensure default.

7. <u>MCOR - Multiple Correlation</u>. This feature allows the user to obtain some indication of whether a model suffers from multicollinearity. It allows the user to estimate the degree to which an independent variable in a model is explained by the other independent variables. If multicollinearity is suspected it is not because an independent variable is collinear with one or more of the other independent variables but rather because, for a specified binary subset of the alternatives, the differenced value of an independent variable (CHOICE VALUE - ALTERNATIVE VALUE) is collinear with one or more of the differenced values of the other independent variables. If the analyst has J alternatives then there are $\frac{1}{2}(J)(J-1)$ independent choice-alternative binary pairs and there are therefore $\frac{1}{2}(J)(J-1)$ difference equations in which a specified independent variable may appear. If in any one of these $\frac{1}{2}(J)(J-1)$ difference equations an independent variable is perfectly or nearly collinear with one or more of the other independent variables, then the estimated multinomial logit coefficient should be regarded as unreliable in that its variance would be biased upwards. Thus if it is suspected that the model may be suffering from multicollinearity, possibly because (a) the significance of a variable is suspected (that is not

to be interpreted as insignificant), or (b) either
the sign or the magnitude of a coefficient is
suspected, the model can be tested by use of this
option. The analyst is required to inform the
program of:

    (a) the number of independent variables (NIV)
    (b) the number of dependent variables (NDV)
    (c) the chosen alternative number (NUM 1)
    (d) the other alternative number (NUM 2)
    (e) the suspected independent variable
        number (NUM 3)
    (f) NAA (= NUM 4).

FORMAL DEFINITION - FEATURES COMMAND

FIELD	FORMAT	DESCRIPTION	STATUS
1	A4	(a) CORR	
		(b) OLSE	
		(c) MLOG	
		(d) BTTE	M[1]
		(e) REST	
		(f) BRES	
		(g) MCOR	
2	4X	4 Blanks	M
3	A4	NIV (Begin Col. 10)	O
4	I4	(NIV)	M
5	A4	NDV (Begin Col. 18)	O
6	I4	(NDV)	M/O[2]
7	A4	NM1 (Begin Col. 26)	O
8	I4	(NUM 1)	M/O[2]
9	A4	NM2 (Begin Col. 34)	O
10	I4	(NUM 2)	M/O[2]
11	A4	NM3 (Begin Col. 42)	O
12	I4	(NUM 3)	M/O[2]
13	A4	NM4 (Begin Col. 50)	O
14	I4	(NUM 4)	M/O[2]

Notes:

        (1)   One and only one of the commands in
field one is mandatory;   (2)   M/O indicates that the
status of the field depends on the feature specified.

    The feature commands, REST and BRES require
additional inputs immediately after the Feature card
and preceding the Equation card. It is at this
point that you are required to specify the nature of
the restrictions. There are three options:

    (a)   Set a restricted coefficient equal to a
constant e.g. $\beta_2 = 2.5$

(b)   Set a restricted coefficient equal to a linear combination of a set of <u>unrestricted</u> coefficients e.g. $\beta_2 = \beta_3 + 2.8 \, \beta_4$

(c)   Set a restricted coefficient equal to a constant plus a linear combination of a set of <u>unrestricted</u> coefficients e.g. $\beta_2 = 2.5 + \beta_3 + 2.8 \, \beta_4$

It is imperative that each restricted coefficient be equated (where appropriate) with only UNRESTRICTED coefficients. Thus if you have a set of economically meaningful restrictions such that the number of restrictions equals NRES you must initially solve the set of NRES restrictions such that there are NRES restricted coefficients. For example, suppose NRES = 2 and they are as follows:

$$\beta_1 + \beta_3 = 4.0 + 2\beta_2 \ldots \qquad (1)$$

$$\beta_2 = 1.0 + \beta_4 \ \ldots \qquad (2)$$

Then substituting for β_2 from (2) in (1) we have

$$\beta_1 + \beta_3 = 4.0 + 2 \, (1.0 + \beta_4) \qquad (3)$$

and subtracting β_3 from both sides of (3) we have

$$\beta_1 = 4.0 + 2.0 + 2\beta_4 - \beta_3.$$

That is

$$\beta_1 = 6.0 + 2\beta_4 - \beta_3$$

$$\beta_2 = 1.0 + \beta_4$$

Thus the two restricted coefficients are β_1 and β_2. (β_2 and β_4, or β_3 and β_2, or β_1 and β_3, β_1 and β_4, or β_3 and β_4, could have been the restricted coefficients by the appropriate transformations.) If restricted estimation fails to converge, then initialise the unrestricted coefficients at something other than zero by means of the option command. Select a sensible value.

FORMAL DEFINITION - RESTRICTION

FIELD	FORMAT	DESCRIPTION	STATUS
1	4X	4 Blanks	M
2	A3	B (Col. 7)	O
3	I3	Restricted coefficient number	M
4	A4	= (Col. 12)	O
5	F10.0	Constant - if zero leave blank	O

FIELD	FORMAT	DESCRIPTION	STATUS
6	A3	+ (centre in field)	O
7	F4.0	The multiplical[1] of an unrestricted coefficient	O
8	A1	B	O
9	I3	Unrestricted coefficient number	M

Fields 6 to 9 may be repeated such that up to four unrestricted coefficients appear on this card. Thus

10-13	As for 6 to 9 above		
14-17	As for 6 to 9 above		
18-21	As for 6 to 9 above		
22	A4	+[2] (Col. 78)	O

Notes:

(1) If a restriction involves subtractions then the appropriate unrestricted coefficient should be multiplied by -1.0. e.g. $\beta_1 = 4.0 + \beta_2 + -1.0\ \beta_3$ is identical with $\beta_1 = 4.0 + \beta_2 - \beta_3$.

(2) If the restriction requires more than one card and you desire to use a continuation card, place a + in column 78 to indicate that the restriction continues onto the next card. Use as many cards as is required.

(3) All variables, including ASCs, are assigned a coefficient number.

FORMAL DEFINITION - CONTINUOUS RESTRICTION

FIELD	FORMAT	DESCRIPTION	STATUS
1	F4.0	(Multiplical)	O
2	A1	B	O
3	I3	(Unrestricted number)	M
4	A3	+ (centred in field)	O
5-8	As for 1 to 4 above		
9-12	As for 1 to 4 above		
13-16	As for 1 to 4 above		O
17-20	As for 1 to 4 above		
21-24	As for 1 to 4 above		
25	As for 1 above		
26	As for 2 above		O
27	As for 3 above		
28	A4	+ (Col. 78)	O

The EQUATION command allows the following options:

(1) Specify NIV independent variables for correlation.

(2)   Specify NIV independent variables and one dependent variable for OLS regression and
(3)   Specify NIV independent variables and NDV dependent variables for multinomial logit estimation.

In all cases the command takes the form

EQUATION v_1 . . . . v_n

(Note in options (2) and (3) above the dependent variable/s must appear last in the list.)

FORMAL DEFINITION - EQUATION

FIELD	FORMAT	DESCRIPTION	STATUS
1	A4	EQUA	M
2	A4	TION	O
3-20	I4	(Variable number)	M[1]

Notes:

Use as many of these fields as appropriate and if you require more than one card continue onto the next and so on until the full list is specified.

FORMAL DEFINITION - CONTINUOUS EQUATION

FIELD	FORMAT	DESCRIPTION	STATUS
1-20	I4	(Variable number)	O

The OPTIONS[1] command allows the following options:

(1)   Specify the maximum number of iterations for multinomial logit estimation (MAX).
(2)   Indicate whether the tolerance for estimation is to be changed (TOL = $\emptyset$ ~ NO, 1 ~ YES).
(3)   Indicate whether the coefficients should be initialised at other than $\emptyset.\emptyset$. These options are designed to enable the analyst to economise on computer time. BET = 0 indicates NO; BET = 1 indicates a full restriction; BET = 2 indicates that initial values of the coefficients using restricted estimation only are to follow; BET = 3 indicates use of initial values for coefficients in unrestricted estimation, the initial values of unrestricted coefficients using restricted estimation are to follow (RES); and BET = 4 indicates initial values of coefficients for unrestricted estimation only. This is particularly relevant in transferability (see later section).
(4)   Indicate whether model variables are to be checked for out-of-range values (NRJ = $\emptyset$ ~ NO, $\neq \emptyset$ ~ YES). If TOL = 1 a card follows specifying

1. This command is not legal with Features Commands CORR or OLSE

354

the new tolerance. If NRJ $\neq$ $\emptyset$, NRJ cards follow
specifying the out-of-range values on which a
specified variable must pass or the observation is
rejected for the purpose of this model estimation.
A bad value is specified by giving a variable number
followed by a lower and upper limit. If BET $\neq$ $\emptyset$,
an appropriate number of cards follow specifying the
initial coefficient values.
  (5) Indicate the desired output (OUT).
1 = LONG, 2 = MEDIUM and 3 = SHORT.

FORMAL DEFINITION - OPTIONS COMMAND

FIELD	FORMAT	DESCRIPTION		STATUS
1	A4	OPTI		M
2	A4	ONS		O
3	A4	(a) MAX		
		(b) TOL	Right	
		(c) NRJ	justified	
		(d) BET		
		(e) OUT		
4	I4			

Notes:
  (1) Repeat fields 3 and 4 to specify desired
options.
  (2) Field 4 is an I4 format containing
appropriate value as explained above.
  (3) The options may appear in any order.

  If you have specified TOL = 1 then the program
will expect a tolerance card which informs it of
the new tolerance.

FORMAL DEFINITION - TOLERANCE

FIELD	FORMAT	DESCRIPTION	STATUS
1	A4	TOL (Right Justified)	M
2	6X	6 Blanks	M
3	F10.0	(New Tolerance)	M

  If you have specified NRJ $\neq$ 0, then the
program will expect NRJ out-of-range value cards
which inform the program of (a) the variable to be
checked — this must be an original or transformed
variable number (CANNOT BE GENERATED VARIABLE
NUMBER), (b) lower limit, (c) upper limit.

FORMAL DEFINITION - OUT-OF-RANGE VALUE

FIELD	FORMAT	DESCRIPTION	STATUS
1	A4	NRJ (Right justified)	M
2	I4	(Variable Number)	M

FORMAL DEFINITION - OUT-OF-RANGE VALUE (Continued)

FIELD	FORMAT	DESCRIPTION	STATUS
3	A4	LOW	O
4	F10.0	(lower limit)	M
5	A4	UP	O
6	F10.0	(upper limit)	M

If you have specified BET = 2 then the program expects a card/s containing NIV initial values of the coefficient.

FORMAL DEFINITION - INITIAL COEFFICIENTS

FIELD	FORMAT	DESCRIPTION	STATUS
1	A4	BET or RES (Right justified)	M
2	6X	6 Blanks	M
3-9	F10.0	(Initial Coefficient)	

Note:

The program expects NIV + NALT-1 coefficients where ASCs are specified, and NIV otherwise for unrestricted estimation (i.e. BET). For restricted estimation (i.e. RES) the program expects (NIV + NALT-1) - NRES coefficients where ASCs are specified, and NIV-RES otherwise. The above card allows 7 values. If NIV > 7, continue onto another card/s until the NIV coefficients have been specified.

FORMAL DEFINITION - CONTINUE COEFFICIENTS

FIELD	FORMAT	DESCRIPTION	STATUS
1-10	F10.0	(Initial Coefficients)	O

Note: See note above (Initial coefficients).

Default is obtained by ignoring these options. The program automatically sets TOLERANCE to the last value, and MAX to the last value. The initial coefficient is set to 0.00. The initial MAX is 25, and the initial TOL is 0.0001. Default output is MEDIUM except in the TEST option where it is always LONG.

The features commands BTTE and BRES require an additional set of inputs immediately preceding the END command dependent on the Method you have specified. We will treat each in turn.

Method 1. You are required to inform the program whether the location parameter is iterated across a given range (MODE = 1) or whether you wish to specify the values of the location parameter (NGCV)

(MODE = 0). There is a choice of output; (a) a
matrix of log-likelihood values and the estimated
coefficients associated with each set of lambda and
location parameter (M1 = 1); (b) just the matrix
of log-likelihood values (M1 = 2).

If MODE = Ø, the program expects a card
containing NGCV given values. If MODE = 1, the
program expects a card containing Minimum value
(CMIN), iteration step value (CIT), and maximum
value (CMAX). The program also expects a card
containing LMIN, LIT and LMAX appropriate to lambda.

Method 2. As for Method 1, except for location
parameter read lambda and vice versa.

FORMAL DEFINITION - METHODS 1 AND 2 - CARD 1

FIELD	FORMAT	DESCRIPTION	STATUS
1	A4	BTT (Right justified)	M
2	6X	6 Blanks	M
3	I4	(Mode)	M
4	I4	(M1)	M
5	I4	(NGCV, NGLV)	O

Note: NGLV is the set of values for lambda.

FORMAL DEFINITION - CARD 2 (a) - GIVEN VALUES

FIELD	FORMAT	DESCRIPTION	STATUS
1	A4	BTT (Right justified)	M
2	6X	6 Blanks	M
3-9	F10.0	(Given values)	O

Note: A maximum of 7 values can be specified.

FORMAL DEFINITION - CARD 2 (b) - ITERATIONS

FIELD	FORMAT	DESCRIPTION	STATUS
1	A4	BTT (Right justified)	M
2	6X	6 Blanks	M
3	F10.0	(Min)	M
4	F10.0	(IT)	M
5	F10.0	(Max)	M

Note: Min. and Max. should be so chosen that a
maximum of 7 values are specified.

FORMAL DEFINITION - CARD 3

FIELD	FORMAT	DESCRIPTION	STATUS
1	A4	BTT (Right justified)	M
2	6X	6 Blanks	M
3	F10.0	(Min)	M

FORMAL DEFINITION - CARD 3 (continued)

FIELD	FORMAT	DESCRIPTION	STATUS
4	F10.0	(It)	M
5	F10.0	(Max)	M

Note: Min. and Max. should be so that a maximum
of 50 values are specified. Card 2(b) and
Card 3 can interchange CMIN and LMIN, CMAX
and LMAX.

Method 3. The analyst requires to inform the
program of the given value of lambda (L) and given
value of Location Parameter (C).

FORMAL DEFINITION - METHOD 3

FIELD	FORMAT	DESCRIPTION	STATUS
1	A4	BTT (Right justified)	M
2	6X	6 Blanks	M
3	F10.0	(lambda)	M
4	F10.0	(Location Parameter)	M

The last card in any Feature is the END card.

FORMAL DEFINITION - END CARD

FIELD	FORMAT	DESCRIPTION	STATUS
1	A4	END (Begin Col. 1)	M

GENERAL INFORMATION

To specify a particular feature the relevant cards
should appear in the following order:

```
            FEATURE
            RESTRICTION  ⎫
            RESTRICTION  ⎪
            RESTRICTION  ⎬  NRES cards if applicable
            RESTRICTION  ⎪
            RESTRICTION  ⎭
            EQUATION
            OPTIONS         if applicable
                            [Note:  Always applicable
                             to BTTE and BRES features,
                             even if blank]
            TOL             if applicable
            NRJ
            NRJ          ⎫
            NRJ          ⎬  NRJ cards if applicable
            NRJ          ⎭
            BET or RES      if applicable
            BTT
            BTT          ⎫  if applicable
            BTT          ⎭
            END
```

358

The minimum requirements to specify a feature are

    FEATURE
    EQUATION
    END

Any number of features may be specified in any program run.

10·3·6 Output

The output of the program run is given below:

   CORR   - a correlation matrix

   OLSE   - Estimated coefficients and associated standard errors and t-statistics, Sigma Squared, Error Sum of Squares, and R^2.

   MLOG   - Estimated coefficients and associated standard errors and t-statistics; Maximum Log-Likelihood, Log-Likelihood at $\emptyset$, Rho Squared, Adjusted Rho Squared; Aggregate Elasticities (obtained by applying the enumeration method), and Prediction Success Table (see Section 3.5 for interpretation).

   BTTE   - Methods 1 and 2 - Matrix of Log-Likelihood; Max. Log Likelihood and associated lambda and Location Parameter and estimated coefficients and associated standard errors and t-statistics if requested (see Section 6.6 for interpretation).

              Method 3 - as for MLOG.

   REST   - As for MLOG (first two groupings) with unrestricted coefficients; As for MLOG with restricted coefficients and Chi-Squared Test of Restriction.

   BRES   - as for BTTE (Methods 1 and 2)
          - as for REST (Method 3).

   MCOR   - R^2; i.e. explanation offered for the variation in the differenced variable specified by all other differenced variables in the equation; Estimated coefficients and standard errors and t-statistics; and Correlation matrix of all differenced variables in the equation.

10·3·7 Some Notes on Use of Features

OLSE - The feature is provided for two purposes:
(1) Estimation of alternative model structure,
e.g. linear logit, and
(2) Multicorrelation of absolute variables.
The dependent variable must be in floating
point form and thus must be defined as an independent
variable. Thus if the analyst wishes to use an
explicitly defined dependent variable as a
dependent variable in OLSE they must transform it
into an independent variable (this may seem contra-
dictory, but it is not in fact). An appropriate
transformation would be by operation 1Ø and operation
16 whereby operation 1Ø creates a constant (e.g.
1.00) and operation 16 creates a new variable by
multiplying a previously defined dependent variable
by a constant variable (1.00).

BTTE - The virtues of BTTE are explained in
Section 6.6.
It would clearly be desirable to estimate the
maximum-likelihood estimates of lambda and the
Location Parameter simultaneously with the estimation of the coefficients. But this is an
extremely time-consuming process which may in the
end prove unfruitful since the estimates may not be
significantly different from one (1) and zero (0)
respectively. Thus we have provided Methods 1 and
2 which allow search over a grid for the maximum
estimates.
It is suggested that the critical search is
over a range of lambda from a Minimum of -2.00 to a
Maximum of +2.00 by a step size of 0.5. The initial
Location Parameter should be chosen to ensure that
for all independent variables in the model
$(X + C) > 0$, where $C \equiv$ Min. Location Parameter. The
maximum Location Parameter should be chosen on the
basis of the data but experience suggests that it is
unlikely to exceed CMIN + 100. Thus set Max. C =
CMIN + 100 with a step size of, say, 2Ø.
Using Method 1, then, you would set MODE = 1,
CMIN = C, CMAX = C + 100, CIT = 20, LMIN = -2.00,
LMAX = + 2.00, LIT = 0.5. The program will then
produce a matrix of log-likelihoods and indicate
the maximum pair of lambda and Location Parameter.
By examination of the matrix you can identify (a)
whether the maximum log-likelihood is likely to be
significantly different from the one (1), zero (0)
Lambda, Location Parameter combination and (b)
where the maximum pair is likely to be located. If
additional searches are likely to be fruitful the

analyst can use Method 1 to zero in on the maximum
likelihood combination. Having isolated that
combination to the users' satisfaction the analyst
can then use Method 3 to obtain normal MLOG output.
Three additional points need to be stressed.

(a)   At Lambda = 1.00, changes in the Location
Parameter from 0.0 will not affect the maximum
log-likelihood;
(b)   The program does not transform alternative-specific constants; and
(c)   Binary dummy variables cannot be
transformed. Thus the program needs to recognise a
variable as such and proceed accordingly. This is
done by placing all such dummies at the end of the
list of variables using the GENERATIONS command.
The analyst then informs the program how many binary
dummy variables there are. This is done via the
GENERATIONS command.

Let us assume that after all generations the
final number of variables is N (i.e. variables 1 - N
exist) and you have informed the program that there
are M binary dummy variables). The program then
assumes that all variables numbered from N-M to N
are binary dummies and treats them accordingly.
In this case we have to redefine the
GENERATIONS command.

FORMAL DEFINITION - GENERATIONS

FIELD	FORMAT	DESCRIPTION	STATUS
1	A4	GENE	M
2	A4	RATI	O
3	A4	ONS (Left justified)	O
4	A4	ARE (Left justified)	O
5	I4	(Number of generations)	M
6	A4	ND (Right justified)	M
7	I4	(Number of dummies)	M

MCOR - As indicated above, this feature is
useful if you suspect the model suffers from
multicollinearity. Confirmation of suspicions is
testable if a few observations are dropped from the
data set and then the model is re-estimated. If
the coefficients alter noticeably (Note: not
significantly) then suspicions are probably
confirmed.
The two alternatives at fault then need to be
isolated. In a small choice set this may be no
problem but if it is large this becomes somewhat
of an art and rests largely on familiarisation with

the problem and the data set. Assuming, then, that there are J choices and the two at fault are alternative i and alternative j. Assuming also there are K independent variables and the offending variable is variable L.

Let $\bar{X}_k = (X_{ik} - X_{jk})$ $k = 1, \ldots, K$

Then the feature MCOR estimates the model

$$\bar{X}_\ell = \beta_1 \bar{X}_1 + \ldots\ldots\ldots + \beta_{k \neq \ell} \bar{X}_{k \neq \ell} + \ldots + \beta_K \bar{X}_K$$

and provides estimates of

$$\beta_{k \neq \ell} = \hat{\beta}_{k \neq \ell}$$

together with associated t-statistics and standard errors.

It also produces an R squared

$$= R^2_{x_\ell - x_k} \quad k \neq \ell$$

Any $\bar{X}_k$ whose variance equals zero is omitted from the model. This would be the case where $X_{ik} = X_{jk}$ for all observations. Regardless of whether or not an alternative-specific constant has been specified, one is provided since otherwise R^2 would be meaningless.

If the resultant output convinces the analyst that the variable in question is indeed multicollinear with the other variables then he must accept that the estimated coefficients in the original model are unreliable. Suggested action on this will be discussed in the next section.

10.3.8 Problems

In this sub-section we look at four (4) common problems and how the program can assist the analyst. These are:

(a)   Model Selection,
(b)   The IIA assumption (see Chapter 5),
(c)   Transferability (see Section 7.3) and
(d)   Multicollinearity.

Although the four problems are by no means independent, they are discussed separately.

362

A.   MODEL SELECTION

A final model should possess the following qualities:

(a)   Its Log-Likelihood should not be significantly different from the maximum Log-Likelihood possible for the given choice set.

(b)   It should include no insignificant variables.

(c)   It should include no variables whose signs or magnitude are meaningless, and it follows that

(d)   It should include no variables whose elasticities are meaningless.

Since point (c) is often difficult to decide, given the nature of multinomial logit models, we would place great stress on point (d). It has been shown (e.g. Hensher & Johnson, 1979) that the use of Box-Tukey transformations is likely to produce significant changes in elasticity estimates such that point (d) is more likely to be satisfied, i.e. it is likely to produce estimates whose significance, sign and magnitude are more meaningful than otherwise. (Note: this is not claimed in all cases, but only in general.)

B.   THE IIA ASSUMPTION (see also Chapter 5)

The Basic Multinomial logit estimation is based on the assumption that the IIA condition holds, but it is often desirable to test this assumption. The program allows this to be done. We will illustrate this with two examples.

(1)   Assume a choice set which allows for three alternatives - A, B, C, for which we have two bits of information, 1 and 2, for each choice. Let there be Q observations. We estimate a model such that:

$$M \sim V_A = \beta_A + \beta_1 X_{1A} + \beta_2 X_{2A}$$

$$V_B = \beta_B + \beta_1 X_{1B} + \beta_2 X_{2B}$$

$$V_C = \beta_1 X_{1C} + \beta_2 X_{2C}$$

Assume now a fourth alternative, D, is included in the choice set for which we have no information except whether it was chosen or not. We then estimate the model,

$$\tilde{M} \sim \tilde{V}_D = \tilde{\beta}_D$$

$$\tilde{V}_A = \tilde{\beta}_A + \tilde{\beta}_1 X_{1A} + \tilde{\beta}_2 X_{2A}$$

$$\tilde{V}_B = \tilde{\beta}_B + \tilde{\beta}_1 X_{1B} + \tilde{\beta}_2 X_{2B}$$

$$\tilde{V}_C = \tilde{\beta}_1 X_{1C} + \tilde{\beta}_2 X_{2C}$$

such that the Log-Likelihood = $\tilde{L}$. We then estimate a further model where

$$\tilde{\beta}_A = \beta_A, \qquad \tilde{\beta}_B = \beta_B, \qquad \tilde{\beta}_1 = \beta_1, \qquad \tilde{\beta}_2 = \beta_2$$

i.e. we use the restricted feature to restrict the above coefficients to their first estimated values. Thus we estimate the model

$$M^* \sim V_D^* = \beta_D^*$$

$$V_A^* = \beta_A + \beta_1 X_{1A} + \beta_2 X_{2A}$$

$$V_B^* = \beta_B + \beta_1 X_{1B} + \beta_2 X_{2B}$$

$$V_C^* = \beta_1 X_{1C} + \beta_2 X_{2C}$$

such that Log-Likelihood = L^*. Now the IIA condition will hold if L^* is not significantly different from $\tilde{L}$.

If you use the REST feature to specify the model, M^*, it will automatically estimate the model, $\tilde{M}$, and provide a CHI-SQUARED TEST STATISTIC of the RESTRICTION.

(2)   As for (1) except we now assume that for the new choice, D, we have the information X_{1D} and X_{2D}.

Two models are then estimated,

$$\tilde{M} \sim \tilde{V}_D = \tilde{\beta}_D + \tilde{\beta}_1 X_{1D} + \tilde{\beta}_2 X_{2D}$$

$$\tilde{V}_A = \tilde{\beta}_A + \tilde{\beta}_1 X_{1A} + \tilde{\beta}_2 X_{2A}$$

$$\tilde{V}_B = \tilde{\beta}_B + \tilde{\beta}_1 X_{1B} + \tilde{\beta}_2 X_{2B}$$

$$\tilde{V}_C = \tilde{\beta}_1 X_{1C} + \tilde{\beta}_2 X_{2C}$$

where Log-Likelihood = $\tilde{L}$ and

$$M^* \sim V_D^* = \beta_D^* + \beta_1 X_{1D} \quad \beta_2 X_{2D}$$

$$V_A^* = \beta_A + \beta_1 X_{1A} \quad \beta_2 X_{2A}$$

364

$$V_B^* = \beta_B + \beta_1 X_{1B} + \beta_2 X_{2B}$$

$$V_C^* = \beta_1 X_{1C} + \beta_2 X_{2C}$$

where Log-Likelihood = $\tilde{L}^*$. If L^* is not significantly different from $\tilde{L}$ then the IIA condition holds. Again the above models may be estimated by using the REST feature.

C.   TRANSFERABILITY (see Section 7.3)

(1)   The REST feature allows the user to:

(a)   Transfer a subset of coefficients from one data set to another and test such a transfer by the provided CHI-SQUARED STATISTIC.

(b)   Transfer a coefficient, or set of coefficients, from one set of data to another, in the form of linear restrictions and test such a transfer. An example of such an application is if in one data set a variable such as TIME was aggregated while in the other it was disaggregated into its components. Then one could restrict the sum of the disaggregated component coefficients in the second data set to be equal to the coefficient of the aggregated variable in the first data set.

(c)   Transfer all but the coefficients of the alternative-specific constants from one data set to another, thus allowing the ASC coefficients to be determined by the new data set while restricting all others.

(2)   Unfortunately the user cannot transfer a complete set of coefficients from one model to another by way of the REST feature since this demands that the number of restrictions be less than the number of variables; but the program nevertheless provides for this possibility.

This is done by using the MLOG feature. You are required to use the OPTION command as follows: Set BET = 1 (the only occasion in which you should do so). This informs the program that a set of initial coefficient values is to be imputed and that these are to be used as restricted values. Thus you must provide the restricted values as described in the relevant section (i.e. under OPTION command).

This method will carry out the CHI-SQUARED test but will not provide Elasticities and Prediction Success Table for the Restricted Model If this output is required, you must re-estimate the model again using the OPTION command with BET = 1 but this time also set MAX = 1.

D.   MULTICOLLINEARITY

Assume that after practising the art of multicollinearity detection the user is convinced that his model suffers from multicollinearity and that as a result the estimates must be assumed unreliable. Assume further that the analyst has isolated the pair of alternatives at fault.

In more traditional OLS estimation we would validly use the estimated coefficients for the purpose of prediction and this remains so for multinomial logit estimation though we would be hesitant to transfer such a set of coefficients to a new data set. Assume, however, that we are more concerned with the reliability of the estimates than with prediction. What can be done?

Clearly the offending variable cannot be dropped from the model since if the variable is significant then its exclusion will leave the estimates as biased. Similarly we cannot leave out the value of the variable for one of the offending alternatives since this will equally leave the estimates biased.

Under OLS estimation two recourses are available. More observations could be obtained and the model re-estimated to see if this corrected the problem; alternatively we could obtain an estimate of the offending coefficient independent of the data and estimate a restricted model. While both options apply equally well to multinomial logit estimation, and particularly to this program, since the user has recourse to the REST feature, multinomial logit has a unique feature which allows the analyst to overcome the multicollinearity problem. We will illustrate this by means of an example.

Assume we wish to estimate a model where the choices are A, B, C, D, for which we have information, 1, 2 and 3. Assume there are Q observations where Q is reasonably large. Assume no ASCs. Let the model be such that

$$V_A = \beta_1 X_{1A} + \beta_2 X_{2A} + \beta_3 X_{3A}$$

$$V_B = \beta_1 X_{1B} + \beta_2 X_{2B} + \beta_3 X_{3B}$$

$$V_C = \beta_1 X_{1C} + \beta_2 X_{2C} + \beta_3 X_{3C}$$

$$V_D = \beta_1 X_{1D} \quad \beta_2 X_{2D} + \beta_3 X_{3D}$$

Assume the offending coefficient is β_3 such that $X_{3C} - X_{3D}$ is multicollinear with $X_{1C} - X_{1D}$ and

$X_{2C} - X_{2D}$. Then Alternatives C and D are the alternatives at fault. Let the Log-Likelihood of this model = L. Now assume that the number of observations for which D was the chosen = M. Then the number of observations for which either A, B, or C was chosen = Q - M. Let M* = (A,B,C,) and $\tilde{M}$ = (A,B,C,D). Now the IIA assumption indicates that a choice from M* is identical with a choice from $\tilde{M}$ and is thus independent of D. Let the number that choose A from M* = a*, B from M* = b*, C from M* = c*, then the proportion that choose A from M* = a*/Q - M, B from M* = b*/Q - M, c from M* = c*/Q - M. Let the number that choose A from $\tilde{M}$ = a, B from $\tilde{M}$ = b, C from $\tilde{M}$ = c; then the proportion that choose A from $\tilde{M}$ = a/Q, B from $\tilde{M}$ = b/Q, C from $\tilde{M}$ = c/Q. Then by the IIA property

$$\frac{a^*/Q-M}{b^*/Q-M} = \frac{a/Q}{b/Q}$$

i.e. $\qquad a^*/_{b^*} = a/_b \qquad \ldots \qquad (10.1)$

and similarly for

$$a^*/_{c^*} = a/_c \qquad \ldots \qquad (10.2)$$

and $\qquad b^*/_{c^*} = b/_c \qquad \ldots \qquad (10.3)$

Let M* be such that

$$V_A^* = \beta_1^* X_{1A} + \beta_2^* X_{2A} + \beta_3^* X_{3A}$$

$$V_B^* = \beta_1^* X_{1B} + \beta_2^* X_{2B} + \beta_3^* X_{3B}$$

$$V_C^* = \beta_1^* X_{1C} + \beta_2^* X_{2C} + \beta_3^* X_{3C}$$

It is clearly the case that equations (10.1), (10.2) and (10.3) above can only be true if

$$\beta_1^* = \beta_1 \quad \beta_2^* = \beta_2 \text{ and } \quad \beta_3^* = \beta_3$$

Since in this case equations (10.1), (10.2) and (10.3) are true because a* = a, b* = b and c* = c, it follows that

$$\beta_1^* = \beta_1, \quad \beta_2^* = \beta_2 \text{ and } \beta_3^* = \beta_3$$

Thus the population parameters β_1^*, β_2^* and β_3^* are identical with the population parameters β_1, β_2 and

β_3 and thus estimates of $\hat{\beta}_1^*$, $\hat{\beta}_2^*$ and $\hat{\beta}_3^*$ will be consistent estimates of β_1, β_2 and β_3.

To begin with we would eliminate alternative D from the choice set and estimate the model M* and obtain the estimates $\hat{\beta}_1^*$, $\hat{\beta}_2^*$ and $\hat{\beta}_3^*$. Then to improve the efficiency of the estimates we would estimate the model

$$\tilde{M}^* \sim \tilde{V}_A = \tilde{\beta}_1 X_{1A} + \tilde{\beta}_2 X_{2A} + \hat{\beta}_3^* X_{3A}$$

$$\tilde{V}_B = \tilde{\beta}_1 X_{1B} + \tilde{\beta}_2 X_{2B} + \hat{\beta}_3^* X_{3B}$$

$$\tilde{V}_C = \tilde{\beta}_1 X_{1C} + \tilde{\beta}_2 X_{2C} + \hat{\beta}_3^* X_{3C}$$

$$\tilde{V}_D = \tilde{\beta}_1 X_{1D} + \tilde{\beta}_2 X_{2D} + \hat{\beta}_3^* X_{3D}$$

where Log-Likelihood of $\tilde{M}^* = \tilde{L}^*$

By an analogous argument to that above it can be shown that $\tilde{\beta}_1$ and $\tilde{\beta}_2$ are consistent estimators of β_1 and β_2 but clearly more efficient than $\hat{\beta}_1^*$ and $\hat{\beta}_2^*$ since more information is included. While the original estimates $\hat{\beta}_1$, $\hat{\beta}_2$ and $\hat{\beta}_3$ were all consistent it would seem reasonable to assume that the new set of estimates (i.e. $\tilde{\beta}_1$, $\tilde{\beta}_2$ and $\hat{\beta}_3^*$) are more reliable.

The above analysis rests wholly on the assumption that the IIA condition holds. This assumption can be tested. Thus if L* is not significantly different from L we can assume the IIA condition holds and the restriction is valid. The above estimation procedure can be carried out by the appropriate use of MLOG and REST features.

Assume you have already estimated the original model (choice set M). Then use the MLOG feature to estimate model M*. (Note the program will automatically adjust the number of observations by including for the purpose of estimation only those observations whose choice was either A, B or C.) Then restrict the coefficient of X_3 to $\hat{\beta}_3^*$ and estimate model $\tilde{M}^*$ using the REST feature.

10·3·9 Program Segmentation

Size limitations require program segmentation as follows:

DRIVE1, containing
SUBD1: BTT, PROB, TRAN, AINV, DERIV, DAINV,
MLOGIT, METHOD 1, METHOD 2, METHOD 3,
TRANDAT, BETAINT, FUNC, EBTT, ELASTR, ELAS,
IERROR, MTAB, RESTD, RESTB, RESTV, CORRM,
CORRX.

The above segment allows for features MLOG, REST,
BTTE, BRES and MCOR.

DRIVE2
SUBD2: TRAN, IERROR, AINV, CORRA, REGR.

This segment allows for features CORR and OLSE.

The inputs for both are identical. The above
means that features specific to both executable
segments within one run cannot be utilised. The
two segments can be combined, if required, by
replacing Lines 394-39 and 406 in DRIVE 1 with the
appropriate CALL statements [Lines 388 and 402] as
per DRIVE 2. Then MAP all elements into DRIVE 1.
(Core storage, however, will exceed 100K.)

Maximum Program Limits

Data Set

Data Set	Note
Independent variables = 200 Alternative (dependent variables) - 40	Apply after all transformations and generations.
Generations (in terms of cards not variables) = 60 cards	
Transformation = 240	There is a facility to backpack to define all variables and transformations.

Features

Features	
CORR = 150 variables	If no variables are specified the first 150 will be correlated. If your system permits this can be extended by redimensioning the XS matrix in subroutine CORRA from 150 x 150 to 200 x 200.

OLS independent variables
= 30

All Other Features

```
Independent variables
(including ASCs)     = 30
Dependent variables = 40
BTTE and BRES: (Methods 1, 2)
   = 10 x 7 log-likelihood
     matrix
No. of features      = unlimited
No. of observations = unlimited
```

Error Codes

200	Expected TEST or ORIGINAL
210	Expected INPUT PARAMETERS card
220	Expects TRANSFORMATION/ GENERATION or END card
240	Expects GENERATION or END card
300	Specified an alternative greater than 40 on a transformation card
400	Expects an ASV or a GEN card
410	On a GENERATION card specified a variable number outside range
420	On a GENERATION card specified a variable with no specific alternative
430	On an ASV card specified an alternative outside range
500	Expects FEATURE or STOP card
510	A feature specifies more than 40 alternatives
520	Feature specified more than 30 independent variables
530	Expects EQUATION card
540	Expects OPTION card
550	Expects TOLERANCE card
560	Expects out-of-range (NRJ) card
570	Expects BTT card
580	Expects RES card
590	Expects END card
600	Expects BTT card

10·4 The Illustrative Input and Output

In concluding the discussion on using BLOGIT, we present the set up of the card deck that the analyst can prepare as input for the test run; and the output.

TABLE 10·2 A Test Run with 25 Observations

1	2	3	4	5	6	7	8	9	10	11	12	13	14	15	16	17	18	19	20	2	22	23	24	25	26	27	28	29	30	31	32	33	34	35	36	37	38	39	40	41	42	43	44	45	46	47	48	49	50
I	N																																																
O	R	I	G	I	N	A	L		J	O	B		=		Y																																		
H	O	R	N	S	B	Y		D	A	T	A		1	1		M	A	Y		1	9	7	9																										
V	A	R	=				4					O	B	S	=			2	5					A	L	T	=				2					F	M	T	=				1						
(	4	F	1	0	·	0	,	2	I	3	)																																						
C	A	R						T	R	N																																							
T	I	M	E	/	C	A	R					A	L	T	=				1																														
C	O	S	T	/	C	A	R					A	L	T	=				1																														
T	I	M	E	/	T	R	N					A	L	T	=				2																														
C	O	S	T	/	T	R	N					A	L	T	=				2																														
T	R	A	N	S	F	O	R	M	A	T	I	O	N	S	=				6		F	N	=				6																						
T	I	M	E	/	C	A	R																	T	R	A	N			2	2				1									1	·	0			
C	O	S	T	/	C	A	R																	T	R	A	N			2	2				2									1	·	0			
T	I	M	E	/	T	R	N																	T	R	A	N			2	2				3									1	·	0			
C	O	S	T	/	T	R	N																	T	R	A	N			2	2				4									1	·	0			

TABLE 10-2 (cont.)

1	2	3	4	5	6	7	8	9	10	11	12	13	14	15	16	17	18	19	20	21	22	23	24	25	26	27	28	29	30	31	32	33	34	35	36	37	38	39	40	41	42	43	44	45	46	47	48	49	50
T	-	$		C	A	R						A	L	T	=				1					T	R	A	N			1	4				1			2				5							
T	-	$		T	R	N						A	L	T	=				2					T	R	A	N			1	4				3			4				6							
		G	E	N	E	R	A	T	I	O	N	S	A	R	E				3																														
		T	I	M	E					G	E	N								V	N		=			1				3																			
		T	-	$						G	E	N								V	N		=			5				6																			
		E	N	D																																													
		M	L	O	G				N	I	V				5		N	D	V			2			N	A	A			4					2														
		E	Q	U	A	T	I	O	N		O				1				2			3				A	A			1																			
		E	N	D																																													
		B	T	T	E				N	I	V				5		N	D	V			2			N	M	1			3		N	A	A				4											
		E	Q	U	A	T	I	O	N		O				1				2			3				4				1					2														
		O	P	T	I	O	N	S																																									
		B	T	T																																													
		E	N	D																																													
		S	T	O	P																																												

TABLE 10·3: Output of the Test Run

```
1            HORNSBY DATA  11TH, MAY 1979            DATE 121279        PAGE    1
0

NUMBER OF ORIGINAL VARIABLE= 4   NUMBER OF OBSERVATIONS= 25   NUMBER OF ALTERNATIVES= 2

0 SPECIFIED FORMAT        (4F10.0,2I3)
0 ALTERNATIVES ARE :  1. CAR   2. TRN.
0

SPECIFIED VARIABLE NAMES ARE :
  1  TIME/CAR
  2  COST/CAR
  3  TIME/TRN
  4  COST/TRN
0---------------------------------------------------------------------------------
   TIME/CAR REJECTED IF  LE   1.0000
   COST/CAR REJECTED IF  LE   1.0000
   TIME/TRN REJECTED IF  LE   1.0000
   COST/TRN REJECTED IF  LE   1.0000
  5  T-$/CAR  = TIME/CAR / COST/CAR              .   ALT=  1
  6  T-$/TRN. = TIME/TRN / COST/TRN              .   ALT=  2
0---------------------------------------------------------------------------------
  7  TIME                                        .   VN =  1  ALT=  1    GENERIC
                                                 .   VN =  3  ALT=  2    GENERIC
                                                 .   VN =  5  ALT=  1
  8  T-$                                         .   VN =  6  ALT=  2    GENERIC
0
```

373

TABLE 10-3 (cont.)

```
                     TRANFORMED DATA FIRST FIVE AND LAST OBSERVATIONS

0 OBS.  1   .70000+02  .50000+02  .64000+02  .39000+02  .14000+01  .16410+01
0 OBS.  2   .50000+02  .23000+03  .60000+02  .32000+02  .21739+00  .18750+01
0 OBS.  3   .50000+02  .70000+02  .58000+02  .40000+02  .71429+00  .14500+01
0 OBS.  4   .60000+02  .10800+03  .93000+02  .62000+02  .55556+00  .15000+01
0 OBS.  5   .70000+02  .60000+02  .68000+02  .26000+02  .11667+01  .26154+01
0 OBS. 25   .17000+02  .20000+02  .78000+02  .35000+02  .85000+00  .22286+01

0 MEAN    43.840    51.200    66.360    37.360    1.0844    1.8699
          .48000    .52000                        .45573    .58032
0 STD.    17.442    43.613    27.024    15.697

0 0 OBS. ARE REJECTED   25 CASES LEFT

1 GENERATED MODEL NO. 1

  ALTERNATIVES ARE  1 CAR   2 TRN.

  ATTRIBUTES ARE :
              ASC-CAR   TIME/CAR   COST/CAR   TIME/TRN   COST/TRN

0 0 OBS. ARE REJECTED   25 CASES LEFT
```

```
       INDEP VARIABLE     ESTIMATE   T-STAT   STD. ERROR

1ASC-CAR                  -1.4664    -.84226   1.7410
2TIME/CAR      ( 1)       -.81346-01 -1.4894    .54616-01
3COST/CAR      ( 2)       -.19595-01 -.70584    .27761-01
4TIME/TRN      ( 3)       -.32489-02 -.69522-01 .46732-01
5COST/TRN      ( 4)       -.16118    -1.8082    .89139-01

0  LOG LIKELIHOOD =-8.9067  LOG LIKELIHOOD(0) =-17.309 RHO SQUARED = .48542 RHO-BAR SW
0 WEIGHTED AGGREGATE ELASTICITY

                    1. CAR    2. TRN.
( 2)TIME/CAR DE=-.75763    .00000
          CE= 2.3539      .00000
( 3)COST/CAR DE=-.19993    .00000
          CE= .53162      .00000
( 4)TIME/TRN DE= .00000   -.41024-01
          CE= .00000      .15341
( 5)COST/TRN DE= .00000   -1.1343
          CE= .00000      3.5771

PREDICTED SUCCESS TABLE
            1 CAR    2 TRN.
 1CAR   ( 12)  9.0843   2.9157
 2TRN.  ( 13)  2.9157  10.084
 TOTAL  ( 25) 12.000   13.000
1          GENERATED MODEL NO. 2
```

375

TABLE 10·3 (cont.)

ALTERNATIVES ARE 1 CAR   2 TRN.
ATTRIBUTES ARE :

0 0 OBS. ARE REJECTED   ASC-CAR   TIME/CAR   COST/CAR   TIME/TRN   COST/TRN
                         25 CASES LEFT

0 METHOD 3   GIVEN LAMBDA AND LOCATION PARAMETER

LAMBA = .000   CONSTANT = .0000

INDEP VARIABLE	ESTIMATE	T-STAT	STD. ERROR
1ASC-CAR	-5.3823	-.92937	5.7914
2TIME/CAR (1)	-2.5166	-1.1642	2.1617
3COST/CAR (2)	-1.3360	-1.0948	1.2202
4TIME/TRN (3)	-.95143	-.34995	2.7187
5COST/TRN (4)	-4.4385	-1.7886	2.4815

0   LOG LIKELIHOOD =-9.6677   LOG LIKELIHOOD(0) =-17.309 RHO SQUARED = .44145 RHO-BAR SQ
0 WEIGHTED AGGREGATE ELASTICITY

	1. CAR	2. TRN.	PREDICTED SUCCESS TABLE
(2)TIME/CAR DE=-.63523	CE= 1.8814	.00000	
(3)COST/CAR DE=-.33722	CE= .99875	.00000	
(4)TIME/TRN DE= .00000	CE= .00000	-.22168	
(5)COST/TRN DE= .00000	CE= .00000	-1.0342	
		3.4043	

PREDICTED SUCCESS TABLE

		1 CAR	2 TRN.
1CAR	(12)	8.9153	3.0847
2TRN.	(13)	3.0847	9.9153
TOTAL	(25)	12.000	13.000

376

NOTES — CHAPTER 10

1. A tape copy of BLOGIT can be obtained from the
    Australian Road Research Board, Box 156 (Bag 4),
    Nunawading, Victoria 3131 Australia.   In
    requesting a copy of the program, a tape must
    be supplied together with the following
    information: the computer at the local
    institution, number of tracks (7, 9 or 16),
    the Bpi (800 or 1,600), number of characters
    per block, ASCII or EBCD configuration, and
    labelled or unlabelled tape. There is a small
    handling charge.

    At the time of publication an additional set
    of subroutines had been added to BLOGIT to
    estimate the Generalised Extreme Value Model.
    It is anticipated that this option will be
    available by mid-1981. The new program will
    be known as GLOGIT.

APPENDIX A

Statistical Tables

TABLE A1: Exponential Functions exp U

μ	0	1	2	3	4	5	6	7	8	9
.0	1.0000	1.0101	1.0202	1.0305	1.0408	1.0513	1.0618	1.0725	1.0833	1.0942
.1	1.1052	1.1163	1.1275	1.1388	1.1503	1.1618	1.1735	1.1853	1.1972	1.2092
.2	1.2214	1.2337	1.2461	1.2586	1.2712	1.2840	1.2969	1.3100	1.3231	1.3364
.3	1.3499	1.3634	1.3771	1.3910	1.4049	1.4191	1.4333	1.4477	1.4623	1.4770
.4	1.4918	1.5068	1.5220	1.5373	1.5527	1.5683	1.5841	1.6000	1.6161	1.6323
.5	1.6487	1.6653	1.6820	1.6989	1.7160	1.7333	1.7507	1.7683	1.7860	1.8040
.6	1.8221	1.8404	1.8589	1.8776	1.8965	1.9155	1.9348	1.9542	1.9739	1.9937
.7	2.0138	2.0340	2.0544	2.0751	2.0959	2.1170	2.1383	2.1598	2.1815	2.2034
.8	2.2255	2.2479	2.2705	2.2933	2.3164	2.3396	2.3632	2.3869	2.4109	2.4351
.9	2.4596	2.4843	2.5093	2.5345	2.5600	2.5857	2.6117	2.6379	2.6645	2.6912
1.0	2.7183	2.7456	2.7732	2.8011	2.8292	2.8577	2.8864	2.9154	2.9447	2.9743
1.1	3.0042	3.0344	3.0649	3.0957	3.1268	3.1582	3.1899	3.2220	3.2544	3.2871
1.2	3.3201	3.3535	3.3872	3.4212	3.4556	3.4903	3.5254	3.5609	3.5966	3.6328
1.3	3.6693	3.7062	3.7434	3.7810	3.8190	3.8574	3.8962	3.9354	3.9749	4.0149
1.4	4.0552	4.0960	4.1371	4.1787	4.2207	4.2631	4.3060	4.3492	4.3929	4.4371
1.5	4.4817	4.5267	4.5722	4.6182	4.6646	4.7115	4.7588	4.8066	4.8550	4.9037
1.6	4.9530	5.0028	5.0531	5.1039	5.1552	5.2070	5.2593	5.3122	5.3656	5.4195
1.7	5.4739	5.5290	5.5845	5.6407	5.6973	5.7546	5.8124	5.8709	5.9299	5.9895
1.8	6.0496	6.1104	6.1719	6.2339	6.2965	6.3598	6.4237	6.4883	6.5535	6.6194
1.9	6.6859	6.7531	6.8210	6.8895	6.9588	7.0287	7.0993	7.1707	7.2427	7.3155
2.0	7.3891	7.4633	7.5383	7.6141	7.6906	7.7679	7.8460	7.9248	8.0045	8.0849
2.1	8.1662	8.2482	8.3311	8.4149	8.4994	8.5849	8.6711	8.7583	8.8463	8.9352
2.2	9.0250	9.1157	9.2073	9.2999	9.3933	9.4877	9.5831	9.6794	9.7767	9.8749
2.3	9.9742	10.074	10.176	10.278	10.381	10.486	10.591	10.697	10.805	10.913
2.4	11.023	11.134	11.246	11.359	11.473	11.588	11.705	11.822	11.941	12.061
2.5	12.182	12.305	12.429	12.554	12.680	12.807	12.936	13.066	13.197	13.330
2.6	13.464	13.599	13.736	13.874	14.013	14.154	14.296	14.440	14.585	14.732
2.7	14.880	15.029	15.180	15.333	15.487	15.643	15.800	15.959	16.119	16.281
2.8	16.445	16.610	16.777	16.945	17.116	17.288	17.462	17.637	17.814	17.993
2.9	18.174	18.357	18.541	18.728	18.916	19.106	19.298	19.492	19.688	19.886
3.0	20.086	20.287	20.491	20.697	20.905	21.115	21.328	21.542	21.758	21.977
3.1	22.198	22.421	22.646	22.874	23.104	23.336	23.571	23.807	24.047	24.288
3.2	24.533	24.779	25.028	25.280	25.534	25.790	26.050	26.311	26.576	26.843
3.3	27.113	27.385	27.660	27.938	28.219	28.503	28.789	29.079	29.371	29.666
3.4	29.964	30.265	30.569	30.877	31.187	31.500	31.817	32.137	32.460	32.786
3.5	33.115	33.448	33.784	34.124	34.467	34.813	35.163	35.517	35.874	36.234
3.6	36.598	36.966	37.338	37.713	38.092	38.475	38.861	39.252	39.646	40.045
3.7	40.447	40.854	41.264	41.679	42.098	42.521	42.948	43.380	43.816	44.256
3.8	44.701	45.150	45.604	46.063	46.525	46.993	47.465	47.942	48.424	48.911
3.9	49.402	49.899	50.400	50.907	51.419	51.935	52.457	52.985	53.517	54.055
4.	54.598	60.340	66.686	73.700	81.451	90.017	99.484	109.95	121.51	134.29
5.	148.41	164.02	181.27	200.34	221.41	244.69	270.43	298.87	330.30	365.04
6.	403.43	445.86	492.75	544.57	601.85	665.14	735.10	812.41	897.85	992.27
7.	1096.6	1212.0	1339.4	1480.3	1636.0	1808.0	1998.2	2208.3	2440.6	2697.3
8.	2981.0	3294.5	3641.0	4023.9	4447.1	4914.8	5431.7	6002.9	6634.2	7332.0
9.	8103.1	8955.3	9897.1	10938	12088	13360	14765	16318	18034	19930
10.	22026									

TABLE A2: Exponential Functions exp−U

μ	0	1	2	3	4	5	6	7	8	9
.0	1.00000	.99005	.98020	.97045	.96079	.95123	.94176	.93239	.92312	.91393
.1	.90484	.89583	.88692	.87810	.86936	.86071	.85214	.84366	.83527	.82696
.2	.81873	.81058	.80252	.79453	.78663	.77880	.77105	.76338	.75578	.74826
.3	.74082	.73345	.72615	.71892	.71177	.70469	.69768	.69073	.68386	.67706
.4	.67032	.66365	.65705	.65051	.64404	.63763	.63128	.62500	.61878	.61263
.5	.60653	.60050	.59452	.58860	.58275	.57695	.57121	.56553	.55990	.55433
.6	.54881	.54335	.53794	.53259	.52729	.52205	.51685	.51171	.50662	.50158
.7	.49659	.49164	.48675	.48191	.47711	.47237	.46767	.46301	.45841	.45384
.8	.44933	.44486	.44043	.43605	.43171	.42741	.42316	.41895	.41478	.41066
.9	.40657	.40252	.39852	.39455	.39063	.38674	.38289	.37908	.37531	.37158
1.0	.36788	.36422	.36060	.35701	.35345	.34994	.34646	.34301	.33960	.33622
1.1	.33287	.32956	.32628	.32303	.31982	.31664	.31349	.31037	.30728	.30422
1.2	.30119	.29820	.29523	.29229	.28938	.28650	.28365	.28083	.27804	.27527
1.3	.27253	.26982	.26714	.26448	.26185	.25924	.25666	.25411	.25158	.24908
1.4	.24660	.24414	.24171	.23931	.23693	.23457	.23224	.22993	.22764	.22537
1.5	.22313	.22091	.21871	.21654	.21438	.21225	.21014	.20805	.20598	.20393
1.6	.20190	.19989	.19790	.19593	.19398	.19205	.19014	.18825	.18637	.18452
1.7	.18268	.18087	.17907	.17728	.17552	.17377	.17204	.17033	.16864	.16696
1.8	.16530	.16365	.16203	.16041	.15882	.15724	.15567	.15412	.15259	.15107
1.9	.14957	.14808	.14661	.14515	.14370	.14227	.14086	.13946	.13807	.13670
2.0	.13534	.13399	.13266	.13134	.13003	.12873	.12745	.12619	.12493	.12369
2.1	.12246	.12124	.12003	.11884	.11765	.11648	.11533	.11418	.11304	.11192
2.2	.11080	.10970	.10861	.10753	.10646	.10540	.10435	.10331	.10228	.10127
2.3	.10026	.09926	.09827	.09730	.09633	.09537	.09442	.09348	.09255	.09163
2.4	.09072	.08982	.08892	.08804	.08716	.08629	.08543	.08458	.08374	.08291
2.5	.08208	.08127	.08046	.07966	.07887	.07808	.07730	.07654	.07577	.07502
2.6	.07427	.07353	.07280	.07208	.07136	.07065	.06995	.06925	.06856	.06788
2.7	.06721	.06654	.06587	.06522	.06457	.06393	.06329	.06266	.06204	.06142
2.8	.06081	.06020	.05961	.05901	.05843	.05784	.05727	.05670	.05613	.05558
2.9	.05502	.05448	.05393	.05340	.05287	.05234	.05182	.05130	.05079	.05029
3.0	.04979	.04929	.04880	.04832	.04783	.04736	.04689	.04642	.04596	.04550
3.1	.04505	.04460	.04416	.04372	.04328	.04285	.04243	.04200	.04159	.04117
3.2	.04076	.04036	.03996	.03956	.03916	.03877	.03839	.03801	.03763	.03725
3.3	.03688	.03652	.03615	.03579	.03544	.03508	.03474	.03439	.03405	.03371
3.4	.03337	.03304	.03271	.03239	.03206	.03175	.03143	.03112	.03081	.03050
3.5	.03020	.02990	.02960	.02930	.02901	.02872	.02844	.02816	.02788	.02760
3.6	.02732	.02705	.02678	.02652	.02625	.02599	.02573	.02548	.02522	.02497
3.7	.02472	.02448	.02423	.02399	.02375	.02352	.02328	.02305	.02282	.02260
3.8	.02237	.02215	.02193	.02171	.02149	.02128	.02107	.02086	.02065	.02045
3.9	.02024	.02004	.01984	.01964	.01945	.01925	.01906	.01887	.01869	.01850
4.	.018316	.016573	.014996	.013569	.012277	.011109	.010052	$.0^{2}90953$	$.0^{2}82297$	$.0^{2}74466$
5.	$.0^{2}67379$	$.0^{2}60967$	$.0^{2}55166$	$.0^{2}49916$	$.0^{2}45166$	$.0^{2}40868$	$.0^{2}36979$	$.0^{2}33460$	$.0^{2}30276$	$.0^{2}27394$
6.	$.0^{2}24788$	$.0^{2}22429$	$.0^{2}20294$	$.0^{2}18363$	$.0^{2}16616$	$.0^{2}15034$	$.0^{2}13604$	$.0^{2}12309$	$.0^{2}11138$	$.0^{2}10078$
7.	$.0^{3}91188$	$.0^{3}82510$	$.0^{3}74659$	$.0^{3}67554$	$.0^{3}61125$	$.0^{3}55308$	$.0^{3}50045$	$.0^{3}45283$	$.0^{3}40973$	$.0^{3}37074$
8.	$.0^{3}33546$	$.0^{3}30354$	$.0^{3}27465$	$.0^{3}24852$	$.0^{3}22487$	$.0^{3}20347$	$.0^{3}18411$	$.0^{3}16659$	$.0^{3}15073$	$.0^{3}13639$
9.	$.0^{3}12341$	$.0^{3}11167$	$.0^{3}10104$	$.0^{4}91424$	$.0^{4}82724$	$.0^{4}74852$	$.0^{4}67729$	$.0^{4}61283$	$.0^{4}55452$	$.0^{4}50175$
10.	$.0^{4}45400$									

TABLE A3: Student's t–Distribution

STUDENT'S *t* DISTRIBUTION

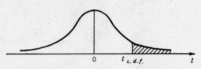

Degrees of Freedom	Probability of a Value Greater in Absolute Value than the Table Entry					
	0.01	0.02	0.05	0.1	0.2	0.3
1	63.657	31.821	12.706	6.314	3.078	1.963
2	9.925	6.965	4.303	2.920	1.886	1.386
3	5.841	4.541	3.182	2.353	1.638	1.250
4	4.604	3.747	2.776	2.132	1.533	1.190
5	4.032	3.365	2.571	2.015	1.476	1.156
6	3.707	3.143	2.447	1.943	1.440	1.134
7	3.499	2.998	2.365	1.895	1.415	1.119
8	3.355	2.896	2.306	1.860	1.397	1.108
9	3.250	2.821	2.262	1.833	1.383	1.100
10	3.169	2.764	2.228	1.812	1.372	1.093
11	3.106	2.718	2.201	1.796	1.363	1.088
12	3.055	2.681	2.179	1.782	1.356	1.083
13	3.012	2.650	2.160	1.771	1.350	1.079
14	2.977	2.624	2.145	1.761	1.345	1.076
15	2.947	2.602	2.131	1.753	1.341	1.074
16	2.921	2.583	2.120	1.746	1.337	1.071
17	2.898	2.567	2.110	1.740	1.333	1.069
18	2.878	2.552	2.101	1.734	1.330	1.067
19	2.861	2.539	2.093	1.729	1.328	1.066
20	2.845	2.528	2.086	1.725	1.325	1.064
21	2.831	2.518	2.080	1.721	1.323	1.063
22	2.819	2.508	2.074	1.717	1.321	1.061
23	2.807	2.500	2.069	1.714	1.319	1.060
24	2.797	2.492	2.064	1.711	1.318	1.059
25	2.787	2.485	2.060	1.708	1.316	1.058
26	2.779	2.479	2.056	1.706	1.315	1.058
27	2.771	2.473	2.052	1.703	1.314	1.057
28	2.763	2.467	2.048	1.701	1.313	1.056
29	2.756	2.462	2.045	1.699	1.311	1.055
30	2.750	2.457	2.042	1.697	1.310	1.055
∞	2.576	2.326	1.960	1.645	1.282	1.036

SOURCE: Reprinted from Table IV in Sir Ronald A. Fisher, *Statistical Methods for Research Workers*, 13th edition. Oliver & Boyd Ltd., Edinburgh, 1963, with the permission of the publisher and the late Sir Ronald Fisher's Literary Executor.

TABLE A4 : Table of the chi–square Distribution

area = 0.10

$f(Y_k)$

Example:
for $k = 10$ degrees of freedom
$P[Y_k > 15.99] = 0.10$

P \ k	0.995	0.99	0.975	0.95	0.90	0.75	0.50	0.25	0.10	0.05	0.025	0.01	0.005	P \ k
1	0.0^4393	0.0^3157	0.0^3982	$0.0^3 93$	0.0158	0.102	0.455	1.323	2.71	3.84	5.02	6.63	7.88	1
2	0.0100	0.0201	0.0506	0.103	0.211	0.575	1.386	2.77	4.61	5.99	7.38	9.21	10.60	2
3	0.0717	0.115	0.216	0.352	0.584	1.213	2.37	4.11	6.25	7.81	9.35	11.34	12.84	3
4	0.207	0.297	0.484	0.711	1.064	1.923	3.36	5.39	7.78	9.49	11.14	13.28	14.86	4
5	0.412	0.554	0.831	1.145	1.610	2.67	4.35	6.63	9.24	11.07	12.83	15.09	16.75	5
6	0.676	0.872	1.237	1.635	2.20	3.45	5.35	7.84	10.64	12.59	14.45	16.81	18.55	6
7	0.989	1.239	1.690	2.17	2.83	4.25	6.35	9.04	12.02	14.07	16.01	18.48	20.3	7
8	1.344	1.646	2.18	2.73	3.49	5.07	7.34	10.22	13.36	15.51	17.53	20.1	22.0	8
9	1.735	2.09	2.70	3.33	4.17	5.90	8.34	11.39	14.68	16.92	19.02	21.7	23.6	9
10	2.16	2.56	3.25	3.94	4.87	6.74	9.34	12.55	15.99	18.31	20.5	23.2	25.2	10
11	2.60	3.05	3.82	4.57	5.58	7.58	10.34	13.70	17.28	19.68	21.9	24.7	26.8	11
12	3.07	3.57	4.40	5.23	6.30	8.44	11.34	14.85	18.55	21.0	23.3	26.2	28.3	12
13	3.57	4.11	5.01	5.89	7.04	9.30	12.34	15.98	19.81	22.4	24.7	27.7	29.8	13
14	4.07	4.66	5.63	6.57	7.79	10.17	13.34	17.12	21.1	23.7	26.1	29.1	31.3	14
15	4.60	5.23	6.26	7.26	8.55	11.04	14.34	18.25	22.3	25.0	27.5	30.6	32.8	15
16	5.14	5.81	6.91	7.96	9.31	11.91	15.34	19.37	23.5	26.3	28.8	32.0	34.3	16
17	5.70	6.41	7.56	8.67	10.09	12.79	16.34	20.5	24.8	27.6	30.2	33.4	35.7	17
18	6.26	7.01	8.23	9.39	10.86	13.68	17.34	21.6	26.0	28.9	31.5	34.8	37.2	18
19	6.84	7.63	8.91	10.12	11.65	14.56	18.34	22.7	27.2	30.1	32.9	36.2	38.6	19
20	7.43	8.26	9.59	10.85	12.44	15.45	19.34	23.8	28.4	31.4	34.2	37.6	40.0	20

TABLE A4 (cont.)

	−2.58	−2.33	−1.960	−1.645	−1.282	−0.674	0.000	0.674	1.282	1.645	1.960	2.33	2.58	
21	8.03	8.90	10.28	11.59	13.24	16.34	20.3	24.9	29.6	32.7	35.5	38.9	41.4	21
22	8.64	9.54	10.98	12.34	14.04	17.24	21.3	26.0	30.8	33.9	36.8	40.3	42.8	22
23	9.26	10.20	11.69	13.09	14.85	18.14	22.3	27.1	32.0	35.2	38.1	41.6	44.2	23
24	9.89	10.86	12.40	13.85	15.66	19.04	23.3	28.2	33.2	36.4	39.4	43.0	45.6	24
25	10.52	11.52	13.12	14.61	16.47	19.94	24.3	29.3	34.4	37.7	40.6	44.3	46.9	25
26	11.16	12.20	13.84	15.38	17.29	20.8	25.3	30.4	35.6	38.9	41.9	45.6	48.3	26
27	11.81	12.88	14.57	16.15	18.11	21.7	26.3	31.5	36.7	40.1	43.2	47.0	49.6	27
28	12.46	13.56	15.31	16.93	18.94	22.7	27.3	32.6	37.9	41.3	44.5	48.3	51.0	28
29	13.12	14.26	16.05	17.71	19.77	23.6	28.3	33.7	39.1	42.6	45.7	49.6	52.3	29
30	13.79	14.95	16.79	18.49	20.6	24.5	29.3	34.8	40.3	43.8	47.0	50.9	53.7	30
40	20.7	22.2	24.4	26.5	29.1	33.7	39.3	45.6	51.8	55.8	59.3	63.7	66.8	40
50	28.0	29.7	32.4	34.8	37.7	42.9	49.3	56.3	63.2	67.5	71.4	76.2	79.5	50
60	35.5	37.5	40.5	43.2	46.5	52.3	59.3	67.0	74.4	79.1	83.3	88.4	92.0	60
70	43.3	45.4	48.8	51.7	55.3	61.7	69.3	77.6	85.5	90.5	95.0	100.4	104.2	70
80	51.2	53.5	57.2	60.4	64.3	71.1	79.3	88.1	96.6	101.9	106.6	112.3	116.3	80
90	59.2	61.8	65.6	69.1	73.3	80.6	89.3	98.6	107.6	113.1	118.1	124.1	128.3	90
100	67.3	70.1	74.2	77.9	82.4	90.1	99.3	109.1	118.5	124.3	129.6	135.8	140.2	100
Z_α	−2.58	−2.33	−1.960	−1.645	−1.282	−0.674	0.000	0.674	1.282	1.645	1.960	2.33	2.58	Z_α

Source: This table is abridged from 'Table of percentage points of the χ^2 distribution' by Catherine M. Thompson, *Biometrika* 32 (1941) pp. 187–91, and is published here by permission of the author and editor of *Biometrika*.

For $k > 100$ take $\chi^2 = \frac{1}{2}(Z_\alpha + \sqrt{(2k - 1)})^2$. Z_α is the standardised normal deviate corresponding to the α level of significance, and is shown in the bottom of the table.

On the Identification of the Functional Form of the Utility Expression and its Relationship to Discrete Choice

Jordan J. Louviere

B·1 Introduction

The purpose of this Appendix is to discuss ways in which the functional form of the utility expression in a choice model may be inferred from data and to demonstrate the relationship between the derivation of the utility function and the outcome(s) of the choice process.

There are two approaches available to assess the functional form of the utility expression. The first is called the 'direct assessment' approach; and the second, the 'choice' approach.

B·2 The `Direct Assessment´ Approach to Identifying the Functional Form of the Utility Expression of a Choice Model

'Direct assessment' refers to defining the utility function by simulating a number of choice alternatives, asking the individual to assign utility values to the alternatives, and then recovering the function from the data. Formally there are at least three approaches which can be shown to provide a useful first approximation to the function. The three approaches are based, respectively, on axiomatic utility theory, conjoint measurement, and functional measurement (see

Keeney & Raiffa, 1976; Krantz & Tversky, 1971;
Anderson, 1974, 1976; Louviere, 1978, 1979). Each
of these theories is a theory about the way in which
data must behave in order to be represented alge-
braically according to some multilinear algebraic
expression which maps the marginal utility values
into an overall utility value. Each approach differs
in the assumptions which it makes about the input
data, and as a result, each leads to a quite
different approach to specification of the function.
We will treat the case of riskless alternatives,
whose attribute levels are known to the individual,
and for which we wish to determine a preference
function. Thus individuals will be asked to
indicate their preferences for a set of alternatives.
Discussion is confined to the theory of functional
measurement because, of the three approaches, it
alone has a well developed theory of errors. From
time to time, however, we shall make reference to
similarities and differences between the functional
measurement approach and the other approaches.

B·2·1 Functional Measurement

Functional measurement refers to both the
theory by which human values may be modelled and
to the philosophy behind the approach to the measurement of subjective quantities which is derived from
the theory. We will term any subjective value
assessment of a set of multiattribute alternatives a
'utility assignment process' provided the values
being assigned have a direct bearing on choice among
the alternatives in a demand context. The values
which an individual assigns to the alternatives and
which are related to his/her choices or the
probabilities of such choices will be referred to as
'utility values', provided they are understood to be
made in the context of a 'utility assignment
process'.[1] Like both axiomatic utility theory and
conjoint measurement, functional measurement
postulates that utility-assignment processes of
humans may be represented by some algebraic
expression which is a subset of the general multilinear form. A multilinear algebraic expression is
one which is additive in its coefficients and
which includes terms in single attributes, products
of attributes and combinations of the two. The
most general form is one which includes all possible
single attribute terms, all possible products of two
attributes at a time, all possible products of three
attributes at a time, etc., up to and including a

final term representing the product of all of the attributes.

We will assume that this more general model or some more restricted form, such as strict addition, is the appropriate multiattribute descriptor of the utility-assignment process and the problem is to identify which of these forms is the 'most appropriate'. In order to do this an isomorphism needs to be developed between the terms in the multilinear 'utility' models and terms in the general-linear statistical model of analysis of variance and multiple-linear regression. In particular, we will regard both analysis of variance and multiple-linear regression as the error theory by which we may diagnose and test various hypotheses about the 'appropriate' forms of multilinear multiattribute 'utility-assignment processes'. We shall develop the algebraic theory behind the use of classical procedures taken from the design and analysis of experiments in statistics, demonstrate that it can be used to make powerful inferences regarding functional form, and illustrate its application in a case study. Following the illustration the necessary connections to choice theory are developed, with a demonstration that the outcome is consistent with the econometric theory developed in the body of the text. Denoting an attribute as a , where $k = 1,2,...,K$; marginal utilities as $u(a_k)$; and the overall utility assigned to a combination of k attribute levels as U, then

$$U = f(u(a_k)) \qquad (B.1)$$

where f is a mapping defined over the k attributes into the overall utility U. These marginal utility values, $u(a_k)$ are assumed to be related to observable attribute levels, denoted as x_k. Thus:

$$u(a_k) = g(x_k) \qquad (B.2)$$

where g is a mapping from x_k into a_k. By substitution we trivially derive:

$$U = f(g(x_k)) \qquad (B.3)$$

which establishes that utility or U must be related to observable components of attributes.[2] Equation (B.1) is emphasised in the discussion below,

although a complete specification must involve all
of the equations above.

Any multiattribute alternative may be expressed
as a combination of different levels of the relevant
attributes which define it. For example,
alternative boxes of ice cream in the grocer's
freezer may be described by at least some of the
following attributes: flavour, price, creaminess,
sweetness, and naturalness. Thus, four packages
may be described as follows:

(1)   Vanilla, $1.59 per half gallon,
moderately creamy, very sweet, mostly preservatives;
(2)   Chocolate, $1.59 per half gallon,
moderately creamy, very sweet, mostly preservatives;
(3)   Vanilla, $1.59 per half gallon,
moderately creamy, very sweet, all natural; and
(4)   Chocolate, $1.59 per half gallon,
moderately creamy, very sweet, all natural.

Suppose we observe choices among these four
packages and note that the fourth package is
selected. Nothing is known about the individual
choice behaviour other than the observation that
number four was selected. We need to either observe
the individual's choices over an extended period of
time and record the proportion of times each of
these four was selected, or observe the choice of a
large number of individuals at one or more points in
time vis-a-vis these four alternatives. Both of
these methods of observation have obvious drawbacks
in terms of time and resources.

Let us adopt a different approach: Suppose we
ask our individual under observation to rank order
preferences for these alternatives (assuming that
the individual can purchase any one of the alternatives and there are no attributes restraining choice
like an allergy to chocolate). The individual ranks
them 2, 4, 1, 3. We already have an immense amount
of information about this individual's preferences
and choices. Price, creaminess and sweetness are
constant over all alternatives and thus, they cannot
have influenced choice or preference. While they
are irrelevant as far as these alternatives are
concerned, they may not be irrelevant as far as
other alternatives are concerned. This is the first
point to note - statistically, we would be forced to
conclude that these three attributes had no
influence on preferences or choices; yet, if we
had examined another set of ice cream packages
over which these attributes took different values,
we may have concluded otherwise. Thus, one

388

objective is to define the set of 'relevant attributes' and assess their influence regardless of their necessary range in the real world.

By examining the way in which the ranks behave as we move from one level to the next, it can be concluded that both flavour and naturalness had an influence on preferences and choices. Note that all possible combinations of the two flavours vanilla and chocolate are paired with the two levels of naturalness, 'all natural' and 'mostly preservatives'; and that vanilla, 'all natural' was picked first. Vanilla, 'mostly preservative' was picked second. This implies that the attribute 'vanilla' dominates the preference ordering, with naturalness being secondary. We would like to be able to derive a simple expression for this pattern of dominance or tradeoff between flavour and naturalness. One procedure, conjoint measurement, could be used to find a set of marginal utility values that would reproduce or preserve the rank ordering of the original preferences. Unfortunately, there are a large number of possible marginal values which could satisfy this criterion - one set is vanilla = 1.0; chocolate = 0.0; all natural = 0.5; mostly preservative = 0.0. If the utility-assignment process is strictly additive, we would have the sums 1, 0.0, 2, and 0.5.[3]

This corresponds directly with the original rank order. But nothing has been learnt from this because we had to estimate four marginal utility values from four observations and there are a very large number of ways to do this and perfectly reproduce the rank order of the preferences.

Consider another approach to the same problem. Instead of having the individual rank order preferences, s/he compares them with a favourite, assigned the number '100' by the individual. The four ice cream alternatives are then assessed between zero and 100 by a response which is relative to one another and the individual's favourite. Suppose the individual assigns the numbers 70, 40, 90, 60. If we assume that each of these numbers represent a random number drawn from a normal distribution about some 'correct' number; and, hence, the individual is attributed a degree of inconsistency or self-measurement error, notions from the statistical theory of analysis of variance or multiple-linear regression can be applied to tell us that the individual has the following values for the attribute levels: vanilla = 80 units; chocolate = 50 units; all natural = 75 units; and mostly preservative = 55 units. This individual does not like chocolate flavouring relative to the other attribute levels.

How are these values derived and how can they be interpreted? The secret to the above analysis is that the ice cream combinations were assigned according to a factorial-design structure. A factorial-design structure is a way of combining attributes and their levels such that all possible combinations are represented. A factorial design is the key to the derivation of U functions.

Consider the following possible alternatives for lunch: a ham and cheese sandwich, a hamburger, and a roast-beef sandwich, as main courses; a coca-cola, a glass of milk, and a beer, as accompanying drinks, and A, B and C as places to buy lunch. There are 27 possible luncheon alternatives that can be identified by systematically combining sandwiches with drinks with places. These 27 alternatives are in actuality combinations of levels of attributes which constitute a complete factorial design. Let us refer to them as factors S for sandwich, factor D for drink, and factor P for eating place. Now, we would like to be able to predict an individual's choice behaviour among these 27 alternatives; to do so requires a U function:

$$U = f(u(S), u(D), u(P)) \qquad (B.4)$$

How can we specify the function f? The most general function in these three factors is

$$U = z_0 + z_1 u(S) + z_2 u(D) + z_3 u(P) + z_4 u(S) u(D) + z_5 u(S) u(P)$$
$$+ z_6 u(D) u(P) + z_7 u(S) u(D) u(P) \qquad (B.5)$$

where z's are scaling constants and $u(a_k)$'s are as previously defined. Let us further index equation (B.5) by subscripting each of the factors to take note of the factorial arrangement. Let there be $n (=1,2,3)$ levels of S, $m (=1,2,3)$ levels of D, and $\ell (=1,2,3)$ levels of P. Now rewrite equation (B.5):

$$U_{nm\ell} = z_0 + z_1 u(S_n) + z_2 u(D_m) + z_3 u(P_\ell) + z_4 u(S_n) u(D_m)$$
$$+ z_5 u(S_n) u(P_\ell) + z_6 u(D_m) u(P_\ell) + z_7 u(S_n) u(D_m) u(P_\ell) \qquad (B.6)$$

If we assume that the same individual interviewed before in the grocery store can provide estimates

of the degree of preference for these 27 alternatives on a scale that ranges from 0 to 100, where
100 is the favourite, then we can prove that the
marginal mean or average of each level of each
subscripted dimension is the desired measure of
$u(a_k)$ on a cardinal scale with arbitrary zero and
unit of measurement. To see this, first consider
the average across all occurrences of S_n. That is,
we average across all $m\ell$ combinations in which S_n
appears. In so doing we derive the following
(see Lerman & Louviere, 1979):

$$U_{n..} = Z_0 + Z_1 u(S_n) \qquad (B.7)$$

where $U_{n..}$ is the marginal mean of the nth dimension,
the Zs are collected terms, and $u(S_n)$ is as
previously defined. Equation (B.7) is an important
result because it says that so long as any multilinear algebraic form is an appropriate description
of the utility-assignment process, the marginal
mean from a factorial design is an estimate of the
'true' marginal utility value up to a linear
transformation. The latter can be seen by
rearranging equation (B.7) to give equation (B.8).

$$u(S_n) = \frac{U_{n..} - Z_0}{Z_1} \qquad (B.8)$$

Thus, the marginal means from the individual's data
are just as good as any other estimate of the
marginal utility values. This result is the key to
the entire theory of assessment of functional form.
We can directly test the coefficients in equations
(B.5) or (B.6) to see whether they are significantly
different from zero and this test permits us to
completely specify the individual's utility-
assignment process. This can be done in one of two
ways:

   (1)   If the individual will complete a minimum
of two replications of the judgments - that is, if
all of the alternatives (factorial combinations)
are judged twice, then repeated measures analysis
of variance can be used to analyse the response
data;
   (2)   If we can be certain that some of the
higher (or lower) order cross-product terms are zero

in theory and not significant in practice, then a test can be developed from only one replication or a single set of judgments about the alternatives. By taking each of the possible cases in turn, we can show how this is done.

B·2·2 Strict Additivity

If the individual were employing a strictly additive utility-assignment process, that is, if the individual was combining the marginal values in an additive manner, as is assumed in most applications of discrete-choice analysis (e.g. Section 4.5 of the text), then the 'true' function would be:

$$U_{nm\ell} = z_0 + z_1 u(S) + z_2 u(D) + z_3 u(P) + e \qquad (B.9)$$

where all terms are as defined before, except e, which is a normally distributed error term with expectation zero. Returning to equation (B.5), such a 'true' state of the world would require that coefficients z_4 to z_7 equal zero in theory and be nonsignificant in practice. Thus, a necessary and sufficient test for strict additivity of equation (B.9) is a test on the coefficients of the cross-product terms in an analysis of variance or multiple-linear regression. Technically, the cross-product terms are known as 'interactions', a term which we will adhere to henceforth in this discussion. Similarly, the marginal utility values would be isomorphic with the 'main effects' in an analysis of variance or regression analysis. Thus, in contradistinction to the usual practice in statistical analysis, we would like to retain the null hypothesis for coefficients z_4 to z_7 in order not to reject additivity. Thus, a key difference in strategy is emphasis on retention of various null hypotheses to define functional form.

B·2·3 Statistical Tests

Technically, we can express our design as a Sandwich x Drink x Place x replications, or 3 x 3 x 3 x 2 factorial design, where 2 refers to 'replications'. In order to use analysis of variance effectively, two replications are required. Assuming that we have them, we are interested in performing an analysis of variance for repeated measures, sometimes referred to as a 'within-subjects' design. In such a design the null hypothesis is evaluated not against residual mean square, as in the usual applications of multiple-linear regression in econometrics, but against the interactions of replications with each of the terms in question. That is, a test of the null hypothesis of no effect for sandwiches would be made by computing mean square for sandwiches and testing it against mean square for sandwiches x replications, the latter being the interaction of replications and the sandwiches effect. This tests whether the effect due to sandwiches is larger than the replication-to-replication variance in its effect. Thus, the variance due to sandwiches must be significantly larger than the variance in its effect across replications. Similarly, a test for the null hypothesis of no sandwiches x drinks inter-action is determined by the ratio of the mean square for the sandwiches x drinks interaction to the mean square of the sandwiches x drinks x replications interaction. As before, this tests whether the variance due to the sandwiches x drinks interaction is larger than the variance within that interaction across replications. Rejection of all interaction effects as to their significance is tantamount to acceptance of strict additivity.

A second method for conducting the test could be employed on a single replication if, and only if, the analyst knew for certain that some of the regression effects were zero in theory. Returning to equation (B.6), we could use each of the marginal means as estimates of their corresponding marginal utility values in a multiple-linear regression analysis. However, they cannot be directly employed because their cross-products would not be independent of one another or of the main effects.

Independence is required to fully utilise the power of the test. Independence is achieved by orthogonalising each of the sets of marginal means with respect to one another. The method for doing this is referred to as the method of orthogonal polynomials and may be referenced in any standard statistical text on factorial experiments. Our problem, however, is somewhat complicated by the fact that it is highly unlikely that the marginal means will be equally spaced in their values. That is, the numerical difference between mean at level 1 and mean at level 2 will not be the same as the numerical difference between mean at level 2 and mean at level 3. When unequal spacing occurs, which

will be the general case in this test, local sets of
orthogonal polynomials must be computed rather than
using available tabled values. A simple method for
computing such values is given by Robson (1959),
permitting any set of marginal means to be
orthogonalised. If there are n levels of an attribute, one must create (n-1) polynomials; hence, a
3-level attribute requires 2 orthogonal polynomials,
and a 5-level attribute requires 4. In the current
example, each attribute would require 2 orthogonal
polynomials. These would be referred to as a linear
and a quadratic polynomial. A complete statistical
representation of these polynomial terms would be
expressed as equation (B.10).

$$U = b_0 + b_1 u(S) + b_2 u(S)^2 + b_3 u(D) + b_4 u(D)^2 + b_5 u(P) + b_6 u(P)^2$$

(all the main effects)

$$+ b_7 u(S) u(D) + b_8 u(S) u(D)^2 + b_9 u(S)^2 u(D) + b_{10} u(S)^2 u(D)^2$$

(all the S x D interactions)

$$+ b_{11} u(S) u(P) + b_{12} u(S) u(P)^2 + b_{13} u(S)^2 u(P) + b_{14} u(S)^2 u(P)^2$$

(the S x P interactions)

$$+ b_{15} u(D) u(P) + b_{16} u(D) u(P)^2 + b_{17} u(D)^2 u(P) + b_{18} u(D)^2 u(P)^2$$

(the D x P interactions)

$$+ b_{19} u(S) u(D) u(P) + b_{20} u(S) u(D) u(P)^2 + b_{21} u(S) u(D)^2 u(P)$$

$$+ b_{22} u(S) u(D)^2 u(P)^2$$

$$+ b_{23} u(S)^2 u(D) u(P) + b_{24} u(S)^2 u(D) u(P)^2$$

$$+ b_{25} u(S)^2 u(D)^2 u(P) + b_{26} u(S)^2 u(D)^2 u(P)^2$$

(all of the three-way interactions)

$$+ e \qquad\qquad (B.10)$$

where all of the terms are as previously defined and
the b's are regression constants. The $u(a_k)^2$ terms
represent an orthogonal polynomial transformation of
$u(a_k)$ such that each of the $u(a_k)$ and $u(a_k)^2$
vectors sum to zero, as do all of the $u(a_k) u(a_{k'})$
cross-products, and all of their inner products are
zero. The logic of this test may be grasped by

noting that if the individual completes only a single replication of the judgment task (judges all 27 combinations only once), the complete statistical representation of the data as given by equation (B.10) would require as many constants as there are observations. This situation could be ameliorated by expressing the dependent variable as a deviation from means and estimating the regression constants through a zero intercept. This would permit a one degree of freedom test on all of the remaining terms. Another approach is to employ stepwise multiple-linear regression, accumulating degrees of freedom into the residual which are statistically not significant. Those readers accustomed to applications of stepwise multiple-linear regression procedures on nonorthogonal data sets might note that stepwise and multiple-regression procedures yield identical results when all attribute vectors are independent (orthogonal). Thus, the resulting coefficients are identical, but the accumulated degrees of freedom should permit a stronger test of the terms than the one degree of freedom test suggested earlier.

Again consider strict additivity. This condition would require that only the b_1, b_3, and b_5 terms be statistically significant; all remaining terms should be nonsignificant. Indeed, as may be noted, this approach constitutes a general diagnosis' and testing method using the error theory of regression and analysis of variance.

B·2·4 Strict Multiplication

Strict multiplication may be represented as equation (B.11).

$$U = z_0 + z_1 u(S) u(D) u(P) + e \qquad (B.11)$$

where all terms are as previously defined, z's are empirically defined scaling constants, and e is a random error term with zero mean. On the surface, equation (B.11) would seem to require that only b_{19} be statistically significant in equation (B.10). Such is not the case, however, and we proceed to prove that strict multiplication requires that all of the nonsquared terms be statistically significant in equation (B.10). First, return to equation (B.8) and substitute the marginal mean as an estimate of the $u(a_k)$'s in equation (B.11). This will result in the following general form:

$$U_{nm\ell} = z_0 + z_1((z_0' + z_1'U_{n..})(z_0'' + z_1''U_{.m.})(z_0''' z_1''' U_{..\ell})) + e \qquad (B.12)$$

where all terms are as previously defined. Equation (B.12) when expanded will yield the expectation that all nonsquared terms in equation (B.10) be statistically significant. In terms of an analysis of variance test, if there are two replications, the equation requires that all terms in the analysis of variance be different from zero. More importantly, however, equation (B.11) requires that all of the variation in the terms in the analysis of variance be concentrated in the linear, linear x linear, linear x linear x linear, etc. terms. This latter test requires a regression test.

B·2·5 Subset Multilinear Forms

Addition and multiplication are two ends of the spectrum of multilinear models. All other reduced forms may be diagnosed and tested by consideration of the procedures outlined for addition and multiplication. For example, suppose the following form is hypothesised:

$$U = z_0 + z_1 u(P)(u(S) + u(D)) \qquad (B.13)$$

This equation implies that individuals treat sandwiches and drinks independently - trade one off for the other in a compensatory manner - but rely heavily on eating place to make their decisions, using it as a multiplicative weighting device. This type of utility-assignment process might hold, for example, if individuals strongly differentiated sandwiches and drinks by eating place, but maintained the same identical preference patterns for sandwiches and drinks within each place.

Returning to equation (B.10) as a basis for statistical testing (or diagnoses) of this hypothesis, equation (B.13) demands that the following coefficients be statistically significant: b_1, b_3, b_5, b_{11} and b_{15}. No other coefficients can be statistically significant. In an analysis of variance context, equation (B.13) requires that all of the 'main effects' of the three factors be significant and the sandwich x place and the drink x place interactions. All other interactions must be zero.

B·2·6 Developing a Mapping from Observables

Once the nature of the utility function is known, the marginal utility function can be estimated in units of the original variables. In the case of sandwiches, drinks and places, our work is done because they have no original measurement units other than those obtained.

Consider a case with original units of measurement: Suppose we have a product, refrigerators, and we are examining individuals' utilities and choices for various alternatives. Suppose that the relevant attributes are price, cubic footage of refrigerator capacity, cubic footage of freezer capacity, and colour. The first three attributes have observable measures and the last does not. Thus, we would like to be able to obtain a mapping of these observable attributes into the marginal utility values with which they correspond. In other words, we wish to estimate equation (B.2), or simultaneously estimate equation (B.3).

Unless there are compelling theoretical reasons for expecting a particular functional relationship between observable values and marginal means or marginal utility values, this part of the functional assessment problem is strictly empirical, that is, it entails curve-fitting to the observed data. However, the approach permits the relationships of interest to be graphed and a form selected among a few 'reasonable' function forms. For example, the following might be common fitted forms:

$$U_{k..} = \alpha_0 + \alpha_1 x + \alpha_2 x_k^2 + e$$

$$U_{k..} = \alpha_0' + \alpha_1' (x_k)^{\alpha_2'} + e$$

$$U_{k..} = \alpha_0'' + \alpha_1'' \exp(\alpha_2'' + \alpha_3'' x_k) + e$$

$$U_{k..} = \alpha_0''' + \alpha_1''' \ln(x_k) + e \qquad (B.14)$$

where $U_{k..}$ is the marginal mean of the evaluations on the kth attribute, x_k is the corresponding observable attribute, and α's are empirical constants to be estimated. The selection of a form depends on the problem, its context, theory which may apply, and the predilections of the analyst.

In the refrigerator example, suppose we asked the individual to make 5 x 2 evaluations, where there were five levels of price ($350, $400, $500, $750 and $900), cubic footage of refrigeration space (14ft.^{3}, 16ft.^{3}, 19ft.^{3}, 23ft.^{3}, and 28ft.^{3}), freezer space (5ft.^{3}, 7ft.^{3}, 10ft.^{3}, 12ft.^{3}, and 14ft. , and two colours (white and gold). The subject's hypothetical response data are given in Figure B.1.

FIGURE B·1

Examples of Marginal Relationships with Objective Attribute Valves

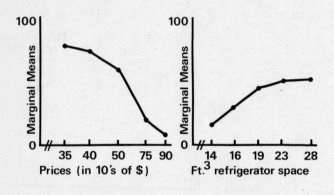

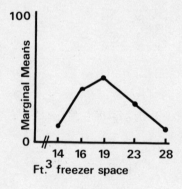

Figure B.1 illustrates several plausible types of marginal relationships. In the case of prices, one could approximate the relationship between actual prices and marginal responses with a linear equation or perhaps an exponential form to catch the curvature evident at the top left-hand portion of the curve. In the refrigeration space graph, there is an evident non-linearity which is described as increasing at a decreasing rate. Several of the curve forms in equation (B.14) might do - an equation in ℓn (refrigeration space), one in refrigeration space and space squared, an exponential form, etc. Freezer space, however, narrows the most likely choice to a polynomial of degree two with freezer space and freezer space squared. The important point is that we need to know the utility-assignment process in order to be able to properly combine these marginal relationships. Suppose the utility-assignment process was found to be multiplicative. We would then estimate either simultaneously or separately[4] the marginals and the overall combination function. In the case of a multiplicative expression, we would now have an equation which would have quite a few terms in it, including both main effects and cross-products. It is this latter general form that would be a candidate for estimation on real choice data.

For example, Lerman & Louviere (1979) developed a simple description of a utility-assignment process for choice of town as a place to live and then estimated this form on real data regarding towns which had been selected as residence places by mining and construction workers in the United States of America Rocky Mountain region. This functional form was then compared for performance against a sizeable number of other functional forms. The utility-assignment process form outperformed all other competing forms in terms of goodness-of-fit, residual error, adjusted fit, and significance of terms. We now proceed to demonstrate the connection between the utility-assignment process and choice behaviour.

B·3 A Choice Theoretic Approach to Determining Functional Form

In a choice context the individual is confronted by some array of alternatives (i.e. a choice set - see Chapter 4) from which only one can be selected (unless we are interested in the choice behaviour of an individual over time). Each of the alternatives differs in some observable manner from the others in the choice set A. Assume that these differences are reflective of differences in levels of the attributes which affect choices, and that the choice set contains only feasible alternatives. These are alternatives which:

(a) are not strictly dominated by other alternatives in A;

(b) can actually be selected, e.g. those which the individual can afford; and

(c) the individual has sufficient information on which to make a choice - i.e. those known to the individual.

Domination refers to any alternative which is worse than a second on all attributes considered by the individual; the former would never be in the set A, while the latter would. In the case of information, we assume that observable dimensions like incomes, locations, etc. serve as important determinants of information use and availability.

Thus, we begin by assuming that the individual is confronted with a set of A alternatives in which there are j feasible alternatives available $(j=1, 2,..., i,...J)$. We now consider how the ith alternative comes to be selected. Let us first consider how many different choice sets there are in A. There are 2^J choice sets in A because an alternative which is feasible may either be available for choice or not. Thus, there are 2^J possibilities, if we include one set in which no alternatives are available and J sets in which only one is available. Suppose there are four sandwiches and drinks in the set A. Then $J = 4$ and there are 16 possible feasible choice sets. Let us say that the sandwiches are a cheeseburger or a hot dog, and the drinks are milk or water. The four alternatives are (1) cheeseburger and milk, (2) cheeseburger and water, (3) hot dog and milk, and (4) hot dog and water. The enumeration of all of the choice sets in A is given in Table B.1. Let us assume that the individual was asked to judge the four alternatives on the 0 to 100 point ratings scale. The individual assigns the numbers 80 to cheeseburger and milk, 60 to hot dog and milk, 50 to cheeseburger and water, and 30 to hot dog and water. We can ascertain from analysis of the utility-assignment process that the individual is strictly additive. We then confront the individual with the 16 choice sets and observe which alternative is selected in each. The

400

TABLE B·1: An Enumeration of the Choice Sets in the Set A

Choice set number	Cheeseburger and milk	Cheeseburger and water	Hot dog and milk	Hot dog and water
1	0	0	0	0
2	0	0	0	1
3	0	0	1	0
4	0	0	1	1
5	0	1	0	0
6	0	1	0	1
7	0	1	1	0
8	0	1	1	1
9	1	0	0	0
10	1	0	0	1
11	1	0	1	0
12	1	0	1	1
13	1	1	0	0
14	1	1	0	1
15	1	1	1	0
16	1	1	1	1

0 = absent from the choice set; 1 = present and available in the choice set.

---

individual is assumed to be consistent; that is, the alternative with the highest U value is always selected whenever it is available. In that case, the individual's marginal choice proportions can be specified as follows: cheeseburger and milk = 1.0; hot dog and milk = 0.5; chesseburger and water = 0.25; and hot dog and water = 0.125. These numbers may be derived directly from Table B.1 by counting the number of times each alternative would be selected when it is available. Cheese-burger and milk is available exactly half of the time and it should be selected every time it is available, or 100%. Hot dog and milk is then available half of the time in the remaining half of the original choice sets. It would be selected every time it was available in that set, or 50 per cent of the time that it was originally available in the whole set. Similarly, each of the remaining two alternatives is available in half of the remaining sets and they are selected in order of utility values half of each of the remaining times choices are made.

This yields the expectation that a geometric series will be the outcome of this choice process. In particular, this geometric series is of the form

FIGURE B·2:

The Relationship Between Utility and Marginal Choice Probability

(a)

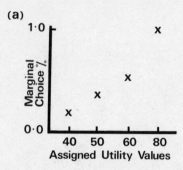

X denotes a co-ordinate point of the cross-product set

(b)

	cheeseburger	hot dog	marginal
milk	1.0	0.5	0.75
water	0.25	0.125	0.1875
marginal	0.625	0.3125	0.46875

$1/2^{(n-1)}$, where n is the order of the U value for the alternative in question. Let us examine the nature of the relationship between utility and marginal probability of choice. This is given in Figure B.2 above.

The results in Figure B.2 (a) can be represented as a 2 x 2 matrix (Figure B.2 (b)). It can now be demonstrated that the U function for choices is strictly multiplicative. If we multiply the marginal probability for cheeseburger (0.625) by the marginal probability for milk (0.75) and divide by the average probability for the entire table (0.46875), we obtain exactly 1.0, the desired result for cheeseburger and milk. Thus, the function is multiplicative in its marginals; and it is an easy matter to convince ourselves that this $\underline{must}$ be true for any choice function in which the individual is strictly ordinally consistent. Hence, we now know that the overall marginal choice function is multiplicative.[5] Thus, assuming the equivalence of relative frequency and probability,

$$\bar{p}(i) = (\bar{p}_A)^{-(k-1)} \prod_k \bar{p}(a_{ik}) \qquad \text{(B.15)}$$

where $\bar{p}(i)$ is the marginal probability of choosing alternative i, given that it is available; $(\bar{p}_A)^{-(k-1)}$ is the reciprocal of the average probability of selecting any of the j alternatives in A raised to the power (k-1), where k is the number of attributes, $\bar{p}(a_{ik})$ is the marginal probability associated with attribute a_{ik}. Equation (B.15) states that the marginal probability of selecting any i from the set of j alternatives in A is a product of the marginals of the marginal probabilities associated with each combination of attribute levels divided by the reciprocal of the grand average of the marginal probabilities raised to the (k-1) power (Anderson, 1974, 1976). This formulation assumes strict independence.

To predict the probability of selecting an alternative i from any choice set with j alternatives, we would write:

$$P(i \mid i \in A \,\forall\, j \in A) = \bar{p}(i) / \sum_{j \in A} \bar{p}(j), \qquad \text{(B.16)}$$

where $P(i \mid i \in A \,\forall\, j \in A)$ is the probability of selecting i, given that i is in the set A for all j in A and $\bar{p}(i)$ and $\bar{p}(j)$ are as previously defined. By substitution then:

$$p(i \mid i \in A \,\forall\, j \in A) = (\bar{p}_A)^{-(k-1)} \prod_k \bar{p}(a_{ik}) / \sum_{j \in A} (\bar{p}_A)^{-(k-1)} \prod_k \bar{p}(a_{jk})$$

$$\text{(B.17)}$$

If we let $\qquad \bar{p}(a_{ik}) = f(x_{ik}),$ $\qquad\qquad$ (B.18)

where f is a mapping from objectively measurable attribute values to marginal probabilities associated with these attribute values; then substituting equation (B.18) in equation (B.17)

403

gives

$$P(i|i \in A \nleftrightarrow j \in A) = (\bar{p}_A)^{-(k-1)} \prod_k [f(x_{ik})] / \sum_{j \in A} (\bar{p}_A)^{-(k-1)} \prod_k [f(x_{jk})]$$

(B.19)

where $f(x_{ik})$ is the tradeoff function implied by the choice behaviour. Equation (B.19) is a form of the multinomial logit model of discrete-choice theory. The multinomial logit form can be deduced by assuming that there is a random error component associated with the attribute functions which is independent of the tradeoff function and distributed as a double exponential.

The remainder of this Appendix presents an illustrative application of the theory development in utility assessment and choice assessment applied to choices among alternative airline tickets for travel to a common destination.

B·4 A Case Study — International Air Fares and Ticket Conditions

The case study deals with the preferences and choices of potential international air travellers for various reduced air fare tickets for travel from Australia to the United States West Coast. We shall concentrate on describing the relationship between preferences, choices and various attributes of reduced fare tickets:

(1)   air fare in Australian dollars;
(2)   advance-purchase requirement or how many days in advance one must pay for a ticket;
(3)   the number of stopovers permitted en route, and
(4)   the cancellation penalty or the per cent of the advance payment that is foregone if a reservation is cancelled.

In order to observe, measure and model preferences and choices among various reduced fare tickets, two experimental designs are developed - one to study preferences and a second for choices.

B·4·1 Analysis of Preferences

A study design can be developed based on principles from the design of factorial experiments in statistics (Winer, 1971) by arbitrarily dividing each of the attributes into 'high' and 'low' values.

This binary classification yields $(2)^4$ possible combinations of 'high' and 'low' values on each attribute. A complete factorial design requires 16 combinations of 'high' and 'low' values. These combinations are displayed in columns 2 to 5 of Table B.2.

TABLE B·2: Complete Factorial Enumeration of Attribute Combinations

FACTORIAL DESIGN

No.	Fare	Advance Payment	No. of Stopovers	Cancellation Penalty
1	L	L	L	L
2	L	L	L	H
3	L	L	H	L
4	L	L	H	H
5	L	H	L	L
6	L	H	L	H
7	L	H	H	L
8	L	H	H	H
9	H	L	L	L
10	H	L	L	H
11	H	L	H	L
12	H	L	H	H
13	H	H	L	L
14	H	H	L	H
15	H	H	H	L
16	H	H	H	H

ACTUAL SAMPLING DESIGN

No.	Fare	Advance Payment	No. of Stopovers	Cancellation Penalty
1	$ 240	14 days	2	25%
2	$ 360	7 days	4	75%
3	$ 480	21 days	15	0%
4	$ 600	0 days	20	50%
5	$ 600	60 days	NONE	40%
6	$ 480	90 days	1	100%
7	$ 360	45 days	7	10%
8	$ 240	120 days	10	60%
9	$ 780	14 days	1	40%
10	$ 900	7 days	NONE	100%
11	$1020	21 days	10	0%
12	$1080	0 days	7	50%
13	$1080	60 days	4	10%
14	$1020	90 days	2	60%
15	$ 900	45 days	20	25%
16	$ 780	120 days	15	75%

A nonsystematic sampling procedure was employed to generate four 'high' and 'low' values for each attribute. These values were then assigned on a nonsystematic basis to each combination in the factorial design with reference to the factorial design code. The purpose of this procedure is to retain as much of the original factorial structure for statistical reasons, while ensuring a wide range of sampling values over the range of each attribute. Interviewees were shown a 'standard' ticket (which was very close to an average: fare = $700; advance payment = 45 days; stopovers = 1 to 2; penalty = 50%) and asked to judge how much 'better' or 'worse' each of the 16 tickets were compared to this standard on a 13 category scale, described on one end by 'very much less desirable than standard'; on the other end by 'very much more desirable than standard'; and, in the middle by 'about the same as standard'. Interviewees checked one of 13 boxes beneath the verbal labels just described that best matched how they evaluated each ticket. Data were recorded as numbers between one and thirteen and were analysed by means of multiple-linear regression and analysis of variance. Thirty-five interviewees volunteered to participate in this study and the following choice study. Results indicate the possibility of only two interactions, one between fare and advance-payment requirement, and a second between advance-payment requirement and stopovers. Of the two, only the first is very large relative to the main effects of the attributes by themselves. This result implies that cost and advance-purchase requirement are not independent of one another. Graphical analysis suggests a multiplicative relationship, which implies that each attribute modifies and/or intensifies the effect of the other, depending upon whether they are respectively at a 'bad' or 'good' level. Despite this result, it is nonetheless true that an additive regression equation should provide a good approximation to the judgment process. We have derived two equations, one relative to the original 13 category judgment scale and a second which is based on a linear transform of the judgment scale such that the largest average score of the 16 combinations is assigned the value 1.0, and the smallest average score receives 0.0. This forces all scores to range between 0.0 and 1.0 so that they might later be compared with the results of the choice analysis.

The two equations are given below:

Judgment
Response = 14.125 - .0089 (fare) - .0271 (Advance Purchase)
         + .0933 (Stops) - 3.066 (Cancellation)
             (Untransformed) R^2 = .98   (B.20)

Judgment
Response = 1.338 - .0093 (fare) - .0037 (Advance Purchase)
         + .0095 (Stops) - .3180 (Cancellation)
             (Transformed) R^2 = .98   (B.21)

Results indicate that fare has the largest effect, followed by advance-purchase requirement, cancellation penalty and stopovers.[6] Thus, if these results were representative of the population, one would achieve the greatest change in choice behaviour by manipulating fare and advance-purchase requirement, particularly because they are slightly jointly multiplicative. This latter result implies that very low fares and low advance-purchase requirements will have considerably more than their independent effects on choice.

Let us now investigate whether this relationship also holds for choices by designing and adminstering a choice experiment based on these same four attributes.

B·4·2 Analysis of Choices

In order to analyse choice behaviour, we need to design a choice experiment which allows us to observe, measure and model individual choices. Following the logic of the body of the Appendix, two experimental designs are created:

(a) a tradeoff design, similar to the factorial design developed to analyse preferences, and (b) a choice design in which the availability of the ticket alternatives developed in (a) are varied.

Let us develop each design in turn. A preference or tradeoff design is developed by creating a fractional factorial design from four attributes. This is done by creating another $(2)^4$ factorial design ('high' and 'low') and selecting half of the 16 combinations in such a way that all of the marginal (or 'main') effects are independent of two-way dependencies (Hahn & Shapiro, 1966). This design is listed in Table B.3. We deliberately include four combinations which are identical in design code to combinations number four and five.

407

TABLE B·3: Trade Off Task Design

FACTORIAL DESIGN

No.	Fare A$	Advance Payment	No. of Stopovers	Cancellation Penalty
1	L	L	L	H
2	L	L	H	L
3	L	H	L	L
4*	L	H	H	H
5**	H	L	L	L
6	H	L	H	H
7	H	H	L	H
8	H	H	H	L
9*	L	H	H	H
10*	L	H	H	H
11**	H	L	L	L
12**	H	L	L	L

ACTUAL SAMPLING DESIGN

No.	Fare A$	Advance Payment	No. of Stopovers	Cancellation Penalty
1	$ 360	21 days	0	75%
2	$ 600	7 days	SOME	40%
3	$ 600	45 days	1-2	10%
4*	$ 240	120 days	SOME	100%
5**	$1020	7 days	0	10%
6	$1020	21 days	SOME	50%
7	$ 780	90 days	1-2	50%
8	$ 900	45 days	SOME	40%
9*	$ 360	90 days	SOME	50%
10*	$ 480	60 days	SOME	60%
11**	$1080	0 days	0	0%
12**	$ 780	14 days	0	25%

* denotes the three combinations which are correlated
  (L H H H)
** denotes the three combinations which are correlated
  (H L L L)

Their purpose is to permit us to test the constant ratio rule or the IIA property of the choice model (see Chapter 5). That is, because two sets of three highly correlated alternatives are deliberately included, it permits direct testing of whether such correlations have a direct effect on the choice process such that they cause IIA to be violated. Now that we have the alternatives, the choice experiment can be designed. To do this each

of the 12 tickets are treated as a factor which can
take the values, present or absent. There are $(2)^{12}$
or 4,096 possible combinations of the alternatives;
each combination represents a choice set because it
enumerates which alternatives are present and which
are absent. There are, however, too many choice
sets. The number needs to be reduced while
retaining statistical independence of each alternative so that unbiased estimates of the marginal
choice frequencies of each alternative can be
obtained. That is, the frequency with which each
alternative is chosen given that it is available
(= present). Once again, we return to principles
from the design of factorial experiments to develop
a fractional factorial design that requires 16
combinations (choice sets), and if the choice model
is correct, permits us to guarantee independence
of the alternatives for statistical estimation.
This design is listed in Table B.4, where the ticks
indicate the alternatives in each choice set.
Fifteen choice sets are required because one is a
null set (i.e. containing no alternatives). This
design indicates which of the choice alternatives
are to be offered with which other alternatives in
a choice set. The interviewees' task is to read
through the choice alternatives offered and choose
one and only one. The analysis is carried out
entirely on the frequency with which each
alternative is chosen in each choice set and the
marginal choice frequencies calculated over all
choice sets. The same 35 individuals who partici-
pated in the preference study also completed the
choice study.
     As a first step in the analysis of the data,
the absolute choice frequencies of each of the 12
tickets in each of the 15 choice sets are tabulated.
Then they are converted to relative frequencies by
the formula:

$$f(i;A) = f'(i)/ \sum_{j \in A} f'(j) \qquad \text{(B.22)}$$

where $f(i;A)$ is the relative frequency of
           alternative i in choice set A.

           $f'(i)$ is the absolute frequency of
           i in A.

           $f'(j)$ is the absolute frequency of
           each $j \in A$.

Either the absolute or relative frequencies may then
be used to determine the marginal frequences of each

409

TABLE B·4: Choice Task Design

	CHOICE	ALTERNATIVES				
1 FARE ($)	1020	1020	780	900	360	600
2 PAY AHEAD (days)	7	21	90	45	21	7
3 STOPOVERS (No.)	0	Some	1-2	Some	0	Some
4 CANCELLATION (%)	10	50	75	40	75	40
1						
2					✓	
3				✓	✓	✓
4				✓	✓	✓
5		✓	✓			
6		✓	✓		✓	
7		✓	✓	✓		✓
8		✓	✓	✓	✓	✓
9	✓		✓		✓	✓
10	✓		✓		✓	✓
11	✓		✓	✓	✓	
12	✓		✓	✓	✓	
13	✓	✓				✓
14	✓	✓			✓	✓
15	✓	✓		✓		
16	✓	✓		✓	✓	
1 FARE ($)	600	360	1080	780	480	240
2 PAY AHEAD (days)	45	90	0	14	60	120
3 STOPOVERS (No.)	1-2	Some	0	0	Some	Some
4 CANCELLATION (%)	10	50	0	25	60	100
1						
2	✓	✓	✓	✓	✓	
3	✓	✓			✓	✓
4			✓	✓		✓
5	✓		✓		✓	✓
6		✓		✓		✓
7		✓	✓			
8	✓			✓	✓	
9	✓	✓	✓	✓		✓
10					✓	✓
11			✓	✓	✓	
12	✓	✓		✓	✓	
13		✓		✓	✓	
14	✓			✓		
15	✓			✓		✓
16		✓	✓		✓	✓

410

TABLE B·4 (cont.) — NOTES

1. FARE ($)   IS THE COST OF THE TICKET in Australian dollars

2. PAY AHEAD (days) IS THE NUMBER OF DAYS BEFORE YOU DEPART that you must pay for your ticket, e.g. 45 days, means that you must pay for your ticket 45 days before you leave.

3. STOPOVERS (No.) IS THE NUMBER OF STOPOVERS YOU MAY MAKE EN ROUTE to your destination, e.g. 4 means you can make 4 stopovers en route.

4. CANCELLATION (%) IS THE PER CENT OF YOUR TICKET COST THAT YOU LOSE IF YOU CANCEL, e.g. 75% means you lose 75% of what you paid.

      √ Indicates that the alternative is available

---

alternative by means of the following formula:

$$f((i;T);A) = \sum_{\forall i \in T} f(i;A)/(T/2) \qquad (B.23)$$

where $f((i;T);A)$ is the relative frequency of the alternative i in all of the T choice sets, T is the set of all choice sets, $f(i;A)$ is as previously defined, and T/2 is the number of choice sets divided by two, this division occurring because the basic design is drawn from a 2^n design which requires each alternative to appear in exactly half of the choice sets.

The choice model predicts that:

$$f(i;A) = f((i;T);A)/\sum_{\forall j \in A} f((j;T);A) \qquad (B.24)$$

where $f((j;T);A)$ is the marginal relative frequency of all of the j alternatives in A, and other terms are as previously defined.

In calculating the marginal frequencies the sums and averages are best least-squares estimates with heteroskedasticity. To correct for this problem we apply the well-known transformation:

$$t(i;A) = SIN^{-1} (f(i;A))^{\frac{1}{2}} \qquad (B.25)$$

where $t(i;A)$ is the transformed relative frequency of i in A, and

SIN^{-1} $(f(i;A))^{\frac{1}{2}}$ is the square root of the Arcsin of the relative frequency of i in A.

A similar transformation is applied to $f((j;T);A)$. All tests are then carried out on the transformed data. The results are illustrated in Figure B.3. A regression test of the results indicates that the best fitting line is given by equation (B.26).

$$f(i;A) = -.007447 + 1.05 \left[f(i;T) / \sum_{j \in A} f((j;T);A) \right] \quad (B.26)$$

FIGURE B.3

Observed Vs. Predicted Choice Frequencies

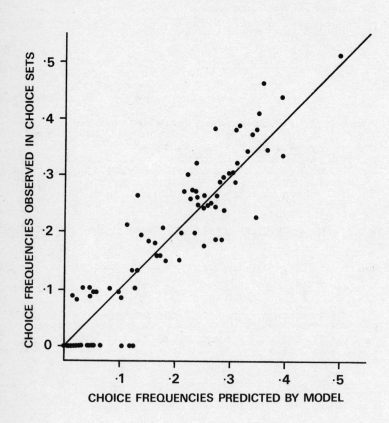

The model accounts for 88 per cent of the variance in the choice proportions. The slope and intercept are within the 95 per cent confidence bands for the theoretical values of zero and unity; hence, the choice model provides an excellent account of the data.

It should be noted that this latter test is utility-function free in that it does not require any assumptions about the form of the utility function. There are a number of ways in which this utility function can be estimated by means of theory developed in the main text. We choose, however, to use a multiple-linear regression approach in order to make estimates comparable with those from the transformed data in the preference study. In general, however, it would be preferable to use the logit estimates. Nonetheless, because independent estimates of the marginals are available from the choice study the marginals can be used directly to estimate a regression equation as a first approximation to the choice function. That is, the following equation is estimated:

$$t[f((j;T);A)] = b_0 + b_1 \text{ (fare)} + b_2 \text{ (advance purchase)}$$
$$+ b_3 \text{ (stopovers)} + b_4 \text{ (cancellation)} + \varepsilon$$

$$(B.27)$$

where $t[f((j;T);A)]$ is the ARCSIN $(f((j;T);A))^{\frac{1}{2}}$

The estimates for this equation are:

$$t[f((j;T);A] = 4.544 - .0029 \text{ (fare)} - .0081 \text{ (advance}$$
$$\text{purchase)}$$
$$+ .0201 \text{ (stopovers)} - .786 \text{ (cancellation)}$$

$$(B.28)$$

which is significant beyond the .001 level and accounts for 95.5 per cent of the variation in the data. All attributes have the right sign and are significant at the .05 level. The comparable equation for the judgments estimated on the transformed judgment data[7] is equation (B.29).

$$t(J(j)) = - 0.56 - .0028 \text{ (fare)} - .0089 \text{ (advance purchase)}$$
$$+ .0332 \text{ (stopovers)} - 1.173 \text{ (cancellation)}$$

$$(B.29)$$

where $t(J(j))$ is the Arcsin square-root transformation of the judgment data which has been normalised to range between 0 and 1. All of these coefficients are within the 95 per cent confidence

413

region for the coefficients estimated from the marginal choice frequencies. These results strongly suggest that both sets of data agree and could be interchanged, with the exception of the intercept, which is only a scaling constant.

Similar results were obtained for the raw frequencies, however, one of the coefficients in the choice marginals has the wrong sign, probably due to heteroskedasticity. The respective equations from this analysis are given as equations (B.30) and (B.31).

$$f((j;T);A) = .7015 - .001 \text{ (fare)} + .0003 \text{ (advance purchase)}$$
$$+ 0.548 \text{ (stopovers)} - .3209 \text{ (cancellation)}$$
$$\text{(B.30)}$$

$$J'(j) = 1.339 - .00094 \text{ (fare)} - .00375 \text{ (advance purchase)}$$
$$+ .009511 \text{ (stopovers)} - .3181 \text{ (cancellation)}$$
$$\text{(B.31)}$$

where $J'(j)$ is the judgment data normalised to lie between zero and one. Except for the intercept, all coefficients are once again within the 95 per cent confidence region of the equation estimated on the raw frequencies. Indeed, the estimates are very close in the case of fare and cancellation penalty.

B·5 Concluding Comments

The results of the preference judgment and choice judgment analysis strongly support their comparability and illustrate the way in which experimental procedures can be used to derive insight regarding functional form of both preference and choice models. Further analysis would involve tests for non-linearity of marginal relationships (which were nonsignificant for these data) and tests for interactions in the choice data (which revealed a slightly significant interaction between fare and advance purchase requirement as in the preference analysis) to assess nonadditivity of the choice function. Additional analysis could be performed on sociodemographic or market segmentation data as a covariance analysis in which one tests for different marginal slopes for different segments. This may be accomplished in a most straightforward manner by estimating separate marginal frequences for each individual, which is possible in this kind of choice experiment or in the preference experiment. These analyses, however, are beyond the scope of this Appendix, the purpose of which is to illustrate the design, execution and analysis of these kinds of experiments.

NOTES — APPENDIX B

1. This nomenclature is deliberately selected so that the intended readership, most of whom will be economists, will feel at ease with use of the term 'utilities'. Psychologists and others will recognise the equivalence to 'values' in general.

2. Psychologists would usually argue that there is an intervening function between equations (B.3) and (B.2) which maps observable attribute levels into perceived or believed levels of the attribute. It is then assumed that it is these believed levels which map into $u(a_k)$.

3. These numbers are invented. The reader is invited to reproduce these numbers so that sums are in the same rank order as the original numbers.

4. If the design is orthogonal, we may reduce the task to several independent 'regression-type' estimations.

5. This is 'true' for an individual; however, when the function is estimated over a group of individuals the group relationship may differ because one is essentially averaging over different marginal functions. Similarly, it is likely to be the case that intercept terms are necessary in predicting from observable attribute values, which adds another complication.

6. This result is obtained from examining the partial-r^2 for each attribute, recalling that the attributes are independent in this design. Hence this comparison is statistically correct and yields the same information as an elasticity measure. For example, fare accounts for 51 per cent of the explained variance, and advance purchase requirement, stopovers and cancellation account respectively for 20 per cent, 11 per cent and 17 per cent of explained variance.

7. The judgments are first transformed to range between 0.0 and 1.0 and then subjected to an Arcsin square-root transformation.

APPENDIX C

Sampling, Specification and Data Errors in Probabilistic Discrete-Choice Models

Joel Horowitz

C·1 Introduction

The standard statistical procedures for estimating the values of the parameters of econometric models assume that the correct functional specifications of the models are known a priori and that the data used for parameter estimation are error-free. In practice, these conditions often are not satisfied. Even when the conditions are satisfied, the forecasts produced by econometric models are subject to errors caused by statistical sampling errors in the estimated values of the models' parameters. The effects of specification, data and sampling errors on the forecasts of linear econometric models have been studied extensively (see, for example, Theil, 1971). The purpose of this Appendix is to examine the effects of these errors on forecasts produced by nonlinear probabilistic discrete-choice models, such as logit and probit models.

The forecasts that are dealt with here consist of estimates of the probabilities with which an individual chooses among the discrete options in the choice set. These probabilities are referred to as 'choice probabilities'. A distinction is made between errors that cause correct models to yield incorrect forecasts (e.g. errors in forecasting explanatory variables and in aggregating disaggregate models) and errors that cause incorrect models to be developed. Only the latter class of errors is treated in this Appendix. Treatments of the former class of errors have been given in Koppelman (1976, 1976a), Reid (1979), Landau (1979), Bouthelier & Daganzo (1979) and Chapter 7.

Sources of errors in probabilistic discrete-choice models are described in Sections C2, C3 and C4. Numerical illustrations of the magnitudes of the errors' effects on choice probabilities are given in Section C5. The findings of Sections C2 through C5 are interpreted in Section C6.

C·2 Statistical Sampling Errors

Sampling errors in probabilistic discrete-choice models, as in other econometric models, arise from the need to estimate the values of the models' parameters from finite data sets. When the parameters are estimated by the method of maximum-likelihood (see Chapter 3), the sampling errors in the parameter estimates are asymptotically jointly normally distributed with zero means and a covariance matrix that can be estimated from the derivatives of the log-likelihood function with respect to the parameters. It is a straightforward matter to compute confidence regions for the parameters. Let b be a column vector of estimated parameter values, β be a column vector of the true parameter values, and A be the inverse of the covariance matrix of b. If L denotes the log-likelihood function, then A is estimated by $- \partial^2 L / \partial b \partial b'$. Define $Q(b, \beta)$ by:

$$Q(b, \beta) = (b - \beta)' A (b - \beta) \qquad (C.1)$$

If there are M parameters in the model, then Q has the chi-square distribution with M degrees of freedom. Let $\chi^2 (\varepsilon, M)$ denote the $1-\varepsilon$ percentile of this distribution. Then the set of β values defined by:

$$Q(b, \beta) \le \chi^2 (\varepsilon, M) \qquad (C.2)$$

defines a joint $100 (1-\varepsilon)$ confidence region for the true parameter values β.

Converting the confidence region for the parameters into a confidence region for the choice probabilities presents a problem, as the relation between the parameters and the choice probabilities is nonlinear. Horowitz (1979a) has described two methods for computing confidence regions for the choice probabilities. One method consists of approximating the choice probabilities by first order Taylor-series expansions in the parameters, thereby linearising the relation between the probabilities and the parameters. Let $\hat{P}$ and P, respectively, represent the estimated and true values of a choice probability. Then, the Taylor-series approximation is:

$$\hat{P} = P + (b - \beta)' \, \partial P / \partial \beta \qquad (C.3)$$

Because of the asymptotic normality of b, $\hat{P}$ in the Taylor-series approximation is normally distributed with mean P and variance

$$V = (\partial P / \partial \beta') \, A^{-1} \, (\partial P / \partial \beta) \qquad (C.4)$$

The numerical value of V can be estimated by substituting b for β in the derivatives. Then, if $Z(\varepsilon/2)$ denotes the $1-\varepsilon/2$ percentile of the standard normal distribution, a $100 \, (1-\varepsilon)$ percent confidence interval for P is:

$$\hat{P} - Z(\varepsilon/2) \, V^{1/2} \leq P \leq \hat{P} + Z(\varepsilon/2) V^{1/2} \qquad (C.5)$$

The Taylor-series method of developing confidence intervals is well known in mathematical statistics and is computationally straightforward. Moreover, the method can be extended to provide joint confidence regions for several choice probabilities (Horowitz, 1979a). However, the Taylor-series method can give erroneous results. For example, consider the single-parameter logit model

$$P(X) = 1/[1 + \exp (\beta X)] \qquad (C.6)$$

where X is the independent variable and P(X) is the probability of choosing alternative one, say, expressed as a function of X. Suppose that the maximum-likelihood estimate of β is b = 3.0 and that the sampling variance of b is 1.0. Then if X = 1.0, inequality equation (C.5) yields $-0.041 \leq P \leq 0.136$ as a 95 percent confidence interval for P. This interval clearly is erroneous, as it permits negative values of P. An exact 95 percent confidence interval for P can be computed for this simple model and is $0 \leq P \leq 0.205$.

In general, the determination of whether equation (C.3) is a good approximation and inequality (equation C.5) is a meaningful confidence interval is very difficult. See Horowitz (1979a) and Daganzo (1979a) for discussions of this problem.

The second method for computing confidence regions for choice probabilities is based on nonlinear programming. There are several ways to formulate this approach, the simplest of which is

419

described here. Alternative approaches are described by Horowitz (1979a). Let P_i (β) be the probability that the ith of J alternatives is chosen when the parameter vector is β and the variables X have given fixed values. Define $b_i(ε)$ and $B_i(ε)$ by the following nonlinear programming problems:

$$\{b_i(ε), B_i(ε)\} = \{min, max\}\ P_i(β), \quad i=1,\ldots,J \quad (C.7)$$

subject to: $Q(b, β) ≤ χ^2(ε, M)$. The max. and min. operations are carried out over values of β, then the inequalities:

$$b_i(ε) ≤ P_i ≤ B_i(ε), \quad i=1,\ldots,J \quad (C.8)$$

define a rectangular joint confidence region for the P_i with confidence level equal to or greater than $100(1-ε)$ percent.

The nonlinear programming method tends to give larger confidence regions than the Taylor-series method does. In addition, the nonlinear programming method is more difficult computationally than the Taylor-series method. However, unlike the Taylor-series method, the nonlinear programming method always gives meaningful results.

The magnitudes of a model's sampling errors are roughly inversely proportional to the square root of the number of observations in its estimation data set and can be reduced by increasing the size of the data set. However, the reduction in sampling errors takes place slowly. For example, the data set size must be quadrupled to halve the sampling errors.

C·3 Specification Errors

Five types of specification errors are considered here: inclusion of an irrelevant explanatory variable in a model, random utility components that are not independently and identically distributed, random taste variations, omission of a relevant explanatory variable from a model, and random utility components that are correlated with the explanatory variables.

C·3·1 Inclusion of an Irrelevant Explanatory Variable

An irrelevant explanatory variable is one that does not affect the choice process that is being modelled. In a choice model with a linear-in-parameters utility function, an irrelevant variable is one whose utility-function coefficient is zero. Because the maximum-likelihood method yields consistent estimates of the utility function parameters, inclusion of an irrelevant variable in a model with a linear-in-parameters utility function will not cause inconsistency or asymptotic bias in the model or its forecasts. However, inclusion of an irrelevant variable will increase the sampling errors.

If the utility function is nonlinear-in-parameters, the effect of an irrelevant explanatory variable depends on whether there exist values of the parameters of the erroneous model that cause the true and erroneous models to coincide. If such parameter values exist, then the irrelevant variable will cause an increase in sampling errors but will not cause the model to be inconsistent. If such parameter values do not exist, then the irrelevant variable will cause the estimated model to be inconsistent. For example, if the true systematic component of the utility function is αX but the systematic component of the utility function of the estimated model is specified as $aX\, Y^b$, where Y is an irrelevant variable and a and b are parameters to be estimated, then the presence of the irrelevant variable Y will not cause inconsistency. However, if the systematic component of the utility function of the estimated model is specified as $aX\, Y$, then the estimated model will be inconsistent.

The following example illustrates the increase in sampling error that can be caused by an irrelevant variable. Suppose that in a binary choice situation the true probability P_1 of choosing alternative one is given by the single-parameter logit model

$$P_1 = 1/(1 + \exp \alpha) \qquad\qquad (C.9)$$

However, assume that the estimated model is specified as

$$P_1 = 1/[1 + \exp (a + b\, X)], \qquad\qquad (C.10)$$

where X is an irrelevant variable. Assume further that the estimation data set contains 2R observations with X = 0 for the first R observations, and X = 1 for the second R. Then the large-sample limit of the matrix A is:

421

$$A = 2RP_1(1 - P_1) \begin{bmatrix} 1 & 1/2 \\ 1/2 & 1/2 \end{bmatrix} \quad (C.11)$$

where $A(1, 1)$ is the (a, a) element, $A(2, 2)$ is the (b, b) element, and so forth. Using the approximation (C.4), the variance of the estimated value of P_1 is $2P_1(1-P_1)/2R$. If the correct specification (C.9) is used in the estimated model, then A is the scalar $2RP_1(1-P_1)$. The variance of the estimated value of P_1 is $P_1(1-P_1)/2R$. Thus, the inclusion of the irrelevant variable X in the estimated model has doubled the sampling variance of the estimated value of P_1.

C·3·2 Random Utility Components that are not Independently and Identically Distributed

In probabilistic choice models based on utility maximisation, the utility U_i of alternative i is given by

$$U_i = V(X_i, \alpha) + \varepsilon_i \quad (C.12)$$

where V is a deterministic function, X_i is a vector of explanatory variables, α is a vector of parameters whose values must be estimated from data, and ε_i is a random variable whose mean value is zero. In the basic multinomial logit model it is also assumed that the random utility components ε_i are independently and identically distributed across alternatives. It is easy to think of examples where this assumption is violated. For example, suppose that the variable 'fuel consumption' is not one of the explanatory variables in a model that forecasts consumers' choices of new cars but that cars with low fuel consumption are preferred to cars with high fuel consumption, other things being equal. Then the random utility components of cars with low fuel consumption will tend to be positively correlated with each other and to be negatively correlated with the random utility components of cars with high fuel consumption.

The functional relation between the choice probabilities and explanatory variables in models with non-IID random utility components is different from the relation in models with IID random

422

components. As an example of this, assume that in a model of choice among three alternatives, the utility of alternative i is

$$U_i = V_i + \varepsilon_i, \qquad (C.13)$$

where V_i is the systematic component of utility and for each i the random component ε_i has the Type I extreme value distribution (i.e. the distribution that leads to the logit model). If, in addition, the ε_i are independent, the choice probabilities are given by the basic logit model. Thus, the probability that alternative one is chosen is:

$$P_1 = \exp V_1 / \sum_{i=1}^{3} \exp V_i \qquad (C.14)$$

Now suppose that ε_1 and ε_2 are correlated with correlation coefficient $\rho \geqslant 0$. Then the probability that alternative one is chosen is (McFadden, 1979):

$$P_1 = \{\exp[V_1/(1-\rho)] + \exp[V_2/(1-\rho)]\} - \rho \exp[V_1/(1-\rho)]$$
$$\qquad (C.15)$$
$$\div (\{\exp[V_1/(1-\rho)] + \exp[V_2/(1-\rho)]\}^{1-\rho} + \exp V_3)$$

Comparing equation (C.14) and equation (C.15) it can be seen that an erroneous assumption that the random utility components are IID causes the relation between the choice probabilities and the explanatory variables to be specified incorrectly.

In principle, violation of the logit model's assumption of IID random utility components causes that model to yield inconsistent parameter and choice-probability estimates. In practice, the parameter estimates obtained from logit models with linear-in-parameters utility functions appear to be robust against violations of the IID assumption. In numerical experiments with a three-alternative model, Horowitz (1979) found that the logit model gave consistent parameter estimates (apart from an arbitrary scale factor), even when the variances of the random components differed by a factor of 16 and had correlation coefficients of 0.75. Subsequent research has shown that this result holds for variance differences of a factor of 100 and correlations of 0.99. However, despite the consistency of the parameter estimates, the basic logit model gives inconsistent estimates of choice probabilities when the IID assumption is violated. Numerical examples of the resulting errors in logit estimates of choice probabilities are given in Section C5.

There are two possible ways of dealing with a model that has non-IID random utility components. One is to include additional explanatory variables in the model in an attempt to achieve an explicit representation of the variables that cause the random components not to be IID. However, this approach is available only to analysts who are able to acquire the necessary data and who are lucky enough to be able to identify the relevant variables. The other approach is to use a model that is more general than the basic logit model. The probit model (Hausman & Wise, 1978; Daganzo, Bouthelier & Sheffi, 1978) permits the random utility components to be correlated and to have unequal variances. The generalised-extreme-value (GEV) model (McFadden, 1979) permits the random utility components to be correlated but not to have unequal variances. Both of these models are computationally unwieldy and are very difficult to apply in problems where there are large numbers of alternatives.

C·3·3 Random Taste Variations

The parameters α in the utility function (equation C.12) represent the effects on choice of individuals' tastes. If tastes vary among individuals in ways that are not accounted for by the explanatory variables X, then the values of the parameters α will tend to vary randomly among individuals. For example, suppose that in a model of consumer choice among different brands of a certain product there are two explanatory variables, cost (C) and quality (Q). Suppose that the utility function is specified as:

$$U = \alpha Q + \beta C + \varepsilon, \qquad (C.16)$$

where α and β are parameters, and ε has a probability distribution that is independent of Q and C. Assume, however, that low-income individuals are more sensitive to cost changes than high-income individuals are, so that the true utility-function specification is

$$U = \alpha Q + \gamma C/I + \varepsilon, \qquad (C.17)$$

where I is income, and γ is a fixed parameter. Comparing equation (C.16) and equation (C.17), it can be seen that equation (C.16) is correct only if the parameter β is considered to be a random variable whose distribution is the same as the distribution of γ/I in the population under consideration. In other words, the specification (C.16) contains random taste variations.

If it is assumed erroneously that the taste parameters of a probabilistic choice model are fixed, then the relation between the model's explanatory variables and the choice probabilities will be specified erroneously. As an example of this, consider a univariate, binary-choice, probit model in which the explanatory variable is denoted by X. Let the utility function for alternative i (i=1, 2) be

$$U_i = \alpha X_i + \varepsilon_i, \tag{C.18}$$

where α is a parameter, and the ε_i are independently distributed with the standard normal distribution. If the value of α is fixed, then the probability P_i that alternative one is chosen is:

$$P_1 = \Phi[\alpha(X_1 - X_2)/\sqrt{2}], \tag{C.19}$$

where Φ is the cumulative standard normal distribution function. Now suppose that α is a normally distributed random variable whose mean is α^* and whose variance is one. Then $U_1 - U_2$ has the normal distribution with mean $\alpha^* (X_1 - X_2)$ and variance $2 + (X_1 - X_2)^2$. The probability that alternative one is chosen is now:

$$P_1 = \Phi\{\alpha^* (X_1 - X_2)/[2 + (X_1 - X_2)^2]^{1/2}\} \tag{C.20}$$

Comparing equation (C.19) and equation (C.20) it can be seen that an erroneous assumption that the taste parameters of a model are fixed causes the relation between the choice probabilities and the explanatory variables to be specified incorrectly.

In general, random taste variations cause fixed-parameters models such as basic logit to yield inconsistent estimates of utility-function parameters and choice probabilities. However, in the case of linear-in-parameters utility functions, the numerical experiments of Horowitz (1979) indicate that the logit model yields consistent estimates of the mean values of the taste parameters (apart from an arbitrary scale factor), although the logit model's estimates of choice probabilities are inconsistent. A numerical example of the magnitudes of the errors in the choice probabilities is given in Section C5.

Random taste variations can, in principle, be dealt with in the same way as non-IID disturbances with fixed tastes. One can expand the set of explanatory variables to account for the taste variations, or one can use a model that permits taste variations. Random taste variations are permitted in the probit model. They are not permitted in the GEV model.

C·3·4 Omission of a Relevant Explanatory Variable

An omitted relevant explanatory variable is a variable that affects behaviour but that is not one of the explanatory variables of the model under consideration. In random-utility choice models, the purpose of the random component of the utility function is to capture the effects of omitted relevant variables. Thus, omission of a relevant variable from a model does not necessarily constitute a modelling error. Rather, the effect of omitting a relevant variable from a model depends on the relations between the omitted and included variables, and on the relations between the distributions of the omitted variable in the population for which the model was estimated and the populations for which forecasts are made.

The effect of omitting a relevant explanatory variable from a model can be illustrated with a binary-choice (independent) probit model. Let there be two explanatory variables, X and Y, in the model, and let the correct utility function specification for alternative i be:

$$U_i = \alpha X_i + \beta Y_i + \varepsilon_i \tag{C.21}$$

Let the parameters α and β be fixed, and let the ε_i be independently distributed with the standard normal distribution. Now suppose that Y is omitted from the specification, so that the utility function is written as:

$$U_i = \alpha X_i + \eta_i \tag{C.22}$$

426

where η_i is a random variable equal to $\beta Y_i + \varepsilon_i$. Then the following statements can be made:

$$E(U_1-U_2) = \alpha (X_1-X_2) + E(Y_1|X_1,X_2) - E(Y_2|X_1,X_2) \qquad (C.23)$$

$$\begin{aligned} Var(U_1-U_2) = 2+\beta^2[Var(Y_1|X_1,X_2) \\ + Var(Y_2|X_1,X_2) - 2Cov(Y_1,Y_2|X_1,X_2)] \end{aligned} \qquad (C.24)$$

If the Ys are normally distributed for each set of values of (X_1,X_2) then the probability that alternative one is chosen is:

$$P_1 = \Phi\{E(U_1-U_2)/ [var(U_1-U_2)]^{\frac{1}{2}}\} \qquad (C.25)$$

By comparing equations (C.23) to (C.25) with equation (C.19), it can be seen that the omission of the variable Y from the utility function causes the usual binary probit specification for P_1 to be incorrect unless Y_1 and Y_2 are distributed independently of X_1 and X_2, and $E(Y_1) = E(Y_2) = 0$.

In general, omission of a relevant explanatory variable from a model will cause the model to yield inconsistent estimates of choice probabilities unless the following conditions are satisfied:

(1) The omitted variable must be distributed independently of the included variables.
(2) Either the omitted variable must have equal mean values in all alternatives, or else alternative-specific constant terms must be included in the utility function to represent the effects of the alternative-specific means of the omitted variable.
(3) Either the omitted variable must be IID across alternatives, or else a model that permits non-IID random utility components must be used.
(4) The omitted variable must have the same distribution in the population for which forecasts are made as in the population from which the values of the model's parameters are estimated.
(5) The omission of the relevant variable must not substantially alter the parametric form of the random component of the utility function. For example, if a probit model is being used, then the omitted variable must be approximately normally distributed.

427

A numerical example of the error in choice probabilities caused by omitting a relevant variable from a model is given in Section C5.

C·3·5 Correlated Random Utility Components and Explanatory Variables

Suppose that in a model of commuter-choice between car and bus for the trip to work, the utility function for alternative i (i = car, bus) is specified as:

$$U_i = \alpha T_i + \varepsilon_i, \tag{C.26}$$

where T_i is the home-to-work travel time for alternative i. If travel cost also affects choice and is correlated with travel time by virtue of the dependence of both on trip length, then ε_i and T_i will tend to be correlated.

Correlation between random utility components and the explanatory variables is a source of modelling error that is a special case of omitting a relevant explanatory variable. For example, let ε_i be the random utility component for alternative i, and let X_i be the vector of explanatory variables for alternative i. If X_i and ε_i are correlated but ε_i is independent of the explanatory variables for alternatives other than i, then the omitted variable is $E(\varepsilon_i | X_i)$. If this variable were included in the utility-function specification, then the random component would become $\varepsilon_i - E(\varepsilon_i | X_i)$, which is uncorrelated with X_i.

Correlation between random utility components and explanatory variables causes estimates of models' parameters and of choice probabilities to be inconsistent. At present, the only means available for dealing with this problem is to identify the variables that cause the correlation and include them explicitly in the specification of the model under consideration.

C·4 Erroneous Data

In general, use of erroneous data to estimate a model will produce an erroneous model. A special case of this that arises frequently in practice is use of group-mean values of explanatory variables. For example, data on individuals' incomes may not be available for use in a model of individual choice, but data giving the mean income of individuals who live in the same neighbourhood may be available (see Section 7.2).

Grouping of data represents a special case of omitting a relevant explanatory variable from a model. The omitted variable is the difference between the individual and group-mean values of the grouped variable. In general, use of grouped data in maximum-likelihood estimation of the values of the parameters of a model of individual choice will produce a model that gives inconsistent estimates of individuals' choice probabilities. The model also will produce inconsistent estimates of group-mean choice probabilities unless the following conditions are satisfied:

(1)   The grouped explanatory variables are not correlated with any nongrouped variables that are included in the model's specification.
(2)   The grouped variables have the same joint distribution function in each group, both in the estimation data set and in the data set used for forecasting.

McFadden & Reid (1975) have described procedures for using grouped data in Berkson-Theil estimation of individual-choice models. However, these procedures are applicable only when there are enough repetitions of each observation to permit use of the Berkson-Theil method.

Bouthelier & Daganzo (1979) have described a procedure for using grouped data in maximum-likelihood estimation of individual-choice (covariate) probit models. This procedure involves modifying the probit likelihood function to compensate for the effects of grouping. The procedure requires the grouped variables to have intragroup distributions that are multivariate normally distributed with known covariance matrices, although it appears to be reasonably robust against departures from the normality assumption. However, use of the procedure can cause substantial increases in sampling errors.

C·5 Numerical Examples

This section presents six numerical examples that illustrate the magnitudes of the forecasting errors that can be caused by sampling, specification and data errors in probabilistic choice models. The examples are explained in the text below. The numerical results of the examples are presented in Table C.1.

Example 1: Sampling Errors. The values of the parameters of a bivariate, three-alternative, basic logit model are estimated using the method of maximum likelihood. The correct choice model is a logit model in which the systematic component of the utility function for alternative i (i=1, 2, 3) is:

$$V(X_i, Y_i) = 5 X_i + Y_i \qquad (C.27)$$

where X and Y are the explanatory variables of the model. The systematic component of the utility function of the estimated model is specified (correctly) as

$$V(X_i, Y_i) = aX_i + bY_i \qquad (C.28)$$

where a and b are the parameters whose values are to be estimated. The values of X and Y in the estimation data set are such that the choice probabilities for all of the alternatives span a range from nearly zero to nearly one. (The same values of X and Y are used in all of the examples presented in this section.)

The RMS absolute and fractional sampling errors in the choice probabilities have been computed for an estimated data set that contains 1000 observations. The errors were computed by averaging, respectively, the sampling variances and squared coefficients of variation of the choice probabilities at each point in the estimation data set and taking the square roots of the results. In addition, 'maximum' absolute and fractional sampling errors were computed by taking the maximum value of the differences between the choice probabilities and their 95 percent confidence limits at each point in the estimation data set.

Example 2: Correlated Random Components of Utility. It is assumed that the true choice model is a bivariate, three-alternative probit model in which the utility function for alternative i is:

$$U(X_i, Y_i) = 5 X_i + Y_i + \varepsilon_i \qquad (C.29)$$

The ε's are normally distributed with means of zero and variances of one. In addition, ε_1 and ε_2 are

TABLE C-1: Examples of the Magnitudes of Errors in Choice Probabilities Caused by Sampling, Specification, and Data Errors

	RMS Absolute Error	Maximum Absolute Error	Fractional Error When the Choice Probabilities are Less than 0.05		Fractional Error When the Choice Probabilities Exceed 0.05	
			RMS	Maximum	RMS	Maximum
Sampling Error	0.016	0.057	0.24	0.77	0.060	0.42
Correlated Random Utility Components	0.022	0.074	120,000,000	620,000,000	0.14	0.77
Random Utility Components with Unequal Variances	0.027	0.13	49,000,000	210,000,000	0.11	0.33
Random Taste Variations	0.069	0.18	150,000,000	560,000,000	0.36	2.29
Omission of Relevant Explanatory Variable	0.32	0.85	980,000,000	2,200,000,000	1.77	9.57
Grouped Data	0.11	0.35	2,600	970	0.57	1.86

431

correlated with a correlation coefficient of $\rho = 0.95$.

The estimated model is specified incorrectly as a basic logit model with the specifications of equation (C.28). If the ε's were IID normally distributed, the resulting multinomial probit model would be virtually indistinguishable from a basic logit model. Thus, the use of a logit model in place of a probit model is not, by itself, a significant source of error.

The large-sample limits of the maximum and RMS absolute and fractional differences between the true probit and logit-estimated choice probabilities have been computed. In this example and in all of the remaining examples, the absolute and fractional differences, respectively, refer to the absolute and fractional differences between the true and estimated choice probabilities at each point in the estimation data set.

Example 3: Random Utility Components with Unequal Variances. It is assumed that the true choice model is a bivariate, three-alternative probit model in which the utility function has the same systematic component as in equation (C.29). The ε_i are assumed to be independent. However, the variances of ε_1, ε_2, and ε_3 are 0.10, 1.0, and 10.0, respectively. The estimated model is specified incorrectly as a basic logit model with the specification of equation (C.28). The large-sample limits of the maximum and RMS absolute and fractional differences between the true probit and logit-estimated choice probabilities have been computed.

Example 4: Random Taste Variation. It is assumed that the true choice model is a bivariate, three-alternative probit model in which the utility function of alternative i is:

$$U(X_i, Y_i) = \alpha\, X_i + \beta\, Y_i + \varepsilon_i \qquad (C.30)$$

The ε_i are IID normally distributed with means of zero and variances of one. In addition, α and β are independently normally distributed with means of 5.0 and 1.0, respectively, and coefficients of variation of 0.10. The estimated model is specified incorrectly as a basic logit model with the specification of equation (C.28). The large-sample limits of the maximum and RMS absolute and

432

fractional differences between the true probit and logit-estimated choice probabilities have been computed.

Example 5: Omission of a Relevant Explanatory Variable. It is assumed that the true choice model is the bivariate, three-alternative logit model of equation (C.27). The estimated model also is a basic logit model, but the systematic component of its utility function is specified incorrectly as

$$V(X_i) = aX_i. \tag{C.31}$$

The large-sample limits of the maximum and RMS absolute and fractional differences between the true and estimated logit choice probabilities have been computed.

Example 6: Grouped Data. It is assumed that the true choice model is the bivariate, three-alternative logit model of equation (C.27). The estimated model is specified correctly as a basic logit model with the specification of equation (C.28). However, the estimation data set contains only group-mean values of Y. In this example, each group contains five observations. The large-sample limits of the maximum and RMS absolute and fractional differences between the true and estimated choice probabilities have been computed.

The results presented in Table C.1 show that the effects of specification and data errors can be large compared to sampling errors and are potentially serious. In the examples, the errors caused by random taste variations, omission of a relevant explanatory variable and grouping of data all are large enough to seriously degrade or destroy the practical value of a model. The errors caused by non-IID random components of utility are smaller, although these errors, as well as sampling errors, clearly can impair a model's practical value. Additional results leading to similar conclusions are presented in Horowitz (1979, 1980).

C·6 Conclusions

Probabilistic discrete-choice models are sensitive to a larger group of specification and data errors than linear econometric models are. Random taste variations and non-IID random components can cause a loss of estimation efficiency in linear models but do not cause bias or inconsistency. Linear models also are less sensitive to data grouping than nonlinear probabilistic models are.

The basic logit model is more sensitive to specification and data errors than the GEV and probit models are. This sensitivity is caused by the basic logit model's requirement that the random components of utility be IID. The limited numerical results that are available indicate that the basic logit model is especially vulnerable to random taste variations, omission of relevant variables and data grouping, whereas it is somewhat more robust in the presence of random utility components that are correlated or that have unequal variances. Comparable numerical results for the GEV model are not available. However, the fact that the main difference between the GEV and basic logit models is that GEV permits correlation of random utility components, whereas basic logit does not, suggests that the GEV model is likely to share the weaknesses of the basic logit model in the presence of random taste variations, omitted relevant variables or grouped data.

In contrast to basic logit and GEV models, probit models offer considerable flexibility. The covariate probit structure automatically permits random taste variations and non-IID random utility components. In addition, probit models can be adapted for use with grouped data. However, to obtain these advantages of probit it is necessary to accept the considerable computational difficulty of probit models. Whether the tradeoff between model flexibility and computational difficulty favours the use of covariate probit models in practical empirical work depends on the extent to which the error conditions that cause logit and GEV models to perform poorly exist in practical empirical models. The empirical research needed to assess the extent of the occurrence of the error conditions has not yet been performed.

The large number of specification errors that can affect probabilistic discrete-choice models and the large potential magnitudes of the resulting forecasting errors imply that diagnostic testing should play an important part in the development of these models. Available diagnostic tests for basic logit models include a set of procedures developed by McFadden, Train & Tye (1977)(see Chapter 5) and testing a basic logit model against a more general

434

covariate probit model (Horowitz, 1979). The McFadden, Train & Tye procedures are computationally easier to use than a test against a probit model, but the probit test appears to be more powerful. Diagnostic tests for nonlogit models are not yet available.

REFERENCES

Adler, T.J. & Ben-Akiva, M.E. (1976). 'Joint choice model for frequency, destination and travel mode for shopping trips', Transportation Research Record, No. 569, 136-150.

Adler, T. & Ben-Akiva, M.E. (1979). 'A theoretical and empirical model of trip chaining behaviour', Transportation Research, 13B(3), 243-258.

Albright, R., Lerman, S. & Manski, C. (1977). Report on the Development of an Estimation Program for the Multinomial Probit Model, prepared for Federal Highway Administration, Washington, D.C.

Amemiya, T. (1973). 'Regression analysis when the dependent variable is truncated normal', Econometrica, 41(6), 997-1016.

Anderson, N.H. (1974). 'Information integration theory: a brief survey', in Krantz, D.H., Atkinson, R.C., Luce, R.D. & Suppes, P. (eds.) Contemporary Developments in Mathematical Psychology, Vol. 2, W.H. Freeman, San Francisco.

Anderson, N.H. (1976). 'How functional measurement can yield validated interval scales of mental quantities', Journal of Applied Psychology, 61, 677-692.

Anscombe, F.J. & Tukey, J.W. (1954). 'The criticism of transformations', Paper presented before the American Statistical Association and Biometric Society, Montreal.

Atherton, T.H. & Ben-Akiva, M.E. (1976). 'Transferability and updating of disaggregate travel demand models', Transportation Research Record, No. 610, 12-18.

Arrow, K.H. (1951). Social Choice and Individual Values, John Wiley & Sons, New York.

Barton, M.F. (1979). 'Conditional logit analysis of FCC decisionmaking', The Bell Journal of Economics, 10(2), 399-411.

Bates, J.J. (1979). 'Sample size and grouping in the estimation of disaggregate models - a simple case', Transportation, 8(4), 347-370.

Becker, G.M., DeGroot, M.N. & Marschak, J. (1963). 'Stochastic models of choice behaviour', Behavioural Science, 8(4), 306-311.

Ben-Akiva, M.E. (1973). <u>Structure of Passenger Travel Demand Models</u>, Unpublished Ph.D. Thesis, Department of Civil Engineering, M.I.T., Cambridge.

Ben-Akiva, M.E. & Koppelman, F.S. (1974). 'Multi-dimensional choice models: alternative structures of travel demand models', <u>Transportation Research Record Special Report</u> No. 149, 129-142.

Ben-Akiva, M.E. & Lerman, S.R. (1974). 'Some estimation results of a simultaneous model of auto ownership and mode choice to work', <u>Transportation</u>, 4(4), 357-376.

Ben-Akiva, M.E. & Atherton, T.J. (1977). 'Choice-model predictions of carpool demand: methods and results', <u>Transportation Research Record</u>, No. 637, 13-17.

Ben-Akiva, M.E. & Atherton, T.J. (1977a). 'Author's closures', <u>Transportation Research Record</u>, No. 637, 20-22.

Ben-Akiva, M.E. (1977). 'Passenger travel demand forecasting: applications of disaggregate models and directions for research', in Visser, E.J. (ed.) <u>Transport Decisions in an Age of Uncertainty</u>, Martinus Nijhoff, The Hague, 183-193.

Ben-Akiva, M.E. (1977a). 'Choice models with simple choice set generating processes', Working Paper, Centre for Transportation Studies, M.I.T. (mimeo).

Ben-Akiva, M.E. & Watanatada, T. (1980). 'Application of a continuous spatial choice logit model', in Manski, C.F. & McFadden, D. (eds.) <u>Structural Analysis of Discrete Data: with Econometric Applications</u>, M.I.T. Press, Cambridge, Massachusetts.

Ben-Akiva, M.E. & Lerman, S.R. (1979). 'Disaggre-gate travel and mobility choice models and measures of accessibility', in Hensher, D.A. & Stopher, P.R. (eds.) <u>Behavioural Travel Modelling</u>, Croom Helm, London.

Ben-Akiva, M.E. (1980). 'Issues in transferring and updating travel behaviour models', in Brog, W., Stopher, P.R. & Meyburg, A.H. (eds.) <u>New Horizons in Behavioural Travel Research</u>, Lexington Books, Lexington.

Bergmann, B.R. (1978). 'Have economists failed?', <u>Studies in Economic Analysis</u>, 2(2), 3-18.

Berkson, J. (1944). 'Application of the logistic function to bio-assay', <u>Journal of American Statistical Association</u>, 39, 357-365.

Berkson, J. (1953). 'A statistically precise and relatively simple method of estimating the bio-assay with quantal response based on the logistic function', Journal of American Statistical Association, 48, 565-599.

Blase, J.H. (1979). 'Hysteresis and catastrophe theory: empirical identification in transportation modelling', Environment and Planning A, 11(5), 675-688.

Bock, R.D. & Jones, K.V. (1968). The Measurement and Prediction of Judgement and Choice, Holden-Day, San Francisco.

Boskin, M.J. (1974). 'A conditional logit model of occupation choice', Journal of Political Economy, 82(2), 389-398.

Bouthelier, F. & Daganzo, C.F. (1979). 'Aggregation with multinomial probit and calibration of disaggregate demand models with aggregate data: a new methodological approach', Transportation Research, 13B(2), 133-146.

Box, G.P. & Tidwell, P.W. (1962). 'Transformations of the independent variables', Technometrics 4, 531-550.

Box, G.P. & Cox, D.R. (1964). 'An analysis of transformations', Journal of the Royal Statistical Society, Series B, 26, 211-243.

Brog, W., Stopher, P.R. & Meyburg, A.H. (eds.) (1980). New Horizons in Behavioural Travel Research, Lexington Books, Lexington.

Brown, H.P. (1979). 'A model of weekend recreational travel demand', Working Paper RP/06/79/Trans, Department of Civil Engineering University of Melbourne, Australia.

Bruzelius, N. (1979). The Value of Travel Time: Theory and Measurement, Croom Helm, London.

Bullen, A.G.R. & Boekenkroeger, R.H. (1979). 'Disaggregate travel models - how strong are the foundations?', Transportation Research Record, No. 728, 44-46.

Bullock, R.G. (1979). MUT-Land Use and Transport Model for Sao Paulo — Calibration of the Transport Model, Report prepared by Marcial Echenique & Partners, Sao Paulo, Brazil.

Cambridge Systematics, Inc., (1975). A Behavioral Model of Car Ownership and Mode of Travel - Vols. 3 & 4, prepared for U.S. Department of Transportation, Washington, D.C.

Cambridge Systematics, Inc., (1977). 'Methodology: specification and estimation of disaggregate behavioural models used in aggregate forecast systems', The SIGMO Study, Part 2 report prepared for Projectbureau IVVS and Netherlands Ministry of Transport.

Cambridge Systematics, Inc., (1979). SLogit, Zuidvleugel Study Report No. 2, prepared for the Netherlands Ministry of Transport.

Charles River Associates, Inc., (1975). The Effects of Automotive Fuel Conservation Measures on Automotive Air Pollution, Final report to the Environmental Protection Agency, Washington, D.C.

Charles River Associates, Inc., (1976). Disaggregate Travel Demand Models, Vols. I & II (Project 8-13, Phase 1, Report, National Cooperative Highway Research Program, Charles River Associates, Boston.

Charles River Associates, (1978). Guidelines for Using the Market Segmentation Technique to Apply Disaggregate Travel Demand Models with Census Data, (Project 8-13, Phase 2, Report, National Cooperative Highway Research Program), Charles River Associates, Boston.

Church, J.G. & Gordon, I.M. (1978). 'Market share models of rural telephone service', Omega, 6(1), 59-64.

Clark, C. (1961). 'The greatest of a finite set of random variables', Operations Research, 9, 145-162.

Clark, F.R. (1957). Constant-ratio rule for confusion matrices in speech communication, Journal of Acoustics Society of America, 29(b), 715-720.

Cochran, M.D. (1964). Sampling Techniques, J. Wiley & Sons, New York.

Communications Research (Australia), (1979) PABX Marketing Study, Final report prepared for Telecom (Australia) Sydney.

Cosslett, S.R. (1978). 'Efficient estimation of discrete-choice models from choice-based samples', Workshop in Transportation Economics Working Paper 7801, Department of Economics, University of California at Berkeley, California.

Cosslett, S.R. (1980). 'Efficient estimation of discrete choice models', in Manski, C.F. & McFadden, D. (eds.) Structural Analysis of Discrete Data: with Econometric Applications, M.I.T. Press, Cambridge, Massachusetts.

Cox, D.R. (1970). The Analysis of Binary Data, Methuen, London.

Cragg, J.G. (1968). 'Some statistical models for limited dependent variables with application to the demand for durable goods', Discussion Paper 8, University of British Columbia, Vancouver, British Columbia.

Cragg, J.G. & Lisco, T.E. (1968). PROLO-User Manual, Department of Economics, University of Chicago (mimeo).

Daganzo, C.F., Bouthelier, F. & Sheffi, Y. (1977). 'Multinomial probit and qualitative choice: a computationally efficient algorithm', Transportation Science, 11(4), 338-358.

Daganzo, C.F. (1978). 'Optimal updating of discrete choice models', Institute of Transportation Studies Working Paper UCB-ITS-WP-79-4, University of California, Berkeley.

Daganzo, C.F. (1979). Multinomial Probit: The Theory and Its Application to Demand Forecasting, Academic Press, New York.

Daganzo, C.F. (1979a). 'The statistical interpretation of predictions with disaggregate demand models', Transportation Science, 13(1), 1-12.

Daganzo, C.F. (1980). 'Calibration and prediction with random utility models: some recent advances and unresolved questions', in Brog, W., Stopher, P.R. & Meyburg, A.H. (eds.) New Horizons in Behavioural Travel Research, Lexington Books, Lexington.

Dagenais, M.G. (1969). 'A threshold regression model', Econometrica, 37(2), 193-203.

Dagenais, M.G. (1975). 'Application of a threshold regression model to household purchases of automobiles', Review of Economics and Statistics, 57(3), 275-285.

Daly, A.J. (1978). 'Issues in the estimation of journey attribute values', in Hensher, D.A. & Dalvi, M.Q. (eds.) Determinants of Travel Choice, Saxon House, Teakfield, Farnborough, England, 335-357.

Daly, A.J. & Zachary, S. (1978). 'Improved multiple choice models', in Hensher, D.A. & Dalvi, M.Q. (eds.) Determinants of Travel Choice, Saxon House, Teakfield, Farnborough, England, 187-201.

Daly, A.J. (1978a). Zuid Vleugel Study: Proposed Model Structure, Report 1, Cambridge Systematics Inc., Netherlands, February (unpublished).

Daly, A.J. (1979). 'Some developments in transport demand modelling', in Hensher, D.A. & Stopher, P.R. (eds.) Behavioural Travel Modelling, Croom Helm, London.

Daly, A.J. (1979a). 'Estimating attraction variables', Cambridge Systematics, Inc., Holland (mimeo).

441

Daly, A.J. (1980). 'Some issues in the implementation of advanced travel demand models', in Brog, W., Stopher, P.R. & Meyburg, A.H. (eds.) New Horizons in Behavioural Travel Research, Lexington Books, Lexington.

De Donnea, F.X. (1971). The Determinants of Transport Mode Choice in Dutch Cities, Rotterdam University Press, Rotterdam.

De Serpa, A.C. (1971). 'A theory of the economics of time', Economic Journal, 81(324), 828-45.

Devletoglou, N.E. (1963). 'Thresholds and rationality', Kyklos, XXI(4), 623-636.

Devletoglou, N.E. (1971). 'Thresholds and transactions costs', Quarterly Journal of Economics, 85(1), 163-170.

Dhrymes, P.J., Howrey, E.P., Hymans, S.H., Kmenta J., Leamer, E.E., Quandt, R.E., Ramsay, J.B., Shapiro, A.T. & Zarnowicz, V. (1972). 'Criteria for evaluation of economic models', Annals of Economic and Social Measurement, 1, 291-324.

Dobson, R. de P., (1979). 'Market segmentation: a tool for transport decision-making', in Hensher, D.A. & Stopher, P.R. (eds.) Behavioural Travel Modelling, Croom Helm, London.

Dobson, R. de P. & Nicolaides, G.C. (1974). 'Preferences for transit service by homogeneous groups of individuals', Proceedings of American Transportation Research Forum, XV(1), 326-335.

Domencich, T. & McFadden, D. (1975). Urban Travel Demand: a Behavioural Analysis, North-Holland Publishers, Amsterdam.

Dunbar, F.C. (1975). 'Evaluation of the effectiveness of pollution control strategies on travel: an application of disaggregated behavioural demand models' Proceedings of the USA Transportation Research Forum, XVI(1), 259-268.

Elsahoff, J.D. & Elsahoff, R.M. (1974). 'Two-sample problems for a dichotomous variable with missing data', Applied Statistics, 23(1), 26-34.

Feige, E. & Watts, H.C. (1972). 'An investigation of the consequences of partial aggregation of micro-economic data', Econometrica, 40(3), 343-360.

Figlewski, S. (1979). 'Subjective information and market efficiency in a betting market', Journal of Political Economy, 87(1), 75-88.

Finney, D.J. (1971). _Probit Analysis_, 3rd edition, Cambridge University Press, Cambridge.

Fischer, G.L. & Nagin, D. (1980). 'Random vs. fixed coefficient quantal choice models: an empirical comparison', in Manski, C.F. & McFadden, D. (eds.) _Structural Analysis of Discrete Data: with Econometric Applications_, M.I.T. Press, Cambridge, Massachusetts.

Freund, J.E. (1962). _Mathematical Statistics_, Prentice-Hall Inc., Englewood Cliffs, New Jersey.

Frisch, R. (1951). 'Some personal reminiscences of a great man', in Harris, S.E. (ed.) _Schumpeter, Social Scientist_, M.I.T. Press, Cambridge, Massachusetts.

Galbraith, R.A. (1979). _The Transferability of Disaggregate Mode Choice Models_, Unpublished B.Sc. (Applied Geography) Honours Thesis, University of New South Wales, Sydney.

Gaudry, M.J.I. & Dagenais, M.G. (1978). 'A class of inverse power transformation probabilistic models', _Research Publication No. 7803_, Department of Economics, University of Montreal.

Gaudry, M.J.I. & Wills, M.J. (1978). 'Estimating the functional form of travel demand models', _Transportation Research_, 12(4), 257-289.

Gaudry, M.J.I. & Dagenais, M.G. (1979). 'The dogit model', _Transportation Research_, 13B(2), 105-12.

Gaudry, M.J.I. & Wills, M.J. (1979). 'Testing the dogit model with aggregate time-series and cross-sectional travel data', _Transportation Research_, 13B(2), 155-166.

Gensch, D.H. & Svestka, J.A. (1978). 'An exact hierarchical algorithm for determining aggregate statistics from individual choice data', _Department of Marketing Working Paper_, University of Wisconsin.

Georgescu-Roegen, N. (1936). 'The pure theory of consumer's behaviour', _Quarterly Journal of Economics_, 1(1).

Georgescu-Roegen, N. (1958). 'Threshold in choice and the theory of demand', _Econometrica_, 26(1), 157-168.

Gillen, D.W. (1975). 'Parking prices and parking restrictions: the effects of urban mode choice and congestion', _Proceedings USA/Canadian Transportation Research Forum_ XV(1), 240-46.

Gillen, D.W. (1977). 'Estimation and specification of the effects of parking costs on urban transport mode choice', _Journal of Urban Economics_, 4(2), 186-199.

Gillen, D.W. (1977a). 'Effects of parking costs on urban transport mode choice', Transportation Research Record, No. 637, 46-51.

Goldberger, A.S. (1964). Econometric Theory. John Wiley & Sons, New York.

Goldfeld, S.M. & Quandt, R.E. (1972). Nonlinear Methods in Econometrics, North-Holland Publishing Co., Amsterdam.

Goldsmith, P.L. & Boddy, R. (1978). 'Critical analysis of factorial experiments and orthogonal fractions', Applied Statistics, 27, 141-160.

Goodman, L.A. (1970). 'The multivariate analysis of qualitative data; interactions among multiple classifications', Journal of American Statistical Association, 65, 225-256.

Goodman, L.A. (1972). 'A modified multiple regression approach to the analysis of dichotomous variables', American Sociological Review, 37, 28-46.

Gottschalk, P. & Goluke, U. (1979). 'Sentencing of drunken drivers', Resource Policy Center Working Paper, Thayer School of Engineering, Dartmouth College, New Hampshire.

Green, J.H.A. (1969). Aggregation in Economic Analysis, Princeton University, Princeton, New Jersey.

Green, J.H.A. (1978). Consumer Theory, revised edition, Macmillan, London.

Green, P.F., Carmone, F.J. & Wachspress, D.P. (1977). 'On the analysis of qualitative data in marketing research', Journal of Marketing Research, XIV(1), 52-59.

Green, P. (1978). 'An AID/logit procedure for analysing large contingency tables', Journal of Marketing Research, XV, 132-136.

Gronau, R. (1974). 'Wage comparisons - a selectivity bias', Journal of Political Economy, 82(6), 1119-1143.

Hahn, G.J. & Shapiro, S.S. (1966). 'A catalog and computer program for the design and analysis of orthogonal symmetric and asymmetric fraction factorial experiments', General Electric Research and Development Center Report No. 66-C-165, General Electric Research and Development Center, Schenectady, New York.

Halldin, C. (1974). 'The choice axiom, revealed preference, and the theory of demand', Theory and Decision, 5, 139-160.

Hansen, S. (1980). 'Pro cross-cultural transferability', in Brog, W., Stopher, P.R. & Meyburg, A.H. (eds.) New Horizons in Behavioural Travel Research, Lexington Books, Lexington.

Hartley, M.J. (1976) 'The tobit and probit models: maximum likelihood estimation by ordinary least squares', Department of Economics, State University of New York at Buffalo (mimeo).

Hausman, J.A. & Wise, D.A. (1978). 'A conditional probit model for qualitative choice: discrete decisions recognising interdependence and heterogeneous preferences', Econometrica, 46(2), 403-426.

Hausman, J.A. (1979). 'Individual discount rates and the purchase and utilisation of energy using durables', Bell Journal of Economics, 10(1), 33-54.

Heckman, J.J. (1974). 'Shadow prices, market wages and labour supply', Econometrica, 42(4), 679-694.

Heckman, J.J. (1976). 'Introduction', Annals of Economic and Social Measurement, 5(4), i-iii.

Heckman, J.J. (1976a). 'The common structure of statistical models of truncation, sample selection and limited dependent variables and a simple estimator for such models', Annals of Economic and Social Measurement, 5(4), 475-492.

Heckman, J.J. (1978). 'Dummy endogenous variables in a simultaneous equation system', Econometrica, 46(4), 931-59.

Heckman, J.J. (1980). 'Statistical models for discrete panel data', in Manski, C.F. & McFadden, D. (eds.) Structural Analysis of Discrete Data: with Econometric Applications, M.I.T. Press, Cambridge, Massachusetts.

Hensher, D.A. (1974). 'A probabilistic disaggregate model of binary mode choice', in Hensher, D.A. (ed.) Urban Travel Choice and Demand Modelling Special Report No. 12, Australian Road Research Board, Melbourne, 61-99.

Hensher, D.A. (1974a). 'The problem of aggregation in disaggregate behavioural travel-choice models with emphasis on data requirements', Transportation Research Board Special Report, No. 149, 85-102.

Hensher, D.A. (1976). 'Use and application of market segmentation', in Stopher, P.R. & Meyburg, A.H. (eds.) Behavioural Travel-Demand Modelling, Lexington Books, Lexington, 271-280.

Hensher, D.A. & McLeod, P.B. (1977). 'Towards an integrated approach to the identification and evaluation of the transport determinants of travel choices', Transportation Research, 11(2), 77-93.

Hensher, D.A. (1977a). Valuation of Business Travel Time, Pergamon Press, Oxford.

445

Hensher, D.A. (1978). 'The demand for location and accommodation - a qualitative choice approach', Paper presented at the National Conference on Housing Economics, Sydney.

Hensher, D.A. (1978a). 'Theories of the allocation of time: state of the art', unpublished paper, Macquarie University.

Hensher, D.A. & Johnson, L.W. (1977). 'A two-period analysis of commuter mode choice: the predictive capability of individual choice models', Logistics and Transportation Review, 13(4), 361-375.

Hensher, D.A. & Dalvi, M.Q. (eds.) (1978). Determinants of Travel Choice, Saxon House, Teakfield, England.

Hensher, D.A., McLeod, P.B. & Stanley, J.K. (1975). 'Usefulness of attitudinal measures in investigating the choice of travel mode', International Journal of Transport Economics, II(1), 51-78.

Hensher, D.A., Smith R.A. & Hooper, P.G. (1978). An approach to Developing Transport Improvement Proposals, Occasional Paper No. 24, Bureau of Transport Economcs, Canberra.

Hensher, D.A. & Bullock, R. (1979). 'Price elasticity of commuter mode choice: effect of 20 per cent rail fare reduction', Transportation Research, 13A(3), 193-202.

Hensher, D.A. (1979). 'Formulating an urban passenger transport policy: a re-appraisal of some elements', Australian Economic Papers, 18(32), 119-130.

Hensher, D.A. (1979a). 'Individual choice modelling with discrete commodities: theory and application to the Tasman bridge reopening', Economic Record, 55(150), 243-260.

Hensher, D.A. & Stopher, P.R. (1979). 'Behavioural-travel modelling', in Hensher, D.A. & Stopher, P.R. (eds.) Behavioural Travel Modelling, Croom Helm, London, 1-47.

Hensher, D.A. & Stopher, P.R. (eds.) (1979). Behavioural Travel Modelling, Croom Helm, London.

Hensher, D.A. & Louviere, J.J. (1979). 'Behavioural intentions as predictors of very specific behaviour', Transportation, 8(2), 167-182.

Hensher, D.A. (1979b). Telecommunication Attribute Selection Modelling: The Determinants of Organisation Communication Requirements, Report prepared for Telecom (Australia) as part of a study by Communications Research (Australia), Sydney.

Hensher, D.A. & Johnson, L.W. (1979). 'External structure of variables in individual choice models of travel demand', International Journal of Transport Economics, VI(1), 51-61.

Hensher, D.A. (1979c). 'Towards a design of future telecommunication options: the contribution of organisation requirements', School of Economic and Financial Studies, Research Paper No. 191, Macquarie University.

Hensher, D.A. (1979d). MLOGPROT User's Manual, School of Economic and Financial Studies, Macquarie University, Sydney.

Hensher, D.A. & Johnson, L.W. (1980). 'Behavioural response and form of the preference function in travel choice models', School of Economic and Financial Studies, Macquarie University (mimeo).

Hicks, J.R. (1946). Value and Capital, 2nd edition, Oxford University Press, Oxford.

Horowitz, J. (1979). 'The accuracy of the multinomial logit model as an approximation to the multinomial probit model of travel demand', Transportation Research, forthcoming.

Horowitz, J. (1979a). 'Confidence intervals for the choice probabilities of the multinomial logit model', Transportation Research Record, forthcoming.

Horowitz, J. (1980). 'Sources of error and uncertainty in behavioural travel-demand models', in Brog, W., Stopher, P.R. & Meyburg, A.H. (eds.) New Horizons in Behavioural Travel Research, Lexington Books, Lexington.

Horowitz, J. (1980). 'Testing the multinomial logit model against the multinomial probit model without estimating the probit parameters', U.S. Environmental Protection Agency, Washington, D.C. (mimeo).

Johnson, L.W. (1979). 'An introduction to generalised functional form and random coefficients in transport modelling. Environment and Planning A, 11(9), 1029-1037.

Johnson, L.W. & Hensher, D.A. (1980). 'Application of multinomial probit to a two-period data set', Paper presented at International Conference on Disaggregate Travel Demand Models, University of Leeds, July.

Johnson, M.A. (1975). 'Psychological variables and choices between auto and transit travel: a critical research review', Urban Travel Demand Forecasting Project Working Paper No. 7509, Institute of Transportation Studies, University of California, Berkeley.

Johnson, N. & Kotz, S. (1972). Distributions in Statistics: Continuous Multivariate Distributions, John Wiley & Sons, New York.

447

Johnson, T. (1972). 'Qualitative and limited dependent variables in economic relationships', _Econometrica_, 40(3), 455-462.

Kaplan, R.S. & Urwitz, G. (1979). 'Statistical models of bond ratings: a methodological inquiry', _Journal of Business_, 52, 231-261.

Kau, J.B. & Lee, C.F. (1976). 'The functional form in estimating the density gradient: an empirical investigation', _Journal of American Statistical Association_, 71, 326-327.

Keeney, R.L. & Raiffa, H. (1976). _Decisions with Multiple Objectives: Preference and Value Tradeoffs_, John Wiley & Sons, New York.

Kemp, M. (1973). 'Some evidence on transit demand elasticities', _Transportation_, 2(1), 25-52.

Kohn, M.G., Manski, C.F. & Mundel, D.S. (1976). 'An empirical investigation of factors which influence college going behaviour', _Annals of Economic and Social Measurement_, 5(4), 391-420.

Koppelman, F.S. (1975). 'Prediction with disaggregate models: the aggregation issue', _Transportation Research Record_ No. 527, 73-80.

Koppelman, F.S. (1976). 'Methodology for analysing errors in prediction with disaggregate choice models', _Transportation Research Record_, No. 592, 17-23.

Koppelman, F.S. (1976a). 'Guidelines for aggregate travel prediction using disaggregate choice models', _Transportation Research Record_, No. 610, 19-24.

Koppelman, F.S. & Ben-Akiva, M.E. (1977). 'Aggregate forecasting with disaggregate travel demand models using normally available data', in Visser, E.J. (ed.) _Transport Decisions in an Age of Uncertainty_, Martinus Nijhoff, The Hague, 159-166.

Krantz, D.H. & Tversky, A. (1971). 'Conjoint measurement analysis of composition rules in psychology', _Psychological Review_, 78, 151-169.

Krishnan, K.A. (1977). 'Incorporating the concept of minimum perceivable difference in the logit model', _Management Science_, 23(11), 1224-1233.

Lancaster, K.J. (1966). 'A new approach to consumer theory', _Journal of Political Economy_, 74(2), 132-157.

Lancaster, K.J. (1971). _Consumer Demand: A New Approach_, Columbia University Press, New York.

Laumas, G.S. & Mehra, Y.P. (1976). 'The stability of the demand for money function: the evidence from quarterly data', _Review of Economics and Statistics_, 58, 463-468.

Lave, C.A. & Train, K.E. (1979). 'A behavioural disaggregate model of automobile-type choice', Transportation Research 13A(1), 1-9.

Lee, L.F. (1975). 'Limited information estimation of some switching regression models', Discussion Paper 75-20, Department of Economics, University of Rochester.

Lee, L.F. (1977a). 'Estimation of a modal choice model for the work journey with incomplete observations', Discussion Paper No. 77-86, Center for Economic Research, University of Minnesota.

Lee, L.F. (1978). 'On the estimation of a probit choice model with censored dependent variables and Amemiya's principle', Discussion Paper No. 78-99, Center for Economic Research, University of Minnesota.

Lee, L.F. (1979). 'Identification and estimation in binary choice models with limited (censored) dependent variables', Econometrica, 47, 977-996.

Lee, L.F. & Trost, R.P. (1978). 'Estimation of some limited dependent variable models with application to housing demand', Journal of Econometrics, 8(4), 357-382.

Leibenstein, H. (1976). Beyond Economic Man: a New Foundation in Microeconomics, Harvard University Press, Cambridge, Massachusetts.

LePlastrier, V. (1980). A Dynamic Discrete Choice Model of the Household's Car Fleet Acquisition Process, unpublished M.Ec.(Hons) Thesis, School of Economic and Financial Studies, Macquarie University, Sydney.

Lerman, S.R. (1975). A Disaggregate Behavioural Model of Urban Mobility Decisions, unpublished Ph.D. Thesis, Department of Civil Engineering, M.I.T. Cambridge.

Lerman, S.R., Manski, C.F. & Atherton, T.J. (1976). Non-Random Sampling in the Calibration of Disaggregate Choice Models, Report No. PO-6-3-0021 prepared for the U.S. Department of Transportation, Federal Highway Administration, Washington, D.C.

Lerman, S.R. (1976). 'Location, housing, car ownership and mode to work: a joint choice model', Transportation Research Record No. 610, 6-11.

Lerman, S.R. & Manski, C.F. (1978). Sample Design for Discrete Choice Analysis of Travel Behaviour, Report UMTA-MA-06-0049-78-8, U.S. Department of Transportation, Washington, D.C. U.S.A.

449

Lerman, S.R. & Manski, C.F. (1979). 'Sample design for discrete choice: state of the art', Transportation Research 13A(1), 29-44.

Lerman, S.R. & Louviere, J.J. (1978). 'On the use of functional measurement to identify the functional form of the utility expression in travel demand models', Transportation Research Record No. 673, 78-86.

Lerman, S.R. & Manski, C.F. (1976). 'Alternative sampling procedures for calibrating disaggregate choice models', Transportation Research Record, No. 592, 24-28.

Li, M.M. (1977). 'A logit model of home ownership', Econometrica, 45(5), 1081-1097.

Liou, P.S., Cohen, G.S. & Hartgen, D.T. (1975). 'Application of disaggregate modal-choice models to travel demand forecasting for urban transit systems', Transportation Research Record, No. 534, 52-62.

Little, I.M.D. (1952). A Critique of Welfare Economics, Oxford University Press, Oxford.

Louviere, J.J. (1978) 'Psychological measurement of travel attributes', in Hensher, D.A. & Dalvi, M.Q. (eds.) Determinants of Travel Choice, Teakfield, Saxon House, England, 148-186.

Louviere, J.J. (1979). 'Attitudes, attitudinal measurement and the relationship between behaviour and attitude', in Hensher, D.A. & Stopher, P.R. (eds.) Behavioural Travel Modelling, Croom Helm, London.

Louviere, J.J. (1979a). 'Modelling individual residential preferences: a totally disaggregate approach', Transportation Research 13A(4), 1-15.

Louviere, J.J. (1979b). 'Applications of functional measurement to problems in spatial decision making', in Golledge, R.G. (ed.) Analysis of Spatial Behavioural Data, University of Minnesota Press, Minesota.

Louviere, J.J. & Hensher, D.A. (1980). 'Demand for international air travel: behavioural models of preferences and choices with particular emphasis on the impact of alternative choice structures', Occasional Paper, Bureau of Transport Economics, Canberra, Australia.

Louviere, J.J. (1980). 'Some comments on premature expectations regarding spatial, temporal, and cultural transferability of travel choice models', in Brog, W., Stopher, P.R. & Meyburg, A.H. (eds.) New Horizons in Behavioural Travel Research, Lexington Books, Lexington.

450

Lovelock, C.H. (1975). 'Segmenting the market for public transit: insights for managers and model builders', Proceedings of the American Transportation Research Forum, XVI(1), 247-258.

Luce, R.D. (1959). Individual Choice Behaviour, John Wiley & Sons, New York.

Luce, R.O. & Raiffa, H. (1957). Games and Decisions. John Wiley & Sons, New York.

Luce, R.D. & Suppes, P. (1965). 'Preference, utility and subjective probability', in Luce, R.D., Bush, R.R. & Galanter, E. (eds.) Handbook of Mathematical Psychology, Volume III, John Wiley & Sons, Inc., New York.

Luce, R.D. (1977). 'The choice axiom after twenty years', Journal of Mathematical Psychology, 15(2), 215-233.

Maddala, G.S. & Lee, L.F. (1976). 'Recursive models with qualitative endogenous variables', Annals of Economic and Social Measurement, 5(4), 525-546.

Maddala, G.S. (1977). Econometrics, McGraw-Hill Book Company, New York.

Manski, C.F. (1973). The Analysis of Qualitative Choice, unpublished Ph.D. Thesis, Department of Economics, M.I.T. Cambridge, Massachusetts.

Manski, C.F. (1977). 'The structure of random utility models', Theory and Decision, 8, 229-54.

Manski, C.F. & Lerman, S.R. (1977). 'The multi-nomial probit model', Transportation Research Record, No. 624.

Manski, C.F. & Lerman, S.R. (1977a). 'The estimation of choice probabilities from choice-based samples', Econometrica, 45(8), 1977-1988.

Manski, C.F., Sherman, L. & Royce Ginn, J. (1978). An Empirical Analysis of Household Choice Among Motor Vehicles, Cambridge Systematics Inc., Boston, Massachusetts.

Manski, C.F. & McFadden, D. (1980). 'Alternative estimators and sample designs for discrete choice analysis', in Manski, C.F. & McFadden, D. (eds.) Structural Analysis of Discrete Data: with Econometric Applications, M.I.T. Press, Cambridge, Massachusetts.

Manski, C.F. & McFadden, D. (eds.) (1980). Structural Analysis of Discrete Data: with Econometric Applications, M.I.T. Press, Cambridge, Massachusetts.

Manski, C.F. (1980). 'Recent advances in and new directions for behavioural travel modelling', in Brog, W., Stopher, P.R. & Meyburg, A.H. (eds.) New Horizons in Behavioural Travel Research, Lexington Books, Lexington.

March, J.G. (1978). 'Bounded rationality, ambiguity, and the engineering of choice', Bell Journal of Economics 9(2), 587-608.

Marschak, J. (1959). 'Binary choice constraints and random utility indicators' in Arrow, K.J. (ed.) Mathematical Methods in the Social Sciences, Stanford University Press, Stanford.

McFadden, D. (1968). 'The revealed preferences of a government bureaucracy', Technical Report No. 17, Department of Economics, University of California, Berkeley, (Published in Bell Journal of Economics, Fall 1975 and Spring 1976 401-406, 51-72).

McFadden, D. (1974). 'Conditional logit analysis of qualitative choice behaviour', in Zarembka, P. (ed.) Frontiers in Econometrics, Academic Press, New York, 105-142.

McFadden, D. (1974a). 'The measurement of urban travel demand', Journal of Public Economics, 3(3), 303-328.

McFadden, D. & Reid, F. (1975). 'Aggregate travel demand forecasting from disaggregated behavioural models', Transportation Research Record, No. 534, 24-37.

McFadden, D. (1975). 'On independence, structure and simultaneity in transportation demand analysis', Urban Travel Demand Forecasting Project Working Paper No. 7511, Institute of Transportation Studies, University of California, Berkeley.

McFadden, D. (1976). 'Quantal choice analysis: a survey', Annals of Economic and Social Measurement, 5(4), 363-390.

McFadden, D. (1976a). 'The theory and practice of disaggregate demand forecasting for various modes of urban transportation', Urban Travel Demand Forecasting Project Working Paper No. 7623, Institute of Transportation Studies, University of California, Berkeley.

McFadden, D., Train, K. & Tye, W. (1977). 'An application of diagnostic tests for the independence from irrelevant alternatives property of the multinomial logit model', Transportation Research Record, No. 637, 39-45.

McFadden, D. (1978). 'Modelling the choice of residential location', in Karlquist, A., Lundquist, L., Snickars, F. & Weibull, J.L. (eds.) Spatial Interaction Theory and Planning Models, North-Holland, Amsterdam.

McFadden, D. (1979). 'Quantitative methods for analysing travel behaviour of individuals: some recent developments' in Hensher, D.A. & Stopher, P.R. (eds.) Behavioural Travel Modelling, Croom Helm, London.

McFadden, D., Berkman, J., Brownstone, D. & Duncan, G.M. (1979). QUAIL 3.0 User's Manual, Department of Economics, University of California, Berkeley.

McFadden, D. (1980). 'Econometric models of probabilistic choice', in Manski, C.F. & McFadden, D. (eds.) Structural Analysis of Discrete Data: with Econometric Applications, M.I.T. Press, Cambridge, Massachusetts.

Miller, D.R. (1974). 'Aggregation problems', Transportation Research Board Special Report, No. 149, 25-30.

Mossin, A. (1968). 'Elements of a stochastic theory of consumption', Swedish Journal of Economics, LXX(3), 210-221.

Muth, R.F. (1966). 'Household production and consumer demand functions', Econometrica, 34(3), 699-708.

Myers, M.H., Hankey, B.F. & Martel, N. (1973). 'A logistic-exponential model for use with response-time data involving regressor variables', Biometrics, 29, 257-269.

Nelson, F. & Olson, L. (1978). 'Specification and estimation of a simultaneous-equation model with limited dependent variables', International Economic Review, 19(3), 695-710.

Nelson, F. & Noll, R. (1978). 'In search of scientific regulation: the UHF allocation experiment', Paper presented at the Annual Meeting of the Public Choice Society.

Office of Director-General of Transport (1978) Metropolitan Adelaide Data Base Study, Phase 3 Report, Travel Model Preparation, prepared by P.G. Pak Poy & Associates and John Paterson Urban Systems Pty. Ltd., Adelaide, South Australia.

Oliveira, J.T. de (1958). 'Extremal distributions', Revistade Faculdada du Ciencia, Lisboa, Serie A, 7, 215-227.

Olsen, R.J. (1978). 'Comment on the effect of unions on earnings and earnings on unions: a mixed logit approach', International Economic Review, 19(1), 259-261.

O'Muircheartaigh, C.A. & Payne, C. (eds.) (1977).
The Analysis of Survey Data: Volume 1 -
Exploring Data Structures, John Wiley & Sons,
London.

Ortuzar, J. D. (1978). 'Mixed mode demand
forecasting techniques: an assessment of
current practice', PTRC Summer Annual Meeting,
L 7(ii) Group 1.

Ortuzar, J.D. & Williams, H.C.W.L. (1978). 'A
geometric interpretation of random utility
models of choice between discrete alternatives',
Institute for Transport Studies Technical Note
3, University of Leeds, Leeds.

Ortuzar, J. D. & Williams, H.C.W.L. (1981).
Research and Applications of Disaggregate
Travel Demand Models, Proceedings of a
conference held at University of Leeds, July
1980 (forthcoming).

Oum, T.H. (1979). 'A warning on the use of linear
logit models in transport mode choice studies',
Bell Journal of Economics, 10(1), 374-388.

Owen, D.C. (1956). 'Tables for computing bivariate
normal probabilities', Annals of Mathematical
Statistics, 27, 1075-90.

Payne, C. (1977). 'The log-linear model for
contingency tables', in O'Muircheartaigh, C.A.
& Payne, C. (eds.). The Analysis of Survey
Data: Volume 2 - Model Fitting, John Wiley &
Sons, London, 105-144.

Peat, Marwick, Mitchell & Co. (1972). Implementation
of the n-Dimensional Logit Model, Final report
to the Comprehensive Planning Organization,
San Diego County, California.

Pindyck, R.S. & Rubinfeld, D.L. (1976). Econometric
Models and Economic Forecasts, McGraw-Hill
Book Company, New York.

Pollakowski, H. (1974). The Effects of Local Public
Service on Residential Location Decision: an
Empirical Study of the San Francisco Bay Area,
unpublished Ph.D. Thesis, Department of
Economics, University of California, Berkeley.

Poirier, D.J. (1976). 'The determinants of home
buying in the New Jersey graduated work
incentive experiment', in Watts, H.W. & Rees, A.
(eds.) Impact of Experimental Payments on
Expenditure, Health and Social Behaviour, and
Studies on the Quality of the Evidence,
Academic Press, New York.

Poirier, D.J. (1978). 'A curious relationship
between probit and logit models', Southern
Economic Journal, 44(3), 40-41.

Punj, G.N. & Staelin, R. (1978). 'The choice process for graduate business schools', Journal of Marketing Research, XV, 588-598.

Quandt, R.E. (1956). 'A probabilistic theory of consumer behaviour', Quarterly Journal of Economics, LXX(4), 507-536.

Quigley, J.M. (1976). 'Housing demand in the short run - an analysis of polytomous choice', Explorations in Economic Research, 3(1), 76-102.

Radner, R.A. (1975). 'A behavioural model of cost reduction', Bell Journal of Economics 6(1), 196-215.

Raiffa, H. & Schlaifer, R. (1961). Applied Statistical Decision Theory, Harvard University Press, Cambridge.

Rao, V.R. & Winter, F.W. (1978). 'An application of the multivariate probit model to market segmentation and product design', Journal of Marketing Research, XV, 361-8.

Ratchford, B.T. (1975). 'The new economic theory of consumer behaviour: an interpretative essay', Journal of Consumer Research, 2(2), September, 65-78.

Reid, F.A. (1978). 'Minimizing error in aggregate predictions from disaggregate models', Transportation Research Record, No. 673, 59-65.

Restle, F. (1971). Mathematical Models in Psychology: An Introduction. Penguin Science of Behaviour, Penguin Books Ltd., Harmondsworth: Ch. 3, 84-113.

Richards, M.G. & Ben-Akiva, M.E. (1975). A Disaggregate Travel Demand Model, Saxon House Studies, Farnborough, England.

Richardson, A.J. (1978). 'A comparative analysis of transport choice models', Department of Civil Engineering Working Paper No. 78/11, Monash University, Victoria, Australia.

Robins, P.K. & Spiegelman, R.C. (1978). 'An econometric model of the demand for child care', Economic Inquiry, XVI(1), 83-94.

Robson, D.S. (1959). 'A simple method for constructing orthogonal polynomials when the independent variable is unequally spaced', Biometrics, 187.

Rosen, S. (1974). 'Hedonic prices and implicit markets: product differentiation in pure competition', Journal of Political Economy, 82(1), 34-55.

455

Ross, R. (1979). 'Disaggregate labour supply function for married women: preliminary estimates for New Zealand' Working Paper No. 37, Department of Economics, University of Sydney (Australia).

Ruiter, E.R. & Ben-Akiva, M.E. (1977). 'The development of a complete system of disaggregate travel demand models', Cambridge Systematics Inc., Boston, March (unpublished).

Sattah, S. & Tversky, A. (1976). 'Unite and conquer; a multiplicative inequality for choice probabilities', Econometrica, 44(1), 78-89.

Schmidt, P. & Strauss, R.P. (1974). 'Estimation of models with jointly dependent qualitative variables' Paper presented at Econometric Society meetings, U.S.A. (unpublished).

Schmidt, P. & Strauss, R.P. (1975). 'Estimation of models with jointly dependent qualitative variables: a simultaneous logit approach', Econometrica, 44, 745-755.

Schmidt, P. & Strauss, R.P. (1976). 'The effect of unions on earnings and earnings on unions; a mixed logit approach', International Economic Review, 17(1), 204-212.

Schmidt, P. (1978). 'Estimation of a simultaneous equations model with jointly dependent continuous and qualitative variables: the union-earnings question revisited', International Economic Review, 19(2), 453-465.

Schmidt, P. (1980). 'Constraints on the parameters in simultaneous tobit and probit models', in Manski, C.F. & McFadden, D. (eds.) Structural Analysis of Discrete Data: with Econometric Applications, M.I.T. Press, Cambridge, Massachusetts.

Scitovsky, T. (1976). The Joyless Economy, Oxford University Press, New York.

Sen, A. (1973). 'Behaviour and the concept of preference', Economica, XL(159), 241-259.

Sheffi, Y. (1979). 'Estimating choice probabilities among nested alternatives', Transportation Research, 13B(3), 189-206.

Silman, L.A. (1977). 'The interpretation of the coefficient of the logsum accessibility variable in the distribution model', memorandum Pb 140/6.513.77.L.S., the SIGMO Project, Project Bureau IVVS and Netherlands Ministry of Transport (unpublished).

Silman, L.A. (1979). 'The time stability of a disaggregate modal-split model', Working Paper, The Israel Institute of Transportation Planning and Research, Tel-Aviv, Israel.

456

Simon, H.A. (1957). <u>Models of Man</u>, John Wiley & Sons, New York.

Sloan, F.A. (1978). 'The demand for physicians' services in alternative practice settings: a multiple logit analysis', <u>Quarterly Review of Economics and Business</u>, 18(1), 41-61.

Smith, B. & Campbell, J.M. (1978). 'Aggregation bias and the demand for housing', <u>International Economic Review</u>, 19(2), 495-505.

Smith, T.E. (1975). 'A choice theory of spatial interaction', <u>Regional Science and Urban Economics</u>, 5(2), 137-76.

Smith, T.M.F. (1976). 'The foundations of survey sampling: a review', <u>Journal of Royal Statistical Society</u>, 1139, part 2, 183-202.

Snyder, D. (1978). 'Economic variables and the decision to have additional children: evidence from the survey of economic opportunity', <u>The American Economist</u>, XXII(1), 12-16.

Sobel, K.L. (1981). 'Travel demand forecasting with the nested multinomial logit model, <u>Transportation Research Record</u>' (in press).

Spitzer, J.J. (1978). 'A Monte Carlo investigation of the Box-Cox transformation in small samples', <u>Journal of the American Statistical Association</u>, 73, 488-495.

Sonquist, J.A., Baker, E.L. & Morgan, J.N. (1971). <u>Searching for Structure</u>, Institute for Social Research, University of Michigan.

Stoner, J. (1977). <u>The Effects of Sampling Error on the Use of Disaggregate Models in the Evaluation of Alternative Transit Schemes</u>, unpublished Ph.D. Thesis, Department of Civil Engineering, Northwestern University, Evanston, Illinois.

Stopher, P.R. (1969). 'A multinomial extension of the binary logit model for choice of mode of travel', The Transportation Center, Northwestern University (mimeo).

Stopher, P.R. & Meyburg, A.H. (1976). 'Behavioural travel-demand models', in Stopher, P.R. & Meyburg, A.H. (eds.) <u>Behavioural Travel-Demand Models</u>, Lexington Books, Lexington, 3-56.

Stopher, P.R. & Wilmot, C.G. (1979). 'Work-trip mode-choice models: a South African datum point', <u>Transportation Engineering Journal of the American Society of Civil Engineers</u>, November.

Stopher, P.R. & Ergun, G. (1979). 'Population segmentation in urban recreation choices', <u>Transportation Research Record</u>, No. 728, 59-64.

457

Stopher, P.R. & Meyburg, A.H. (1979). Survey Sampling and Multivariate Analysis for Social Scientists and Engineers, Lexington Books, Lexington, Massachusetts.

Strotz, R.H. (1957). 'The empirical implications of a utility tree', Econometrica, 25(4), 269-280.

Strotz, R.H. (1959). 'The utility tree - a correction and further appraisal', Econometrica, 27(3), 482-488.

Struyk, R.J. (1976). Urban Homeownership - The Economic Determinants, Lexington Books, Lexington.

Swets, J.A. (1967). 'Detection theory and psychophysics', in Edwards, D.W. & Tversky, A. (eds.) Decision-Making, Penguin Modern Psychology, London.

Talvitie, A.P. (1973). 'Aggregate travel demand analysis with disaggregate or aggregate travel demand models', Transportation Research Forum Proceedings, XIV(1), 583-603.

Talvitie, A.P. (1976). 'Disaggregate travel demand models with disaggregate data, not aggregate data, and how', Urban Travel Demand Forecasting Project Working Paper No. 7615, Institute of Transportation Studies, University of California, Berkeley.

Talvitie, A.P. & Kirschner, D. (1978). 'Specification, transferability and the effect of data outliers in modelling the choice of mode in urban travel', Transportation, 7(3), 311-331.

Talvitie, A.P. (1980). 'Inaccurate or incomplete data as a source of uncertainty in econometric or attitudinal models of travel behaviour', in Brog, W., Stopher, P.R. & Meyburg, A.H. (eds.) New Horizons in Behavioural Travel Research Lexington Books, Lexington.

Theil, H. (1969). 'A multinomial extension of the linear logit model, International Economic Review, 10(2), 251-259.

Theil, H. (1970). 'On the estimation of relation-ships involving qualitative variables', American Journal of Sociology, 76(1), 103-154.

Theil, H. (1971). Principles of Econometrics, John Wiley & Sons, New York.

Thurstone, L.L. (1927). 'A law of comparative judgement', Psychological Review, 34, 278-286.

Thurstone, L.L. (1927a). 'Psychophysical analysis', American Journal of Psychology, 38, 368-389.

Tobin, J. (1955). 'The application of multivariate probit analysis to economic survey data', Cowles Foundation Discussion Paper No. 1, Yale University, New Haven, Connecticut.

Tobin, J. (1958). 'Estimation of relationships for limited dependent variables', _Econometrica_, 26(1), 24-36.

Train, K.E. (1978). 'The sensitivity of parameter estimates to data specification in mode choice models', _Transportation_, 7(3), 301-310.

Train, K.E. & McFadden, D. (1978). 'The goods/ leisure trade off and disaggregate work trip mode choice models', _Transportation Research_, 12, 349-353.

Truong, T.P. & Hensher, D.A. (1980). 'Valuation of commodity time savings and budget time', School of Economic and Financial Studies, Macquarie University, Sydney.

Tukey, J.W. (1957). 'On the comparative anatomy of transformations', _Annals of Mathematical Statistics_, 28, 602-632.

Tversky, A. (1972). 'Elimination by aspects: a theory of choice', _Psychological Review_, 79, 281-299.

Uhler, R.S. & Cragg, J.G. (1969). 'The demand for automobiles', _Discussion Paper No. 27_, Department of Economics, University of British Columbia.

Van der Gaag, P. & Van de Ven, W.P. (1978). 'The demand for primary health care', _Medical Care_, XVI(4), 299-312.

Van de Ven, W.P. & Van Praag, B. (1979). 'The demand for deductibles in private health insurance', _Working Paper 77.02B_, Centre for Research in Public Economics, Leiden University, The Netherlands.

Wald, A. (1947). 'A note on regression analysis', _Annals of Mathematical Statistics_, 18, 586-589.

Warner, S.L. (1962). _Stochastic Choice of Mode in Urban Travel: a Study in Binary Choice_, Northwestern University Press, Evanston, Illinois.

Warner, S.L. (1963). 'Multivariate regression of dummy variates under normality assumptions', _Journal of the American Statistical Association_, 58, 1054-1063.

Warner, S.L. (1967). 'Asymptotic variances for dummy variate regression under normality assumptions', _Journal of the American Statistical Association_, 62, 1305-1314.

Watson, P.L. & Westin, R.B. (1975). 'Transferability of disaggregate mode choice models', _Regional Science and Urban Economics_, 5(3), 229-249.

Westin, R.B. (1974). 'Predictions from binary choice models', _Journal of Econometrics_, 2(1), 1-16.

Westin, R.B. (1975). 'Statistical models for inter-related discrete and continuous choices', Paper presented at the Third World Congress of the Econometric Society, Toronto. (mimeo).

Westin, R.B. & Gillen, D.W. (1978). 'Parking location and transit demand — a case study of endogenous attributes in disaggregate mode choice models', Journal of Econometrics, 8(1), 75-101.

Westin, R.B. & Manski, C.F. (1979). 'Theoretical and conceptual developments in demand modelling', in Hensher, D.A. & Stopher, P.R. (eds.) Behavioural Travel Modelling, Croom Helm, London, Ch. 17.

Whelan, J., Seaton, E. & Cunningham-Day, E. (1976). Aftermath — The Tasman Bridge Collapse, AIC, Hobart.

Wilkie, W.L. (1971). An Empirical Analysis of Alternative Bases of Market Segmentation, unpublished Ph.D. Thesis, Graduate School of Business, Stanford University, California.

Wilks, S.S. (1962). Mathematical Statistics, John Wiley & Sons, Inc., New York.

Williams, H.C.W.L. (1977). 'On the formation of travel demand models and economic evaluation measures of user benefit', Environment and Planning A, 9(3), 285-344.

Williams, H.C.W.L. & Ortuzar, J.D. (1979). 'Behavioural travel theories, model specification and the response error problem', Institute for Transport Studies Working Paper 116, University of Leeds, Leeds.

Winer, B.J. (1971). Statistical Principles in Experimental Design, John Wiley & Sons, New York.

Wrigley, N. (1975). 'Analysing multiple alternative dependent variables', Geographical Analysis, 7(2), 187-195.

Wrigley, N. (1976). An Introduction to the Use of Logit Models in Geography, Concepts and Techniques in Modern Geography No. 10, Geo Abstracts Ltd., University of East Anglia, Norwich.

Wrigley, N. (1977). 'Probability surface mapping: a new approach to trend surface mapping', Institute of British Geographers Transactions, 2(2), 129-139.

Wrigley, N. (1979). 'Developments in the statistical analysis of categorical data', Progress in Human Geography, 3.

Wrigley, N. (1980). 'Paired comparison experiments and logit models: a review and illustration of some recent developments', Environment and Planning A, 12, 21-40.

Yellott, J.I. (1977). 'The relationship between Luce's choice axiom, Thurstone's theory of comparative judgement, and the double exponential distribution', Journal of Mathematical Psychology, 15, 109-144.

Zarembka, P.C. (1974). 'Transformation of variables in econometrics', in Zarembka, P.C. (ed.) Frontiers in Econometrics, Academic Press, New York, 81-104.

INDEX

467

468